Under Sentence of Death

Under Sentence of Death

Lynching in the South

Edited by W. Fitzhugh Brundage

The University of North Carolina Press

Chapel Hill & London

© 1997

The University of North Carolina Press

Manufactured in the United States of America

The paper in this book meets the guidelines for

permanence and durability of the Committee on

Production Guidelines for Book Longevity of the

Council on Library Resources.

Library of Congress Cataloging-in-Publication Data

Under sentence of death: lynching in the South /

edited by W. Fitzhugh Brundage.

p.   cm.

Includes bibliographical references and index.

ISBN 0-8078-2326-0 (cloth: alk. paper).–

ISBN 0-8078-4636-8 (pbk.: alk. paper)

1. Lynching–Southern States–History. 2. Afro-Americans–

Crimes against–History. 3. Southern States–Race relations–

History. 4. Racism– Southern States–History. I. Brundage,

W. Fitzhugh (William Fitzhugh), 1959-   .

HV6464.U49   1997

364.1'34–dc20   96-30204

CIP

01 00 99 98 97   5 4 3 2 1

Thomas G. Dyer's essay was previously published as " 'A Most
Unexampled Exhibition of Madness and Brutality': Judge Lynch
in Saline County, Missouri, 1859," *Missouri Historical Review* 89
(April and July 1995): 269- 89, 367–83. It is reprinted here by
permission of the State Historical Society of Missouri.
Nancy MacLean's essay was previously published as "The Leo
Frank Case Reconsidered: Gender and Sexual Politics in the
Making of Reactionary Populism," *Journal of American History* 78
(December 1991): 917–48. It is reprinted here by permission of
the Organization of American Historians.

To the memory of

the courageous southerners

who waged the crusade

against lynching

Every Negro in the South knows

that he is under a kind of sentence

of death; he does not know when

his turn will come, it may never

come, but it may also be any time.

—*John Dollard, 1937*

Contents

Acknowledgments

I am grateful to the contributors for
their diligence and their commitment
to this project. Despite the complicated
logistics and our harried schedules, I am
gratified that my respect for and friend-
ship with the contributors actually has
deepened during the compiling of this
book. A large debt for the completion
of this project is due to the staff of the
University of North Carolina Press and
especially to Lewis Bateman. He was
patient when patience was needed and
always helpful. I also would like to thank
Robert Malcolmson, chair of the Department of History at Queen's University, for
his help with this project. Finally, the
National Humanities Center provided an
ideal setting in which to complete this
collection. For this privilege I am grateful
to W. Robert Connor, Kent Mullikin, and
the staff of the NHC.

Under Sentence of Death

Introduction

W. Fitzhugh Brundage

I n 1901, Mark Twain penned a stinging indictment of American civilization when he called lynching "this epidemic of bloody insanities." At a time when American missionaries proselytized to "heathen" peoples across the globe, Twain wondered about the principles of a nation where cheering crowds urged on the mobs that had brutally executed more than two hundred men and women during the past two years. Hoping to overcome the apathy of his countrymen, he appealed to them to "Picture the scene."

> Place 203 in a row, allowing 600 feet of space for each human torch, so that there may be viewing room around it for 5,000 Christian American men, women, and children, youths and maidens; make it night, for grim effect; have the show in a gradually rising plain, and let the course of the stakes be uphill; the eye can then take in the whole line of twenty-four miles of blood-and-flesh bonfires unbroken. . . . All being ready now, and the darkness opaque, the stillness impressive—for there should be no sound but the soft moaning of the night wind and the muffled sobbing of the sacrifices—let all the far stretch of kerosene pyres be touched off simultaneously and the glare and the shrieks and the agonies burst heavenward to the Throne.[1]

His hellish vision was evocative precisely because scenes of baying hounds and armed whites chasing black men across moonlit swamps, of frenzied mobs torturing and mutilating their victims, and of festive crowds of white men, women, and children gathering to gawk at the dangling or charred bodies of lynching victims were so commonplace. As Twain well understood, the horror of lynching at once manifested some of the deepest, most tenacious prejudices held by Americans and raised troubling questions about the prospects for any measure of justice and civility in the United States.

Seven decades later, when Benjamin E. Mays chronicled his distinguished career as a black educator and activist, he too saw the lynch mob as a tragic symbol of race relations in the American South. "The first thing I remember is a white mob looking for a Negro to lynch [in 1898]. I remember a crowd of white men who rode up on horseback with rifles on their shoulders. . . . They cursed my father, drew their guns and made him salute, made him take off his hat and bow down to them several times. Then they rode away. I was not yet five years old, but I have never forgotten them." The lynching party, May regretted, did not spare other blacks in Greenwood County, South Carolina, and in subsequent years the black community there endured periodic white violence. "Never a year passed," he recalled, "that there were not several brutal incidents involving Negroes and whites."[2]

The accumulation of news accounts, oral testimonies, and lived experiences of racist violence were a constant reminder to Mays and all African Americans of their oppression. Lynching was a powerful tool of intimidation that gripped blacks' imagination whether they lived in a mob-prone part of the South or in the relative safety of a border state. Across the region and through time, W. E. B. Du Bois in Atlanta, Benjamin Mays in rural South Carolina, Richard Wright and Medgar Evers in the Deep South, and generations of other southern blacks experienced the fear, insecurity, and rage provoked by racial violence.[3]

The scale of lynching and the severity of the scars it has left on American society have caused both blacks and whites to struggle to explain this grisly manifestation of humankind's capacity for hate and violence. Indeed, so pronounced was the penchant for lynching in the United States that early observers considered it a measure of American distinctiveness. To explain the prevalence of mob violence was to explain much about American attitudes about social order, justice, and race. As early as the 1830s, when collective violence flared in Illinois and Ohio, as well as Virginia and Louisiana, concerned observers scrutinized American institutions and democratic mores for the roots of what Abraham Lincoln called the "mobocratic spirit" and the "ill-omen amongst us."[4] Some early commentators traced the violence to moral decay, others to the evils connected with immigrants, Catholics, and various "conspiratorial" groups. Others saw the violence as evidence of the dangers of unbridled democracy.[5]

As the sectional conflict escalated, more and more observers focused on the regional divergence in extralegal violence. It persisted in the North throughout the antebellum period, but accelerating economic development and urban growth there promoted the permanent and dependable exercise of state authority to protest capital and property. Consequently, courts and law enforcement agencies, including recently created urban police forces, worked to preserve social order by actively suppressing violent crowds. In the South no comparable institutional opposition developed to discourage collective violence.[6]

Abolitionists traced southern extralegal violence to the region's debased traditions and institutions. Lynching in the South, they insisted, originated in the institution of slavery, which entailed coercion of slaves as well as the intimidation of nonslaveholders by white slave owners. Slavery at once perpetuated and strengthened a peculiarly southern code of honor, with its corollaries of the glorification of motherhood and feminine virtue. Abolitionists claimed that the defense of white feminine virtue—the very symbol and repository of white racial purity—was at the heart of an elaborate code of honor. This code required white men to respond to challenges to their honor, especially offenses by black men against white women, by acting outside of the law.

Southern whites dismissed these critiques of regional folkways by defending the necessity and legitimacy of extralegal violence. Popular justice, they boasted, reflected the vigor of both democratic and communal values in the South; lynchers defended, rather than endangered, civilization by protecting it against the threat of slave revolts and abolitionist sedition. And southern honor, however ambiguously defined, was a legitimate code of conduct in a society that venerated virtue, courage, and community standing. Antebellum northerners, who were blinded by their commitment to social leveling and commercialism, may have had difficulty understanding the idea of honor, but white southerners believed that they were upholding a rich and sacred tradition that stretched back for centuries.

Although the charges and countercharges which antebellum northerners and southerners hurled at each other framed much of the subsequent debate over mob violence, it also was shaped by images of frontier traditions of extralegal violence. Enthralled by the adventure and romance of the newly opened West, journalists and adventure-seekers before and especially after the Civil War depicted lynching as an inevitable feature of the conquest and settlement of the frontier; it was a lamentable but necessary form of justice which persisted until formal institutions could take its place. By evoking images of cowboys, cattle rustlers, and a purportedly wholesome tradition of spontaneous communal justice, these genteel accounts of western vigilantism at once served to legitimate the defiance of legal authority and to undercut any subsequent appeals for scrupulous obedience to the law by opponents of lynching.[7]

But even as vigilante violence in the West held the attention of many Americans, mob violence became a pervasive and chronic feature of southern life. Lynching, like slavery and segregation, was not unique to the South. But its proportions and significance there were unparalleled outside the region. Drawing upon traditions of lawlessness rooted in slavery and the turmoil of Reconstruction, lynch mobs in the South continued to execute alleged wrongdoers long after lynching had become a rarity elsewhere in the nation. By the late nineteenth century, mob violence had become a prominent feature of race relations in the South that for many symbolized black oppression. Lynching also came to define southern distinctiveness every bit as much as the Mason-Dixon line marked the boundary of the region.

The proportion of lynchings that occurred in the South rose with each succeeding decade after the Civil War, increasing from 82 percent of all lynchings in the nation during the 1880s to more than 95 percent during the 1920s. In the Northeast, where lynchings occurred rarely, lynchers killed only two whites and seven blacks between 1880 and 1930. The Midwest proved more fertile soil for collective violence; there 181 white and 79 black victims died at the hands of mobs. And in the Far West, where vigilantism and lynching flourished throughout the late nineteenth century, mobs lynched 447 whites and 38 blacks. The toll of mob violence outside the South, however sizable, is greatly overshadowed by the estimated 723 whites and 3,220 blacks lynched in the South between 1880 and 1930. Casualties of extralegal violence in some lynch-prone states in the South equaled or exceeded the totals of entire regions outside the South. For example, the 492 victims lynched in Texas surpassed the number in the thirteen states of the Far West.[8]

Many whites responded with puzzlement to the violence allegedly committed in the defense of their civilization, but few expressed outright horror or condemnation of the practice. Instead, most whites responded with ambivalence. Although a few, like Mark Twain, forcefully denounced lynching, others, like reformers Frances Willard and Jane Addams, equivocated even while they voiced contempt for what they termed the sadism and lawlessness of lynch mobs. Countless other whites simply accepted lynching as an inevitable part of the rhythm of life in the United States and as a curiosity that merited comment only when it assumed unusually barbaric forms.

Blacks, however, refused to allow the epidemic of lynching that swept the South in the late nineteenth century to pass without protest. Ida B. Wells-Barnett, Frederick Douglass, John Mitchell, and others forthrightly challenged contemporary justifications of mob violence and developed trenchant and enduring critiques of antiblack violence. They were the first to attempt to explode myths about the causes of this violence by making careful empirical studies of lynching. By compiling lists of lynching victims and collecting news accounts of incidents, they demonstrated that, for example, alleged sexual offenses against white women were not the principal cause of lynchings. Moreover, they ventured that most accusations of sexual offenses against blacks were specious and argued that white men and women, despite their professed concern for racial purity, routinely engaged in consensual sexual relations with blacks. Rather than punish criminals, lynchers actually sought to crush black economic aspirations, squelch black activism, and perpetuate white hegemony over a cowed and inarticulate black population. Once the myths were discredited, they believed, lynching would be understood for what it was—a crude and brutal tool of white supremacy. Far from a defense of the hallowed traditions of civilization, lynching, blacks insisted, was an indefensible assault on them.[9]

Southern defenders of lynching responded by setting out to discredit black activists and their exposés. These apologists gave voice to a wide range of white supremacist attitudes. Some saw lynchings as the unfortunate consequence of misguided, even criminal, social engineering after the Civil War; others saw them as the natural and laudable response of whites to black depravity. But whether the defenders were hand-wringing moderates who lamented but excused extralegal executions or bellicose radicals who looked to lynchers to hasten the passing of the black race in the South, they defined the terms of all subsequent debate and discussion. Scholars who sought to explain lynching and activists who set out to suppress it necessarily had to address the arguments of lynching's defenders. With seemingly endless reservoirs of stamina, black activists repeatedly stressed that most lynchings were not provoked by alleged sexual offenses by black men against white women, that blacks invariably received harsh and swift justice at the hands of the courts, and that mob violence weakened rather than strengthened the rule of law. Thus as long as lynching persisted as part of southern life, the National Association for the Advancement of Colored People (NAACP), the Commission on Interracial Cooperation, and later the Association of Southern Women for the Prevention of Lynching were inextricably engaged in a debate with defenders of lynching. Both antilynching activists and lynching's defenders well understood that their struggle was profoundly important and that its outcome had far-reaching implications for the "moral economy" of white supremacy.

The first generation of professional social scientists joined the campaign to expose and dramatize the reality concealed by the myths of lynching. Lynching attracted scholarly attention in part because its increase during the late nineteenth and early twentieth centuries coincided with the maturation of American social sciences. Practitioners of both sociology and psychology viewed lynching as a glaring example of social pathology that their respective disciplines were committed to explaining. American sociology in particular had emerged at a time when problems of social order and control seemed especially important. The discipline thus dwelled on the mechanisms of social order precisely when the effects of the "great migrations" of immigrants and blacks to cities exacerbated the problems of social and cultural diversity in the nation. Similarly, the discipline promoted techniques of social control to remedy the swashbuckling capitalism, political corruption, and weak social institutions that characterized the age.[10]

Early sociological explorations of lynching had a clear intellectual debt to sociologist Robert Park's theory of collective behavior. Park saw human society as made up of interdependent individuals and groups who were divided by competition for economic and political dominance but were held together by shared values and purposes. When social controls, which served the vital function of softening the competitive struggle for existence, weakened, Park predicated that collective violence became more likely. Although Park said little about lynching, his theories influenced both the methods and conclusions of subsequent scholarship on mob violence. Intent on explaining the underlying sources of competition and conflict that culminated in lynchings, researchers learned from Park to immerse themselves in the social and economic context that generated collective violence. His approach also encouraged scholars to view participants in collective violence as disproportionately deviant and isolated, in short, individuals poorly integrated into the larger society.[11]

As social scientists turned the cold light of science on lynching, they added their voices to a growing social critique of southern society that emerged in the Progressive Era of the early twentieth century. They intended their conclusions to consign lynching to the primitive past of the South, a past they believed should not be allowed to contaminate the modern age. Although few in number and subject to strenuous attacks from conservative critics, these social scientists were early participants in the larger intellectual transformation from the Victorian values that had dominated southern discourse during the late nineteenth century to a set of cautiously modern values that were far less encumbered by the regional chauvinism and prejudices of the past. In their quest to overcome the ignorance of the southern masses and enlighten public opinion, they laid the foundations for all subsequent studies of lynching.[12]

Southern sociologists, especially those associated with the University of North Carolina, including Howard W. Odum, Arthur F. Raper, Rupert B. Vance, and Thomas J. Woofter Jr., disposed of the shibboleths of conventional white supremacy and hammered home their central point that lynchings could not be separated from the region's far-reaching social and economic difficulties. Sociologists and activists alike shared a powerful yearning for order and control along with a sincere desire to eliminate the social ills of mob violence and brutal racial discrimination. Mob violence, they contended, was the harvest of weak educational, religious, and civic institutions, exploitative economic relationships, poverty, and ineffective law enforcement agencies, all of which failed to instill sufficient respect for the rule of law or human dignity. The statistics and evidence gathered by sociologists demonstrated that lynching went hand in hand with a rural culture corrupted by drunkenness, irreligion, illiteracy, poverty, and excessive license. The object of the reformers was to initiate change and inculcate values that were all too obviously absent in a region where lynchers routinely committed acts they considered inhuman and brutal. They assumed that the modernization of the southern economy would eradicate many of the causes of mob violence. They predicted that as the South became increasingly urban and industrial, the mechanisms for social control in time would became strong enough to discourage extralegal violence and discredit the values that sustained it.[13]

Early psychologists, powerfully influenced by Freudian theory, looked to individual psychopathologies rather than social conditions to explain antiblack violence. The ritualized mutilation of some lynching victims, the seeming frenzy of mobs, and the fixation of defenders of lynching on black sexuality prompted psychologists to attribute extralegal violence to deeply rooted psychological tensions about gender and sexuality. In 1933, for instance, Philip Resnikoff suggested that whites projected forbidden fantasies onto blacks and then vented their anger on the object of their own creation, the black rapist. Similarly, W. J. Cash, in his classic study, *The Mind of the South*, addressed white southerners' alleged twin obsession with race and sex. He suggested that the "rape complex" that gripped the white South demanded the violent defense of white feminine honor because "any assertion of any kind on the part of the Negro constituted in a perfectly real manner an attack on the Southern women." But it was William Faulkner, in his novel *Light in August*, who gave the richest and most provocative psychological interpretation of lynching. When Joanna Burden, a white woman, is killed in confused circumstances by Joe Christmas, a deeply disturbed man of unclear racial ancestry, the local community responds with obvious relish. At the climax of the novel, Christmas serves as the scapegoat for the thwarted sexual longings of Percy Grimm, the leader of the mob that murders and mutilates him. Black men were said to represent for white men a sexual liberation that they wanted but could not achieve without contradicting their race's professed mores. Tortured by their frustration, white men thus projected their thoughts upon black men and symbolically eradicated those desires by lynching hapless blacks.[14]

Alternatively, psychologist John Dollard attributed southern violence to the socially accepted channels for aggression in the region. Dollard's and subsequent scholars' work led to the claim that violent behavior is caused by a collective psychic state of frustration and resentment. Social conventions in the South permitted the release of white frustrations on blacks, a defenseless group who were associated with whites' repressed fears and desires. The violent tone of southern race relations thus was the culmination of "free-floating" aggression seeking an outlet.[15] Scholars subsequently located a variety of sources for the frustrations of whites that seemed to breed violence against blacks. In 1940, Carl Hovland and Robert Sears claimed that high correlations existed between lynching rates in the South and indicators of economic performance such as the per acre value of cotton. The frequency of lynching, they suggested, was a barometer of the economic frustration of white southerners. Poor economic conditions bred frustration by "blocking individual goal-directed behavior." This frustration, they contended, found its expression in lynchings of blacks, rather than other forms of violence, for two reasons. First, the actual sources of the frustration—landlords, merchants, and speculators— were powerful and hence actions taken against them would likely have been punished. Second, many of those lynched had already been arrested or were being sought for alleged crimes and thus had already acted as "frustrating agents" for whites.[16]

Other social scientists argued that lynching and violence helped maintain a caste system in the South. Custom alone was not enough to keep blacks in their place; only continual vigilance by whites maintained white superiority. Because all whites were said to share economic and psychic benefits both from the exploitation of blacks and from the caste system, they were united in their devotion to preserving white dominance. Lynching, then, was just one tool to perpetuate the privileges of whiteness. By resorting to extralegal violence, whites drew caste boundaries and reaffirmed their seemingly limitless power both to themselves and to blacks.[17]

By the 1940s, social scientists had produced a substantial and diverse body of work on both the structures of southern society and lynching which reinforced many of the charges made by antilynching activists. By combining techniques derived from ethnography, anthropology, and history with often deft social commentary, scholars began to chart the broad social forces, such as illiteracy, religious fundamentalism, poverty, and cultural isolation, that were said to create the conditions conducive to lynching. They had also addressed the complex psychological tensions that allegedly found release in violent behavior. Even so, for all of the innovation in explanations of lynching, a host of questions remained unanswered. One glaring gap in the literature was the lack of any careful survey of the historical evolution of lynching. Indeed, some of the interpretations of lynching ignored the historical complexities of the phenomenon. For example, early attempts to discover the socioeconomic causes of lynching, such as Arthur Raper's *Tragedy of Lynching*, outlined the conditions that produced contemporary extralegal violence, with the assumption that the same conditions could be traced throughout the history of lynching. Raper argued that mobs flourished in isolated, backward communities such as those that dotted the vast expanse of south Georgia. And yet mob violence had been chronic when the same region had been undergoing rapid development and could not, in any real sense, be described as stagnant or backward.[18] Psychological approaches also failed to provide any convincing explanation for regional variations in lynching or its ebb and flow over time. Rather, psychological analyses of lynching ignored its complex and widely varying characteristics and instead emphasized the individual psychology of lynchers. These and many other unresolved questions about the variation in lynching over time and place, however, would remain unaddressed for decades.

As the rate of lynching declined during the 1940s and virtually ended during the 1950s, scholarly study of lynching waned as well. The attention of sociologists and psychologists, in keeping with the present-minded orientation of their disciplines, shifted increasingly to more contemporary forms of racial violence and to the conflicts surrounding the civil rights movement. Historians, meanwhile, displayed little interest in violence.

Historians of the South recognized that violence occupied a prominent place in the region's past, but with the notable exceptions of John Hope Franklin and Vernon L. Wharton, few writing before the 1970s displayed an interest in the role of violence in shaping southern life.[19]

It is noteworthy that no historian addressed the topic of lynching in a major scholarly work until the late 1970s. For their analysis of lynching, historians seem to have been content to rely on sociologist Arthur Raper's *Tragedy of Lynching*, published in 1933, a cautiously scientific study rich in descriptive material but lacking in explanatory power.[20] Lack of interest in the subject of lynching is evident, for example, in the work of C. Vann Woodward, who devoted less than two pages to the topic in his classic work, *Origins of the New South*.[21] The silence of southern historians on lynching merely reflected the prevailing lack of interest in the subject before the 1960s. It also was partly a reflection of the grip C. Vann Woodward's work had on generations of scholars who traced the implications of his work. Perhaps, above all, historians were hindered by the simple fact that the history of violence in America, let alone in the South, was as yet poorly understood.

In 1971, Richard Hofstadter observed that American historians had not yet explored the subject of violence in the nation's past. Only since the 1960s did historians and other social scientists, prodded by urban riots, student unrest, and chronic violence throughout the nation, "rediscover" violence. The work of historians and sociologists Eric Hobsbawm, George Rudé, Charles Tilly, and others argued for the importance of studying collective violence in Europe and elsewhere by suggesting that crowd action is purposeful, rational, and continuous with other forms of social behavior. Collective action, they argue, is not a result of failed social control or exceptional social and psychological states. Instead, it arises out of ongoing political and economic contests present in all societies: violence is a by-product of "normal" collective action. Participants in collective violence are not isolated deviants, but rather often representative, well-integrated members of society. Historical collective violence no longer could be dismissed as an epiphenomenon of only passing interest. It moved, along with conflict in general, to the heart of social life. The study of riots, lynchings, and all manner of violence thus held the promise of enriching long-standing debates about topics as varied as resistance to modernization and traditions of community regulation.[22]

Spurred on by these new concepts and methods, scholars have reconsidered the purposes animating crowds and the relation between the participants in violence and the interests reflected in their actions. The influence of modern feminism has also helped scholars to understand the place of violence in the evolution of gender roles and behavior. The full record of violence against women, which, like lynching, has been too often overlooked, is now understood as a key element in the historical subordination of women. In a flood of new scholarship, historians have examined the central importance of violence to the dispossession of native peoples of their land and culture, to the social upheavals both before and after the American Revolution, to the opposition to immigration and various manifestations of dissent during the nineteenth century, and to the suppression of labor activism. Indeed, there now seems to be widespread agreement that conflict and violence have not been peripheral but rather are central to the nation's evolution.[23]

Southern history could not long escape the reevaluation of violence in general and lynching in particular. In recent years our understanding of the place of racial violence in southern history has been advanced by new viewpoints as well as by continuing work along older lines. The work that first lifted the historical study of lynching to a new level of sophistication was Jacquelyn Dowd Hall's *Revolt against Chivalry*.[24] Hall's biography of the white antilynching activist Jessie Daniel Ames attempts to reveal the complex motivations that incited lynchers in their bloody work. Although many of Hall's themes had been hinted at by antilynching activists decades earlier, she displays an uncanny eye for the place of lynching in the long span of southern history. The roots of extralegal violence, she explains, may be traced to the patriarchal vision of proslavery ideologues, to the dislocations of modernization in the South, and to the deeply traditional sexual and racial order of the South. Her concise analysis of lynching argues that lynching was never simply the blood sport of hayseeds and rednecks. Instead, she argues that lynching was a drama that helped to cement the entire southern social order. The dramatic spectacle of each lynching taught all southerners, male and female, black and white, precisely where in the social hierarchy they stood. For black men and women, lynchings graphically demonstrated their vulnerability and debasement; for white women, the violence reaffirmed their dependence upon white men; and for white men, lynching was a ritual that manifested their intention to occupy the loftiest position in the racial and gender hierarchy of the South. The enduring influence of Hall's work has been demonstrated by a spate of recent work that has expanded and deepened its line of argument.[25]

For all of the insights of Hall's work, which after all is a biography of a woman reformer rather than a monograph on lynching, there is still much work to be done to explain in greater detail the variations in lynching over time and place and the values that sustained extralegal violence. Several major works published during the 1980s have begun to tackle these topics. Joel Williamson, in *The Crucible of Race*, outlined the myriad ways in which violence became incorporated into the racial philosophies of the New South. The rantings of the Feltons, Tillmans, and Dixons of the South, he suggests, were much more than crude tactics of rabble rousing by twisted personalities. Rather, the rhetoric of "radical racists" and the violent actions of mobs existed in a symbiotic relationship, giving justification and legitimacy to each other while drowning out voices of restraint and moderation.

Williamson is struck by the coincidence of the sharp rise of lynching in and after 1889 and the increasing popularity of the radical idea that African Americans, free from the civilizing restraints of slavery, were "retrogressing" to the savage state that was their true nature. Both, he argues, were propelled by psychosexual tensions rooted in the worsening economic condition of southern whites. Trapped by an international market economy and all too aware of the shrinking gap that separated white farmers from their black counterparts, white men confronted the unthinkable possibility that the entire racial hierarchy would collapse. Unable to guarantee the economic security of their wives and families, white men became gripped by psychological tensions so profound that many of them found peace only in the catharsis of mob violence.

Central to Williamson's work is his belief that the balance of forces which shaped southern race relations was never static. Though by no means an advocate of a fixed value system in the South, historian Bertram Wyatt-Brown traces the roots of southern violence much further back than Williamson. In his study of antebellum southern culture, *Southern Honor*, Wyatt-Brown offers an all-encompassing interpretation of southern mob violence bolstered by examples drawn from the eighteenth, nineteenth, and twentieth centuries.[26] The key to lynching is the preeminent role that the culture of honor played in southern society. Unlike the ethos of dignity and self-restraint which prevailed in the North, the code of honor in the South encouraged and sanctioned violence. Lynch mobs, he explains, mobilized deep cultural traditions in a collective defense of community honor.

Edward L. Ayers, in *Vengeance and Justice*, also has stressed the importance of honor in understanding southern violence. But he contends that honor by itself is only a partial explanation for the spasm of racial violence that plagued the New South. In addition to honor, which endured with diminishing power once the crucial support of the institution of slavery was removed by the Civil War, Ayers explains the surge of mob violence by pointing to the economic dislocation of the depression of the 1890s and the dogma of republicanism which imposed sharp limitations on the courts and the authority of the states. A final catalyst he identifies was the growing alienation of postwar blacks and whites. In his recent study, *The Promise of the New South*, Ayers has added that lynchings were rife in precisely those areas of the South—the Gulf Plain stretching from Florida to Texas, and the cotton uplands of Mississippi, Louisiana, Arkansas, and Texas—where white insecurities were fueled by the prevalence of "what they called 'strange niggers,' blacks with no white to vouch for them, blacks with no reputation in the neighborhood, blacks without even other blacks to aid them."[27] The bloodshed, then, was the product of "apparently immutable features of the nineteenth-century South: race hatred, sexual fears, honor, intense moralism, and localistic republicanism."[28]

Other scholars recently have explored the diffuse and episodic character of lynching in the South by writing detailed case studies of notorious lynchings or histories of violence in individual states. With an eye for the setting, the historical context, and the consequences of specific lynchings, historians have added layers of texture and a level of precision to the topic.[29] At the same time, sociologists have displayed renewed interest in historical sociology and have reappraised older interpretations of all manner of collective violence, including lynching. This new scholarship reflects the increasing use of and interest in approaches to the study of social behavior that incorporate time as a dynamic rather than a static process.[30]

Taken together, this recent work provides scholars with many of the materials needed for a nuanced portrait of the history of lynching in the South. We, the contributors to this collection, owe a large debt to the scholars who have preceded us. These debts are evident in our conclusions and our sources. And yet this collection is intended to underscore that still more needs to be known about lynching and all forms of extralegal violence in the South. Much empirical research still needs to be done. Our understanding of the history of antiblack violence in the South remains severely circumscribed because of the excessive generalization that pervades the scholarship. Scholars know enough to differentiate the upper South from the deep South, the Piedmont from the Piney Woods, and plantation districts from the up-country. Scholars also have a deeper understanding of the complex balance of continuity and change that has characterized southern life during the past century and a half. But until recently historians and social scientists have not done the hard work of refining their analysis to take into account the regional and temporal complexities of southern society that the new scholarship has revealed.

Advances in the future, then, will almost certainly emerge both from the introduction of new theories, hypotheses, and methods and from deeper research into all aspects of lynching, extralegal violence, class structure, and southern mores. This collection is intended to bring together a broad and representative sample of important research on lynching and to demonstrate how theories, hypotheses, and methods, old as well as new, can be rigorously applied and tested. This volume brings together, in a comparative context, some of the best recently published essays on lynching with work published here for the first time. This book is not intended to be comprehensive, much less definitive. Instead, it is one more contribution to the growing number of sophisticated, in-depth studies of southern racial violence—studies that can help us to refine, deepen, correct, and if necessary replace vitally important ideas about the history of the South, American race relations, and the nature of American violence.

With essays that range in time from the close of the antebellum era to the mid-twentieth century and in place from Kentucky to Mississippi, this volume attempts to clarify and explain a distinct phase—the most southern and virulently racist phase—in the history of lynching in the United States. Admittedly, most of the essays are devoted to the postbellum era, in large part because it was then that lynching became such a conspicuously southern and racial phenomenon. Even so, two essays draw our attention to antebellum and Civil War antecedents to postbellum mob violence. And though the focus here is largely on the American South—the heartland of lynching— we speak to patterns of violence, injustice, racism, and oppression that have plagued the entire nation.

The essays in this volume do not exhaust the subject. Many aspects of the history of lynching remain to be investigated. We need to know more about the lasting effects of lynching on the cultural sensibilities of blacks and whites. We are familiar with the powerful renderings of mob violence in fiction, art, and music, but the connections between modernist aesthetics and depictions of lynching in the arts, for instance, have yet to be analyzed fully.[31] We also need to understand better the fusion of masculinity, status, racial identity, and work privileges that played a large role in mob violence. Various works have revealed the sexual politics that mobilized the lynch mobs that executed alleged rapists and black men who defied conventions of sexual propriety. The linkages of gender, race, and class in the lynchings of black men accused of rape are perhaps almost self-evident. But the same linkages were also fundamental to other manifestations of racial violence, ranging from riots against black industrial workers to attacks on black sharecroppers. Rather than applying gender analysis to some lynchings (i.e., lynchings of alleged sexual offenders) and class analysis to others (i.e., lynchings of black sharecroppers), scholars should continue to work to reveal the salience of class and gender in all lynchings. Much also remains unclear about both the role of collective violence in the maintenance of class structures and the participation of different classes in and their varied reactions to racial violence.[32]

The role of "contagion" effects on the pattern of lynchings is another question deserving further attention. Scholars need to determine whether lynchings increased or decreased the likelihood of further mob violence in a given area. Did lynchings, or other racial violence, release pent-up social tensions so that further violence was unlikely until tensions built up again? Or did lynchings, along the lines of a contagious disease, breed further violence until the contagion ran its course? Or, finally, were lynchings random events that had little causal effect on the likelihood of other violence in a given area? Almost certainly any attempt to answer these questions will raise interesting and complex methodological problems that will have implications far beyond the study of lynching.

In addition, much more work should be done on resistance to mob violence. Neither the character of extralegal attacks on ethnic minorities in the South, such as Mexican Americans in Texas and Italians in Louisiana, nor the response of those groups to mob violence has received adequate scholarly attention. Similarly, too little is known about the responses of black ministers and congregations to white violence.[33] Scholars have begun to chart the antilynching activities of national church bodies but have yet to describe how black ministers addressed extralegal violence in their sermons and fit it into their respective theologies. The response of black churches across the South and the nation to the exceptionally vicious and highly publicized 1899 lynching of Sam Hose in Georgia is but one example of a rich field for study that remains untapped.[34] Finally, this collection leaves unaddressed the question of the historical memory of lynching in the South. Since, as Benjamin Mays's and Richard Wright's reminiscences demonstrate, the memory of this violent past is so profoundly intertwined with the basic identities of African Americans and white southerners, there are many lingering questions about how generations of blacks and whites repressed, forgot, and reshaped their memories of lynching.[35]

We present this collection in the hope that it brings together useful and thought-provoking work that will reveal the scope of research done so far and, above all, will stimulate further efforts to understand the tragedy that was lynching in the American South.

NOTES

1. Mark Twain, *Collected Tales, Sketches, Speeches, and Essays, 1891– 1910* (New York: Library of America 1992), 485.

2. Benjamin E. Mays, *Born to Rebel: An Autobiography* (Athens: University of Georgia Press, 1987), 1, 17.

3. W. E. B. Du Bois, *Dusk of Dawn* (New York: Schocken Books, 1968), 67; Mrs. Medgar Evers with William Peters, *For Us, the Living* (New York: Ace, 1970); and Richard Wright, *Black Boy: A Record of Childhood and Youth* (New York: Harper & Row, 1966), 190.

4. Abraham Lincoln, *Speeches and Writings, 1832–1858* (New York: Library of America, 1989), 29.

5. Paul A. Gilje, *The Road to Mobocracy: Popular Disorder in New York City, 1763– 1834* (Chapel Hill: University of North Carolina Press, 1987); Leonard L. Richards, *"Gentlemen of Property and Standing": Anti-Abolition Mobs in Jacksonian America* (New York: Oxford University Press, 1970).

6. Lawrence M. Friedman, "The Law between the States: Some Thoughts on Southern Legal History," in *Ambivalent Legacy: A Legal History of the South*, ed. David J. Bodenhamer and James W. Ely Jr. (Jackson: University Press of Mississippi, 1984), 30–46; and Michael S. Hindus, *Prison and Plantation: Crime, Justice, and Authority in Massachusetts and South Carolina, 1767–1878* (Chapel Hill: University of North Carolina Press, 1980).

7. Robert Maxwell Brown, *Strain of Violence: Historical Studies of American Violence and Vigilantism* (New York: Oxford University Press, 1975).

8. For lynching totals, see Monroe Work, ed., *The Negro Yearbook: An Annual Encyclopedia of the Negro, 1931–1932* (Tuskegee: Negro Year Book Publishing Co., 1931), 293. The totals for Virginia and Georgia, which are lower than those recorded in the *Negro Year Book*, are derived from my research. The totals for Kentucky are from George C. Wright, *Racial Violence in Kentucky, 1865–1940: Lynchings, Mob Rule, and "Legal Lynchings"* (Baton Rouge: Louisiana State University Press, 1990), 71. Stewart E. Tolnay and E. M. Beck have counted 2,805 lynchings between 1882 and 1930 in ten southern states, excluding Texas and Virginia. See Tolnay and Beck, *A Festival of Violence: An Analysis of Southern Lynchings, 1882–1930* (Urbana: University of Illinois Press, 1995), 269–70.

9. The best survey of black responses to white violence is Herbert Shapiro, *White Violence and Black Response: From Reconstruction to Montgomery* (Amherst: University of Massachusetts Press, 1988). See also the discussion of Ida B. Wells's critique of lynching in Gail Bederman, *Manliness and Civilization: A Cultural History of Gender and Race in the United States, 1880–1917* (Chicago: University of Chicago Press, 1995), chap. 2.

10. On the currents in early American sociology, see Lewis A. Coser, "American Trends," in *A History of Sociological Analysis*, ed. Tom Bottomore and Robert Nisbet (New York: Basic Books, 1978); and Anthony Oberschall, "The Institutionalization of American Sociology," in *The Establishment of Empirical Sociology*, ed. Oberschall (New York: Harper & Row, 1972).

11. Coser, "American Trends," 311–17; Robert E. L. Faris, *Chicago Sociology, 1920–1932* (Chicago: University of Chicago Press, 1970); and James B. Rule, *Theories of Civil Violence* (Berkeley: University of California Press, 1988), 95–104.

12. W. Fitzhugh Brundage, *Lynching in the New South: Georgia and Virginia, 1880–1930* (Urbana: University of Illinois Press, 1993), chap. 8; Dewey W. Grantham, *Southern Progressivism: The Reconciliation of Progress and Tradition* (Knoxville: University of Tennessee Press, 1983), 28–32; Daniel Joseph Singal, *The War Within: From Victorian to Modernist Thought in the South, 1919–1945* (Chapel Hill: University of North Carolina Press, 1982), esp. chap. 5.

13. Arthur F. Raper, *The Tragedy of Lynching* (Chapel Hill: University of North Carolina Press, 1933), esp. 41–43, 51–54. See also Earl Fiske Young, "The Relations of Lynching to the Size of Population Areas," *Sociology and Social Research* 12 (March–April 1928): 348–53; and W. E. Wimpy, "Lynchings: An Evil of County Government," *Manufacturers' Record* 76 (December 25, 1919): 49–50. The best summary of this interpretation of lynching is in Gunnar Myrdal, *An American Dilemma: The Negro Problem and Modern Democracy* (1944; rpt. New York: Pantheon, 1972), 560–66.

14. Philip Resnikoff, "A Psychoanalytic Study of Lynching," *Psychoanalytic Review* 20 (October 1933): 421–27; W. J. Cash, *The Mind of the South* (New York: Knopf, 1941), 116–20. This line of argument predated psychoanalytic scholarship. For earlier versions, see William Archer, *Through Afro-America: An English Reading of the Race Problem* (London: Chapman and Hull, 1910), 216–17; Thomas P. Bailey, *Race Orthodoxy in the South* (New York: Neale, 1914), 44; Sir Harry H. Johnston, *The Negro in the New World* (London: Methuen, 1910), 462.

15. John Dollard, *Caste and Class in a Small Southern Town* (New Haven: Yale University Press, 1937); Dollard et al., *Frustration and Aggression* (New Haven: Yale University Press, 1939).

16. The correlation between cotton prices and lynchings is described in Carl Iver Hovland and Robert R. Sears, "Minor Studies of Aggression: VI. Correlation of Lynchings with Economic Indices," *Journal of Psychology* 9 (April 1940): 301–10; and Raper, *Tragedy of Lynching*, 30–31. For a methodological critique of Hovland and Sears, see Alexander Mintz, "A Re-Examination of Correlations between Lynchings and Economic Indices," *Journal of Abnormal and Social Psychology* 41 (1946): 154–65. For a sophisticated modern treatment of this topic, see E. M. Beck and Stewart E. Tolnay, "The Killing Fields of the Deep South: The Market for Cotton and the Lynching of Blacks, 1882–1930," *American Sociological Review* 55 (August 1990): 526–99. The psychoanalytical theories have continued to inform scholarship. Historian Joel Williamson has offered an influential reworking of the psychoanalytic theory in *The Crucible of Race: Black-White Relations in the American South since Emancipation* (New York: Oxford University Press, 1984). Similarly, sociologists E. M. Beck and Stewart Tolnay have given new life to the frustration-aggression theory in their study of lynching, *Festival of Violence*, chap. 5.

17. Allison Davis, Burleigh B. Gardner, and Mary R. Gardner, *Deep South: A Social Anthropological Study of Caste and Class* (Chicago: University of Chicago Press, 1965); and Dollard, *Caste and Class in a Southern Town*. Although Oliver C. Cox rejected the application of caste to southern race relations, his conclusions about the role of racial violence complemented those associated with the so-called caste school of scholars. See Cox, *Caste, Class, and Race: A Study in Social Dynamics* (New York: Doubleday, 1948), 548–64.

18. Contrast Raper, *Tragedy of Lynching*, Part III, with Brundage, *Lynching in the New South*, chap. 4.

19. John Hope Franklin, *The Militant South* (Cambridge, Mass.: Harvard University Press, 1941); Vernon Lane Wharton, *The Negro in Mississippi, 1865–1890* (Chapel Hill: University of North Carolina Press, 1947). A minor classic also deserving mention is Jack K. Williams, *Vogues in Villainy: Crime and Retribution in Antebellum South Carolina* (Columbia: University of South Carolina Press, 1959).

20. Historians less often cited Walter White's far more daring and penetrating study of lynching, *Rope and Faggot: A Biography of Judge Lynch* (New York: Knopf, 1929).

21. C. Vann Woodward, *Origins of the New South, 1877–1913* (Baton Rouge: Louisiana State University Press, 1951), 351–52. Similarly, lynching receives only passing mention in Woodward's other classic, *The Strange Career of Jim Crow* (New York: Oxford University Press, 1955), 43, 87, 114– 15, 173–74. In contrast, George Tindall, in *The Emergence of the New South* (Baton Rouge: Louisiana State University Press, 1967), 170–80, devoted considerable space to lynching, especially to the antilynching campaigns.

22. Richard Hofstadter and Michael Wallace, *American Violence: A Documentary History* (New York: Vintage Press, 1971), 4; Ted Robert Gurr, *Why Men Rebel* (Princeton: Princeton University Press, 1970); George Rudé, *The Crowd in the French Revolution* (Oxford: Oxford University Press, 1959); and Charles Tilly, *The Vendée* (Cambridge, Mass.: Harvard University Press, 1964). See also Rule, *Theories of Civil Violence*, chaps. 6–7.

23. For a sampling of works that have charted the role of violence in American society, see Richard Maxwell Brown, *The South Carolina Regulators* (Cambridge, Mass.: Harvard University Press, 1963); Brown, *Strain of Violence: Historical Studies of American Violence and Vigilantism* (New York: Oxford University Press, 1975), esp. 91–180; Dickson D. Bruce Jr., *Violence and Culture in the Antebellum South* (Austin: University of Texas Press, 1979); Richard Drinnon, *Facing West: The Metaphysics of Indian-Hating and Empire-Building* (New York: New American Library, 1980); Michael Fellman, *Inside War: The Guerilla Conflict in Missouri during the American Civil War* (New York: Oxford University Press, 1989); Eric Foner, *Reconstruction: America's Unfinished Revolution, 1863–1877* (New York: Harper & Row, 1988), 119–23; Gilje, *Road to Mobocracy*; Elliot J. Gorn, " 'Gouge and Bite, Pull Hair and Scratch': The Social Significance of Fighting in the Southern Backcountry," *American Historical Review* 90 (February 1985): 18–43; Hugh Davis Graham and Ted Robert Gurr, *Violence in America: Historical and Comparative Perspectives* (Beverly Hills: Sage, 1979); Ray Granade, "Violence: An Instrument of Policy in Reconstruction Alabama," *Alabama Historical Quarterly* 30 (Fall–Winter 1968): 181–202; Patricia Nelson Limerick, *The Legacy of Conquest: The Unbroken Past of the American West* (New York: Norton,

1987); Richard B. McCaslin, *Tainted Breeze: The Great Hanging at Gainesville, Texas, 1862* (Baton Rouge: Louisiana State University Press, 1994); Neil R. McMillen, *Dark Journey: Black Mississippians in the Age of Jim Crow* (Urbana: University of Illinois Press, 1989); Phillip S. Paludan, *Victims: A True Story of the Civil War* (Knoxville: University of Tennessee Press, 1981); George C. Rable, *But There Was No Peace: The Role of Violence in the Politics of Reconstruction* (Athens: University of Georgia Press, 1984); Richards, *"Gentlemen of Property and Standing"*; Thomas P. Slaughter, *The Whiskey Rebellion: Frontier Epilogue to the American Revolution* (New York: Oxford University Press, 1986); Slaughter, *Bloody Dawn: The Christiana Riot and Racial Violence in the Antebellum North* (New York: Oxford University Press, 1991); Richard Slotkin, *Regeneration through Violence: The Mythology of the American Frontier, 1600–1860* (Middletown, Conn.: Wesleyan University Press, 1973); Slotkin, *The Fatal Environment: The Myth of the Frontier in the Age of Industrialization, 1800–1890* (New York: Atheneum, 1985); Allen W. Trelease, *White Terror: The Ku Klux Klan Conspiracy and Southern Reconstruction* (New York: Harper & Row, 1979); Robert M. Utley, *The Indian Frontier of the American West, 1846–1890* (Albuquerque: University of New Mexico Press, 1984); Michael Wallace, "The Uses of Violence in American History," *American Scholar* 40 (Winter 1970–71): 81–102.

24. Jacquelyn Dowd Hall, *Revolt against Chivalry: Jessie Daniel Ames and the Women's Campaign against Lynching* (New York: Columbia University Press, 1979).

25. Laura F. Edwards, "Sexual Violence, Gender, Reconstruction, and the Extension of Patriarchy in Granville County, North Carolina," *North Carolina Historical Review* 68 (1991): 237–60; Martha Hodes, "The Sexualization of Reconstruction Politics: White Women and Black Men in the South after the Civil War," *Journal of the History of Sexuality* 3 (1993): 402–17; Nancy MacLean, "The Leo Frank Case Reconsidered: Gender and Sexual Politics in the Making of Reactionary Populism," *Journal of American History* 78 (1991): 917–48; Robyn Wiegman, "The Anatomy of Lynching," *Journal of the History of Sexuality* 3 (1993): 445–67.

26. Bertram Wyatt Brown, *Southern Honor: Ethics and Behavior in the Old South* (New York: Oxford University Press, 1983).

27. Edward L. Ayers, *The Promise of the New South* (New York: Oxford University Press, 1992), 157.

28. Edward L. Ayers, *Vengeance and Justice: Crime and Punishment in the 19th Century South* (New York: Oxford University Press, 1984), 265.

29. Ann Field Alexander, "Like an Evil Wind: The Roanoke Riot of 1893 and the Lynching of Thomas Smith," *Virginia Magazine of History and Biography* 100 (April 1992): 173–206; W. Fitzhugh Brundage, "The Darien 'Insurrection' of 1899: Black Protest during the Nadir of Race Relations," *Georgia Historical Quarterly* 74 (Summer 1990): 234–53; Brundage, *Lynching in the New South*; Brundage, "Varn Mill Riot: Violence and Justice in the New South," *Georgia Historical Quarterly* (Summer 1994): 257–80; Beth Crabb, "May 1930: White Man's Justice for a Black Man's Crime," *Journal of Negro History* 75 (Winter–Spring 1990): 29–40; Juanita W. Crudele, "A Lynching Bee: Butler County Style," *Alabama Historical Quarterly* 42 (Spring–Summer 1980): 59–71; Jack E. Davis, "'Whitewash' in Florida: The Lynching of Jesse James Payne and Its Aftermath," *Florida Historical Quarterly* 68 (January 1990): 277–98; Leonard Dinnerstein, *The Leo Frank Case* (1968; rpt. Athens: University of Georgia Press, 1987); Mary Louise Ellis, "'Rain Down Fire': The Lynching of

Sam Hose" (Ph.D. diss., Florida State University, 1992); Robert P. Ingalls, *Urban Vigilantes in the New South: Tampa, 1882–1936* (Knoxville: University of Tennessee Press, 1988); Todd E. Lewis, "Mob Justice in the 'American Congo': 'Judge Lynch' in Arkansas during the Decade after World War I," *Arkansas Historical Quarterly* 52 (1993): 156–84; James R. McGovern, *Anatomy of a Lynching: The Killing of Claude Neal* (Baton Rouge: Louisiana State University Press, 1982); Howard Smead, *Blood Justice: The Lynching of Charles Mack Parker* (New York: Oxford University Press, 1986); James M. SoRelle, "The 'Waco Horror': The Lynching of Jesse Washington," *Southwestern Historical Quarterly* 86 (April 1983): 517–36; Stephen J. Whitfield, *A Death in the Delta: The Story of Emmett Till* (New York: Free Press, 1988); Edward C. Williamson, "Black Belt Political Crisis: The Savage-James Lynching, 1882," *Florida Historical Quarterly* 45 (April 1967): 402–9; Jon L. Wilson, "Days of Fear: A Lynching in St. Petersburg," *Tampa Bay History* 5 (Fall–Winter 1983): 4–26; Wright, *Racial Violence in Kentucky*.

30. See, e.g., Larry J. Griffin, "Temporality, Events, and Explanation in Historical Sociology: An Introduction," *Sociological Methods and Research* 20 (May 1992): 403–27; Griffin, "Narrative, Event-Structure Analysis and Causal Interpretation in Historical Sociology," *American Journal of Sociology* 98 (March 1993): 1094–1133; and Tolnay and Beck, *Festival of Violence*.

31. For four provocative forays into this area, see Jane Gaines, "Fire and Desire: Race, Melodrama, and Oscar Micheaux," in *Black American Cinema*, ed. Manthia Diawara (New York: Routledge, 1993), 49–70; Trudier Harris, *Exorcising Blackness: Historical and Literary Lynching and Burning Rituals* (Bloomington: Indiana University Press, 1984); Marlene Park, "Lynching and Antilynching: Art and Politics in the 1930s," *Prospects* 18 (1994): 311–66; and Judith L. Stephens, "Antilynching Plays by African-American Women: Race, Gender, and Social Protest in American Drama," *African-American Review* 26 (Summer 1992): 329–40.

32. For a modest attempt to incorporate gender and class more fully into accounts of mob violence, see W. Fitzhugh Brundage, "Class, Gender and Mob Violence in the South," in *Xenophobia, Racism, Nativism, and National Identity in Germany and the United States: A Comparative Perspective on Conditions of Intolerance*, ed. Norbert Finzsch and Dietmar Schirmer (New York: Cambridge University Press, 1997).

33. Two works that have begun to fill this void are Evelyn Brooks Higginbotham, *Righteous Discontent: The Women's Movement in the Black Baptist Church, 1880–1920* (Cambridge, Mass.: Harvard University Press, 1993); and Ralph E. Luker, *The Social Gospel in Black and White: American Racial Reform, 1885–1912* (Chapel Hill: University of North Carolina Press, 1991).

34. On the Hose lynching, see Ellis, " 'Rain Down Fire.' "

35. For one attempt to explore the historical memory of lynching in one community, see Charlotte Wolf, "Construction of a Lynching," *Sociological Inquiry* 62 (Winter 1992): 83–97.

Part I

Approaches to Racial Violence and Lynching

More than three decades ago, sociologist Neil Smelser asked, "What determines whether an episode of collective behavior of any sort will occur? What determines whether one type rather than another will occur?"[1] Roberta Senechal de la Roche and Larry J Griffin, Paula Clark, and Joanne C. Sandberg ask similar questions of collective violence, and in particular lynching. The "repertoires" of collective violence, to borrow Charles Tilly's phrase, have long been the focus of scholarly interest, and these two essays both draw upon and contribute to that rich tradition. They are excellent examples of the continuing value of theoretical innovation in the study of lynching. Both essays seek to explain variation in violence at the level of the case or individual incident of violent conflict.

Griffin, Clark, and Sandberg explore the importance of temporal order, sequence, and contingency in lynchings. Their essay, which has implications for students of all social events, demonstrates the advantages of the methodological approach of "event-narrative analysis" by carefully reconstructing the sequence of events in a lynching in Mississippi. Griffin, Clark, and Sandberg, like Senechal de la Roche, reveal a nuanced understanding of the importance of the circumstances specific to each lynching. But they, to a far greater extent than Senechal de la Roche, are interested in developing a methodology that takes into account the temporal sequence of collective actions such as lynchings. Rather than approaching lynchings as historical facts, they look at them as events that might have turned out differently. Simply put, they insist that each lynching is a narrative and that theories which seek to explain lynchings should avoid mechanistic models of the unfolding of lynchings and instead should take into account the inherently open-ended, contingent nature in any narrative event—the novel twists, turns, and unexpected happenings that shape what actually happened.

Among the implications of Griffin, Clark, and Sandberg's approach is the vitally important point that mob violence was not random; it appeared so only because the circumstances that could culminate in mob violence were so commonplace. In addition, their analysis demonstrates that any understanding of the origins and unfolding of lynching will remain incomplete unless attempted lynchings, no less than accomplished lynchings, are taken into account. Historians and social scientists understandably have concentrated on race riots and lynchings, the most visible and dramatic instances of racial violence, but have paid far less attention to much more frequent minor racial disturbances and attempted lynchings. But as long as historians interested in mob violence concentrate only on accomplished lynchings, they risk ignoring suggestive evidence of circumstances that either impeded or even thwarted lynchers. Given the frequency of and widespread support for mob violence in the South, the fact that many lynching attempts were frustrated begs for explanation. Close scrutiny of the flow of events in Bolivar County, Mississippi, in 1930 and elsewhere demonstrates that each incident of mob violence was contingent upon a range of possibilities and constraints, which themselves were shaped by circumstances, place, and prior actions, no less than the South's social structure and racial mores.

Senechal de la Roche encourages us to understand southern lynching in the context of a broader and more general theory of collective behavior. Implicit in her argument is that lynching in the South varied according to principles that also apply to group violence across the world and in different historical periods. Her essay, which establishes with new clarity and precision the social conditions that predict and explain variations in the likelihood and severity of lynching, provides some answers to knotty questions that historians and social scientists have long overlooked. Why, for the same alleged offense, did southerners lynch in one situation and not in another? Why might lynchers kill one alleged offender in one case and multiple victims in another? What accounts for the variation in the severity seen from one lynching to another?

Senechal de la Roche's theory is new in that it seeks to explain collective violence such as lynching without regard to psychological or motivational factors (e.g., frustration caused by economic hardship or repressed sexuality) or broad, shared social values (e.g., racism or the southern code of honor). Instead, she draws upon the paradigm and concepts of sociologist Donald Black and treats lynching as a means of social control—one of many ways humans handle the misconduct of others. Following Black, and taking the single case of conflict as the unit of analysis, she offers propositions that predict and explain the likelihood and severity of lynching in the postbellum South. Her formulations draw attention to the vital importance of "the social structure of the case of conflict," which is determined by the degree of intimacy, cultural similarity, interdependence, and inequality between the parties in the conflict. The theory informs us that for any instance of collective violence to occur, a variety of necessary conditions must be fulfilled. Moreover, its propositions underscore that no incident of collective violence can be adequately explained by a single "cause" or variable. Her propositions are testable: the theory is falsifiable. Because it addresses only observable behavior, the theory yields statements for which, in principle, contrary evidence may be adduced. Unlike most historians, who often are unclear about concepts, who offer variables that are not directly observable or measurable, and who seldom offer testable statements about how changes in one factor predict changes in the likelihood of another, Senechal de la Roche offers a theory that can and undoubtedly will be tested and applied to lynchings and other forms of collective violence.

These two essays should encourage future scholars to wring more analytical significance out of the important details of each lynching, details that may explain much about the different forms of racial violence. These essays also reveal the vigor of the new burst of methodological innovation in the study of lynching, which promises greatly to enrich our understanding of both collective and racial violence.

NOTE

1. Neil Smelser, *Theory of Collective Behavior* (London: Routledge & Kegan Paul, 1962), 12.

Narrative and Event
Lynching and Historical Sociology

Larry J. Griffin, Paula Clark,

and Joanne C. Sandberg

S ociologists study southern lynching in ways that are strikingly
different from the approaches taken by most historians. By de-
sign, they generally explore aggregate lynching rates, most often
with statistical techniques and equipped with theories of social
organization, group relations, and social control which emphasize the
structural impetus to, and support for, lynching—its roots in the economics and politics of cotton and oppressive Jim Crow laws. Their findings have proven invaluable in systematically documenting the socially
determined nature of lynchings and in forging causal generalizations of
broad theoretical and comparative potential. But because their structural
emphasis and aggregate/statistical research designs often require sociologists to freeze history, strip lynchings of their historical specificity, and
relegate context and narrative to the void of "background," "data," and
"illustration," we seldom see what actually happened as lynchings unfolded, why they happened as they did, and how, once under way, they
might have been stopped. We perceive the powerful and anonymous or
not-so-anonymous forces at work behind the backs of southerners but not
enough of their own moral and causative agency and thus too little of what
racial violence reveals about the makeup and subtle operation of white
supremacy.

By narrating richly detailed, fluid accounts of lynchings squarely situated in their cultural contexts and centered on the behavior of real people,
historians generally do better here. Agency is depicted in motion, and
possibilities cunningly realized, blundered upon, or permitted to seep
away are often insightfully examined to show how threatened lynchings
were expedited or stymied. Lynchings are windows to the soul of white

supremacy and African American life in the South, and historians more readily than sociologists exploit the prismatic nature of incidents of racial violence or near violence, seemingly relishing the intricacies of the Jim Crow South refracted there. But the assumptions and reasoning behind the analyses of historians, particularly those in the case study tradition, often remain untheorized, implicitly contained in and swept along by the dramatic flow of actions and events. Although historians' inferences are usually illuminating, how they reached and empirically verified them is sometimes unclear, as are the generalizability and theoretical implications of their conclusions.

Useful disciplinary conventions, then, entail costs, occasionally unacceptably high costs. Racial violence and its implications about the South and the region's relationship to the nation, its economic and political structures, and its norms and cultural constructions (of race, gender, class, and justice, among others) are too important to sustain an artificially neat division of intellectual labor that unfortunately misses as much about the dynamics of lynchings as it clarifies. Sociologists and historians have much to learn from each other, not just facts or how to write compelling narrative, on the one hand, or theories and techniques, on the other, but also fundamental ways of thinking about and analyzing lynchings.

By synthesizing important strengths of each approach, we attempt in this essay to bridge partially these methodological and substantive differences. Our synthesis joins the concreteness and contingency of historical case studies to the analytic explicitness and comparative grounding of sociological analyses.[1] We canvass a wide variety of incidents of real or incipient racial violence that demonstrate that the actions and reactions of southerners were conflicted and thus surprisingly rich and nuanced; use this empirical generalization to make several methodological points about threatened lynchings as historical happenings; and then apply both the comparative and theoretical insights to the analysis of a single lynching that occurred in Mississippi in 1930.

COMPLEXITIES, CONTRADICTIONS, PUZZLES

White supremacy did not unalterably script or encode what southerners would do when confronted by racial conflict or potentially lethal racial situations. Consider what happened in two nearly adjacent West Tennessee counties in an eighteen-hour period in 1931. In Obion County, a white mob stormed the jail, "overpowered" the sheriff and his deputy, and lynched George Smith, an African American prisoner, while in Carroll County white vigilantes were stopped by the wife of the sheriff. She misled the mob about her husband's absence and, referring to the mob's intent to take the prisoner, told them, "You couldn't run anything like that over me." Ultimately, the black man, Henry Mauford (also named Joe Wauford and Henry Wanford in the newspapers), was moved to four different jails to protect him from various lynch mobs. These are not isolated incidents. A year earlier, in 1930, a police officer in Kemper County, Mississippi, reportedly leaked to potential lynchers crucial information about the time and route of transporting two black prisoners, an act that, if true, resulted in a double lynching, while the sheriff in the adjacent Mississippi hill county, Neshoba—a county equally poor and equally white supremacist—spirited his prisoner away, thereby saving his life.[2]

The essential unpredictability of both action and the resolution of action seen in these racial episodes was widely replicated throughout the Jim Crow South. Two episodes from Adams County (Natchez), Mississippi, in the 1930s indicate that possible lynchings could be short-circuited even before they got started. In the first, a white woman accused an African American male of striking her in an argument over property lines and had him arrested. The judge threw the case out of court after the man, a black professional, claimed that he had merely knocked a pistol from the woman's hand. In the second example, a black man, again a respected professional, killed a drunken white man in a traffic accident. Not only was the African American not arrested, but important whites rushed to his defense, labeling him "a great influence for good in the community."[3] Either incident might have led to a lynching or threatened lynching, but neither did. In these cases, African Americans who might have been seen to be in the wrong by prevailing racist standards, and thus vulnerable to mob violence, were almost entirely excluded from punishment by "Judge Lynch's law" because of how whites constructed and understood the incidents.

As we have already seen from what happened in West Tennessee and the Mississippi hill country, even after mobs were organized and, smelling blood, had begun to move, threatened lynchings could be—and often were—prevented by the actions of white southern law enforcement officials. Estimates of the number of prevented lynchings range from 648 during the years 1915–32 (Arthur Raper) to 762 for the 1915–42 period (Jessie Daniel Ames). If only suggestive of the exact number, these data nonetheless indicate that between one-half and two-thirds of threatened lynchings failed, largely because of the active intercession of the authorities.[4] What white authorities did vis-à-vis both African American prisoners or fugitives and fellow whites in the lynch mob thus was often critical to whether an attempted lynching became a lynching in fact. An archetypic expression of a firm antilynching stance comes from a small-town Louisiana jailer, who reportedly averted a lynching in 1926 by telling five vigilantes, "You may kill me, but you can't get the negro." Virtually every detailed scholarly analysis of particular lynchings or averted lynchings, moreover, powerfully reiterates the central role of law, either as a deterrent before or after the fact of mob formation or as a deliberate or inadvertent facilitator of vigilante hopes.[5]

African Americans did not always rely on white law to prevent mob violence against themselves and other blacks: they also took matters into their own hands, improvising courageously within the interstices of white supremacy. In 1924, William Lewis, a prosperous African American farmer in Clarion, Virginia, successfully fought off a white mob, escaping to Pittsburgh when would-be killers left to get reinforcements. More tragically, some African Americans preferred suicide to mob vengeance. Even as vigilantes were battering down the jail door in Texas in 1923, Clarence Smith killed himself in view of his jailer with a homemade knife after the guard ignored his pleas to save him. Black resistance to lynchings, moreover, did not stop with individual acts of defiance. African Americans also armed themselves and engaged in full-fledged defensive collective action. This seemed generally to occur in the early days of Jim Crow, before it became so tightly institutionalized. The events in Darien, Georgia, in 1899 and in Muskogee, Oklahoma, in 1915 are cases in point. In the latter incident, hundreds, possibly even a thousand, African American men and women organized to prevent a lynching and fired their weapons above the white mob, thereby dispersing it.[6] These incidents defy most expectations about what blacks would or could do when confronted with a potential lynching.

Whites without official authority also helped halt threatened lynchings. They both initiated or were otherwise involved in the preventive steps taken by police officers and intervened directly, persuading mobs to disband or sheltering African Americans. When the infamous 1927 Little Rock public lynching and burning unleashed several days of white frenzy against many blacks, a white man forced his way to the front of an angry crowd surrounding an armed African American, reportedly "denounced the mob and urged them to permit the negro to be taken to the city jail." The African American was then rushed out of the crowd and taken to the jail for safekeeping.[7]

Threatened lynchings could be derailed at virtually any point, even at what seemed to be almost the logical end of the event. White mobs in physical possession of African Americans accused of a crime (or of a violation of racist norms) occasionally were persuaded by authorities to release a suspect, or they evaluated what was construed to be "evidence" and freed someone they adjudicated innocent. This sometimes resulted from the unwillingness of alleged white victims to identify a particular African American as the culprit of some real or imaginary wrong. Probably more rarely, some mobs chose to stop the lynching before they committed murder. In 1915, would-be lynchers in Deadon, Tennessee, reportedly placed a noose around a black man's neck, but when the white husband of the alleged sexual assault victim refused to kill the African American, they returned the prisoner to the jail. Similarly, an Anson County, North Carolina, African American wrongly thought to have killed a white man in 1924 was jailed after he was captured by a lynch party because some mob members ("cooler heads," in the newspaper account) convinced the other whites to allow the law to take its course.[8]

These ironies, contradictions, and ambiguities of meaning and purpose, which riddle the entire history of race in the South, pose genuine challenges to conventional sociological approaches to the study of lynching, especially those that denude cases of their historicity and rely on historically tenuous generalizations and causal determinism. Even though the power to define the meaning of situations and persons and to act on those definitions was as one-sidedly "colored" as is possible in what passed for a liberal democracy, whites and blacks possessed and used, individually and collectively, such a surprisingly large repertoire of possible responses to incidents of racial violence or near violence that any certainty about the event's unfolding or denouement was precluded. This is not to suggest that these and similar events are inexplicable random happenings or that all we can do is tell stories about them. Each has an interpretable logic conjoining social structure and circumstance, cultural pattern and particularity. To discern and understand that logic, however, storytelling must be transcended even as narrative, as the medium through which we know events, must be retained and analytically exploited.

Averted lynchings and episodes of near violence undoubtedly are of genuine moral and analytical importance in their own right. Or they may be used, as we do here, to help us think more systematically about lynchings as a generic happening, about how to study them, and about how to use them to penetrate the surface of white supremacy and unpeel layers of meaning.

"LYNCHINGS-IN-THE-MAKING" AS EVENT
AND NARRATIVE

As historical events, completed and prevented lynchings (which we group together under one term, "lynchings-in-the-making") have formal and substantive properties that set them off from other classes of phenomena and yield valuable clues about how to analyze, explain, and interpret them.

Formally, an event is a particular happening that is constituted by a particular sequence of temporally ordered actions and occurs in a particular historical context. These characteristics give the event its identity as a certain kind of happening (say, a lynching versus a prevented lynching), imbue it with general meaning, and create and convey its central theme or pattern of action. They, along with the event's theme, produce another of the event's formal properties, its holistic, configurational makeup: each sequence in an event is functionally related to its theme (if not, a particular action would not be included in its description) and temporally configured with the other sequences constituting the event. Events, finally, are analytic composites that fuse the historically particular and the theoretically general so thoroughly that the distinction between the two is largely moot. The selection of particular actions into the narrative of an event, for example, presupposes both general categories and general expectations about sequencing. Thus events synthesize empirical generalizations, theoretical concepts and hypotheses, and the historical specifics of action and context.[9]

Several important analytical implications follow from these formal properties. First, events can be theoretically comprehended as coherent historical happenings only by grasping the sum total of their unfolding sequences and placing them in their cultural contexts. The final identity of a lynching-in-the-making as either a completed or a prevented lynching, for example, is entirely a function of the precise sequences of actions constituting the event and how they unfolded through time. Events are complex relational wholes, not analytically isolated facts or aggregates.[10] Second, it follows that events should be analyzed partly in terms of their particular contextual and temporal makeup rather than, as many sociologists do, simply aggregate isolated facts from narratives of lynchings and then explain the occurrence or frequency of the aggregate. No two events, including those of the same theoretical class (such as lynching), have the same actors, temporal unfolding, and historical context. We have repeatedly seen, in fact, that what happened in one lynching-in-the-making cannot be accurately predicted even from what happened in other incidents possessing the same identity and having identical actions at an abstract level (e.g., allegations of racial transgressions, mob formation, and pursuit). Third, the dual character of events—their fusion of the particular and the general—must be acknowledged. Thus as we examine the event's specific context and sequencing, we must also place it in a comparative and theoretical frame. By perceiving how one event is similar to and different from others, we comprehend more clearly both the causal forces responsible for its particular unfolding and its general significance.[11]

The substantive properties of events must also be considered. Events display the anatomy and dynamism of social structures: how they are put together, how and where they produce social tension, and how the possibilities for human liberation and constraint are organized. They thus serve as the repository and (perhaps temporary) resolution of social conflicts and reveal how multiple or contradictory social relations and cultural meanings surface and are held in check or how they are suppressed and the tensions this induces. The event's unfolding sequences function, in the words of Barrington Moore, much as a "series of switching points with forces pushing in several directions," and each link in the event's characteristic "enchainment" of action thus is "actually a contest among opposing forces" impelling the event forward in time. "Any historical moment is both a result of prior process," writes E. P. Thompson, "and an index towards the direction of its future flow."[12]

But only in exceptional circumstances (and then generally toward the event's termination) does a single action clearly determine a contested present and an as yet unmade future. Events therefore are inherently contingent because they did not have to happen as they did. Because neither the event's context nor its early actions entirely prefigure what will subsequently happen, events are capable of what Dale Porter calls the "production of novelty" at virtually any point in their unfolding, the unexpected turn—an armed intervention, an act of resistance by the intended victim, a man refusing to sanction mob death—which may be decisive for subsequent action and thus for the event's ultimate identity. Through their unfolding, events, then, encapsulate and display historically contested structural practices and potentialities, simultaneously pointing to possible avenues of both cultural change and continuity.[13]

To realize the analytical promise inherent in events, however, they must be systematically "unpacked" and theoretically reconstituted as explicit interpretive and explanatory devices. An effective way to do this is to ask and answer counterfactual questions about each action in the event—to explore, that is, the event's range of contestations for possible actions and meanings and for what they say about social structure—because explanations of what did not happen impart understanding of what did happen and why it happened as it did. What did *not* happen in the lynching we analyze below, for example, was that David Harris's murder by whites was prevented, and it was not prevented because of how particular individuals acted and refrained from acting. Their behavior, in turn, can be interpreted in light of what the lynching's prior unfolding had presented to them as opportunities for future action and their own understandings of the culturally sanctioned and socially structured possibilities for their own agency and that of others. To understand the actions that kept this lynching from being averted is to go a long way toward explaining the lynching itself.

Prevented lynchings function as "historical counterexamples" to completed lynchings and, as such, are analytically indispensable to the analysis of lynchings. In grasping why and how threatened lynchings were averted, we more cogently perceive the alternatives for action and the room for maneuvering in any given completed lynching. Through the use of historical counterfactuals and historical counterexamples to unpack an event, then, we can both understand why a lynching-in-the-making becomes a lynching in fact rather than a prevented lynching and reveal what it says about contested social structures and cultural meanings.[14]

THE LYNCHING OF DAVID HARRIS:
BOLIVAR COUNTY, MISSISSIPPI, 1930

The power of any methodology to clarify thinking and sharpen inferences is most profoundly observed when that methodology must grapple with pressing substantive questions. By conducting a detailed and substantive analysis of a single lynching in which we merge the traditions of historical case studies and sociological approaches, we explore what can be learned from thinking of lynchings as open-ended, contingent happenings, simultaneously historically singular and historically general.

The account of this lynching is taken from Arthur F. Raper's book *The Tragedy of Lynching*. Either Raper or his assistant, Walter Chivers, from Atlanta University, visited the sites of each of the incidents described in the book. To gather as much information as possible on these events, they interviewed participants and their family members, bystanders, "leading citizens," and others, pored over court records and newspapers, and gathered extensive information on the histories, politics, and economies of the communities. All quoted words or phrases below that express sentiment and action are Raper's attributions.[15]

The Narrative

David Harris was a tenant farmer and bootlegger who killed a white tenant farmer, Clayton Funderberg, in a dispute on April 23, 1930, in Bolivar County, Mississippi. Accounts of the origins of the argument differ by race. Blacks maintained that Funderberg and two white friends went to Harris's home, from which he sold moonshine, and "demanded" liquor. Funderberg allegedly had not paid off previous liquor debts so Harris "refused" Funderberg's demand. Funderberg then "threatened" Harris, and Harris "retaliated" by shooting and killing Funderberg. Whites held that Funderberg went to Harris's home to confront him with the theft of Funderberg's groceries; the African American "denied the theft" and killed Funderberg in an ensuing argument.

After Funderberg's friends reported his death, white tenant farmers in the area organized a "search party" and notified two law enforcement officials of the killing. One of them, a deputy sheriff, went to the site and was "assured" by whites there that the mob was already searching for Harris. He reportedly expressed "satisfaction" with what he heard and returned to his office. The other officer, the sheriff, was "engaged in court" and "did not respond" to the call. Neither officer apparently did anything else that overtly facilitated or hindered subsequent events. Several hundred members of the "search party" tracked Harris and captured him when his hiding place was "revealed" by another African American. Harris was then taken to the Mississippi River levee, tied to a tree, and shot to death. The African American who disclosed where Harris was hiding was thought to be "associated" with other bootlegging interests and allegedly was himself subsequently killed by "the Harris crowd" in a vengeance killing.

To account for what happened in the lynching, we ask and answer questions about possible causal forces suggested by the narrative's unfolding. (Their general form is, What is the effect of a prior action on a subsequent action?) Our answers synthesize our knowledge of the lynching's temporalities and immediate context, general theories of race relations and collective action, historical generalizations about the Jim Crow South, comparable events, and imaginative reconstruction of the mentalities of the actors involved. Because we must reason about both particularity and generality, we also necessarily probe beneath the lynching proper to uncover what it conveys about social structure and cultural understandings.[16]

As an example of our methodology and where it leads us, consider the following sequence from the African American version of the lynching: "Funderberg demands liquor," "Harris refuses," and "Funderberg threatens Harris." What is the significance of the first two actions to the third? Couched in more abstract terms, what we have here is the assertion of a racist demand, African American resistance to that demand and what it implies, and a racist threat. Our reading of the history of white supremacy is that whites generally did not "need" to be provoked, by black resistance or anything else, to threaten African Americans. For a variety of sadly familiar reasons, whites could usually do so with impunity. So we attach no significance for what subsequently happened *in this event*—including the racist threat—to the first two actions in the chronology. Temporal order made possible the question, but, in this particular instance, it did not provide us with the answer. Thus we have begun to unpack the lynching and analytically reconstitute it as an explicit causal interpretation. Understanding the lynching, then, has begun to surpass the cognitive act of simply following narrative flow.

Similar questions must be asked of every sequence in the event. What, for example, was the importance of the noninterventions of two law enforcement officers in the lynching? This can be a significant cause of what subsequently happened only if the (counterfactual) intervention of these two was a genuine possibility allowed, deliberately or otherwise, to lapse unrealized. Was intervention possible?

There is little question that the deputy could have done something to try to stop the mob. He possessed knowledge of the first killing and of the mob's subsequent activities and, to our knowledge, was not otherwise precluded from acting. But by apparently "expressing" satisfaction with the "assurance" he received from whites, he openly aligned himself with their (and the mob's) racist aspirations. Had the deputy not been satisfied that the mob was trailing Harris, he would have acted differently, possibly attempting to stop the mob, calling for assistance, or searching for Harris himself. So his inaction signifies that he consciously chose not to try to prevent a lynching-in-the-making.

Whites in the mob knew of the nonpresence of both the deputy and the sheriff, and they probably understood the deputy's absence to mean what he apparently intended, a deliberate "hands-off" stance. No direct evidence exists about the sheriff's intention in not responding to the information he received about Funderberg's death or that he even knew of the existence of the lynch mob. Thus he may not have been in a position to intervene. But in the three decades preceding the murder of Harris, African Americans were lynched, on the average, once every four years in Bolivar County. Even if one or more of these lynchings were not known to the sheriff, which seems unlikely, he at least knew the area's general racial norms and dynamics. It is probable, therefore, that, knowing a black man killed a white man, he would have suspected that a lynch party likely would be organized and that intervention might be required. Yet he, too, did nothing. Thus, in our estimation, both police officers deliberately provided much of the political opportunity needed for the lynchers to act.[17]

If the sheriff and deputy had attempted to stop the mob, might the lynching have been averted? Historical generalizations are shaky on this, perhaps the most crucial question we confront. On the one hand, lynch mobs often prevailed against even determined antilynching actions by authorities. On the other hand, a large number of lynchings were averted. But neither Ames nor Raper, the compilers of those data, identified either the regional location of the event or the race of the intended victims. Thus the applicability of this historical generalization to what happened in Bolivar County is murky.

Fortunately, in *The Tragedy of Lynching*, Raper listed 127 prevented lynchings occurring from January 1, 1930, to January 1, 1933, almost exactly at the time of the Harris lynching. Ninety-two (or 72 percent) of these occurred in the South and African Americans were the intended victims. This is almost three times the number of recorded lynchings (thirty-two) during the same time period in the region. In each of these ninety-two cases, moreover, the murder of an African American was prevented by white law enforcement officials acting to obstruct the mob. Officials used one or more of three general antilynching strategies: force to disperse the mob, removing prisoners to safer jails elsewhere, and calling in the National Guard or state militia to protect prisoners. Table 1 lists, by state, the number of times each of these actions was used. These statistics and actions certainly warrant the suspicion that had the Bolivar County officers intervened to stop the lynching, Harris might have lived.[18]

Even more germane is what happened in Mississippi itself during the same time frame. There police officers acted to prevent fourteen lynchings during the years 1930–32. Indeed, there is one comparable historical counterexample to the Bolivar County incident. Six months after Harris was lynched, a black man named Tom Hill (or Tom Fisher) was tried in Coahoma County, Mississippi, for the attempted rape of two white women. Unlike Harris, however, he was not lynched. City authorities so feared for the African American's safety that they cleared the courtroom and placed extra guards, perhaps troops from the National Guard, around the courthouse, thereby sparing him from a possible lynching.[19]

TABLE 1. *Actions Taken by Law Enforcement Officials to Prevent Lynchings of African Americans in the South, 1930–1932*

State	Force used	Removal of prisoner	National Guard	Total lynchings prevented	Total lynchings completed
Alabama	2	4	2	8	2
Arkansas	0	7	0	7	1
Florida	0	4	0	4	4[a]
Georgia	2	10	2	14	6[b]
Kentucky	3	4	0	7	0
Louisiana	1	4	1	6	1
Mississippi	1	10	2	13	7[a]
North Carolina	1	4	1	6	1
South Carolina	2	6	1	9	2
Tennessee	3	3	1	7	1
Texas	0	6	3	9	4[b]
Virginia	0	0	2	2	1[b]
Total	15	62	15	92	30

Source: Complied from information in Arthur Raper, *The Tragedy of Lynching* (Chapel Hill: University of North Carolina Press, 1933, pp. 469–70), and Fitzhugh Brundage, personal communication.
[a]Includes one double lynching in each state.
[b]Includes killings in Georgia, Texas, and Virginia that Raper questionably categorizes as lynchings.

There was a clear difference here, as in the other accounts we describe, in how law enforcement officials responded to a potential lynching situation, a mortal difference, in fact, and one that could not have been expected or predicted given that the two counties were virtually identical in terms of the variables favored by sociologists who study lynching patterns—racial composition, occupational and class structures, rurality, and racial history. Bolivar and Coahoma Counties are contiguous counties located in what James Cobb has called "the most Southern place on earth," the Mississippi Delta. Sixty-five years ago, both were overwhelmingly and equally rural, African American, and poor, overwhelmingly and equally dominated by the economics and politics of cotton, and overwhelmingly and equally steeped in white supremacy and a history of lethal mob violence against African Americans. From Reconstruction to 1945, for example, Bolivar County witnessed a total of thirteen lynchings of blacks, Coahoma County, nine.[20] Nor could the divergent outcomes—death in Bolivar, life in Coahoma—stem from what we presume motivated mob action: both involved extremely severe violations of white supremacist norms, the killing of a white man in one case (Bolivar County) and an alleged sexual assault of white women by a black man in the other (Coahoma County). Yet the latter allegation—the ultimate defense of lynching in the white southern mind—did not prevent Coahoma County officials from protecting their prisoner.[21]

Evidence addressing counterfactual questions, by its very nature, can never be conclusive. But considering all of it and placing the most weight on the counterexample of the averted lynching in Coahoma County, we conclude that determined intervention by officials in the Mississippi Delta could, in fact, have prevented Harris's lynching. Thus the absence of such action in Bolivar County, in our judgment, morally as well as causally implicates both officers in the lynching of Harris and in the second murder—that of Harris's betrayer—that logically followed from the first.

By giving "assurance" as to the mob's activities to the deputy, white civilians, largely tenant farmers, were also causal and moral agents in these two killings. But their efficacy and culpability extends beyond the influence they exercised on the understanding and actions of peace officers. White civilians were, in our interpretation, also directly responsible for Harris's lynching. If they had defied the vigilantes *and* "indifferent" or racist law enforcement officers in Bolivar County, as sometimes happened in southern lynchings and near lynchings we have discussed, the mob's activities would have been hindered, if not prevented altogether. *Either* systematically racist police practices *or* systematically racist civil practices, therefore, adequately licensed racist mob violence in this lynching.

Racist "assurance" by white civilians and legal inaction also explain, again in our view, the act of the African American who revealed Harris's hiding place. This conclusion is neither obvious nor incontestable. Disclosing the hiding place of a suspect accused of a killing might be sensible in another culture as an indicator of "good citizenship." That does not seem plausible here, where African Americans were not granted citizenship rights in this community and where, on the whole, they justifiably felt great apprehension about white supremacist law. The informer may also have been tortured or promised a private reward of some sort or merely seized upon a chance to ingratiate himself among whites. But there is absolutely no evidence of any of this. Because Harris's betrayer allegedly was associated with other bootleggers, his action may have been motivated by the economics of the illicit liquor industry. Indeed, the informer may have shrewdly capitalized on widely known white supremacist practices in the area to use the mob to do something—remove a competitor—that he himself was unable or unwilling to do. Venality, then, may be all that lies behind the racial betrayal.

Although this interpretation cannot be dismissed on evidentiary grounds, it is woefully incomplete because it ignores the reality of black life and white law in Jim Crow's Mississippi. That the law generally was not color-blind and, averted lynchings notwithstanding, was in fact "white law" in both its personnel and its functioning *is* incontrovertible. Law was seldom oriented or implemented to ensure in practice the U.S. constitutional rights of southern African Americans as citizens of this country. Many southern blacks both fiercely and subtly resisted the oppression and degradations of segregation and mob rule. But others adopted a survival mechanism—aiding white vigilantes—that extended beyond acquiescence to Jim Crow. Blacks even infrequently joined white mobs in the search for fleeing African Americans. Those actions, like this one, where one African American, doubtless with generally accurate foreknowledge of the narrow range of the almost certainly devastating consequences for Harris, betrayed another African American hounded by a lynch mob, are fully intelligible only if one understands the structural relationship between African Americans and white legal institutions.[22]

Whether or not the particular African American who told whites where Harris was hiding knew that the deputy and sheriff had washed their hands of the affair, all blacks knew the racist nature of Jim Crow's legal system. Racial betrayal of this sort reflected the cumulative and corrupt consequences of racist actions and nonactions such as those dramatized by the deputy and other agents of the white legal establishment. This is true whether or not the African American was forced into his betrayal or was promised a reward for his knowledge. The absence of an effective legal check on racist action is, in this context, the root condition of both racial coercion and racial paternalism. Unlike the more complex relationship between the white mob and white law, which really allows no definitive historical generalization, that between African Americans and southern "justice" was generalized in daily practice and institutionally anchored in the very fabric of social life. Racial betrayal, then, signified one of the cardinal social relationships, that between law and race, which both defined the South's white supremacist structure and was recreated every time the law failed to treat all of its citizens, black and white, equally.

There can be little doubt that the disclosure of Harris's hiding place facilitated his capture and subsequent lynching. Would this have happened in the absence of the betrayal? There were other racial betrayals that culminated in lynchings, but such incidents appear rare indeed.[23] Generally African Americans were not apprehended because of an action of this sort. Using what happened in comparable cases as the historical standard here, then, we do not give it weight as a cause of Harris's murder. The racial betrayal, however, did have consequences of mortal significance, namely the "vengeance" killing of the informer by Harris's friends. We interpret this murder to mean that the capacity for African American resistance to white dominance, though necessarily muted and only sporadic in Mississippi by the 1930s, was never entirely extinguished. Under what likely were the most racially oppressive conditions known to "free" African Americans in this country—white supremacy, Mississippi Delta style—blacks persisted in implementing, in one of the few ways available to them, solidaristic understandings of social control in opposition to members of their own race who were thought to have gone "too far" in their subservience to Jim Crow. They punished and removed them from the scene.

Just as the racial betrayal is grounded in the historical context of white supremacy, the solidaristic vengeance killing also has deep cultural and structural roots. Again, we point especially to the racist underpinnings of southern law. Because black people were not deemed fully human, their death at the hands of other blacks was seldom punished to the full extent of the law: white authorities often turned their backs on the killing of African Americans by African Americans.[24] White supremacist law enforcement practices thus unintentionally facilitated this expression of African American solidarity and social control.

Comments on the Interpretation

Our causal interpretation of the lynching is a precise and explicit consequence of how we merged the particularities of the lynching with theoretical knowledge, imaginative reconstruction, historical generalizations, and information from comparable cases to understand the event's sequences and their temporal connectedness. This is evident in several ways.

First, the lynching's logic of action indicates how causality is formed by and embedded in temporality even as the "inner connections" of actions transcend sequence per se. Some sequences were interpreted to be of no consequence for ensuing action or to be ritualistic embellishments on, rather than causal prerequisites for, a more fundamental action (e.g., carrying Harris to the levee and tying him to a tree). Main story lines are accentuated, and "subplots" (such as the themes of racial dominance and resistance played out by Funderberg and Harris in their initial interaction about liquor, and of the solidaristic vengeance killing) are defined in a way that is often masked by narrative sequence.

Second, the analysis reveals those actions which, in a precise sense, are most significant to the entire event. These include, of course, the actions of the white townspeople and policemen. Another event-defining action is the report to others of Funderberg's death by his friends. On the surface, this simple act would seem to have at most instrumental significance. (People can act on something only if they have knowledge of its existence.) Although what was actually reported by Funderberg's friends is not known, it is all too plausible to imagine the general racist construction of the incident.[25] In a real sense, it was the "telling" of Funderberg's death rather than the killing per se that molded its meaning for whites and thereby motivated and channeled their subsequent action. Three different paths of action or branching points in the lynching's unfolding, in fact, flow from the telling (the formation of the mob and the noninvolvement of each of the two police officers), and they, in turn, establish the probable limits and content of future action.

Finally, unpacking the lynching highlights the causal efficacy of human agency, contingency, and the cumulative consequences of past actions and how these, in turn, are temporally structured to form the logical backbone of the lynching. If the actions we have identified as significant had been very different in content and meaning (intended and understood) from what they in fact were, the event likely would have been transformed into a nonlynching. Whites, through their action in informing authorities of the first killing, for example, introduced two contingencies—the possible involvement of the two law officers—which, as we know from other threatened lynchings, they could not control and which might have altered the course of the event. But the analysis also shows how these possible "lynching-averting" contingencies were circumvented by the actions of both white civilians and the two policemen. The consequences of nonintervention increasingly accumulated as the event unfolded, reducing the possibility for alternative choices and actions. By the time the mob had physical control of Harris, the likelihood that he would be lynched was high.

Yet, even then, the lynching was not inevitable. Lynchings-in-the-making, to repeat a basic theme, are contingent historical unfoldings. Neither knowledge of the lynching's white supremacist context nor of its origins in a violation of racist norms would have enabled accurate prediction of what ultimately happened. David Harris was not destined to die after he killed Funderberg, nor after the lynch mob was formed, nor even after it captured him. Until virtually the end, his lynching might still have been averted. His murder thus was the contingent outcome of a number of unfolding sequences that, finally, were brought together through cultural understanding, conscious choice, and purposive action that resulted in two criminal deaths. And in understanding that, we also understand more about the general logic and practice of white supremacy.

CONCLUSION

Neither the statistics on averted lynchings nor the specific examples of it we have discussed imply in any way that life in the Jim Crow South was somehow less brutal for African Americans than is typically portrayed. White southerners began to prevent lynchings in large numbers only after white supremacy was securely entrenched and, even then, not until they realized that unless they dampened their addiction to the rope and faggot, the federal government, in the form of the Dyer Bill of 1919 and after intense prodding from the NAACP, was likely to pass federal antilynching legislation. That lynchings were often averted, or that African Americans accused of a crime sometimes had the "opportunity" to taste the "justice" dispensed by the southern legal system, moreover, did not necessarily mean that blacks escaped vigilante-tinged deaths. Often legal sentencing and execution were conducted in an atmosphere of mob pressure and racial hysteria, rendering the state-sanctioned death little more than a "legal lynching." None of these circumstances must ever be forgotten.[26]

With great poignancy, John Dollard captured the essence of the above paragraph and then profoundly tied it to the inherent contingency of racial violence during the Jim Crow era. In *Class and Caste in a Southern Town,* his study of Indianola, Mississippi, in the 1930s, Dollard wrote, "Every Negro in the South knows that he is under a kind of sentence of death; he does not know when his turn will come, it may never come, but it may also be at any time."[27]

That insight, which, as Dollard intimates, was no insight at all to African Americans in the South, begs for acknowledgment, understanding, and use by historians and sociologists alike. Its human dimension is almost perfectly crystallized in an incident uncovered by Allison Davis, Burleigh Gardner, and Mary Gardner in their study of another Mississippi town, Natchez, in the 1930s. Their source is a white informant, who captured an African American accused of attacking a white woman and turned him over to another white man, named Ted, with instructions to take the prisoner to the sheriff. Ted had been in a mob that earlier had searched for the black man and that had "raved around about what they would do" if they captured the suspect, and Ted too had been "talking big." According to the informant, "After all the talking Ted had done, he walked through a quarter of mile of woods with the Negro and never did a thing; so I figured it was mostly talk. They might have done something if the whole crowd had been there, but by the time they knew about it, the Negro was in jail."[28]

The entire episode is deeply telling, and not only about what separates lynchings from nonlynchings: it also encapsulates and expresses each of the analytical points we have made about threatened lynchings as historical events. First, the segment of the event just recounted clearly reveals the sociological dynamics of lynching only contingently present: when group hysteria and mob mentality were replaced with individual responsibility or timidity, a potential lynching was apparently transformed into a nonlynching. Second, it repeatedly produces novel turns in its unfolding: the black man escapes the mob, but the white informant freely admits that he might have shot the African American if he had believed the assault allegation, which, to echo once more the theme of novelty, he thought both unsubstantiated and unlikely on the surface. So, again, we see how tenuous is the line separating life from death. Third, it demonstrates that the entire temporal makeup of events is key to their analytical utility and that events have to be followed through to their conclusion to ascertain their full significance. Continuing his story, the white informant stated, "Of course, they hung him legally after the trial. There was so much feeling that he was bound to hang. You couldn't get a jury *not* to convict him. . . . But they had to hang him; there was nothing else they could do under the circumstances."[29] So we see here the all-too-present reality of legal lynching.

The kind of contingency Dollard identified was tightly circumscribed, to be sure; it was without doubt criminal and terrible in its living and for a time nurturing of white supremacy. But, still, it represented an indeterminateness predicated on and fostering agency. Every lynching-in-the-making, like that episode, in fact consists of and refracts historical contestation and possibility, both literal and at the level of meaning: white mobs and white law officers battling each other, thereby contesting the meaning and future structural implementation of law and order; prisoners and jailers contesting the meaning of decency and social place; lynch mobs and African Americans clashing, thereby contesting and structuring the meaning of race and justice; white southern women contesting their imposed dependence on white men for protection from black men and thus rejecting accepted meanings and roles of gender and race. Such contestation may culminate in a completed or an averted lynching, a suicide, a confession, or an insurrection. Mob members may be killed, celebrated, or imprisoned, and African Americans may organize, individually resist, or remain horrified onlookers. "Betrayers of a race," black or white, may be rewarded or vilified, voted out of office, or murdered. When historians and sociologists teach each other about how to approach, frame, and analyze episodes of racial violence, each of these acts and the contested, transformative possibilities they express, whether obvious or buried deeply under the event's surface, whether intended or known by its protagonists, can be recaptured and harnessed to better understand both lynchings-in-the-making and the culture that produced them.

NOTES

1. Examples of the case study approach include James R. McGovern, *Anatomy of a Lynching: The Killing of Claude Neal* (Baton Rouge: Louisiana State University Press, 1982); Howard Smead, *Blood Justice: The Lynching of Mack Charles Parker* (New York: Oxford University Press, 1986); Stephen J. Whitfield, *A Death in the Delta: The Story of Emmett Till* (1988; rpt. Baltimore: Johns Hopkins University Press, 1991); and Nancy MacLean, "The Leo Frank Case Reconsidered: Gender and Sexual Politics in the Making of Reactionary Populism," *Journal of American History* 78 (December 1991): 917–48. Aggregate and/or statistical sociological studies include James M. Inverarity, "Populism and Lynching in Louisiana, 1889–1896: A Test of Erikson's Theory of the Relationship between Boundary Crises and Repressive Justice," *American Sociological Review* 41 (April 1976): 262–80; Jay Corzine, Lin Huff-Corzine, and James C. Creech, "The Tenant Labor Market and Lynching in the South: A Test of Split Labor Market Theory," *Sociological Inquiry* 58 (Summer 1988): 261–78; James L. Massey and Martha A. Myers, "Patterns of Repressive Social Control in Post-Reconstruction Georgia, 1882–1935," *Social Forces* 68 (December 1989): 458–88; and most recently, the fine study by Stewart E. Tolnay and E. M. Beck, *A Festival of Violence: An Analysis of Southern Lynchings, 1882–1930* (Urbana: University of Illinois Press, 1995). To be sure, these intellectual and stylistic differences are not insurmountable. In *Lynching in the New South: Georgia and Virginia, 1880–1930* (Urbana: University of Illinois Press, 1993), 269, for example, W. Fitzhugh Brundage combines elements of both case studies and statistical analysis/generalization, and MacLean adeptly merges social theory and historical case study. From the other shore, so to speak, Tolnay and Beck admirably contextualize their sociological inferences in the historical experiences of the southern people and in social practices that were historically motivated and institutionalized. Context and narrative nevertheless continue to serve as workhorses for most historians of lynching, just as formal

and replicable analytic methods and explicit theorizing are the tools of choice for sociologists.

2. The Tennessee events are reported in the *Atlanta Constitution*, April 19, 1931. The behavior of Mrs. J. R. Butler (no first name could be found), the sheriff's wife, was praised in several newspapers, and she was awarded a medal of heroism from the Commission on Interracial Cooperation. See the *Memphis Commercial Appeal*, April 19, 1931, the *New York Times*, November 10, 1931, and several Nashville papers, including the *Banner*, October 27, 1931, the *Tennessean*, October 27, 1931, and the *Globe*, November 13, 1931. A similar incident occurred in Bowling Green, Missouri, in 1915, when a sheriff's wife persuaded a large mob to disperse (*New York Evening Post*, September 2, 1915). The pair of Mississippi incidents are described by Arthur F. Raper, *The Tragedy of Lynching* (Chapel Hill: University of North Carolina Press, 1933), 85–93, 476.

3. Allison Davis, Burleigh B. Gardner, and Mary R. Gardner, *Deep South: A Social Anthropological Study of Caste and Class* (Chicago: University of Chicago Press, 1941), 477.

4. Jessie Daniel Ames, *The Changing Character of Lynching: Review of Lynching, 1931–1941, with a Discussion of Recent Developments in the Field* (Atlanta: Commission on Interracial Cooperation, 1942), 11; Raper, *Tragedy of Lynching*, 484. Both Ames and Raper base their estimates on the information collected by the Tuskegee Institute (now University). Brundage, *Lynching in the New South* (269, 161–244), reports that from 1886 to 1908 officials in the eleven states of the former Confederacy relied on the militia almost two hundred times to prevent lynchings. He recounts numerous instances of decisive antimob actions in Virginia and Georgia, including the indictment and successful conviction of lynch party members and the use of force and injunctions to thwart mob violence. Police also shot and killed mob members in Dallas, Lexington, and elsewhere. See *Dallas Express*, May 23, 1925; John D. Wright, "Lexington's Suppression of the 1920 Will Lockett Lynch Mob," *Register of the Kentucky Historical Society* 84 (Summer 1986): 263–79.

5. The Louisiana incident is reported in the *New York Times*, February 6, 1926, and the *St. Louis Argus*, February 6, 1926. Similar attitudes were expressed by white officers elsewhere. A Mississippi sheriff, for example, apparently dispersed a mob after he said he would "kill any man who comes to get the nigger" (*Atlanta Journal*, May 8, 1931; *Atlanta Constitution*, May 7, 1931). Scholarly treatments of the legal opposition to lynching include, among many others, Raper, *Tragedy of Lynching*, and the historical case studies we previously cited.

6. Clarion, Va.: *Baltimore Afro-American*, August 1, 1924. Lewis's escape north is not uncommon. Arthur F. Raper, in *Preface to Peasantry: A Tale of Two Black Belt Counties* (1936; rpt. New York: Atheneum, 1968), 208–9, described the permanent exodus of dozens of black residents from Greene County, Georgia, because of a lynching there in 1920. Orange, Tex. (Clarence Smith): *Knoxville East Tennessee News*, April 26, 1923. Another example of a suicide under very similar conditions appeared in the *Chicago Defender*, April 23, 1921. Darien, Ga.: W. Fitzhugh Brundage, "The Darien 'Insurrection' of 1899: Black Protest during the Nadir of Race Relations," *Georgia Historical Quarterly* 74 (Summer 1990): 234–53. Interpretations of what happened in Muskogee vary. Compare the *Chicago Defender*, December 27, 1915, and January 1, 1916, with the *Montgomery Advertiser*, December 27, 1915. In yet

another twist on the theme of the willingness and ability of blacks to stop vigilante "justice," an African American woman in Vicksburg confessed to the murder of a white for which a black man had been accused and spared him from possible mob action (*Memphis Commercial Appeal*, August 13, 1924). We also encountered a few incidents of behind-the-scenes interracial cooperation that defused tense racial situations. See, e.g., Hortense Powdermaker, *After Freedom: A Cultural Study of the Deep South*, preface by Elliott M. Rudwick (1939; rpt. New York: Atheneum, 1968), 33.

7. Examples of white civilians working with or pressuring the authorities to act are numerous. See, e.g., Raper, *Tragedy of Lynching*, 462–67, and Lewis T. Nordyke, "Ladies and Lynchings," in Ames, *Changing Character of Lynching*, 63–68, which tells of an instance when the Association of Southern Women for the Prevention of Lynching mobilized legal protection. For a sampling of the many times when whites not directly in the mob either hindered officers or ridiculed or criticized them, see Raper, *Tragedy of Lynching*, 445, 459. The quoted phrase about the Little Rock incident is from the *Montgomery Advertiser*, May 5, 1927. A similar incident occurred in Bowling Green, Mo., reported in *New York Times*, September 2, 1915.

8. Deaden, Tenn.: *Montgomery Advertiser*, September 4, 1915; Anson, County, N.C.: *Raleigh News and Observer*, July 23, 1924. Neil R. McMillen, *Dark Journey: Black Mississippians in the Age of Jim Crow* (Urbana: University of Illinois Press, 1989), 243, 398, discusses two cases of what he calls "spontaneous acquittals" by Mississippi mobs. He goes on to note accurately, however, that these and similar incidents may have been "calculated acts in a theater of white terror designed to feature black leaders as object lessons for the race in general" (243). In another incident, white lynchers in Mississippi took two black men accused of shooting a wealthy white man from a local sheriff, who argued that the evidence against one was "slight" and successfully pleaded for his life. After returning him to the sheriff, the mob then lynched the other African American (*Montgomery Advertiser*, February 17, 1914). On the unwillingness of whites to identify a particular African American, see the *Knoxville East Tennessee News*, December 2, 1920, the *St. Louis Argus*, July 29, 1921, and the *Clinton* (S.C.) *Chronicle*, September 22, 1921. Raper, in *Tragedy of Lynching* (459), also discusses a Georgia white man's efforts to protect an African American who, under suspicious circumstances, confessed to an attack on the white man's wife and daughter.

9. Here we have adapted and merged several definitions. See Gordon Leff, *History and Social Theory* (1969; rpt. Garden City, N.Y.: Anchor Books, Doubleday, 1971), 42–90; Dale H. Porter, *The Emergence of the Past: A Theory of Historical Explanation* (Chicago: University of Chicago Press, 1981), 40–98; Philip Abrams, *Historical Sociology* (Ithaca, N.Y.: Cornell University Press, 1982), 196–226; Paul K. Conkin and Ronald N. Stromberg, *Heritage and Challenge: The History and Theory of History* (Arlington Heights, Ill.: Forum Press, 1989), 3; Larry J. Griffin, "Temporality, Events, and Explanation in Historical Sociology: An Introduction," *Sociological Methods and Research* 20 (May 1992): 403–27.

10. Louis O. Mink, "History and Fiction as Modes of Comprehension," *New Literary History* 1 (Spring 1970): 541–58; Jill Quadagno and Stan J. Knapp, "Have Historical Sociologists Forsaken Theory? Thoughts on the History/Theory Relationship," *Sociological Methods and Research* 20 (May 1992): 481–507.

11. E. P. Thompson, *The Poverty of Theory and Other Essays* (New York: Merlin

Press, 1978), 42–44; Griffin, "Temporality, Events, and Explanation in Historical Sociology."

12. Barrington Moore, *Injustice: The Social Bases of Obedience and Revolt* (White Plains, N.Y.: M. E. Sharpe, 1978), 393; Thompson, *Poverty of Theory*, 47. See also William H. Sewell Jr., "Three Temporalities: Toward an Evenemental Sociology," in *The Historic Turn in the Human Sciences*, ed. Terrence McDonald (Ann Arbor: University of Michigan Press, forthcoming).

13. Abrams, *Historical Sociology*, 190–226, 300–335; Porter, *Emergence of the Past*; Leff, *History and Social Theory*; Sewell, "Three Temporalities"; Larry J. Griffin, "Narrative, Event-Structure Analysis and Causal Interpretation in Historical Sociology," *American Journal of Sociology* 98 (March 1993): 1094–1133. In "A Theory of Structure: Duality, Agency, and Transformation," *American Journal of Sociology* 98 (July 1992): 1–29, William H. Sewell Jr. eloquently argues that social structures are always "at risk," if sometimes only minimally, in every social encounter.

14. Moore, *Injustice*; Griffin, "Narrative, Event-Structure Analysis"; Geoffrey Hawthorne, *Plausible Worlds: Possibility and Understanding in History and the Social Sciences* (New York: Cambridge University Press, 1991). The origins of this form of causal and interpretive reasoning go back to Max Weber, *Max Weber on the Methodology of the Social Sciences*, trans. and ed. Edward A. Shils and Henry A. Finch with a foreword by Edward A. Shils (Glencoe, Ill.: Free Press, 1949). In several articles, Brundage has also pointed to the complexities of, and suppressed possibilities contained in, incidents of violence and near violence, urging especially the analytical utility of averted lynchings. See Brundage, "The Darien 'Insurrection' of 1899," 235; and W. Fitzhugh Brundage, "The Varn Mill Riot of 1891: Lynchings, Attempted Lynchings, and Justice in Ware County, Georgia," *Georgia Historical Quarterly* 73 (Summer 1994): 257–80.

15. This account is contained in Raper, *Tragedy of Lynching*, 94–106. Details of the research procedures are found on p. vi.

16. Our interpretation of the lynching was facilitated by the use of an analytic procedure known as event-structure analysis (ESA). ESA and its associated computer program, ETHNO, elicit the analyst's understanding of the causal connections between the temporal sequences that constitute a narrative. It does this by transforming a chronology of actions constructed by the analyst into a series of "yes/no" questions and then asking the analyst/expert if a temporal antecedent is necessary for a subsequent action to occur. Responses to the questions are diagrammed by ETHNO to create a logical structure displaying the imputed causal connectedness of all actions analytically defining the narrative in question. The structure of the diagram can then be used to identify actions of particular significance to the event's theorized, reconstructed unfolding and to follow the various paths of action as they have been defined by the analyst through this interrogatory process.

ESA's value is merely heuristic, relentlessly prodding users to think more deeply about their construction and interpretation of the event than they might otherwise have. No extant computer algorithm or formal logic can anticipate all novel possibilities—that is, what might have happened—at each and every moment in an event's unfolding. Given this essential indeterminacy, no formal logic can explain what actually happened. ESA assumes that the analyst, not the algorithm, possesses the requisite knowledge to anticipate, counterfactualize, and explain. Causality and historical significance thus are not "discovered" through its use, and event structures are nothing more than explicit depictions of interpretations made by the analyst. See Larry J. Griffin and Charles Ragin, "Some Observations on Formal Qualitative Analysis," *Sociological Methods and Research* 23 (August 1994): 4–21. See also Griffin, "Narrative, Event-Structure Analysis," where much of the analysis and interpretation of this lynching first appeared.

17. On the concept of political opportunity and its importance to collective action, see Charles Tilly, *From Mobilization to Revolution* (Reading, Mass.: Addison-Wesley, 1978).

18. Among the many examples of the mob overcoming law enforcement officials, see Raper, *Tragedy of Lynching*; McGovern, *Anatomy of a Lynching*; McMillen, *Dark Journey*; and George C. Wright, *Racial Violence in Kentucky, 1865–1940: Lynchings, Mob Rule, and "Legal Lynchings"* (Baton Rouge: Louisiana State University Press, 1990). The statistics on prevented lynchings in the South are from Raper, *Tragedy of Lynching*, 473–79. The number of prevented lynchings in Mississippi which we use in the next paragraph in the text were calculated from information on page 476.

19. Accounts of the Hill/Fisher incident are found in the *Memphis Commercial Appeal*, August 21, 1930, September 25, 1930, and the *Pittsburgh Courier*, October 18, 1930. Raper, *Tragedy of Lynching*, 476, states that authorities called in the National Guard in Coahoma County, but we were unable to verify this assertion.

20. For both counties, more than 70 percent of the population was African American; urban and nonfarm rural dwellers together accounted for less than 30 percent of their inhabitants; more than 75 percent of all "gainful workers" were employed in agriculture; cotton accounted for more than 97 percent of the total value of all agricultural land and buildings; and more than 90 percent of all African American families and more than 65 percent of all white families were tenant or sharecropper families. Demographic, employment, and agriculture data are from various 1930 population and agricultural censuses (Washington, D.C., 1932). The lynching statistics are from McMillen, *Dark Journey*, 231. See James C. Cobb, *The Most Southern Place on Earth: The Mississippi Delta and the Roots of Regional Identity* (New York: Oxford University Press, 1992), for a cogent inquiry into the Mississippi Delta.

21. See, e.g., Ames, *Changing Character of Lynching*; Jacquelyn Dowd Hall, *Revolt against Chivalry: Jessie Daniel Ames and the Women's Campaign against Lynching* (New York: Columbia University Press, 1979); Joel Williamson, *A Rage for Order: Black-White Relations in the American South since Emancipation* (New York: Oxford University Press, 1986); and McLean, "The Leo Frank Case Reconsidered."

22. No one has made this point more powerfully than McMillen in *Dark Journey*, 197–253. He also refers (383) to an interracial lynch party searching for an African American.

23. Raper, *Tragedy of Lynching* (358), recounts a similar case of an African American disclosing the hiding place of another black person hounded by a mob.

24. In *The Tragedy of Lynching*, Raper (105), for example, reports that he heard that not until a month after this lynching did Bolivar County courts sentence an African American to death for the murder of another black person.

25. This interpretation is supported by two facts. The first is that Harris was tracked by a mob of over two hundred men and then shot over two hundred times while the law did nothing. The second is that whites constructed an alternative version of the

altercation between Harris and Funderberg. Their version, which casts Funderberg as the innocent victim merely trying to undo a wrong done him, most likely emanated from his friends.

26. The upsurge in the number of prevented lynchings in the 1920s and lynching's ultimate demise in the 1940s and 1950s are quite different phenomena. They have different cultural meanings and were caused by different forces. Lynching ended because white southerners understood that it was an increasingly costly and, finally, unacceptable form of racial control and sanctioning. This understanding, in turn, resulted from an entire complex of factors, some internal to the South and others external to it. On this point, see Brundage, *Lynching in the New South*, 245–59. The doomed history of federal antilynching legislation is explored in Nancy J. Weiss, *Farewell to the Party of Lincoln: Black Politics in the Age of FDR* (Princeton: Princeton University Press, 1983), 96–119, and McGovern, *Anatomy of a Lynching*, 115–39. For a vivid example of the group hysteria of whites, see Dan T. Carter, *Scottsboro: A Tragedy of the American South* (Baton Rouge: Louisiana State University Press, 1979). Legal lynching has been systematically examined by Wright, *Racial Violence in Kentucky*.

27. John Dollard, *Class and Caste in a Southern Town* (New Haven: Yale University Press, 1937), 359.

28. Davis, Gardner, and Gardner, *Deep South*, 27.

29. Ibid., 26–27.

The Sociogenesis
of Lynching

Roberta Senechal de la Roche

The popular view of lynching in the postbellum American South has several elements. First, lynching was "a peculiarly American institution."[1] An explanation of lynching therefore requires a theory grounded entirely in a configuration of characteristics unique to the United States. Second, southern whites were capable of lynching any black for even the slightest offense or for no reason at all. The reasons given by whites were merely "excuses" for lynchings "which ultimately would have occurred on virtually any pretext."[2] Third, if unable to capture the alleged offender, whites might lynch any convenient black in the community as a surrogate: "The black community as a whole was accountable, and one black victim for the lynch mob would serve as well as another."[3] Lynched blacks were frequently innocent and hapless victims of racist mobs. Fourth, blacks were often lynched in mass public spectacles that featured torture and sexual mutilation by whites variously characterized as frenzied, sadistic, barbaric, hysterical, savage, inhuman, ferocious, or suffering from a collective mental illness.[4] All of these popular conceptions, however, distort the reality of southern lynching. And before an effective theory of lynching can be developed, a more accurate portrait is needed.

As we shall see, southern whites seldom lynched capriciously. Lynchings usually followed allegations of serious criminal conduct such as murder and rape; not all blacks were potential targets, and crowds did not invariably mete out severe punishments when blacks committed crimes against whites. Nor was lynching a uniquely American or southern practice explainable with regional or national conditions alone. Why, then, might two alleged offenses by blacks occur in the same community but only one end in a lynching? Why did lynchers kill some offenders swiftly while subjecting others to prolonged torture before execution when the alleged crime, say, the murder of a white, was the same? And why did lynching occur at all? Why did not more rioting or widespread terrorism occur that might have punished and intimidated blacks all the more successfully? Existing theories do not explain variation in lynching across particular cases of conflict. Instead, they explain only variation in the rate of lynching in large geographic units such as counties, regions, or states with broad characteristics of those units, such as their level of economic prosperity or degree of economic or political competition, and cannot order case-by-case variation.[5] By contrast, the purpose of this essay is to offer a theory of lynching that explains variation across specific cases of conflict.

LYNCHING AND THE BLACKIAN PARADIGM

My theory of lynching derives from and extends the general theory of social control pioneered by sociologist Donald Black.[6] First, lynching is social control—a process by which people define or respond to deviant behavior.[7] For example, in ten southern states from 1882 to 1930, alleged crimes constitute the overwhelming majority—at least 90 percent—of the occasions that precipitated lynchings. The most common was murder (nearly 40 percent), followed by sexual assault (30 percent), nonsexual assault (10 percent), theft, robbery, and arson (nearly 10 percent). Less frequent were such miscellaneous offenses as kidnapping, killing livestock, train wrecking, and grave robbing.[8] Although it may seem morally repugnant to modern observers, southern lynching typically was a form of "popular justice" directed against conduct widely regarded as criminal.

Second, the theory employs Black's strategy of predicting and explaining a social phenomenon with what he calls its location and direction in social space, that is, with how it is situated along a number of structural dimensions. Here the unit of analysis is the single case of conflict. In particular, the social characteristics of the parties involved in each case, such as whether they are intimates or strangers, equal or unequal, individuals or organizations, predict and explain how the conflict will be handled.[9] The primary intent is to identify which variables are associated with the likelihood and severity of lynching when a specific grievance arises. The theory thus predicts and explains lynching with the social structure of each conflict.

Finally, the theory of lynching elaborated below also deliberately follows Black's paradigm by excluding motivational and other psychological factors sometimes emphasized by students of the subject.[10] How people perceive, interpret, intend, or experience lynching is beyond its scope.[11] It neither assumes nor denies that social strains frustrate or otherwise incline people to aggression, that people learn the violence they inflict, that violence is goal-directed, socially constructive or destructive, or that the participants rationally weigh or calculate its costs and rewards.[12] Neither does the theory address ritualistic aspects of lynching or assume or deny that it serves a larger function such as the clarification of moral boundaries in a community or society.[13] Instead, it orders observable behavior alone. It is purely sociological.[14]

DEFINITIONS

Lynching and other forms of collective violence can readily be defined and distinguished along two major dimensions: their breadth of liability and degree of organization. Liability is a condition of accountability for a deviant act such as the accountability of a burglar for a crime or a motorist for an accident.[15] It may be collective (when members of a group or social category are held accountable for the conduct of a fellow member) or individual (when only a single person is held accountable).[16] A second dimension of collective violence is its degree of organization. It may be highly or even formally organized and endure for weeks or years, or it may be relatively unorganized, spontaneous, and short-lived. Lynching involves a logic of individual liability and a low degree of organization.

In lynching accountability lies only with an alleged wrongdoer or group of wrongdoers, while uninvolved people associated with the offender are not subject to harm or any other form of social control (as is the case in riots and terrorist violence). Like a modern court, lynchers punish only the alleged offender, then disband. The vast majority of southern lynching incidents—well over four-fifths—thus involved the punishment of a single alleged offender.[17] Accomplices or others directly associated with the offense, such as those who harbored or otherwise supported an alleged wrongdoer, appear to account for most of the small number of lynching incidents in which more than one person was punished. Whites also might lynch more than one black in cases in which those suspected of wrongdoing forcibly resisted arrest or extralegal actions such as beatings or whippings. Especially if gunfire was exchanged and if whites were wounded or killed by a group of resisting blacks, violence was likely to escalate and anyone deemed a party to the resistance might be beaten or executed.[18]

Lynchings also lack the high level of organization and capacity for sustained collective action seen in vigilantism and terrorism. Although lynchings may involve some amount of planning and organization, they nonetheless are highly situational, spontaneous, and temporary. Indeed, they may last but hours or minutes before participants disband. Participation in a lynching is relatively open and fluid. Nearly everyone in a community is welcome to join. In the minority of southern lynchings involving large crowds, people from all walks of life attended and celebrated the lynching of a black accused of a crime.[19] Although white women were usually bystanders only, on occasion they incited hesitant males to violence, "to do their 'manly duty.'"[20] White women also sometimes appeared at the forefront of active violence, joining attacks on jails to seize alleged offenders, helping repulse authorities sent to suppress crowd violence, or inflicting punishment on a suspect.[21] On some occasions, even black residents attended.[22] Police or other authorities might also appear as spectators.[23] Vigilantism, by contrast, is formally organized, with centralized decision making, officers, and limited access to membership. For example, the South's Ku Klux Klansmen during Reconstruction, the 1920s, and the 1960s typically operated as vigilantes. Like lynchers, however, they used a logic of individual liability. Speaking of the Reconstruction-era Klan, one historian notes: "The operating procedure of various Klan dens was surprisingly consistent. Dens would hold regular meetings . . . in which the behavior of certain 'obnoxious' individuals was discussed. Eventually a victim was agreed upon. If . . . warnings were disregarded or if the victim was black, the den would then hold a 'trial' and pass a sentence, which was carried out during a raid."[24]

Lynching, then, is a form of collective violence characterized by informal organization and a logic of individual liability.[25] So defined, lynching was not a peculiarly American practice. It has appeared in such diverse places as ancient Greece and republican Rome, Africa, China, South Asia, early modern Europe, and in some earlier, traditional Native American societies. Lynching has been used to punish not only homicide or rape but also such diverse offenses as theft, witchcraft, adultery, assault, incest, bestiality, spousal abuse, being a werewolf, arson, bullying, and greed.[26] Lynchers sometimes punish members of their own group, outsiders, or both and might operate openly in large crowds or covertly in small bands. Moreover, lynching has not passed away. It continues in both rural and urban settings, in the United States and elsewhere.[27] In American cities, for instance, bystanders who witness a crime might seize the wrongdoer and subject him to a severe beating.[28] Beatings and damage to property also sometimes occur when a member of an ethnic or racial group offends someone in the "wrong" neighborhood.[29] Nor was the lynching of blacks in the American South distinctive for the levels of brutality it sometimes reached. For example, in traditional China in the late nineteenth century, one missionary reported that in cases of theft, lynchers often killed suspects by burying them alive. Some caught stealing corn or fruit were burned to death after lynchers forced them to light the pyre themselves.[30] In response to adultery, he continued, "Sometimes the man's legs are broken, sometimes his arms, and very often his eyes are destroyed by rubbing into them quicklime."[31] But however old and widespread the practice of lynching, however diverse the cultures, norms, traditions, and histories of one setting versus another, all lynchings occur under similar structural conditions.

THE SOCIAL STRUCTURE OF LYNCHING

Collective violence such as lynching sometimes arises where law is lacking, weak, or openly partisan.[32] Yet lynching can also occur where legal agencies are well established. Lynchers may even compete with law by forcibly abducting suspects from police, jails, or courts to punish them in their own fashion. We therefore need to explain why lynching rather than some other form of social control (including law) occurs. Black suggests that every form of social control has a distinctive social structure composed of the social characteristics of all the parties associated with a conflict—offenders, complainants, partisans, and anyone else with knowledge of it.[33] What structural arrangement, then, is associated with lynching? Lynching arises with specifiable combinations of the following structural variables:[34]

1. *relational distance*
2. *functional interdependence*
3. *vertical direction*
4. *cultural distance*

Relational Distance
Relational distance, or intimacy, is "the degree to which [people] participate in one another's lives" and is measurable by such elements as the number and type of ties people have to one another, the frequency and duration of contacts between them, and the age of their relationship.[35] My first proposition is that *lynching varies directly with relational distance*. In

other words, all else constant, the greater the relational distance between the parties to a conflict, the greater is the likelihood and severity of a lynching. Regularized contact between people in a neighborhood, workplace, or organization, for instance, increases intimacy and makes a lynching among them less likely.[36] If a lynching does occur, moreover, intimacy moderates the severity of violence.

Although no data have yet been systematically gathered on the relational distance between the parties in conflicts that led to lynchings in the South, scattered evidence suggests that its significance was considerable. All of the black lynching victims in Georgia and Virginia whose length of residence could be determined from newspaper accounts, for example, were newcomers.[37] Simply being a stranger, such as a black vagrant or itinerant laborer, was often enough in and of itself to provoke suspicion and hostility among whites in small southern towns or rural communities.[38] The comparatively few whites who were killed by lynchers in the South also exhibited a high degree of relational distance from those they offended in many instances. Of the whites subject to lethal lynchings in Georgia and Virginia in the late nineteenth and early twentieth centuries, for instance, nearly half were strangers or recent arrivals in their communities.[39] In contrast, violent conflicts between those with closer ties, such as white employers and black workers, seem to have been less severe. After emancipation, for example, some white employers continued to punish their black workers with beatings and whippings by small groups of whites—a mild form of lynching—but they usually resorted to lethal violence only if a black resisted punishment or sought retaliation for it. In cases in which the parties in conflict had regular contacts, blacks might not be punished at all for threatening or even committing violence against a white.[40]

Within southern communities, interracial intimacy was unevenly distributed. The least intimacy existed between white women and black men. Black boys and white girls who were childhood friends were separated at an early age, and thereafter black men carefully maintained as much distance as possible from females of the other race. Noting the infrequent, limited, and superficial character of contacts between white women and black men, one student of race relations in Mississippi in the 1930s remarked: "Negro men are careful not to look or act offensively in the presence of a white woman, and in general attempt to minimize contacts with them in order to avoid the too-ready suspicion of white men."[41] Much more contact and intimacy prevailed between white men and blacks of both sexes and between women of both races.[42] The relatively great relational distance between black men and white women therefore helps explain why alleged misconduct by black males against these women—including but not limited to sexual offenses—was apparently more likely to result in a lynching and to be handled more harshly than the same offense committed in any other inter- or intraracial combination of parties. Three-quarters of the twenty-three blacks fatally lynched for allegedly killing white women in Georgia and Virginia from 1880 to 1930 were punished more severely than blacks who had allegedly killed a white man. Brundage thus notes that "mutilation and perverse degradation of the corpse . . . were most commonplace" when a black man killed a white woman.[43]

If a black man accused of misbehavior toward a white woman was a complete stranger, the likelihood of lethal punishment was all the greater. And some evidence suggests that this was true of many blacks subjected to lethal lynchings for the alleged rape of white women. In the late nineteenth and early twentieth centuries, those black males with whom a white woman would have had the most contact, however circumscribed, were most often servants, employees, or other subordinates of her husband's, such as farm laborers, tenants, and sharecroppers, but fewer than 20 percent of the 157 men killed for alleged rapes in Georgia and Virginia were drawn from this more intimate group.[44] It also appears that those blacks most vulnerable to being killed for so-called trivial offenses against white women—such as not being adequately deferential or looking at a white woman the "wrong" way—were strangers.[45] For example, in 1926 a black laborer was lynched in Florida after he approached a house to ask for a drink of water and a white woman fled in alarm. Had he been relationally closer, say, an employee of her husband, the lynching almost certainly would never have occurred.[46] Similarly distant was a black railroad porter accused of insulting a white woman on his train. Arrested in Florida, the man was seized and killed by a group of angry whites, all strangers to him.[47] In a more famous case, Emmett Till, a Chicago teenager on a visit to his southern relatives in Mississippi in 1954, had been in the community only a week before he was badly beaten and then shot to death for allegedly making suggestive remarks—or possibly "wolf-whistling"—to a local white female shopkeeper. Had Till not been a stranger, a lethal lynching would have been less likely. As one historian of this case notes: "If a black stranger did something peculiar, the small-town and rural South in particular could explode on impact . . . and even the most innocent of gestures could be dangerous."[48] Although systematic evidence is lacking, the relatively high level of intimacy between the parties in southern interracial conflicts probably prevented many lethal lynchings of blacks. The seriousness of an alleged offense was not simply a function of the nature of the infraction itself, then, but also depended on who offended whom.

Functional Interdependence

A second variable relevant to the likelihood and severity of lynching is the degree of functional interdependence between the parties in conflict—the extent to which they rely on one another economically, politically, militarily, or otherwise: *Lynching varies inversely with functional interdependence.* People are comparatively unlikely to attack those who are important to their well-being but prefer to kill or maim those they can do without.[49] And when a lynching does occur, a degree of functional interdependence tends to reduce the severity of the violence inflicted. In the South, therefore, we would predict that blacks functionally interdependent with whites would be less vulnerable to a lynching—and one accompanied by more severe violence—than those independent of their adversaries. And apparently they were.

With the end of slavery, the South witnessed a simultaneous and large-scale decrease in the degree of functional interdependence between the races and an equally unprecedented rise in the lynching of blacks. But where southern whites in the postbellum era continued to rely heavily on black labor in agriculture and industry, the economic tie of employer-employee apparently provided a degree of protection for blacks. Thus, for example, on farms and in isolated timber industry settlements, white employers tended to handle many conflicts with and among black workers privately.[50] Acts of defiance such as insulting or arguing with an employer and even violence short of murder or rape seem to have resulted at most in a beating inflicted by a small group of whites related to or working for the owner. Scattered evidence also suggests that when interdependence increased between workers and employers, such as during labor shortages or just before harvest time, both the likelihood and severity of violence against blacks diminished even further.[51]

Where a low degree of functional interdependence prevailed between those embroiled in interracial conflicts, however, the result was more likely to be a lethal lynching of great severity, that is, with torture and mutilation. For example, most blacks executed by whites in Georgia and Virginia for alleged sexual misconduct against white women were accused of offending women outside of their employers' families.[52] Over one-quarter of blacks subject to lethal lynchings in Georgia for assault or murder were accused of attacking policemen. And these lynchings were among the most violent.[53] Moreover, black vagrants, transient workers, and other newcomers to communities were structurally vulnerable to lynchings partly because of their lack of interdependence with any whites at all. Any white they offended was likely to be completely independent of them.

Whether a black "in trouble" had what John Dollard called a white "angel"—usually an employer—could be crucial to his physical well-being. Dollard suggests that interdependence with a powerful white gave some blacks—including "disreputable, killers, and very dangerous men"—"extraordinary liberty to do violent things to other Negroes."[54] This interdependence could also mitigate or prevent retaliation against black workers who offended whites. At times, for example, whites might try to prevent the lynching of a black employee by corroborating his alibi or by persuading lynchers to spare him, or they might fend off efforts by whites to drive "their" blacks from the community.[55] White employers might also intercede during a lynching to lessen the severity of the punishment inflicted on a black employee.[56] A white employer might also submit petitions for pardon to authorities, even if a black employee had been sentenced to jail or prison for victimizing a white.[57] Thus, where a high degree of functional interdependence prevailed, planters and other white employers might intervene on behalf of workers in conflicts with either blacks or whites, saving them from prison terms or worse.[58]

Vertical Direction

Inequality of status, measured by wealth and other variables, is another factor associated with the likelihood of lynching. Lynching virtually always takes place between those of unequal status, and who offends whom—the vertical direction of the alleged offense—is the critical factor. As with law, an upward offense—one by a social inferior against a superior—is treated more seriously and results in more punitiveness than a downward offense by a social superior.[59] When an offense is upward, the direction of the complaint or grievance is downward. Accordingly: *Downward lynching is greater than upward lynching.*[60] And the vertical distance is important as well. As the degree of inequality between the parties in such a downward case increases, so does the severity of the violence inflicted. In other words, upward offenses against those of far higher status are more likely to end in lethal lynchings than those involving parties who are unequal to a smaller degree. In the rare instances where an upward lynching might occur and in the absence of other kinds of social distance (relational and cultural, for example), we would expect less severe violence and never death: Such cases are virtually unknown. When social inferiors have griev-ances against their superiors, they far more often resort to nonconfronta-tional and covert forms of social control such as running away, theft, sabotage, noncooperation or slowness in performing tasks, and gossip.[61] For southern blacks, this repertoire of upward social control might also include individual attacks on offending whites from ambush, boycotts, withholding deference, subtle humor and jokes at the expense of whites, and the use of magical revenge.[62]

Many whites lynched for victimizing other whites in Virginia and Geor-gia appear to have committed upward offenses. At least half of the offend-ers had characteristics that lowered their status: problems with drugs or al-cohol, a history of previous criminal behavior, vagrancy, or vagabondage.[63] But whites rarely lynched the typical offender in a white-on-white case such as homicide or rape—one that involved parties largely equal in status and often acquainted with each other. The legal response was milder as well.[64] The same applies to many black-on-black offenses, most of which occurred among equals, including much violence and homicide.[65]

Low status was part of the overall structural vulnerability of black men in relation to whites in the late nineteenth- and early twentieth-century South, but the vertical distance involved in any conflict varied, and with it the likelihood and severity of a lynching. Black transient workers or va-grants were particularly vulnerable to lynchings, for example, for nearly any offense by them against a white crossed a greater gulf of inequality than the same offense committed by a better-established local black. An alleged offense by a black against a white employer or police officer also traversed a considerable vertical distance and so was likely to provoke a severe downward response. Fitzhugh Brundage found, for example, that of 205 cases of lynchings for alleged black killings of or assaults against whites in Georgia, at least half involved attacks on employers or police—all upward offenses.[66] Many of the most violent lynchings of blacks followed the murder of white police officers: dramatically upward offenses against the polity itself. Torture as well as execution of the offender often re-sulted.[67] Cases involving less vertical distance between the parties or a different vertical direction would be less conducive to lynching. For exam-ple, a black's alleged offense against a low-status white woman regarded as promiscuous or otherwise unrespectable was more likely to go unavenged by a lynching than if the woman was of high status.[68] In cases of a down-ward offense by a social superior, however, as when southern white police-men beat or killed black suspects, a lynching was virtually inconceivable, and legal action was unlikely as well.[69] Finally, many of the rare and seemingly anomalous cases in which a white was threatened with lynching by whites for killing a black can also be explained with the vertical direction of the offense. If a white was sufficiently poor and unrespectable, he risked severe punishment if he killed a wealthier, well-established black.[70] In Virginia in 1893, for instance, a poor white who was an ex-convict and violent drunk was threatened with a lynching and later sentenced to hang for killing a black who "stood well in his community as a deserving and peaceable citizen."[71]

Milder lynchings seem to occur in response to upward offenses between parties relatively close in status. A major example is the charivari, the ritualized and public shaming and humiliation of deviants by members of small communities widespread in Europe from ancient times. Charivaris also occurred in rural America, especially among whites in the South, until the twentieth century. In these cases the treatment of offenders normally was limited to low levels of violence such as tarring and feathering, minor property damage, rough handling, and beating, and cases involving verbal harassment alone without any physical aggression or property destruction were also common.[72]

Cultural Distance

Cultural distance refers to differences between individuals and groups in the expressive and symbolic aspects of their social life such as language, religion, cuisine, clothing, and entertainment.[73] As these differences increase, so does the probability and severity of a lynching: *Lynching varies directly with cultural distance.*

Although the late nineteenth- and early twentieth-century South was less diverse ethnically than much of the rest of the United States, cultural distance still contributed to lynching. One major cultural divide was between black and white. Although middle-class blacks in towns might have assimilated some white culture, most southern blacks maintained a separate culture to some degree. A distinctive dialect, food, styles of music and religious worship, humor, and other folkways distinguished the majority of southern blacks from whites.[74] Cultural distance of this sort helps explain why a lynching was more likely in an interracial than an intraracial conflict. When an offense of a particular kind occurred, such as a homicide or rape, a black was more likely to be lynched by whites, followed distantly by white-on-white lynchings, while the smallest number of lynchings stemmed from black-on-black offenses.[75]

Cultural distance was also present in some incidents in which whites lynched other whites. In late nineteenth-century Georgia, Alabama, Kentucky, Tennessee, and North Carolina, for example, proselytizing by Mormon missionaries was sometimes met with beatings, whippings, and killings. By contrast, itinerant ministers of the South's two dominant faiths, Baptist and Methodist, virtually never risked lynching for spreading their beliefs. Southerners apparently reacted not only to the alien content of Mormon theology and religious practice but to the missionaries' largely northern background and manners as well.[76] Similarly distant were Italians, eleven of whom were killed at once in 1891 in New Orleans following the murder of a police officer.[77] Cultural distance also sometimes was present in incidents of vigilantism, such as when Jewish merchants, landowners, and lumber company operators in southern Mississippi became prominent targets of turn-of-the-century "Whitecappers."[78]

Cultural distance between blacks and whites was unevenly distributed across the South and with it the likelihood of lynching. Interracial conflicts involving blacks from outside the South or those from distinct subcultures within the South entailed a greater degree of cultural distance between the parties and a greater likelihood of lynching. Blacks raised in the North or who lived there long enough to assimilate its urban black culture stood out from their southern counterparts in dress, speech, and demeanor, and this relatively greater degree of cultural distance from whites increased their vulnerability to lynching. One example noted earlier was the lynching of Emmett Till in 1954: Till grew up in Chicago and, with his fashionable clothes, spending money, and self-assurance, "did not act like his Southern cousins."[79] One of the whites who attacked Till later admitted telling the youth: "Chicago boy, I'm tired of 'em sending your kind down here to stir up trouble."[80]

The second and more important source of increased interracial cultural distance was the existence of distinct black subcultures, some associated with particular occupations. For example, the turpentine, lumber, and sawmill industries that boomed in the late nineteenth century largely employed black workers and in the young, predominantly male lumber and turpentine camps, a rough-and-tumble, almost frontierlike lifestyle emerged. As one student of the timber industry in Mississippi notes: "In the 'early days'—around the turn of the century—transient laborers, drifters, and lawless men flocked to the lumber towns. Gambling, drinking, and crimes of violence were common."[81] Turpentine workers in particular were recognized by both races as especially unique and "backward" in attitude and customs.[82] Insofar as these predominantly black occupations involved workers in a distinctive subculture, they would be more vulnerable to severe punishment if they offended whites than blacks such as sharecroppers or servants whose occupations entailed more cultural closeness to the dominant population. Although little systematic data on the occupations of blacks lynched yet exist, it is suggestive that those regions in the South where the timber industry flourished—such as northern Florida, southern and western Georgia, east Texas, and central and southern Mississippi—had relatively high lynching rates.[83]

LYNCHING AND SOCIAL POLARIZATION

Lynching is most likely to appear in cases of conflict that cross large expanses of social space. This is why lynching was not equally likely to appear everywhere in the late nineteenth- and early twentieth-century South, even when identical offenses such as homicide and rape were allegedly committed by blacks against whites. Lynching occurred most often in rural or small-town settings and exhibited temporal variation as well. It occurred less during slavery, for example, more as the late nineteenth century progressed, still more during the economic depression of the 1890s, and went into a long-term decline after 1900.[84] My theory explains the varying rates of lynching across time and place.

The degree of social polarization is the combined degree of relational distance, cultural distance, inequality, and functional independence present in a case of conflict. The more of each, the more polarization. And the more polarization, the greater the likelihood and severity of lynching. Thus, as communities experience growing social polarization between groups and individuals, the probability of lynching rises. In the late nineteenth-century South, for example, interaction between blacks and whites gradually lessened over time. Intimate contacts, forged earlier under slavery, diminished as former masters and slaves died off and blacks and whites increasingly lived and worked in different settings: "A new generation of blacks and whites faced each other across an ever-widening chasm. The 'best' whites and blacks seldom had contact with one another, as both races increasingly withdrew into their own neighborhoods and churches."[85] As blacks and whites polarized, the rate of lynching rose.

Because the degree of social polarization of the races was unevenly distributed across the South, the rate of lynching was unequally distributed as well. As a minority group presence in a community or region increases through in-migration or desegregation, for instance, rates of lynching rise. As the number of strangers functionally independent and otherwise socially distant from the original residents increases, so does lynching.[86] It follows, for example, that lynching in the South should be higher in areas with higher in-migration by blacks. And it was. One scholar estimated that while the average county in the South between 1880 and 1910 saw its black population increase by 48 percent, counties in the Gulf Coast subregion stretching from Florida to Texas experienced black population increases ranging from 71 to 131 percent. This Gulf Coast subregion, moreover, had the highest lynching rate over this period.[87] Other subregions that experienced heavy black in-migration in the late nineteenth century such as the cotton uplands of Mississippi, Arkansas, and Louisiana, as well as southwestern Georgia and southwestern Virginia, also experienced higher rates of lynching.[88] Whether black migrants' destinations were cotton plantations or lumber and coal mining camps, the result was the same: more lynchings. Edward Ayers notes that lynchings "tended to flourish where whites were surrounded with what they called 'strange niggers,' blacks with no white to vouch for them, blacks with no reputation in the neighborhood, blacks without even other blacks to aid them."[89]

An economic depression also could increase interracial polarization by raising levels of transiency and vagrancy among blacks. During the depression of the 1890s, for instance, unemployed strangers of both races became more visible than ever in many communities and were accused of increasing crime of all kinds. And this was the peak decade for lynching. Scattered evidence also suggests that many of those who became involved in interracial disputes were itinerant workers.[90] After 1900, however, those whom whites might regard as "tramps" or "suspicious strangers" increasingly sought destinations far removed from cotton fields and lumber camps, and their departure reduced the potential for lynching. With heavy migration out of the South to cities in the North (especially during and after World War I), the numbers of young, single blacks who previously circulated within the rural South fell, social polarization also fell, and lynching rates began a steep decline.[91]

A NOTE ON RIOTING

Under conditions of still greater social polarization, liability broadens and another form of collective violence appears: rioting. In the relatively rare cases when a lynching in a small community was followed by indiscriminate attacks on blacks, a high degree of polarization apparently prevailed not only between the adversaries but also between many members of each race. Such levels of polarization might be reached, for instance, when many out-of-town whites attend a lynching of a black.[92] A high degree of social polarization between newly arrived groups of black workers and local whites might also create conditions conducive to rioting. During the Corbin, Kentucky, riot of 1919, for example, whites attacked hundreds of black railroad construction workers following rumors that a railroad worker had assaulted a white night watchman. Most long-term black residents who worked for whites—those with strong local ties of interdependence and intimacy—were permitted to remain in town unharmed, but hundreds of railroad workers were roughed up and permanently expelled.[93] Antiblack riots increased as blacks migrated to urban settings and lost whatever protection against collective liability their intimacy and interdependence with whites had provided in the rural South. In the North, rapid and heavy in-migration of blacks during and immediately after World War I created a sudden and extreme degree of interracial polarization and was accompanied by a wave of antiblack rioting much greater in severity and frequency than in southern cities.[94]

Some evidence suggests that in the South the degree of polarization between the races varied from city to city and that the likelihood of both rioting and lynching varied accordingly. In slow-growing, older cities such as Savannah and Charleston, the races were less polarized and collective violence was rare or absent. In Charleston, for example, whites maintained what Don Doyle calls "traditions of intimacy and paternalism" with many blacks. He notes that there was little residential segregation, much daily contact between the races, and a "tradition of interdependence . . . an intricate network of personal dependencies, knitted together by hundreds of acts of daily kindness."[95] Understandably, therefore, Charleston had no rioting or lynching in the postbellum period. Newer, faster-growing cities such as Atlanta and Nashville showed a different pattern. The races were far more segregated residentially, and higher proportions of both races were recent migrants. They also lacked a paternalistic tradition with its high degree of interdependence: "In these faster growing cities, blacks and whites met more often as strangers with no personal knowledge of one another, no ties between them."[96] And they had more rioting and lynching: Atlanta in 1906 witnessed large-scale antiblack rioting, while Nashville in the late nineteenth century had at least three lynchings involving large crowds of whites.[97]

Although social polarization between the races in the South grew over time, only in places with many newcomers, such as fast-growing towns and cities, did it reach the high levels conducive to rioting. In rural and small town settings, social proximity between the races was fostered by the interdependence of employer and employee or seller and customer, by the cultural closeness of some blacks to whites, and by the inevitable intimacy involved in regular face-to-face interactions, and the breadth of liability remained narrow. However serious they may have deemed the conduct of a particular black and however severe the resulting violence inflicted on the offender, only rarely did whites injure or kill other blacks in the community because of his wrongdoing. Lynching—not rioting—was the usual response. In this sense, southern lynching was a sign of closeness between blacks and whites.

CONCLUSION

Lynching is social control: it defines and responds to conduct as deviant. Following Black's general theory of social control, the central claim of this essay is that the likelihood and lethality of lynching varies with the social structure of a conflict.[98] The following propositions have been offered:

1. *Lynching varies directly with relational distance.*
2. *Lynching varies inversely with functional interdependence.*
3. *Downward lynching is greater than upward lynching.*
4. *Lynching varies directly with cultural distance.*

What happens in a conflict depends on who does what to whom: on how intimate, interdependent, and culturally similar the antagonists are and on the vertical direction of the alleged offense. When social distance along any of these dimensions is present to a high degree and an upward offense occurs, lynching is more likely. And when social distance of all kinds between the parties is greatest—as when a low-status, culturally distant offender who is a stranger offends a social superior—the most extreme violence is most likely: a fatal lynching, possibly accompanied by torture before the execution and mutilation of the corpse afterward.

These propositions seem to explain patterns of lynching in the postbellum American South. The degree of social distance between those involved in interracial conflicts was strongly associated with whether whites chose to lynch an alleged offender or instead allowed the law to take its course. An impoverished and unemployed black stranger who allegedly beat, robbed, killed, or raped a high-status, respected white, for example, was more likely to face a lynching. But an interracial conflict with a substantially different structure—such as when a well-known, respected black with strong ties of interdependence with whites was accused of beating, robbing, killing, or raping a disreputable, poor white stranger—was likely to have a far different outcome: a trial in court. Conflicts between lower-status antagonists were less likely to result in lynchings, regardless of their race.[99]

This essay, then, represents an initial step in the effort to clarify the circumstances under which lynchings occur and the conditions associated with their varying severity. It also represents the first application of the Blackian paradigm to the phenomenon of lynching at the level of the case. Thus, although scattered evidence supports my propositions, no systematic empirical inquiry into the differential handling of conflict in the postbellum South has yet been attempted. A fuller assessment of the predictive and explanatory power of my propositions will require further study. Quite possibly other structural variables not yet discovered may prove pertinent as well. In any event, we now have testable formulations applicable to lynching not only in the postbellum South but whenever and wherever it occurs.

NOTES

1. James Elbert Cutler, *Lynch Law: An Investigation into the History of Lynching in the United States* (London: Longmans, Green, 1905), 1, 267, 270. Scholars typically bring to the subject matter a purely southern focus. Variation in lynching among states, regions, and counties within the South has been compared and contrasted, but comparison of southern lynching with lynching elsewhere in the world—or even elsewhere in the United States—is virtually nonexistent. Significant exceptions to an exclusively southern focus on lynching and other violence in that region would include Bertram Wyatt-Brown, *Southern Honor: Ethics and Behavior in the Old South* (New York: Oxford University Press, 1982); and Edward L. Ayers, *Vengeance and Justice: Crime and Punishment in the Nineteenth-Century American South* (New York: Oxford University Press, 1984). By contrast, those who study rioting and vigilantism have long been aware of the possible benefits of comparative work in understanding collective violence. See, e.g., Hugh Davis Graham and Ted Robert Gurr, eds., *Violence in America* (New York: Bantam Books, 1969); Paul A. Gilje, *The Road to Mobocracy: Popular Disorder in New York City, 1763–1834* (Chapel Hill: University of North Carolina Press, 1987); and Gilje, *Rioting in American History* (Bloomington: Indiana University Press, 1996); H. Jon Rosenbaum and Peter C. Sederberg, eds., *Vigilante Politics* (Philadelphia: University of Pennsylvania Press, 1976); and James F. Short and Marvin E. Wolfgang, eds., *Collective Violence* (Chicago: Aldine-Atherton, 1972).

2. Andrew F. Henry and James F. Short, *Suicide and Homicide: Some Economic, Sociological and Psychological Aspects of Aggression* (Glencoe, Ill.: Free Press, 1954), 51. See also Richard Maxwell Brown, *Strain of Violence: Historical Studies of Ameri-*

can *Violence and Vigilantism* (New York: Oxford University Press, 1975), 214, 217; and Howard Smead, *Blood Justice: The Lynching of Charles Mack Parker* (New York: Oxford University Press, 1986), x.

3. Herbert Shapiro, *White Violence and Black Response: From Reconstruction to Montgomery* (Amherst: University of Massachusetts Press, 1988), 30.

4. Ibid., 30–31. Another writer describes lynching as "the quintessence of passion . . . composed of a crowd gathering in the dark, high emotion mixed with hard liquor, and a frightening lust for blood vengeance" (Charles David Phillips, "Exploring Relations among Forms of Social Control: The Lynching and Execution of Blacks in North Carolina, 1889–1918," *Law and Society Review* 21 [1987]: 361–74). Similar assertions are frequent in the literature on lynching and have been in circulation for a long time. See, e.g., Arthur F. Raper, *The Tragedy of Lynching* (Chapel Hill: University of North Carolina Press, 1933), 1, 8–11, 41, 44–48. Moralistic evaluations of participants in collective violence contribute little or nothing to a scientific understanding of the sources of variation in such behavior. They are not, for example, falsifiable in the face of the known facts about such violence, especially when they involve attributions of collective mental disorder. See, e.g., John Dollard, *Caste and Class in a Southern Town* (1937; rpt. Garden City, N.Y.: Doubleday, 1957), chap. 15; Gilje, *Rioting in American History*, chap. 5; and Joel Williamson, *The Crucible of Race: Black-White Relations in the American South since Emancipation* (New York: Oxford University Press, 1984), 151–52.

5. Especially since interracial competition is commonly cited as a cause of lynching. See Carl I. Hovland and Robert R. Sears, "Minor Studies of Aggression: Correlations of Economic Indices with Lynchings," *Journal of Psychology* 9 (1940): 301–10; Henry and Short, *Suicide and Homicide*, 51–60; Jay Corzine, Lin Huff-Corzine, and James C. Creech, "The Tenant Labor Market and Lynching in the South: A Test of Split Labor Market Theory," *Sociological Inquiry* 58 (Summer 1988): 261–78; James C. Creech, Jay Corzine, and Lin Huff-Corzine, "Theory Testing and Lynching: Another Look at the Power Threat Hypothesis," *Social Forces* 67 (March 1989): 626–33; E. M. Beck, James L. Massey, and Stewart E. Tolnay, "The Gallows, the Mob, the Vote: Lethal Sanctioning of Blacks in North Carolina and Georgia, 1882 to 1930," *Law and Society Review* 23 (1989): 317–31; E. M. Beck and Stewart E. Tolnay, "The Killing Fields of the Deep South: The Market for Cotton and the Lynching of Blacks, 1882–1930," *American Sociological Review* 55 (August 1990): 526–99; Susan Olzak, "The Political Context of Competition: Lynching and Urban Racial Violence, 1882–1914," *Social Forces* 69 (December 1990): 395–421; Olzak, *The Dynamics of Ethnic Competition and Conflict* (Stanford: Stanford University Press, 1992), 109–34; Sarah A. Soule, "Populism and Black Lynching in Georgia, 1890–1900," *Social Forces* 71 (December 1992): 431–49; W. Fitzhugh Brundage, *Lynching in the New South: Georgia and Virginia, 1880–1930* (Urbana: University of Illinois Press, 1993); Stewart E. Tolnay and E. M. Beck, *A Festival of Violence: An Analysis of Southern Lynchings, 1882–1930* (Urbana: University of Illinois Press, 1995). Virtually all work on collective violence—regardless of its theoretical strategy—is macrostructural in orientation and seeks to uncover what are often termed the deeper conditions or processes underlying collective violence. As one sociologist notes, the search for larger underlying causes has "an extremely long pedigree in the history of social and political thought." See James B. Rule, *Theories of Civil Violence* (Berkeley: University of California Press, 1988), 3.

6. Donald Black, *The Behavior of Law* (New York: Academic Press, 1976); Black, "Common Sense in the Sociology of Law," *American Sociological Review* 44 (February 1979): 18–27; Black, "Compensation and the Social Structure of Misfortune," *Law and Society Review* 21 (1987): 563–84; Black, "Crime as Social Control," *American Sociological Review* 48 (February 1983): 34–45; Black, "The Elementary Forms of Conflict Management," in *New Directions in the Study of Justice, Law, and Social Control*, Prepared by the School of Justice Studies, Arizona State University (New York: Plenum Press, 1990); Black, "The Epistemology of Pure Sociology," *Law and Social Inquiry* 20 (Summer 1995): 829–70; Black, *The Manners and Customs of the Police* (New York: Academic Press, 1980); Black, "Social Control as a Dependent Variable," in *Toward a General Theory of Social Control*, Vol. 1: *Fundamentals*, ed. Black (Orlando: Academic Press, 1984); Black, *Sociological Justice* (New York: Oxford University Press, 1989); and Black, *The Social Structure of Right and Wrong* (San Diego: Academic Press, 1993). See also Mark Cooney, "Behavioural Sociology of Law: A Defence," *Modern Law Review* 49 (March 1986): 262–71. For a fuller discussion of the theory of unilateral collective violence, see Roberta Senechal de la Roche, "Collective Violence as Social Control," *Sociological Forum* 11 (March 1996): 97–128.

7. While some collective violence is predatory (as when stores are looted during a power blackout) or recreational (as when young people destroy property to celebrate a sports victory), most expresses a grievance. For examples of nonmoralistic collective violence, see Gary Marx, "Issueless Riots," in *Collective Violence*, ed. James F. Short Jr. and Marvin E. Wolfgang (Chicago: Aldine-Atherton, 1972); Robert Curvin and Bruce Porter, *Blackout Looting! New York City, July 13, 1977* (New York: Gardner Press, 1979); Francis Russell, *A City in Terror: The 1919 Boston Police Strike* (New York: Viking Press, 1975). Predatory violence committed as a means for some gain is behaviorally distinct from that which seeks to right a wrong or to punish deviant behavior and is more appropriately explained and ordered by a theory of predation than a theory of social control. Therefore, the present discussion excludes all instances of predatory, nonmoralistic collective violence. For example, the beating, killing, or violent expulsion of blacks by whites so as to acquire land, houses, or other property in the postbellum South (which other scholars sometimes count as "lynchings") is viewed here as predatory behavior and not social control. Similarly, because their behavior is predatory and opportunistic rather than moralistic, those engaged exclusively in looting during riots are not counted as "rioters." Indeed, behaviorally speaking, little distinguishes much of the looting behavior that accompanies social disruptions such as riots from that following massive power failures or police strikes in cities. Some predatory behavior such as theft does involve the expression of a grievance and thus can qualify as social control. See, e.g., Black, "Crime as Social Control," and James Tucker, "Employee Theft as Social Control," *Deviant Behavior* 10 (1989): 319–34. To conceptualize violence as social control is not to say that one can explain such phenomena as lynchings and riots as a simple result of crime or other offenses. A concept is not an explanation. While deviant behavior must occur in order for there to be social control, the offense itself, be it a minor infraction or an act considered a serious crime, does not entirely determine what, if anything, will happen in its wake. As discussed below, what happens and to what degree depends on the social structure of a case of conflict.

8. Percentages are calculated from Tables 2-3 and 2-4 (after eliminating the 3.2

percent of cases in which no reason for the lynching could be discovered) of Tolnay and Beck, *Festival of Violence*, chap. 2. See also Raper, *Tragedy of Lynching*, 469–79; George C. Wright, *Racial Violence in Kentucky, 1865–1940: Lynchings, Mob Rule, and "Legal Lynchings"* (Baton Rouge: Louisiana State University Press, 1990), 77; and Brundage, *Lynching in the New South*.

9. Black, *Behavior of Law*, "Social Control as a Dependent Variable," and *Sociological Justice*. See also Allan V. Horwitz, *The Logic of Social Control* (New York: Plenum Press, 1990); and Mark Cooney, "The Social Control of Homicide: A Cross-Cultural Study" (S.J.D. diss., School of Law, Harvard University, 1988).

10. Compare, e.g., Allen D. Grimshaw, "Interpreting Collective Violence," in *Collective Violence*, ed. Short and Wolfgang, 41, and Ted Robert Gurr, ed., *Violence in America*, Vol. 2: *Protest, Rebellion, Reform* (Newbury Park, Calif.: Sage, 1989). References to white lynchers' motives and psychological states as explanatory factors are still common in the literature. See, e.g., Tolnay and Beck, *Festival of Violence*, and Brundage, *Lynching in the New South*.

11. Black, *Behavior of Law*, 7–8.

12. Compare, e.g., Neil J. Smelser, *Theory of Collective Behavior* (New York: Free Press, 1963); Richard Maxwell Brown, "Historical Patterns of Violence in America," in *Violence in America*, ed. Davis and Gurr, 45–84; Charles Tilly, *From Mobilization to Revolution* (Reading, Mass.: Addison-Wesley, 1978); and Natalie Zemon Davis, *Society and Culture in Early Modern France* (Stanford: Stanford University Press, 1975).

13. Compare, e.g., James M. Inverarity, "Populism and Lynching in Louisiana, 1889–1896: A Test of Erikson's Theory of the Relationship between Boundary Crises and Repressive Justice," *American Sociological Review* 41 (April 1976): 262–80; and Dennis B. Downey and Raymond M. Hyser, *No Crooked Death: Coatesville, Pennsylvania, and the Lynching of Zachariah Walker* (Urbana: University of Illinois Press, 1990).

14. Black, "Epistemology of Pure Sociology."

15. See, e.g., Klaus-Friedrich Koch, "Liability and Social Structure," in *Toward a General Theory of Social Control*, ed. Black, 1:95–129; and Black, "Compensation and the Social Structure of Misfortune," 566, 573–76. For a fuller discussion of the differences between the four forms of collective violence, see Senechal de la Roche, "Collective Violence as Social Control."

16. Sally F. Moore, "Legal Liability and Evolutionary Interpretation: Some Aspects of Strict Liability," in *The Allocation of Responsibility*, ed. Max Gluckman (Manchester: Manchester University Press, 1972); and Koch, "Liability and Social Structure." See also Black, *The Manners and Customs of the Police*, 37–38, and "Crime as Social Control," 38.

17. For example, Tolnay and Beck estimate that, for the ten southern states they examined from 1882 to 1930, in approximately 86 percent of lynching incidents a single alleged offender was executed. See *Festival of Violence*, chap. 2. Similarly, Brundage finds that in Georgia and Virginia from 1880 to 1930, approximately 88 percent and 95 percent of lynchings, respectively, involved the lynching of single offenders. Indeed, cases of lynching involving the punishment of three or more offenders at a time were rare: 4.8 percent of lynchings in Georgia and 2.6 percent in Virginia. (Percentages were calculated from *Lynching in the New South*, 262, Appendix A, Table 2.) In addition, a list of persons lynched along with the alleged offense has

been compiled for Kentucky for the years 1866 to 1940. Although it is not possible to calculate with any accuracy the percentage of those incidents which involved the killing of more than one individual, it nonetheless is clear that at least in many apparent multiple-offender lynchings, those executed were deemed to have shared the guilt for the offense. For example, in 1877, a crowd seized five white men, all members of the Simmons gang—notorious horse and cattle thieves and murderers—and killed them. See Wright, *Racial Violence in Kentucky*, 307–23.

18. On rare but dramatic occasions, such white casualties helped to transform what would have been a lynching into violence with a logic of collective liability: an anti-black riot. See Brundage, *Lynching in the New South*, 111–13, 146–48; Tolnay and Beck, *Festival of Violence*, chap. 2; and Wright, *Racial Violence in Kentucky*, 123–24. See also Neil R. McMillen, *Dark Journey: Black Mississippians in the Age of Jim Crow* (Urbana: University of Illinois Press, 1989), 225–26. For an example of black resistance to lynching precipitating rioting, see Maxine Jones, Larry E. Rivers, David R. Colburn, R. Tom Dye, and William R. Rogers, "A Documented History of the Incident Which Occurred at Rosewood, Florida, in January 1923," Document submitted to the Florida Board of Regents, December 22, 1993.

19. Brundage uses a four-part taxonomy of types of lynching groups: mass mobs, private mobs (fewer than fifty persons), terrorist mobs, and posses. He finds that in Georgia and Virginia, mass mobs accounted for 34 and 40 percent of lynchings in each state, respectively (*Lynching in the New South*, 17–48).

20. Raper, *Tragedy of Lynching*, 12.

21. For examples of women at large-scale lynchings, see, e.g., Raper, *Tragedy of Lynching*, 12–13, 143, 206, 236, 323, 326; Brundage, *Lynching in the New South*, 37–38, 41–42; Wright, *Racial Violence in Kentucky*, 93–95; and Ann Field Alexander, "'Like an Evil Wind': The Roanoke Riot of 1893 and the Lynching of Thomas Smith," *Virginia Magazine of History and Biography* 100 (April 1992): 193, 195, 200–201. White women also were present during, and sometimes active in, antiblack violence in the North in the early twentieth century. See, e.g., Elliott Rudwick, *Race Riot at East St. Louis, July 2, 1917* (Carbondale: Southern Illinois University Press, 1964); Downey and Hyser, *No Crooked Death*; and Roberta Senechal [de la Roche], *The Sociogenesis of a Race Riot: Springfield, Illinois, in 1908* (Urbana: University of Illinois Press, 1990), 28, 30, 38, 103–4.

22. For examples of black spectators at the lynching of another black, see Alexander, "'Like an Evil Wind,'" 194–95, and Brundage, *Lynching in the New South*, 45.

23. On the role and behavior of authorities in lynchings and the seizure of black suspects from them, see, e.g., Raper, *Tragedy of Lynching*, 13–15, 207–8; Wright, *Racial Violence in Kentucky*, 89–98, 112–13, 117; McMillen, *Dark Journey*, 246–51, and Brundage, *Lynching in the New South*, 30–31, 33–34, 36.

24. Wyn Craig Wade, *The Fiery Cross: The Ku Klux Klan in America* (New York: Simon & Schuster, 1987), 61, 259–63. Wade quotes a Klan leader in the 1960s as saying, "Instead of hitting the 'mass enemy,' the Klan should target the 'individual enemy'" (338). Although the Klan sometimes punished many in a single raid, it nonetheless singled out those deemed "guilty." The "Whitecappers" of the Mississippi Piney Woods region in the 1890s and 1900s, "regulators" in North Georgia in the late nineteenth century, and "Night Riders" of the tobacco-growing regions of Kentucky and Tennessee at the turn of the century also operated as vigilantes according to the

definition used here. See William F. Holmes, "Whitecapping: Agrarian Violence in Mississippi, 1902–1906," *Journal of Southern History* 35 (May 1969): 165–85; Holmes, "Whitecapping in Mississippi: Agrarian Violence in the Populist Era," *Mid-America* 55 (April 1973): 134–48; Ayers, *Vengeance and Justice*, 255–64; Brundage, *Lynching in the New South*, 128–29; and Christopher Waldrep, *Night Riders: Defending Community in the Black Patch, 1890–1915* (Durham: Duke University Press, 1993). Holmes describes Mississippi's Whitecap clubs as highly organized with "an elaborate committee system" that displayed a pattern of individual liability: "One committee determined who should be punished, another prescribed the kind of punishment, and still another inflicted the punishment" ("Whitecapping in Mississippi," 136). On definitions of vigilantism, compare, e.g., Brown, *Strain of Violence*, 21–22, 103; David A. Johnson, "Vigilance and the Law: The Moral Authority of Popular Justice in the Far West," *American Quarterly* 33 (Winter 1981): 560; and Rosenbaum and Sederberg, *Vigilante Politics*, 3–17. Although a few exceptions may exist, the postbellum rural South seems not to have been fertile ground for terrorism—including antiblack terrorism—which by definition here is highly organized collective violence that operates according to a logic of collective liability.

25. One form of white collective action against blacks that falls beyond the boundaries of the definition of collective violence as used here is expulsion. At different times and places in the postbellum South, such as in western Kentucky and Tennessee in the 1900s and parts of north and southwest Georgia in the late nineteenth and early twentieth centuries, whites drove most or all blacks out of their communities. The details of such expulsions are far from clear, but some historians suggest that whites subsequently may have acquired land and other property owned by blacks (see note 10 above for comments on predation). See, e.g., Wright, *Racial Violence in Kentucky*, 137–43; Waldrep, *Night Riders*, 140–60; and Brundage, *Lynching in the New South*, 24–25. Expulsion of persons from a social setting (when not an instance of predation), regardless of whether it is accompanied by violence or simply intimidation and the threat of violence, is a form of social control behaviorally distinct from collective violence. We do know that, like much of violence or criminal law, it is penal in style, a punishment inflicted for conduct regarded as deviant (see Black, *Behavior of Law*, 4–5, and "Social Control as a Dependent Variable," 8–10). It occurs in a wide variety of settings and conflicts and varies in amount from short or temporary ostracism or exile, as when a child is isolated for misbehavior, to permanent banishment. It may operate according to a logic of individual or collective liability, as when states prohibit the presence of whole ethnic groups or subcultures from their territory. For examples of variation, see Black, *Behavior of Law*, 73, 127, 129, 137. A theory that predicts and explains the likelihood, severity, and scope of expulsion with variation in the social structure of conflicts has not yet been fully developed.

26. See, e.g., A. W. Lintott, *Violence in Republican Rome* (London: Oxford University Press, 1968), 4, 6–13, 24–26; Robert B. Edgerton, "Violence in East African Tribal Societies," in *Collective Violence*, ed. Short and Wolfgang, 166–67; Paul Bohannan, "Homicide among the Tiv of Central Nigeria," in *African Homicide and Suicide*, ed. Paul Bohannan (Princeton: Princeton University Press, 1960), 37–39, 62; L. A. Fallers and M. C. Fallers, "Homicide and Suicide in Busoga," in *African Homicide and Suicide*, ed. Bohannan, 82, 93; Arthur H. Smith, *Chinese Characteristics* (New York: Fleming H. Revell, 1894), 210–12, 214–15; Smith, *Village Life in China: A*

Study in Sociology (New York: Fleming H. Revell, 1899), 163–65, 222; A. B. Saran, *Murder and Suicide among the Munda and Oraon* (Delhi: National Publishing House, 1974), 13, 19, 69–70, 78–79, 81, 84–86, 108–9, 119, 121–22, 202–3, 221–24; Pieter Spierenburg, *The Spectacle of Suffering: Executions and the Evolution of Repression, from a Preindustrial Metropolis to the European Experience* (New York: Cambridge University Press, 1988), 14, 17–18; Richard van Dulman, *Theatre of Horror: Crime and Punishment in Early Modern Germany* (Cambridge, Eng.: Polity Press, 1990), 113–18; Stephen Wilson, *Feuding, Conflict and Banditry in Nineteenth-Century Corsica* (Cambridge: Cambridge University Press, 1988), 364; Caroline Oates, "Metamorphosis and Lycanthropy in Franche-Comté," in *Fragments for a History of the Human Body*, ed. Michel Feher (New York: Urzone, 1989), 308, 346–47; and E. Adamson Hoebel, *The Law of Primitive Man: A Study in Comparative Legal Dynamics* (Cambridge, Mass.: Harvard University Press, 1967), 81, 87–90, 140–42, 168, 276–77, 300. On variation in the size of lynch "mobs," see Brundage, *Lynching in the New South*.

27. See, e.g., Leonard Bloom and Henry I. Amatu, "Nigeria: Aggression, a Psychoethnography," in *Aggression in Global Perspective*, ed. Arnold P. Goldstein and Marshall H. Segall (Elmsford, N.Y.: Pergamon Press, 1983), 360–64; Ali Mazrui, "Black Vigilantism in Cultural Transition: Violence and Viability in Tropical Africa," in *Vigilante Politics*, ed. Rosenbaum and Sederberg, 208–15; R. Lance Shotland, "Spontaneous Vigilantes," *Society* 13 (March–April 1976): 30–32; Gary David Comstock, *Violence against Lesbians and Gay Men* (New York: Columbia University Press, 1991), 13, 19, 26, 46–47, 60–70; Michael H. Bond and Wang Sung-Hsing, "China: Aggressive Behavior and the Problem of Maintaining Order and Harmony," in *Aggression in Global Perspective*, ed. Goldstein and Segall, 69–70; and Jonathan Rieder, *Canarsie: The Jews and Italians of Brooklyn against Liberalism* (Cambridge, Mass.: Harvard University Press, 1985), 175, 178–79, 182, 199–202.

28. Shotland, "Spontaneous Vigilantes," 30–32. The same practice is seen in rural and urban Nigeria. See Bloom and Amatu, "Nigeria," 362–64.

29. See, e.g., Rieder, *Canarsie*, 178–79, 200–201; and Dominic J. Capeci Jr. and Martha Wilkerson, *Layered Violence: The Detroit Rioters of 1943* (Jackson: University Press of Mississippi, 1991), 202–3.

30. Smith, *Chinese Characteristics*, 210–11, 215.

31. Ibid., 210.

32. This is compatible with Black's theory that other means of social control tend to arise where law is not available to settle disputes (*Behavior of Law*, 6–7, 105–11).

33. Black, "Elementary Forms of Conflict Management," 43–69.

34. The model of lynching offered here is largely a synthesis of Black's models of vengeance and discipline and rebellion in his theory of self-help (ibid., 43–49).

35. The variables used here are drawn from Black's theory of law and other social control. See Black, *Behavior of Law* and "Elementary Forms of Conflict Management," 43–49.

36. Max Gluckman, *Custom and Conflict in Africa* (Oxford: Basil Blackwell, 1956), 19–24; and Senechal [de la Roche], *Sociogenesis of a Race Riot*, 141–51.

37. Brundage, *Lynching in the New South*, 81–82, 90–91. Brundage found that one-fifth and one-third of blacks discussed in Georgia and Virginia newspapers after they were killed in lynchings were described as strangers. The length of residence of

the rest mentioned in the press remains an open question. Apparently the press often had little to say about length of residence of black lynching victims. Some blacks might have been long-term residents. Nonetheless, it is highly likely that the actual proportion of offenses by black strangers is much higher, especially in light of the figures for recently arrived whites killed in lynchings. See also Robert P. Ingalls, *Urban Vigilantes in the New South: Tampa, 1882–1936* (Knoxville: University of Tennessee Press, 1988), 210. Holding constant the alleged offense, strangers tend to be treated more severely, both when law and other kinds of social control are brought to bear. See, e.g., Black, *Behavior of Law*, 40–48; Black, *The Manners and Customs of the Police*, 29–32; Black, *Sociological Justice*, 11–12, 58–62; and Senechal de la Roche, "Collective Violence as Social Control." See also Black, "Common Sense in the Sociology of Law," 25. Strangers who commit homicide in modern America are much more likely to receive capital punishment than those who kill intimates or acquaintances. See Samuel R. Gross and Robert Mauro, "Patterns of Death: An Analysis of Racial Disparities in Capital Punishment," *Stanford Law Review* 37 (1984): 58–59.

38. See, e.g., Ayers, *Vengeance and Justice*, 167–69, 250–55, 260–61; Ayers, *The Promise of the New South: Life after Reconstruction* (New York: Oxford University Press, 1992), 156–58; and Brundage, *Lynching in the New South*, 81–84.

39. Brundage, *Lynching in the New South*, 90–91.

40. Ibid., 74–76, 80. See also Dollard, *Caste and Class in a Southern Town*, 292–93. Blacks who were well known by whites and who had cultivated ties with employers and neighbors were less likely to be lynched than those with few or no ties, holding constant the offense. Charles S. Johnson noted "one unfailing rule of life" among the Alabama blacks he observed: "If they would get along with the least difficulty, they should get for themselves a protecting white family. 'We have mighty good white folks friends, and ef you have white folks for your friends, dey can't do you no harm'" (*Shadow of the Plantation* [Chicago: University of Chicago Press, 1934], 27). See also Brundage, *Lynching in the New South*, 83–84; Ayers, *Promise of the New South*, 157–58; and Waldrep, *Night Riders*, 33, 81.

41. Dollard, *Caste and Class in a Southern Town*, 165. See also McMillen, *Dark Journey*, 14–16; Stephen J. Whitfield, *A Death in the Delta: The Story of Emmett Till* (New York: Free Press, 1988), 5–12, and Ayers, *Promise of the New South*, 158.

42. See, e.g., Dollard, *Caste and Class in a Southern Town*, 135–72.

43. Brundage, *Lynching in the New South*, 77–79. This high level of severity was also seen when white police were allegedly killed by blacks.

44. Ibid., 60–61.

45. For an extensive list of reasons given for lynchings, see Tolnay and Beck, *Festival of Violence*, chap. 2. For examples of "trivial" offenses by blacks, see Brundage, *Lynching in the New South*, 53–58, 60–61, 81; McMillen, *Dark Journey*, 236; and Ayers, *Promise of the New South*, 158.

46. Jerrell H. Shofner, "Judge Herbert Rider and the Lynching at Labelle," *Florida Historical Quarterly* 59 (1981): 292, 297–99.

47. Tolnay and Beck, *Festival of Violence*, chap. 3.

48. Whitfield, *A Death in the Delta*, 12, 15–23.

49. Black, "Elementary Forms of Conflict Management," 45–47. See also Senechal de la Roche, "Collective Violence as Social Control."

50. On employers' discipline of black workers, see, e.g., Nollie Hickman, *Mississippi Harvest: Lumbering in the Longleaf Pine Belt, 1840–1915* (University: University of Mississippi Press, 1962), 143–46, 251; Raper, *Tragedy of Lynching*, 56–57; and McMillen, *Dark Journey*, 124–26.

51. McMillen noted that "violence . . . could be counterproductive; whites who employed it too freely risked a sullen and uncooperative workforce. . . . Because dependency cut both ways, even the hardest riding bosses foreswore corporal punishment lest their hands leave them with crops still in the field" (*Dark Journey*, 125–26). It has been suggested that fear of black labor shortages because of heavy black migration to the North beginning in the World War I era also moved some whites to press for a end to lynching (Tolnay and Beck, *Festival of Violence*, chap. 7).

52. Brundage, *Lynching in the New South*, 61.

53. Ibid., 76–77, 79.

54. Dollard, *Caste and Class in a Southern Town*, 282–83. See also W. E. B. Du Bois, ed., *Some Notes on Negro Crime* (Atlanta: Atlanta University Press, 1904), 45–46; H. C. Brearley, "The Pattern of Violence," in *Culture in the South*, ed. W. T. Crouch (Chapel Hill: University of North Carolina Press, 1934), 690; and Ayers, *Vengeance and Justice*, 178–79.

55. See, e.g., Brundage, *Lynching in the New South*, 45, 63–64, 84; Waldrep, *Night Riders*, 81.

56. Dollard, *Caste and Class in a Southern Town*, 338–39.

57. Ayers, *Vengeance and Justice*, 205–7.

58. Du Bois, *Some Notes on Negro Crime*, 45–46; Dollard, *Caste and Class in a Southern Town*, 282–83; Brearley, "Pattern of Violence," 690; and Ayers, *Vengeance and Justice*, 178–79.

59. Black, *Behavior of Law*, 21–28.

60. For variation in the handling of legal cases with stratification and the relative rank of the parties in conflict, see Black, *Behavior of Law*, 11–36, and *Sociological Justice*, 7–13.

61. M. P. Baumgartner, "Social Control from Below," in *Toward a General Theory of Social Control*, ed. Black, vol. 1.

62. Dollard, *Caste and Class in a Southern Town*, 287–314.

63. Brundage, *Lynching in the New South*, 86–102.

64. Ibid., 88. A study of homicide among whites in a mountainous region near the Kentucky-Tennessee border in the nineteenth and twentieth centuries found that most killings occurred between equals or near equals, the vast majority of whom were friends, neighbors, or relatives. Such cases drew little severity at law and prompted no lynchings. Indeed, in some cases, the homicides were never brought to the attention of the authorities. See William Lynwood Montell, *Killings: Folk Justice in the Upper South* (Lexington: University Press of Kentucky, 1986).

65. Exceptions did exist. Blacks might lynch a "desperado" who had preyed on more respectable blacks in a community. See Brundage, *Lynching in the New South*, 30. On black violence and the legal system, see Ayers, *Vengeance and Justice*, 230–36. On rare occasions, whites might lynch low-status blacks accused of killing a higher-status black. See, e.g., Wright, *Racial Violence in Kentucky*, 98–100. Whites might also lend their support to the prosecution of upward crimes by whites against blacks, though this, too, was rare. See Raper, *Tragedy of Lynching*, 172–202, for an example.

Status differences between victim and offender help account for the thirty cases from the eighteenth century to the 1940s—most in the South—in which whites were legally executed for victimizing blacks. The majority of the whites executed in the postbellum era were of low status and had victimized relatively high-status blacks. See Michael L. Radelet, "Executions of Whites for Crimes against Blacks: Exceptions to the Rule?" *Sociological Quarterly* 30 (Winter 1989): 529–44.

66. Brundage, *Lynching in the New South*, 73, 76. Twenty-seven percent of the cases involved alleged attacks on police and 24 percent attacks by blacks on white employers. Another 7 percent of cases involved the alleged killing of a white woman by a black. The relative status of the remainder of the parties in the 205 cases is not given. It is possible that many of the remaining cases also involved a high degree of vertical distance between the parties.

67. Ibid., 73, 76–77, 79. See also James L. Massey and Martha A. Myers, "Patterns of Repressive Social Control in Post-Reconstruction Georgia, 1882–1935," *Social Forces* 68 (December 1989): 458–88; Horwitz, *Logic of Social Control*, 108–13; and Downey and Hyser, *No Crooked Death*.

68. See, e.g., Brundage, *Lynching in the New South*, 63–64; Martha Hodes, "The Sexualization of Reconstruction Politics: White Women and Black Men in the South after the Civil War," *Journal of the History of Sexuality* 3 (January 1993): 411; and Wright, *Racial Violence in Kentucky*, 55. Courts also might take into account the status and degree of respectability of both black and white women who accused black men of raping them. Low standing and low repute on the part of the woman accuser might lead to acquittal or lesser charges. See Samuel Norman Pincus, "The Virginia Supreme Court, Blacks, and the Law, 1870–1902" (Ph.D. diss., University of Virginia, 1978), 250–55.

69. See, e.g., Pincus, "The Virginia Supreme Court, Blacks, and the Law," 304–7; and Howard N. Rabinowitz, *Race Relations in the Urban South, 1865–1890* (Urbana: University of Illinois Press, 1980), 54–55.

70. For example, of the seventeen known cases of whites who were legally executed for killing blacks between 1867 and 1944, ten involved assailants with tainted reputations: they either had criminal records or had been labeled as alcoholics, "tramps," or "dissipated" characters. Another five had killed blacks of higher status (Radelet, "Executions of Whites for Crimes against Blacks"). See also Pincus, "The Virginia Supreme Court, Blacks, and the Law," 308–11. Though also rare, whites might assist in attempts to arrest and prosecute other whites who killed a high-status black. See Raper, *Tragedy of Lynching*, 172–202. Black defines respectability as normative status. He notes that more legal authority is brought to bear on an individual of low normative status who offends someone who is more respectable than the reverse (*Behavior of Law*, 111–17). Extending Black's formulation from law to lynching, it appears that *lynching is greater in a direction toward less respectability than toward more respectability*. With respect to interracial lynchings, this would mean, for example, that a black of low normative status who offended a more respectable white would be more likely to be lynched than a black of higher normative status, such as a minister with a morally unblemished past. Also, the former would be subject to more severe violence. The severity with which blacks accused of killing or wounding white police officers were lynched may be in part traceable to great differences in the degree of respectability between some alleged offenders and the police. Most of the killings of

white police occurred "when officers attempted to arrest criminals charged with such petty crimes as gambling, petty theft, or vagrancy" (Brundage, *Lynching in the New South*, 76). On violence among blacks in the late nineteenth and early twentieth centuries, see W. E. B. Du Bois, *The Philadelphia Negro* (Philadelphia: Publications of the University of Pennsylvania, 1899), chap. 13; Du Bois, *Some Notes on Negro Crime*, 6, 38; Johnson, *Shadow of the Plantation*, 189–92; Dollard, *Caste and Class in a Southern Town*, 267–86; Brearley, "Pattern of Violence," 690–91; Ayers, *Vengeance and Justice*, 231–36; Roger Lane, *Roots of Violence in Black Philadelphia, 1860–1900* (Cambridge, Mass.: Harvard University Press, 1986), 144–61; Lawrence W. Levine, *Black Culture and Black Consciousness: Afro-American Folk Thought from Slavery to Freedom* (New York: Oxford University Press, 1977), 407–20.

71. Pincus, "The Virginia Supreme Court, Blacks, and the Law," 308–11.

72. Lintott, *Violence in Republican Rome*, 8–9; Brown, *Strain of Violence*, 25, 150–51; Davis, *Society and Culture in Early Modern France*, 97–123; Wyatt-Brown, *Southern Honor*, 435–61; and Ingalls, *Urban Vigilantes in the New South*, 14–15, 184.

73. Black, *Behavior of Law*, 61–62.

74. Dollard, *Caste and Class in a Southern Town*; Johnson, *Shadow of the Plantation*; Levine, *Black Culture and Black Consciousness*; and Ayers, *Vengeance and Justice*, 229–37.

75. For statistics on the racial characteristics of lynchers and their victims, see Tolnay and Beck, *Festival of Violence*; Brundage, *Lynching in the New South*; Wright, *Racial Violence in Kentucky*, 61–125; Inverarity, "Populism and Lynching in Louisiana," 263–64; Phillips, "Exploring Relations among Forms of Social Control," 368–69; and McMillen, *Dark Journey*, 225–53.

76. Gene A. Sessions, "Myth, Mormonism, and Murder in the South," *South Atlantic Quarterly* 57 (1976): 212–25; Ken Driggs, " 'There Is No Law in Georgia for Mormons': The Joseph Standing Murder Case of 1879," *Georgia Historical Quarterly* 73 (Winter 1989): 745–72; and Ayers, *Vengeance and Justice*, 255–56. On the importance of cultural differences between Mormons and those of southern background in the antebellum era, see Stephen LeSueur, *The 1838 Mormon War in Missouri* (Columbia: University of Missouri Press, 1987), 3, 16–19, 36, 246–47.

77. Richard Gambino, *Vendetta* (New York: Doubleday, 1974).

78. William F. Holmes, "Whitecapping: Anti-Semitism in the Populist Era," *American Jewish Historical Quarterly* 63 (March 1974): 244–61; and Hickman, *Mississippi Harvest*, 239.

79. Whitfield, *A Death in the Delta*, 16.

80. Ibid., 21.

81. Hickman, *Mississippi Harvest*, 251. See also Gavin Wright, *Old South, New South: Revolutions in the Southern Economy since the Civil War* (New York: Basic Books, 1986), 96–97.

82. Hickman, *Mississippi Harvest*, 139–40.

83. Brundage, *Lynching in the New South*, 114–18, 138; McMillen, *Dark Journey*, 157, 159, 230–31; and Holmes, "Whitecapping in Mississippi."

84. See, e.g., Tolnay and Beck, *Festival of Violence*; and Brundage, *Lynching in the New South*.

85. Ayers, *Vengeance and Justice*, 182, 236–38, 241. See also McMillen, *Dark Journey*, 6, 11, 23–24; Du Bois, *Souls of Black Folk*, 148–51; and Cutler, *Lynch Law*, 275.

86. Some claim that as the numbers of a minority group increase through in-migration or desegregation, rates of collective violence rise due to increased inter-group competition. My analysis, however, implies that these population changes will increase the likelihood of collective violence whether competition exists or not. Compare, e.g., Olzak, *Dynamics of Ethnic Competition and Conflict*; Susan Olzak, Suzanne Shanahan, and Elizabeth H. McEneaney, "Sources of Contemporary Racial Unrest in the United States: From the 1960s through 1990s" (paper presented at the annual meeting of the Social Science History Association, Baltimore, 1993); Tolnay and Beck, *Festival of Violence*, chap. 2; and Beck and Tolnay, "The Killing Fields of the Deep South," 533.

A study of American race riots from 1960 to 1992 found that the likelihood of rioting increased with desegregation. See Olzak, Shanahan, and McEneaney, "Sources of Contemporary Racial Unrest in the United States." Although desegregation in-creases the presence of a racial or ethnic group in a neighborhood or city, ties of intimacy, functional interdependence, or growing cultural closeness do not automat-ically follow. At least for the short term, it appears that newly arrived racial and ethnic groups maintain a high degree of social distance from the original residents.

87. Ayers, *Promise of the New South*, 156–57, 496–97. The one exception to the pattern was Louisiana, which received a far smaller share of black migrants and had a correspondingly low rate of lynching.

88. Ibid., 157; Raper, *Tragedy of Lynching*, 28; McMillen, *Dark Journey*, 259–61; Hickman, *Mississippi Harvest*, 133; Brundage, *Lynching in the New South*, 138, 143–49; and Tolnay and Beck, *Festival of Violence*, chaps. 2, 5, 7. Tolnay and Beck find that in southern counties where cotton growing predominated in the late nineteenth and early twentieth centuries (holding constant their economic variables), "increases in the absolute and relative sizes of the black population are associated with more frequent black lynchings" (128). Also suggestive is the pattern of violence seen in the highly lynch-prone southwestern region of Virginia, which witnessed a substantial in-migration of blacks attracted to the coal mining and timber industries there. Both black and white workers lived in timber and mining camps in Virginia, but lethal lynching among them was virtually unknown. Lynchings of blacks tended instead to occur in towns and small cities and, at least in many of the cases cited, entailed conflicts with a higher degree of social polarization, for example, between black miners from camps and white townsmen. See Brundage, *Lynching in the New South*, 114–18, 138.

89. Ayers, *Promise of the New South*, 157. See also Brundage, *Lynching in the New South*, 81–84, 90–91.

90. The rate of arrest, incarceration, and legal execution of blacks also rose in the 1890s and seems to have been in part owing to the greater number of offenses attributed to socially distant transients set in motion by hard times. See Ayers, *Vengeance and Justice*, 250–55. See also Tolnay and Beck, *Festival of Violence*, chap. 4; Phillips, "Exploring Relations among Forms of Social Control"; Beck, Massey, and Tolnay, "The Gallows, the Mob, and the Vote"; and Du Bois, *Some Notes on Negro Crime*, 6, 10, 22, 29, 31–33.

91. For an extensive discussion of the possible relationships between rates of lynchings and black migration, see Tolnay and Beck, *Festival of Violence*, chap. 7.

92. Regardless of time and place, rioters generally tend to be socially distant from

those they attack. See Senechal de la Roche, "Collective Violence as Social Control."
For examples of lynchings followed by rioting committed by out-of-town attackers,
see Jones et al., "A Documented History of the Incident Which Occurred at Rosewood, Florida, in January 1923"; Raper, *Tragedy of Lynching*, 321–22, 334; and Alexander, "'Like an Evil Wind.'"

93. Wright, *Racial Violence in Kentucky*, 144–47.

94. See, e.g., Rudwick, *Race Riot at East St. Louis*; and William M. Tuttle Jr., *Race
Riot: Chicago in the Red Summer of 1919* (New York: Atheneum, 1970). On the role of
relational distance in rioting in the North, see Senechal [de la Roche], *Sociogenesis of
a Race Riot*, 141–48; Capeci and Wilkerson, *Layered Violence*, 61, 68, 77, 106–7, 109;
and Alexander, "'Like an Evil Wind.'"

95. Don H. Doyle, *New Men, New Cities, New South: Atlanta, Nashville, Charleston, Mobile, 1860–1910* (Chapel Hill: University of North Carolina Press, 1990), 261,
297–98, 302. See also Laylon Wayne Jordan, "Police and Politics: Charleston in the
Gilded Age, 1880–1900," *South Carolina Historical Magazine* 81 (January 1980): 38–
39. Similarly, in Savannah, one contemporary noted that "a leaven of the old house-
servant class is still living beside the sons of their former masters and mutual understanding is much better [than in Atlanta], and perhaps even runs into laxness in cases
where punishment of Negroes would be salutary" (Du Bois, *Some Notes on Negro
Crime*, 52).

96. Doyle, *New Men, New Cities, New South*, 261–62.

97. Ibid., 262; Rabinowitz, *Race Relations in the Urban South*, 52–54; and Charles
Crowe, "Racial Massacre in Atlanta, September 22, 1906," *Journal of Negro History*
54 (April 1969): 150–73. For the same phenomenon of rapidly increasing polarization
in southern cities accompanied by collective violence, see also Alexander, "'Like an
Evil Wind,'" and Ingalls, *Urban Vigilantes in the New South*. The greater frequency of
antiblack rioting in southern cities immediately after emancipation is in part traceable
to temporarily high levels of social polarization that prevailed in many places. Cities
like Memphis and New Orleans in the late 1860s were inundated with black refugees
(dramatically increasing relational distance), who were often former Union soldiers or
Republicans (increasing cultural distance from white Confederate Democrats) and
who were often unemployed and desperate (a very low degree of interdependence).
See Gerald David Jaynes, *Branches without Roots: Genesis of the Black Working Class
in the American South, 1862–1882* (New York: Oxford University Press, 1986), 264;
George C. Rable, *But There Was No Peace: The Role of Violence in the Politics of
Reconstruction* (Athens: University of Georgia Press, 1984), 33–58; Melinda Meek
Hennessey, "Race and Violence in Reconstruction New Orleans: The 1868 Riot,"
Louisiana History 20 (Winter 1979): 77–91.

98. See, e.g., Black, *Behavior of Law*, "Elementary Forms of Conflict Management," and *The Social Structure of Right and Wrong*. See also Senechal de la Roche,
"Collective Violence as Social Control."

99. Law is less available to and used less by low-status parties as well. See Black,
Behavior of Law, 11–30.

Part II
Lynching in the Local and Regional Context

As Mark Twain lamented in 1901, many, if not most, white southerners (indeed, most white Americans) either acquiesced to or openly celebrated mob violence. Virtually all observers and scholars of lynching suggest that whites used mob violence to shore up racial boundaries in the face of some perceived threat or, more simply, to "keep blacks in their place." But because white fears about the maintenance of the racial hierarchy varied considerably both across time and from region to region within the South, the frequency of mob violence also varied. Whatever their proclaimed commitment to white supremacy during the nineteenth and twentieth centuries, white residents of different regions of the South did not share the same proclivity to take the law into their hands.

The three essays in this section help to explain some of the complexities of the historical and geographical variation of lynching. Despite differences in setting and focus, these essays share several similarities. The authors, in their various ways, all pay close attention to the salience of place and moment in incidents of mob violence. And together the essays invite scholars to extend the study of racial violence to include border states such as Missouri, overlooked periods of time such as the closing months of the Civil War, and seldom mentioned aspects such as intraracial mob violence.

In the first two essays, Professors Thomas G. Dyer and Joan E. Cashin achieve a narrative precision that brings to mind anthropologist Clifford Geertz's method of "thick description." By virtue of their richly textured detail alone, these two model case studies offer as full and fascinating accounts of individual lynchings and their aftermath as we are likely to get. Dyer recounts in careful detail the circumstances surrounding and the consequences of a lynching in Missouri in 1859. This essay, which joins a short list of sophisticated studies of both antebellum and border state mob violence, highlights the unique qualities of antebellum mob violence as well as some of the antebellum precedents for postbellum lynching. Joan Cashin reconstructs the events that preceded and followed the lynching of Saxe Joiner in South Carolina at the end of the Civil War. Like Dyer's essay, Cashin's increases our understanding of how, during the Civil War, the practice of lynching in the South began to assume its postwar character.[1]

Both Dyer's and Cashin's essays reveal how long-simmering social tensions and anxieties found release in lynchings. In Saline County, Missouri, the tensions were an outgrowth of the worsening sectional crisis and mounting fears over the threat abolitionists posed to the racial order. The lynching in Union County, South Carolina, Cashin explains, cannot be understood fully without taking into account the different ideas about masculinity, propriety, and temperance that emerged among the male elite during the antebellum era. These long-standing differences were perpetuated, even exacerbated, by the transformation in gender and race relations wrought by the Civil War. Thus at times of great flux in the social and racial order, mobs in Saline County and in Union County resorted to lynchings to restore and reinforce the traditional social order by teaching local residents, male and female, black and white, precisely where they stood.

But as both Dyer's and Cashin's accounts make clear, some of those lessons were murky. These essays encourage us to recognize that lynch mobs gave expression to diverse and even contradictory attitudes about the obligations of white masculinity, white prerogatives, and black deference. Of course, whatever divisions the lynchings may have exposed and even heightened among whites, they did not provide any protection for blacks caught in the middle, even when they had the support of some whites. The divisions between whites that were evident in these lynchings are important not because they somehow ameliorated the effects of mob violence upon blacks—they most emphatically did not—but because they remind us that lynchings were much more than mechanistic expressions of the uncontested values and beliefs of white southerners.

E. M. Beck and Stewart Tolnay address a further complexity of mob violence—intraracial lynching—that has received little scholarly attention. Unlike the case studies by Dyer and Cashin, Beck and Tolnay's essay draws upon the entire record of postbellum lynchings in the South. Using a comprehensive catalog of lynchings that they have compiled, Beck and Tolnay analyze variations in intraracial mob violence over time and place. Their provocative conclusions about intraracial lynchings in turn help to clarify the role of race in all lynchings by revealing possible motivations for mob violence which defy simple models of racism. In particular, their contention that intraracial lynchings were a violent expression of contempt for a distant and lax system of criminal justice by citizens who had ample reason to be skeptical about the courts sheds light on the important interrelationship between legal and extralegal justice. In a region where contempt for legal institutions and tolerance for violence as a defense of personal honor were deeply rooted, it is perhaps not surprising that white and black communities periodically resorted to "popular justice" to execute members who violated community standards.

But the significance of these intraracial lynchings far exceeds the comparatively small number of such occurrences. First, they are another reminder of the pervasiveness of extralegal violence in the South. In addition, they provided defenders of lynching and critics of the criminal justice system, who pleaded for speedier justice with fewer technicalities, with evidence to rebut contrary arguments that lynchings were nothing more than weapons of racial domination or that the courts already moved swiftly enough. Even many opponents of mob violence conceded that the punishment of criminals needed to be made swifter and harsher, drawing the same conclusions from intraracial lynchings that their opponents did: the great mass of southerners during the late nineteenth century had lost faith in the courts. In fact, while intraracial lynchings played a crucial role in the justifications for the campaign for swift and rigorous justice, it was chiefly blacks who were victimized by the legal system (as George Wright's essay vividly demonstrates). Thus in both subtle and obvious ways, the occasional lynching of a white or a black by members of their own race contributed to an atmosphere in which blacks often faced the prospect of "legal lynchings" in the courtroom and mob murder in the streets.

NOTE

1. As long as the Civil War lasted, lynching became intertwined with the far more deadly violence of the war itself. Throughout the conflict, spasms of mob violence erupted in southern communities when whites feared imminent slave insurrections. Clarence Mohr, in his study of Georgia, has revealed that large numbers of slaves were executed in gruesome spectacles aimed at intimidating the slave community into submission and loyalty. And in the backcountry, where allegiances often were divided

between the Union and the Confederacy, partisans on many occasions summarily executed their opponents in a manner that cannot easily be distinguished from lynching. See Michael Fellman, *Inside War: The Guerilla Conflict in Missouri during the American Civil War* (New York: Oxford University Press, 1989); Richard B. McCaslin, *Tainted Breeze: The Great Hanging at Gainesville, Texas, 1862* (Baton Rouge: Louisiana State University Press, 1994); Clarence L. Mohr, *On the Threshold of Freedom: Masters and Slaves in the Civil War* (Athens: University of Georgia Press, 1986), 32–36, 219–20; Phillip S. Paludan, *Victims: A True Story of the Civil War* (Knoxville: University of Tennessee Press, 1981); James Smallwood, "Disaffection in Confederate Texas: The Great Hanging at Gainesville," *Civil War History* 22 (December 1976): 349–60; and William W. White, "The Texas Slave Insurrection of 1860," *Southwestern Historical Quarterly* 52 (January 1949): 259–85.

A Most Unexampled Exhibition of Madness and Brutality

Judge Lynch in Saline County, Missouri, 1859

Thomas G. Dyer

In the space of three days in July 1859, whites in Saline County, Missouri, lynched four slaves accused of unrelated crimes in four different locations. Because extensive sources rarely survive concerning such incidents, there have been virtually no case studies of slave lynchings in the antebellum South and certainly none of such occurrences along the western perimeter of slavery in volatile pre–Civil War Missouri. Although the episode bore some resemblance to a slave insurrection panic, the causes ran much deeper and tapped a tradition of frontier and racial violence which had been intensified by the border warfare of the 1850s, reinforced by the ideological legacy of collective violence in the revolutionary and Jacksonian eras, and linked by the participants themselves to the widespread experience with vigilantism in the last years of the decade.[1]

Saline County, located in a seven-county area called Little Dixie, stretches along the Missouri River, approximately 170 miles west of St. Louis. Settled largely by emigrants from western Virginia, Tennessee, and Kentucky, the region exhibited a decidedly southern character and culture. Politics, religion, architecture, and economic life all partook heavily of southern practices and traditions although a mix of influences from other regions was present as well. Although the county was located near the western and the northern edges of slave territory, slavery pervasively affected life there and especially the system of commercial agriculture that developed soon after the first waves of settlement had passed.[2]

Slavery in Saline County was a vigorous institution. Verdant, prosperous, and ideally suited to a variety of crops including hemp, corn, oats, and wheat, the county had by the late 1850s become home to nearly ten thousand whites and almost five thousand blacks, virtually all of whom were slaves.[3] The slave population grew by 79 percent during the decade of the 1850s, by far the greatest increase of any county in Little Dixie, the area of heaviest slave ownership in the state. By 1860, Saline County ranked fourth among Missouri counties in slave population and had the second highest percentage of slaves to total population. Forty percent of the county's families owned slaves, and the average number of slaves per slaveholder had increased since 1850 from 5.4 to 6.9. Slavery appears to have been profitable for Saline County farmers, most of whom experienced substantial increases in crops, acreage, slaves, and value of their farm lands.[4]

Violence was familiar to blacks and whites who lived in Little Dixie in the late antebellum period. Conflicts settled by gunplay or fisticuffs seemed almost routine, and vigilante lynchings of whites accused of horse stealing or other crimes were not unknown; lynchers, for instance, dispatched two alleged horse thieves in Clay County early in 1859. Violence against slaves, ranging from casual whippings to brutal beatings, occurred with dreadful regularity in the seclusion of the farms and plantations. Accounts of some of the most heinous of these acts became part of the black oral tradition. Ed Craddock, born a slave, told of his father's recollection of an especially brutal Saline County master who, as an object lesson, chained a recalcitrant slave to a hemp brake on a bitterly cold winter night, where he slowly froze to death.[5]

The border wars that had begun in 1854 added to the violent atmosphere, heightening the anxieties of slave owners about the security of the slave system. Bloody conflicts along the Missouri-Kansas border and occasional abolitionist raids into Missouri occurred throughout most of the remainder of the decade and prompted sizable numbers of Saline County citizens repeatedly to go the seventy miles or so into Kansas, where they participated in proslavery raids or cast ballots in elections with the aim of thwarting the establishment of yet another free state on Missouri's borders.[6] In this uncertain and fear-laced setting, anxious whites in Saline County became agitated over what they saw as an insufficiently obsequious slave population and the effects of abolitionism on it.

White concerns were exacerbated by alarmist proslavery newspapers, particularly the *Marshall Democrat*. The newspaper was founded in 1858 by prominent Saline County Democrats and edited by John S. Davis, a transplanted Virginian with sharply prosouthern views. During the events that led to and followed the lynchings, the newspapers played important parts in shaping events through commentary and hyperbolic reporting.[7]

For more than a year, the *Democrat* had noted that an increasing number of runaway slaves were seeking freedom by escaping on the underground railroad that ran through the free states and territory bordering Missouri on three sides. At least twelve Saline County slaves were reported as having escaped between January 1858 and September 1859. Some were captured; others were not. The number of runaways may not have been large considering the size of the slave population, but there had been a steady stream of escapes from the area since the beginning of the Kansas troubles in 1854. In September of that year, nine slaves had escaped in a week's time, prompting the editor of the *Lexington Express* to speculate that a "branch" of the underground railroad operated in the area.[8] The *Democrat* warned that slaveholders must be "vigilant in watching the itinerant population who infest the community at this season of the year. Everyone found talking with the slaves should be spotted and their movements closely watched."[9]

The escapes continued, local fears grew, and still more disquieting news arrived in late 1858 with reports of the murders of a white jailer by a slave, seventy miles away in Callaway County, and of an overseer in nearby Lafayette County who had "found it necessary to correct, for some misconduct, two negro men." Later in the year, slaves on a farm fifty miles to the east in Randolph County killed their master.[10] Such reports of violence had the double effect of raising white anxiety about slave violence and shoring up an angry determination to take further measures to control the slave population.

Even more alarming and galling was a sudden daring raid into Missouri by the militant abolitionist John Brown. During the night of December 20–21, 1858, Brown and two columns of men crossed from Kansas into Vernon County, where they killed a farmer and liberated eleven slaves. Brown's audacity made proslavery Missourians angry and fearful. The proslavery press spewed out a torrent of vitriol, and for a time it appeared that the civil war which had raged along the border would erupt again. About six weeks later, a similar exploit was undertaken by three abolitionists who went into Clay County and took fourteen slaves to Kansas. Pursuing Missourians, however, recaptured the bondsmen and returned them to their owners.[11]

The proximity of Saline County to the border and the sites of abolitionist raids (particularly the Clay County incursion), as well as the knowledge that many antislavery men going to Kansas traversed the county or passed around it on the Missouri River, persuaded slaveholders that the menace from Kansas and from abolitionists was real. Under the circumstances, it was a reasonable concern and certainly had more basis in fact than the wild reactions to supposed abolitionist plots which Deep South slaveholders perceived in the wake of Brown's subsequent raid on Harpers Ferry in October 1859.[12]

By the spring of 1859, still more escapes had occurred. In mid-May, however, concern over runaways suddenly became secondary when fears of black violence toward Saline County whites materialized with the murder of thirty-three-year-old Benjamin Hinton. The son of a prominent farmer, Hinton lived in a shanty and ran a woodyard several miles west of Miami on the Missouri River. There, he and a partner, Giles Kiser, chopped and sold wood to the passing steamboatmen. Each man also owned a slave who worked in the enterprise.[13]

On Saturday morning, May 14, Hinton's slave awoke and went to his master's cabin to rouse him and build his fire. As he drew near the cabin, the startled slave saw Hinton sprawled in the doorway, partially clad, "his head complete[ly] mashed, and the brains and blood spattered all over the threshold." Inside the cabin, a bloody ax lay near Hinton's split-open steamer trunk, from which, it was later discovered, about fifty dollars had been taken. Initial reports held out the possibility that either whites *or* blacks could have committed the crime. The *Saturday Morning Visitor*, published in neighboring Lafayette County, used the occasion to call for a stronger police to protect the countryside from "desperate characters prowling about in quest of victims to gratify their thirst for blood and plunder."[14]

Two days later, Giles Kiser's slave, John, was arrested for the crime, "upon the very strongest circumstantial evidence," and taken to Marshall, where he was put in heavy irons and "confined in a very secure jail." In a hearing before Justice of the Peace H. D. Doak, Martin A. Gauldin, a prosperous slave-owning farmer, testified that he had been told that John had proposed to two other slaves that they kill Hinton for his money. Gauldin also claimed that John had "deposited" ten blood-covered dollars with another slave and that, on the morning after the murder, his clothes had been covered with blood. Gauldin's hearsay testimony was enough to keep the slave in custody.[15]

According to the *Marshall Democrat*, John soon confessed to the crime, giving as his motive that he held a grudge against Hinton for "a threatened or actual chastisement." The *Democrat* confidently accepted John's confession, declaring that there was virtually no chance of his innocence. To an "outraged community," the evidence proved "indubitably" that John had murdered Hinton.[16]

The *Saturday Morning Visitor* presented a slightly different account. On the day after the murder, the newspaper declared, a greatly excited John had reported the murder to residents of a nearby farm where his wife lived. According to the paper, John claimed to have seen the murdered Hinton in his cabin near the river "laid out—the hands crossed and feet placed together." John also claimed that he had gotten all of the money from Giles Kiser's other slave, Dick, whom he blamed for the murder. Not so, the newspaper averred; John was guilty. He had told other slaves of his plans, and he likely had accomplices—raising the possibility of a slave conspiracy. "Hanging [is] too good for him," the editor concluded. "He does not deserve a longer existence, only with the hope of finding his accomplices, that they may all suffer together."[17]

Word of John's confession rapidly spread to Hinton's friends and neighbors in Saline and Lafayette Counties who decided to take matters into their own hands. "Judge lynch would hold a special term," it was said, "and try the murderer with *fire!*"[18] Before dawn on Friday, May 27, several wagonloads of men together with others on horseback gathered a few miles north of Marshall, headed south, and while it was still early clattered into the town. Arriving at the jail, they demanded that John be handed over. They were outraged to learn that a forewarned Sheriff Jacob H. Smith had the day before spirited the slave to jail in Boonville, forty miles away.[19]

Shortly thereafter, the thwarted mob dissolved into a stormy meeting at the courthouse where they were joined by some residents of the town. The conclave, according to the *Marshall Democrat*, was presided over by "one of our prominent citizens" and featured speeches pro and con for going on to Boonville and lynching the slave. In the end, some unnamed Marshall citizens persuaded the group to petition Russell Hicks, judge of the circuit court for Saline and six other counties, for a special term of the court to try John. The persuasive powers of the Marshall citizens notwithstanding, public sentiment seemed solidly arrayed against the slave. The *Democrat* observed that publication of John's confession had "added fuel to the flame, insomuch as to nerve some of them [the mob] to the hazardous undertaking of inflicting punishment on the criminal without the sanction of law."[20]

For three weeks, a tense quiet settled on the county in anticipation of the special session of the court. Then, on June 22, a slave in Arrow Rock, fifteen miles east of Marshall, allegedly attacked William Durrett, a prosperous slave owner and farmer. The *Democrat* reported that the slave, whose name was Holman, had stabbed the white man, wounding him seriously.[21]

Arrested and jailed in Arrow Rock, Holman was soon taken from custody by his owner, Virginia Howard, who sent him out of the county with the intention of selling him, thus protecting her investment.[22] Holman got about thirty miles away before he was captured a few days later, returned to Arrow Rock, and transferred to the jail in Marshall. Howard's action angered those who believed that such behavior contributed to criminality among slaves. The incident inspired the *Marshall Democrat* to argue that the time had come for direct action. "If a few healthy examples were made," the editor wrote, "no doubt we would hear of fewer crimes committed by our slave population."[23]

Meanwhile, slaves continued to run away, adding to a brittle nervousness among whites. On July 1, the *Marshall Democrat* complained that "almost every week, we hear of some outrage committed in this or adjoining counties by negroes." Then, on July 12, an incident two miles east of Marshall incensed the white population and caused the increasingly shrill *Democrat* to raise the prospect of a county-wide "servile insurrection." Jim, a slave belonging to James M. White of rural Marshall, was arrested and jailed for the attempted rape of Mary Habecot, a white woman. Habecot lived on a farm with her mother, sister, and husband, who had gone to nearby Marshall for the evening. At twilight, the women became frightened when a group of boisterous slaves passed the house and again later when Mary thought that she saw a black man lurking in her garden. According to Habecot, Jim broke into the house after she had gone to bed and unsuccessfully attempted to rape her.[24]

Two days after his arrest, Jim appeared before L. R. Parsons, a justice of the peace. During the proceedings that followed, Jim had counsel, probably hired by his owner, because the identity of Habecot's attacker (and therefore Jim's guilt) was in doubt.[25] His attorney, Samuel Boyd, a twenty-four-year-old lawyer and Kentucky native, had recently emigrated from Illinois. Boyd also edited the *Saline County Standard*, the American Party organ in the county, and was in the midst of a feud with the editor of the *Democrat*, John S. Davis, who later in the year would attempt to shoot Boyd. In 1859 Boyd was still in his legal novitiate but already showed signs of lawyerly craftiness.[26] He had serious doubts that Jim had been justly accused and on the way to the hearing told him to change hats with another slave in an apparent effort to confuse Habecot, who would be called upon to identify her attacker in court. When word of Boyd's tactic leaked out, it enraged some citizens who thought that the legal system was too lax in dealing with slaves and that such "tricks" were execrable.[27]

The prosecutor brought the other slave into the courtroom and asked

Habecot whether he was the assailant. She said no. Jim was then brought in, and despite the hat switching, she identified him as the man who had attacked her. But Mary Habecot's answers to Boyd's questions indicated that the lawyer raised substantial doubts about the accuracy of her identification of Jim. Nevertheless, the slave was bound over and remained in jail to await the action of a grand jury. The public mood would likely have allowed nothing else.[28] Unlike Boyd, the newspapers expressed few doubts about Jim's guilt. The *Saline County Herald* showed some sympathy for dealing with the matter through mob action, raised the issue of whether the punishment for rape (castration) was sufficient for so serious a crime, and called for legislation to make rape a capital offense.[29]

Meanwhile, Judge Hicks had set in motion the machinery for a special term of the circuit court to try John for the murder of Benjamin Hinton. As a result of lost mail, however, the special term was not scheduled until July 19. The delay prompted John W. Bryant, the circuit attorney in Marshall, to write Hicks, warning that he feared that "if a trial was not held soon, an outbreak of popular violence" would occur.[30]

By Monday, July 18, excitement in the county had spiraled higher. On that day, as reported by the *Democrat*, "another brutal outrage was perpetrated by a negro" man. Some children had gone out to pick blackberries, the paper reported, when one of the group, a little girl between ten and twelve years old, "was picked up by a negro man and carried into the woods close by, where he perpetrated a most diabolical outrage on her person." A man heard the girl's cries and hurried to her aid "but not in time . . . to prevent [the black's] fiendish designs." The alleged assailant escaped, but he was soon identified by the children as a slave belonging to Dr. William Price of Arrow Rock. Reports circulated that the slave had been nude when he confronted the children.[31]

That same day, citizens of Arrow Rock took swift retribution. An extralegal "committee" arrested the unfortunate man, then tried and summarily hanged him before a crowd estimated at nearly a thousand people, leaving the body hanging overnight as a warning to the slave community of the consequences of such deviant behavior. The *Saline County Herald* reported that the incident had driven public sentiment against slaves in the county to "an uncontrollable pitch."[32]

Meanwhile, Judge Russell Hicks again started for Marshall, where John, Holman, and Jim were incarcerated and where he would hold the special term of court the next day, Tuesday, July 19. Hicks, fifty-one years old and a native of Massachusetts, had been reared and educated in New York, emigrating to Missouri in 1826. After reading law in Old Franklin, he became a successful lawyer and was elected to the circuit court in 1856. In the more than thirty years that he had resided in the state, the well-regarded Hicks had become a slave owner and developed strongly pro-southern sympathies.[33]

Early on July 19, Sheriff Smith and Circuit Attorney Bryant, obviously excited, called on the judge at his hotel and reported the incidents involving Holman and Jim and rumors about the hanging in Arrow Rock. Hicks asked whether they thought that mob violence was likely. Yes, the two men replied. Hicks said that a posse should be raised immediately to try to prevent it. No reliable posse could be raised, the sheriff said. Hicks then asked whether violence could at least be avoided during the court proceedings. That might be possible, Smith and Bryant thought, but they offered no guarantees concerning what might transpire once the court session had ended.[34]

Bryant and Smith left, and Hicks quickly consulted others about the level of public agitation, seeking advice on what course to follow "in the approaching crisis." In those hurried conversations, he learned that at least "three distinct, exasperated parties" had already gathered at the courthouse: friends and relatives of Benjamin Hinton, Mary Habecot, and William S. Durrett. Nevertheless, the judge resolved to proceed with the court session, placing his trust in the moral power of the court "at least for a time, not in the least suspecting an outbreak [of violence] until evening."[35]

After opening court, Hicks impaneled the grand jury and then turned his attention to the spectators.[36] Mildly but firmly, Hicks spoke to them about the rumors of violence. He hoped that the reports were baseless, he said, but if there were those who contemplated violence, they should remember "that however well they could justify themselves to themselves for wresting the prisoner[s] from the officer of the law, and inflicting summary justice upon them, it would not be so easy to justify themselves to the world," especially since a duly constituted court was in session. Alluding to the predictable reaction of the antislavery and abolitionist press, the prosouthern Hicks hinted "distinctly enough to be understood, that the enemies to our institutions would rejoice in and triumph over such a scene."[37]

Let justice take its course, Hicks calmly told the crowd. If there were guilty verdicts, then "in a short time the prisoners would receive in a legal manner the punishment due their crimes," and "however much their [the crowd's] feelings were irritated and exasperated," the judge added, "they should think and consider if they acted in a summary manner at the present time."[38] Disgrace and injury would result from violence, Hicks went on, and he stated that he was determined to do his duty, though "limb should be torn from limb."[39] He concluded with an admonition to the "old and thinking men of the crowd to keep down popular excitement" and to control the hotheads.[40]

His remarks finished, the judge surveyed the room, measuring the expressions on the faces of his listeners. Thinking that he read approval on the majority and seeing "looks of defiance" on only a few, he decided to move ahead with the proceedings. The grand jury then retired from the courtroom to the jury room, where it quickly returned formal indictments against John for the murder of Benjamin Hinton, Jim for the attempted rape of Mary Habecot, and Holman for assault with intent to kill William Durrett. The indictments in hand, Hicks assembled a petit jury to try John, who was then brought in.[41] Hicks appointed John P. Strother and Joseph L. Hutchinson to represent John, who until that point had had no attorney. Still in their twenties and recent emigrants from Kentucky, Strother and Hutchinson were not yet well established in the local legal fraternity.[42]

On such short notice, Strother and Hutchinson obviously could mount no credible defense, but motions for delay would have been unthinkable given the tension in the courtroom and the ugly mood of the crowd. Thus John entered a plea of "not guilty," and the trial proceeded. Among the witnesses for the state were Martin A. Gauldin, who had provided testimony at the earlier hearing; two slaves, Harvey and Banjo, who testified that John approached them about killing Benjamin Hinton; the jailer W. W. Arnett; George, the slave who allegedly received the blood-stained ten dollars from John; George's owner, Robert Kirkley; and three other slaves, one of whom was summoned to testify about John's whereabouts during the early morning hours after Hinton's slaying. The calling of slaves as prosecutorial witnesses was a common practice in slave trials; they could be expected to give testimony as directed by whites or be punished when they returned home. No witnesses appeared for the defense. The indictment and the trial that followed took about two and one-half hours. The jury swiftly found John guilty of murder in the first degree.[43]

Apparently convinced that the crowd was under control, Judge Hicks routinely remarked to the defendant's attorneys that before sentencing he would entertain motions for a new trial or to set aside the verdict. Hicks instantly realized that his procedural correctness had further angered the impatient crowd, which wanted only to hear the death sentence. "The thought flashed across my mind," the judge remembered, "that if the prisoner was publicly ordered back to jail, he would never reach there."

Hicks therefore directed that John remain in the courtroom while he began Jim's trial for the attempted rape of Mary Habecot.[44]

Just before noon, after a jury was impaneled and sworn for Jim's trial, Hicks ordered a one-hour recess. By that time, the crowd had begun to press into the area where the lawyers, the judge, and the prisoners sat. In a voice loud enough to be heard throughout the courtroom, Hicks told the sheriff to keep the two prisoners (John and Jim) in the courthouse during the break for the "dinner hour." A few minutes later, however, he whispered to Sheriff Smith that as soon as the crowd had dispersed, he must take John back to the safety of the jail.[45]

Hicks remained on the bench for a few moments longer, nervously watching the people in the room, hoping they would leave. Some did, but many in the menacing crowd stayed, and suddenly they moved toward the prisoners. As rapidly as he could, the crippled Hicks stepped down from the bench, walked over to the prisoners, stood by their side, and turned boldly to the crowd and announced that the prisoners were "in no danger in the presence of the court." Hicks then ordered Sheriff Smith to take John to the jail, declaring that he would personally escort them.[46]

The sheriff, the judge, the slave, and a deputy then pushed through the angry, milling crowd out the courtroom door, down the stairs to the first floor and outside. From there, they strode rapidly toward the jail, approximately one hundred yards away. Just before reaching a gate that opened to the street, Hicks looked to his right and saw a crowd of men hurdling the fence around the courthouse yard and running down the street toward the jail. In an effort to reach the safety of the jail, John and Sheriff Smith broke into a run. The crippled Hicks could not keep up. Smith got his prisoner to the jail safely and turned him over to the jailer, W. W. Arnett, who hurried the slave to his cell.[47]

By then, the gathering crowd had become a mob in fury, full of wild noise and pressed against the jail, where, according to Judge Hicks, they were harangued and incited to violence by James M. Shackleford, a local farmer, justice of the peace, and neighbor of Mary Habecot. In the confusion of the riot, Hicks found Circuit Attorney Bryant and urged him to calm the mob. Bryant refused. "If such men [as Shackleford] had taken the matter in hand," he said, "it was all over with the prisoners." Shackleford was, Bryant added, "as respectable as any man in the county."[48]

When Shackleford finished, the mob stormed the jail, threatened the sheriff and jailer with sledgehammers, and demanded that they surrender John. The jailer refused. The mob overpowered him, opened the cells, and dragged out John and also Holman, who had remained in the jail during the morning. Meanwhile, a part of the mob rushed back to the court-house, where it forced two sheriff's deputies to surrender Jim.[49]

Loud, furious, and profane, the two mobs then converged, pulling, shoving, beating, and dragging their prisoners through the dust of the streets around the square in a swirl of savage force that took them finally to a ravine in a quiet grove about two hundred yards from the courthouse. Of the three slaves, Jim struggled hardest during the melee, causing minor injuries to some of his tormentors.[50]

In the grove, John, barefoot and stripped to the waist, was chained to a walnut tree, all the while talking rapidly with his captors.[51] According to the *Marshall Democrat*, the slave "had an intelligent and open counte-nance, and conversed very freely with all those who indicated a willingness to hear him while chained to the stake." The frantic man now claimed that he had an accomplice in the murder of Benjamin Hinton, but the charge caused no one in the mob to halt the awful work. While the slave talked, white men gathered dry wood and other combustibles which they piled around John's bare feet at the base of the tree. Only when the mob set fire to the wood did John seem to comprehend that he was to be burned alive. The newspaper's grisly account provides the hideous details:

> He was heard through, and the match applied beneath the combusti-bles piled around him. When the flames began to hiss about him, and the fire to penetrate his flesh, he first seemed to realize that he was to expiate his crime in that dreadful manner, for all along he had fed upon the fond belief that an honest confession would mitigate his punish-ment. We did not hear of his having made his peace with a more terrible Judge than Lynch, and in his dying agony he prayed more to those around him than to One above him. He lived from six to eight minutes from the time the flames wrung the first cry of agony from his lips, the inhalation of the blazing fire suffocating him in a short time. His legs and arms were burnt off, and his body but remained, a charred and shapeless mass.[52]

The *St. Louis Democrat* offered more details. The ghastly effects of the fire could be seen "in the futile attempts of the poor wretch to move his feet. As the flames gathered about his limbs and body, he commenced the most frantic s[h]rieks and appeals for mercy, for death, for water! He seized his chains; they were hot and burned the flesh off his hands. He would drop them and catch at them again and again. Then he would repeat his cries; but all to no purpose. In a few moments he was a charred mass, bones and flesh alike burned into powder."[53]

Meanwhile, Holman had been taken to another walnut tree where a hangman's noose was placed around his neck. The crowd then took the rope, threw it over a limb, jerked Holman from the ground, and suspended the slave until he also died, "apparently easy," as the Marshall newspaper unpersuasively noted. The mob also intended to burn Jim, but, having witnessed John's horrible immolation, decided against this manner of death for the slave accused of attempted rape. Jim was "swung up on the same limb with Holman, where he struggled for some time, dying hard."[54]

Its work finished, the satisfied mob dispersed. Described by one observer as "ribald," the mob may have carried out its plans in an atmosphere of Saturnalia, characteristic of Jacksonian era mobs two decades before.[55] At least some of the men, however, were sickened and horrified by the affair. The *St. Louis Democrat* reported, "Many, very many of the spectators, who did not realize the full horrors of the scene until it was too late to change it, retired disgusted and sick at the sight." Throughout the afternoon and into the evening, the bodies of Jim and Holman hung from the limb of the walnut tree while John's charred remains smoldered until the fire died out. Not until the next morning were the three buried in a common grave nearby.[56]

The slaves were dead, four lynched within the space of three days, one in Arrow Rock, three in Marshall, all by horrible means. The absence of any records showing the immediate effect upon the slave community makes it impossible to say with certainty what the reactions of the families of the four slaves might have been—if indeed they had families. Of the four, only John is known to have had a wife. Whether the others had wives or children will never be known. But almost certainly there was great grief among the survivors and, presumably, great fear engendered among the county's slaves—at least that was the intention of the mob and its leaders.[57]

Within forty-eight hours after the killings, James M. Shackleford, who had harangued the mob at the jail, composed a justification for the murders and delivered it to the *Marshall Democrat*. In this and subsequent letters to newspapers, Shackleford, who was widely regarded as a primary leader of the mob and would become its principal apologist, employed clear and sometimes clever arguments to explain its brutal actions. That Shackleford wrote the letters and the newspaper published them indicates a need in the community for justification and explanation.

Little is known about James Shackleford. He was a farmer who owned 160 acres of land approximately five miles east of Marshall. Circuit Attorney Bryant thought him well regarded in the community, and his election as justice of the peace suggests that he had the respect of his neighbors. The clarity and force with which he presented his arguments suggest that he had more than ordinary education. It also appears that he had journalistic pretensions or experience because he claimed to have been offered the editorship of a local party organ during the election of 1856. A Democrat who had been a Whig but evidently not a slave owner, Shackleford had strongly prosouthern political views.[58]

Altogether five lengthy letters from the thirty-seven-year-old native of Kentucky survive. These, together with a detailed letter from Judge Russell Hicks explaining his view of the mob action, provide rare commentary from two of the principals involved in the trial and lynchings of the slaves. Editorial observations and letters published in area newspapers supply additional insight into the rationale advanced for mob violence and provide a glimpse into divisions among whites in the aftermath of the murders.[59]

Shackleford's first letter explained the events leading to the murders, portraying the slaves in the most egregious light and depicting the whites involved as tragic victims of black brutes. Benjamin Hinton, "a most estimable young man," had been murdered. William Durrett, "in attempting to correct a slave whom he had forbidden to come on his place," had lost the use of his hand. Mary Habecot, "a poor, defenceless, delicate woman," had been the victim of an attempted rape. And "a little girl, about eleven years of age, gathering blackberries, was caught by a naked negro and a rape attempted upon her."[60]

In addition, Shackleford touched upon a theme that he and others would repeatedly emphasize: by providing inadequate penalties for attempted murder and rape by slaves, Missouri slave law was inherently unfair to whites. The crimes had been heinous, Shackleford went on, had followed "each other in rapid succession, [and] excited the public mind to the highest pitch." The people had therefore resolved to take action that would "make the penalty suit the crime" and set "a terrible example" that would quell the "spirit of insubordination" among the slaves.[61]

Shackleford emphasized the ultimate power of the people to dispense justice. The people had been forced to act, he wrote, because the legislature, by failing to revise the criminal code as it applied to slaves, had not satisfied public opinion. "The law that is not based upon public opinion," Shackleford wrote, "is but a rope of sand. An enlightened public opinion is the voice of God, and when brought into action it has a power and an energy that cannot be resisted." An "enlightened people," Shackleford went on, "will ever discriminate in the use of illegal power. If we are advancing in civilization, as I believe we are, the use of this power will become less frequent; the law will have more reverance [sic] because it will be clothed with the sanctity of justice. If we are retrograding, if we are going backwards, the abuse of unlawful power will cure itself; the strong arm of military power will do the work." Likening the action of the mob to that of the crowds during the French and American revolutions, Shackleford observed that there was "no reason why we should not have a little mob law in the State of Missouri, and County of Saline, when the *occassion* [sic] *imperiously; and of necessity* demands it."[62]

Shackleford found precedent for the lynchings in the extralegal activities of Andrew Jackson, noting with admiration that "it was mob law when Jackson drove the legislature of Louisiana from their halls and closed the door" and when Jackson "bombarded Pensacola and hung [Alexander] Arburthnot [sic] and [Robert] Ambrister." Such appeals to Jacksonian precedent fit well with Shackleford's emphasis on popular sovereignty as a justification for mob law. This view posited mob law as a complementary extension of the common law and an expression of the public will, a position entirely compatible with Shackleford's explanation for the mob violence in Saline County. His stress on the responsibility of the people to substitute their will for an inadequate legal system (the differential punishments for crimes committed by blacks and whites) calls to mind a common justification in nineteenth-century America for vigilante justice.[63]

Shackleford and other Saline Countians clearly knew about the extensive vigilante activity throughout the western and southwestern United States during the late 1850s. The most famous of these actions, the San Francisco vigilance committee, had administered "justice" in the California city for much of 1856 and was cited in the *Saturday Morning Visitor* by J. F. Yancey, a Waverly farmer, to justify and explain the action of the Saline County mobs. Like Shackleford, Yancey defended the Saline County hangings as vigilante actions taking the place of a failed legal system.[64]

The *Marshall Democrat* endorsed the general logic and echoed Shackleford's views a week later and several times during the coming months. "A series of the most dastardly and diabolical outrages" and "a spirit of insubordination" among the slave population had "wrought the minds of the people to the highest pitch of excitement; and nothing less than the lives of the criminals could possibly satisfy them," the newspaper added.[65]

By contrast, the *Lexington Express*, published in neighboring Lafayette County, strongly condemned the entire affair and specifically singled out Shackleford as the mob leader. The *Express*'s unequivocal denunciation of the murders—a "most unexampled exhibition of madness and brutality"—provoked responses from several area residents who quickly labeled the *Express* a "negro-outrage-loving," antisouthern newspaper. Shackleford referred to it as "that silly and contemptible Lexington sheet, its negroism being so thinly covered that the most ordinary penetration may see it." In a long letter to the *Express*, which was reprinted in the *Democrat*, Shackleford revisited the issues, expanded upon his earlier parallels between the American Revolution and the action of the mob, and vilified the newspaper for its "niggerish" sympathies.[66]

J. F. Yancey also complained about the *Express* article in the *Saturday Morning Visitor* and defended the lynchings much as Shackleford had. Yancey, like Shackleford, employed antiblack rhetoric which foreshadowed that used by proponents of mob action in the postbellum period, writing of "fiendish" slaves driven to the rape of white women by "hellish lust." It was well known, Yancey went on, that Saline County's slaves had laughed at, even exulted over, the failure of the first mob to take John from the jail and burn him. Yancey also condemned slave owners for complicity in crimes committed by their slaves. The slaves, he concluded, "regard[ed] this as a license to committ [*sic*] crime after crime." Yancey suggested that if Missouri were to adopt statutes compensating slave owners for slaves executed at law, then they would stop shielding their chattels.[67]

Some Saline Countians questioned the lynchings and criticized the mob. The day after the killings, the *Saline County Herald* condemned the "disgusting scenes" surrounding the murders of the slaves and decried the disregard for law and "the rule of anarchy . . . that bodes ill to the permanency of our institutions." Editor George Allen seemed especially concerned that the lynchings might be only the beginning of a protracted period of vigilante law which would be socially destructive to the white population.[68]

Meanwhile, Judge Russell Hicks sent a long letter to the *Lexington Express* concerning his understanding of the entire affair and including a detailed account of his own involvement. Part of Hicks's motivation lay in making the record straight from his point of view in the belief that the lynchings would soon be reported widely throughout the United States and abroad. Running to nearly two thousand words, Hicks's minute account of the circumstances surrounding the trial and lynchings occupied most of the space, but he concluded with a strikingly personal response to the travesty that he saw in the action of the mob.[69]

The judge felt betrayed. "My feelings as a man as well as a Judicial officer have been cruelly wounded," Hicks wrote. He had presided over the seven-county district for nearly three years and "was proud of the

Circuit." "All had gone smoothly," he explained, "until the unfortunate special term in Saline." He elaborated:

> To find myself, both morally and physically, without the aid of the people, unable to administer the laws; to be unable, with the assistance of the proper officers, to protect the prisoners at the bar of the court while upon their trial; to keep them from being dragged from the hall of Justice by violence, and hung and burnt in sight of the Court house, was a blow I was not prepared to receive.—But it came, and came like a thunderbolt in a cloudless sky, and has created such feelings as I never before experienced, and hope and trust I never shall again, in any situation in which I may be placed.[70]

Within days, Hicks resigned his judgeship, in clear protest against the vigilante perversion of judicial process in Saline County and as a result of profound personal disillusionment.[71]

Other glimmers of dissent appeared later when local authorities issued a warrant against James Shackleford for disturbing the peace. The origins of the warrant and its disposition cannot be determined with certainty, but it likely resulted from a complaint by Benjamin Chase, a sixty-four-year-old engineer and New York native, whom Shackleford said was a member of the "Know Nothing," or American party "clique" in Marshall. Chase evidently charged Shackleford with having acted illegally during the violence and with violating his oath as a justice of the peace. Shackleford took refuge in natural law theory to deal with the question of his oath, the charge that troubled him most, because failure to adhere to an oath would normally bring dishonor in southern society. When the law fails to provide adequate protection to the people, he wrote, and is "weak, powerless, and impotent," then citizens are justified in acting extralegally. "I, for one," Shackleford said, "shall ever act in accordance with the natural law when I believe the safety of society requires it. No oaths, no religious or political organizations shall have binding influence to deter me from acting, when the welfare, the peace and the safety of society require me to act."[72]

The *Saline County Herald* provided a forum for Chase and published a letter in which he excoriated Shackleford. Unfortunately, no files of the *Herald* exist, and it is impossible to know the contents of that letter, how fully the newspaper may have departed from the positions of the pro-lynching group, or how much community support Chase attracted. Shackleford claimed that Chase acted alone in promoting the peace warrant against him or, at most, in concert with two or three other persons. Shackleford treated the warrant with contempt and, claiming that he "alone [had been] selected out of the numerous and highly respected gentlemen of Saline who were more implicated in the matter," demanded an immediate jury trial on the charges the same day that he was served. But no trial took place and the matter appears to have been dropped.[73]

The probability remains that the majority of the white population in Saline County harbored few reservations about the correctness of the lynchings. Within a week, Lizzie Marshall, a farm woman who lived in the southwest part of the county, wrote to her sister that there had been "great excitement amongst the people of the county." Marshall reported that "the Negroes are getting Smarter than the White folks here" and in matter-of-fact language observed that as a result "there was two negroe's [sic] hung and one burnt."[74]

Although no significant information survives from which to draw conclusions concerning the effects of mob violence on slave crime, it appears to have had little immediate impact on escape attempts. In fact, the murders may have stimulated slaves to run away. Only days after the lynchings five slaves belonging to Ossamus Hurt, who lived in the southern part of the county, escaped and tried to make their way to the underground railroad in Iowa. When the slaves were captured, the *Saturday Morning Visitor* noted approvingly that they would be sold south.[75]

After the lynchings, an unusually strong anxiety prevailed in the county concerning how its reputation might be damaged when newspapers elsewhere reported the incident. In tones later associated with community boosters, the *Marshall Democrat* worried openly about damage to the community's image as a result of the lawless episode. In fact, much of the justification printed by the *Democrat* seems to have been aimed at newspapers in other locales, which would often, in the nineteenth-century fashion, reprint entire articles from other newspapers.[76] The *Saline County Herald* showed the same concern and, on the day after the lynchings, expressed its hope that "reproach may not rest upon our beautiful county, for the sins of a few misguided men who do not realize that one of the great duties of a good citizen, is to obey the law of the land."[77]

Reproach came solidly to rest on Saline County, however, and it came in part from the hated abolitionist press. Two weeks after the incident, the *National Anti-Slavery Standard* reprinted a lengthy article from the *St. Louis Democrat* which told the story as graphically as had the *Marshall Democrat*.[78] Months later, the American Anti-Slavery Society reported the lynchings in its annual report for 1859–60 within a section entitled "Barbarity to Slaves."[79] And finally, when Union troops arrived in Marshall during the Civil War, they goaded local citizens with the remark: "Ah! here is the place where you burn men at the stake, is it?"[80]

Several questions of interest to scholars arise from the incidents in Saline County. One concerns the frequency of slave lynchings in antebellum America. Eugene Genovese, drawing upon the work of Clement Eaton and W. J. Cash, observed that such events were rare and estimated that of three hundred persons lynched in the South during the period from 1840 until 1860, probably less than 10 percent were black. Slave owners had no interest in seeing their valuable property lynched, Genovese pointed out, preferring that the law execute convicted slaves since owners in some states could expect to be compensated by the state for their value.[81]

In contrast, Kenneth Stampp concluded, "Mobs all too frequently dealt with slaves accused of murder or rape. . . . Their more fortunate victims were hanged; the others were burned to death." In addition, Bertram Wyatt-Brown points to burnings and castrations as "common tortures" inflicted in cases in which slaves "were denied even the most perfunctory of trials" although neither he nor Stampp supplies much documentation. In his study of slave law in Virginia from 1705 to 1865 Philip Schwarz sees an "ominous change" occurring in antebellum Virginia as threats of lynchings as well as actual lynchings of slaves accused of the rape of white women "began to occur regularly." Historians agree that just before the Civil War in 1860–61 and during the war itself, the number and frequency of slave executions grew frightfully as whites, fearful of insurrections, sought to maintain rigid control over the slave community.[82]

If Genovese's estimate is accurate, slave lynchings occurred with comparative frequency in Missouri. In the thirteen years from 1847 through 1859, at least eleven slaves were lynched in various parts of the state—most in or near Little Dixie. Harrison A. Trexler noted five and possibly six lynchings of blacks, two of which were burnings, in Missouri during the seven years from 1847 through 1853. Douglas Hurt, in *Agriculture and Slavery in Missouri's Little Dixie*, states that residents of the seven counties he studied "frequently resorted to lynch law to cower the slave population, particularly as abolitionist activity increased." In support, he offers three examples of lynchings which occurred between 1850 and 1860: one in Clay County in 1850, another in Boone County in 1858, and the incidents in Saline County in 1859. In his pioneering 1905 study of the history of lynching in the United States, James E. Cutler documented yet another in Carroll County in 1856.[83] Thus, if Genovese's estimate is correct, over one-third of all slave lynchings from 1840 through 1860 occurred in

Missouri during the thirteen years from 1847 through 1859. A more plausible conclusion would be that slave lynchings throughout the South were much more numerous than previously thought.

Because of the absence of case studies of slave lynchings, very little is known about the composition, behavior, and leadership of mobs in the antebellum South. Scholars have studied related subjects, however, including Jacksonian and antiabolitionist mobs and the more general topics of vigilantism and violence in pre–Civil War America. In part, the Saline County mobs of 1859 drew upon the models of their Jacksonian predecessors twenty to thirty years earlier. James Shackleford's explanations rested solidly upon his perception that the "anarchic hero" Andrew Jackson had specifically engaged in and endorsed such violence. Shackleford's admiration for Jackson in this regard was shared by the members of urban mobs who roamed American cities during the Jacksonian era. The second Marshall mob resembled the Jacksonian mobs in the inclination toward Saturnalia, as implied in the *Herald*'s description of its "ribald" character, in the "total self-righteousness" of the apologists, and in the conviction that social and individual wills blended perfectly in the mob actions.[84]

More broadly, the Saline County mobs drew upon the American tradition of vigilantism. Whites' perception of a crisis of law and order and a breakdown of the legal system provided much of the impetus to extralegal action. Whites were concerned with disorder among the slaves, the inability of slave owners to control their slaves, and the different punishments for slaves who committed serious crimes as opposed to the penalties for whites. Fear of an organized slave revolt in Saline County played a decidedly secondary role.

Saline Countians displayed a strong affinity for the frontier vigilante practice of dealing directly with problems related to law and order. Significantly, proponents of mob action saw themselves as acting in the vigilante tradition and argued for action on the bases of self-preservation (drawn from natural law) and popular sovereignty (as an extension of common law). As in many vigilante movements, the lynchings carried warnings to the lower orders of society and to the society at large. To the black population, the lynchings said that blacks would be subject to increased repression and terror and that the values of the white community with respect to boundaries between black and white must be observed. The hangings also warned slave owners that they must control their slaves and stop protecting them from the penalties of the law.[85]

The Saline County mobs also behaved similarly to the mass mobs that routinely attacked blacks in postbellum America. These groups had from fifty to a thousand or even thousands of members and "punished alleged criminals with extraordinary ferocity and, on occasion, great ceremony." Mass mobs tended to act quickly in reaction to crimes they viewed as particularly egregious—attempted rape, rape, and murder—often drawing the largest number of people to take part in mobs that frequently lynched more than one victim. No clear conclusions can be drawn about the composition of these mobs along lines of class although one scholar argues that they tended to reflect the "status of the victim of the alleged crime and local perceptions of the alleged crime."[86]

Three mobs operated in Saline County in 1859, and all three bore at least some resemblance to the racially motivated postbellum mass mobs. The unsuccessful mob that first sought to lynch the slave John at Marshall likely was composed of several hundred persons. Obviously organized and not spontaneous, it was frustrated by John's removal and persuaded to channel its fury into a request for a special court term to try the accused slave.

The mob at Arrow Rock, which lynched the nameless slave accused of raping the young girl, was probably the largest and the most spontaneous of the three. It contained as many as a thousand members, virtually the entire population of the town and its environs, according to newspaper accounts. This group reflected a concern for ritual, securing an identification by the alleged victim, trying the accused slave by "committee," and then leaving the body to hang overnight as a macabre symbol. Like postbellum mobs, this group acted swiftly to deal with rape, possibly spurred on in part by reports of the attempted rape of Mary Habecot.

The second Marshall mob also acted swiftly (once the slave John had been returned to Marshall) but in a deliberate way that indicated careful organization. Its size is uncertain, but various accounts suggest that it was quite large, perhaps as big as the Arrow Rock throng. It also followed some rituals associated with postbellum lynchings, including the hearing of John's confession and leaving the bodies on display. Scant evidence exists as to the composition of this mob, although James Shackleford claimed that it contained prominent citizens. He also was careful to note that workingmen composed a large percentage of the participants and that the violence stemmed from their rage. Various other accounts indicate that relatives and friends of the three white victims were also present. Thus it is likely that the mob included a cross section of the county.[87]

For all of the links to the past and portents of the future, the actions of the Saline County mobs derived a particularity of their own from local circumstances. The first Marshall mob, thwarted in its effort to lynch

John, provided a foundation from which the deadly resolve of the county's whites gradually increased, culminating in its reconstitution and expansion into the group of lynchers who gathered on July 19. The second Marshall group responded not only to the murder of Benjamin Hinton but also to the cumulative effects of the fracas between Holman and William Durrett, the attempted rape of Mary Habecot, and possibly the assault against the little girl in Arrow Rock, which likely was known to members of the mob. The Arrow Rock attack and the Habecot incident introduced elements into the equation which had not been present before: sexual assaults upon a child and a woman. These considerations likely were of great importance in stimulating the second Marshall mob to such profound blood lust.

The broad base of the three mobs makes it unlikely that their actions indicated a division of the community along class lines arraying slaveholders against nonslaveholders. Moreover, nearly all of the principals involved in the affair on both sides owned slaves except James Shackleford, Benjamin Chase, and the three young lawyers who defended Jim and John. Although some resentment simmered against slaveholders who were thought to exercise insufficient control over slaves or who sought to evade prosecution of their charges by selling them, Saline Countians seemed united across class lines in asserting racial supremacy over blacks through vigilante justice. What proportion of the mobs were slaveholders will never be known. Nor do we know how much community pressure may have accrued against the owners of the offending slaves, although a resolution passed at a proslavery mass meeting in Marshall in December 1859 called for compensation to owners of legally executed slaves at three-fourths of the slave's value.[88]

The vigilantism that characterized the Saline County affair offers a contrast to the process by which slaves charged with criminal behavior were brought to justice in the Deep South about the same time. Michael Wayne has shown that in Adams County, Mississippi, in 1857 the planting class dominated the legal process at every step in bringing slaves accused of murder to justice and that they "interpret[ed] the behavior of slaves for society as a whole, especially when slaves acted in ways that appeared to contradict the racial assumptions of planters." Wayne contends that "other communities" in the South would have dealt similarly with such matters "in substance if not necessarily in form," with the "plain folk" deferring to planters. This control of the process indicates, Wayne argues, that planters believed that it was their "right and responsibility" to take charge when slave behavior "became a matter of public concern." Nonslaveholders in Mississippi thought this arrangement in their best interest. "Perhaps most striking," Wayne concluded, "is how little was left to the elected officials."[89]

Although the principal officials in Saline County (the jailer, the sheriff, the circuit attorney, and the judge) were unsuccessful in preventing the lynchings, they clearly exercised their legal responsibilities and did not abdicate in favor of a planter class. The jailer, the sheriff, and the judge each ran considerable personal risk in doing so, and the judge, in resigning his post, took the most significant step possible given the circumstances. Nor is there any indication that wealthy slave owners dominated the jury selection process as they did in Mississippi. The sheriff, who was responsible for selecting the members of the jury, appears to have complied with Missouri law in summoning jurors who were geographically representative of the county. Thirty-six men were summoned for service, twenty-nine of whom can be identified through the census. The panel basically reflected the county's slave-owning patterns and included only two members who owned more than twenty slaves. In addition, the panel included eleven men who owned no slaves. All of the jurors were farmers, except two who were overseers. By Deep South standards, this was a panel composed largely of "plain folk" but including men of a range of financial means. There is no evidence that they took their ideological cues from the wealthy slaveholders in the county.[90]

Equally significant in distinguishing the Missouri from the Mississippi case are the repeated suggestions from various quarters in Saline County that the institution of slavery was not sacrosanct and that slave owners acted with gross impropriety in shielding their slaves from the law, primarily through attempts to "run them off." In addition, the editorial declarations of the Waverly newspaper concerning the desirability of selling slaves south point to the existence of a much freer dialogue on questions pertaining to slavery than would have been tolerated in the Deep South. If anyone "interpreted" the behavior of slaves for the Saline County public, it was not the silent slaveholding elite but the nonslaveholding James Shackleford and other apologists for the lynchings who used the pages of local newspapers to argue for the imposition of vigilante justice.

The citizens, editors, and local officials who criticized the mobs were unified by the fear that this was not a transitory incident of vigilantism and that Saline County might experience protracted vigilante law similar to that which had persisted for months, even years, elsewhere. The resignation of the judge, the resistance of the sheriff and the jailer, the fear expressed by the *Herald*, and the criticism put forward by Benjamin Chase all reflected desires to preserve the established legal institutions. Concern for the victims played a decidedly secondary if not negligible role. The picture emerges of a tense society enmeshed in slavery, wearied by years of border warfare, and apprehensive that the established legal system would yield to a powerful, perhaps protracted, vigilante impulse. James Shackleford recognized the fear and in his first letter to the *Democrat*, published three days after the lynching, addressed the issue, declaring that he did not believe that the "action of the people on the 19th" would become "a precedent for the abuse of illegal power."[91]

In the end, the events in Saline County in the summer of 1859 graphically illustrate the harshness and brutality of the slave system in the border regions and show how the white population could, at any time, let loose a fearful reign of terror against the subject blacks. From the standpoints of motivation, organization, composition, process, and propensity to murderous violence, the mobs drew upon the traditions and practices associated with vigilantism and, to a lesser extent, Jacksonian mobs, while anticipating practices of postbellum lynchers. Products of a culture beset with civil unrest, conditioned to frontier and racial violence, and consumed by a desire to assert control over blacks, the lynchings in Saline County in 1859 belonged both to the future and to the antebellum past.

NOTES

1. Brief mentions of the incidents in Saline County in 1859 are found in Robert Duffner, "Slavery in Missouri River Counties, 1820–1865" (Ph.D. diss., University of Missouri, 1974), 73; and R. Douglas Hurt, *Agriculture and Slavery in Missouri's Little Dixie* (Columbia: University of Missouri Press, 1992), 250–51. Duffner incorrectly dates the lynchings to 1852. A more thorough report of the episode is found in *History of Saline County, Missouri* (St. Louis: Missouri Historical Company, 1881), 259–65. I have found no references to the incident in standard works, including Harrison Anthony Trexler, *Slavery in Missouri, 1804–1865*, Johns Hopkins University Studies in Historical and Political Science, ser. 32, no. 2 (Baltimore: Johns Hopkins University Press, 1914), and Herbert Aptheker, *American Negro Slave Revolts* (New York: International Publishers, 1969).

2. I have relied on the geographic definition of Little Dixie as set out in Hurt, *Agriculture and Slavery*, ix–xiii.

3. Ibid., 220.

4. Ibid., 218, 220–22; Duffner, "Slavery in Missouri River Counties," 10, 13, 15–16, 21, 23–29. Donnie D. Bellamy, in "Slavery, Emancipation, and Racism in Missouri, 1850–1865" (Ph.D. diss., University of Missouri-Columbia, 1971), concludes that slavery in Missouri was not in decline during the 1850s and, in fact, was "holding its own" (100). See also Michael Fellman, "Emancipation in Missouri," *Missouri Histor-*

ical Review 83 (October 1988): 36–56; Fellman, *Inside War: The Guerilla Conflict in Missouri during the American Civil War* (New York: Oxford University Press, 1989); Lyle Wesley Dorsett, "Slaveholding in Jackson County, Missouri," *Missouri Historical Society Bulletin* 20 (October 1963): 25–37; James William McGettigan Jr., "Boone County Slaves: Sales, Estate Divisions and Families, 1820–1865," *Missouri Historical Review* 72 (January and April 1978): 176–97, 271–95; George R. Lee, "Slavery and Emancipation in Lewis County, Missouri," *Missouri Historical Review* 65 (April 1971): 294–317; and Philip V. Scarpino, "Slavery in Callaway County, Missouri, 1845–1855," *Missouri Historical Review* 71 (October 1976, April 1977): 22–43, 266–83. Also see Melton McLaurin, *Celia, a Slave* (Athens: University of Georgia Press, 1991).

5. Hurt, *Agriculture and Slavery*, 245–72; Duffner, "Slavery in Missouri River Counties," 83–90; Narrative of Ed Craddock, in George P. Rawick, gen. ed., *The American Slave: A Composite Autobiography* (Westport, Conn.: Greenwood Press, 1977), Supplement, Ser. 1, Vol. 2, pp. 154, 158.

6. *History of Saline County*, 257–59.

7. Claiborne F. Fox, a future governor, and Circuit Attorney John W. Bryant were among the founders of the *Democrat*. During the prelude to the lynchings, the *Democrat* fed the fires of unrest among the county's whites and drew enthusiastic support from the *Saturday Morning Visitor*, published in Waverly, just over the county line in Lafayette County. See *History of Saline County*, 389–95; Census of the United States, Saline County, Missouri, 1860.

8. *Marshall Democrat*, April 30, June 11, August 27, 1858, February 11, July 1, 8, 29, November 4, 1859; Hurt, *Agriculture and Slavery*, 257–58. On the runaway rate and the underground railroad in Missouri, see Duffner, "Slavery in Missouri River Counties," 74–75; and Bellamy, "Slavery, Emancipation, and Racism," 91–92, respectively.

9. *Marshall Democrat*, August 20, 1858.

10. Ibid., December 3, 10, 17, 1858.

11. Stephen B. Oates, *To Purge This Land with Blood: A Biography of John Brown* (Amherst: University of Massachusetts Press, 1984), 261–62; Hurt, *Agriculture and Slavery*, 259.

12. *History of Saline County*, 257–59. For accounts of post–Harpers Ferry violence against slaves, see Clarence L. Mohr, *On the Threshold of Freedom: Masters and Slaves in Civil War Georgia* (Athens: University of Georgia Press, 1986), 1–11; and Randolph B. Campbell, *An Empire for Slavery: The Peculiar Institution in Texas* (Baton Rouge: Louisiana State University Press, 1989), 224–28.

13. *Marshall Democrat*, May 20, 1859; Census of the United States, 1850, Lafayette County, Missouri.

14. *Marshall Democrat*, May 20, 1859; *Waverly and St. Thomas Saturday Morning Visitor*, May 14, 1859 (hereinafter cited as *Saturday Morning Visitor*).

15. *Marshall Democrat*, May 20, 27, 1859; case file, *State* v. *John, a Slave*, Circuit Court of Saline County, Saline County Court House, Marshall, Missouri.

16. *Marshall Democrat*, May 20, 27, 1859; *Saturday Morning Visitor*, May 28, 1859.

17. *Saturday Morning Visitor*, May 21, 1859.

18. Ibid., May 28, 1859.

19. *Marshall Democrat*, June 3, 1859.

20. Ibid.; *Saturday Morning Visitor*, May 28, 1859; *Revised Statutes of the State of Missouri*, 2 vols. (Jefferson City, 1856), 1:545.

21. *Marshall Democrat*, July 1, 1859; case file, *State* v. *Holman, a Slave*, Circuit Court of Saline County, Saline County Court House.

22. *Marshall Democrat*, July 1, 1859; Mark Tushnet, *The American Law of Slavery, 1810–1860: Considerations of Humanity and Interest* (Princeton: Princeton University Press, 1981), 188–90.

23. *Marshall Democrat*, July 1, 1859.

24. Ibid., July 1, 15, 1859; case file, *State* v. *Jim, a Slave*, Circuit Court of Saline County, Saline County Court House.

25. Case file, *State* v. *Jim, a Slave*. The Missouri constitution allowed the assignment of counsel to slaves in capital cases. There was no statutory or constitutional provision pertaining to appointment of counsel in noncapital cases.

26. Census of the United States, 1860, Saline County, Missouri; *History of Saline County*, 390, 771–72.

27. Case file, *State* v. *Jim, a Slave*.

28. Ibid.

29. *Saline County Herald* in *Saturday Morning Visitor*, July 23, 1859; *Revised Statutes of the State of Missouri*, 1:565. By contrast, the Waverly paper argued for castration as a more fitting punishment for rapists. Hanging and burning were "too good in cases of rape" (*Saturday Morning Visitor*, July 23, 1859).

30. Russell Hicks to editors, *Lexington Express*, published in *Marshall Democrat*, August 5, 1859; J. W. Bryant to Claiborne F. Jackson, July 8, 1859, folder 69, John Sappington Collection, Western Historical Manuscript Collection, University of Missouri-Columbia (hereinafter cited as WHMC-Columbia).

31. *Marshall Democrat*, July 22, August 5, 26, 1859.

32. *St. Louis Democrat* quoted in *National Anti-Slavery Standard*, August 6, 1859; *Saline County Herald* in *Saturday Morning Visitor*, July 23, 1859.

33. *History of Saline County*, 265; W. Z. Hickman, *History of Jackson County, Missouri* (Topeka, Kans., and Cleveland, Ohio: Historical Publishing Company, 1920), 239.

34. Hicks to editors, *Lexington Express*.

35. Ibid.

36. Ibid.; case files, *State* v. *John a Slave*, *State* v. *Holman a Slave*, *State* v. *Jim a Slave*.

37. Hicks to editors, *Lexington Express*.

38. Ibid.

39. *Saline County Herald* in *Saturday Morning Visitor*, July 23, 1859.

40. Hicks to editors, *Lexington Express*.

41. Ibid.; case files, *State* v. *John a Slave*, *State* v. *Jim a Slave*, *State* v. *Holman a Slave*.

42. Case file, *State* v. *John a Slave*; Census of 1860, Saline County, Missouri.

43. Case file, *State* v. *John a Slave*.

44. Hicks to editors, *Lexington Express*.

45. Ibid.

46. Ibid.

47. Ibid.

48. Ibid.

49. Ibid.

50. *Saline County Herald*, in *Saturday Morning Visitor*, July 23, 1859; *Marshall Democrat*, July 22, 1859; *History of Saline County*, 260.

51. *St. Louis Democrat* quoted in *National Anti-Slavery Standard*, August 6, 1859.

52. *Marshall Democrat*, July 22, 1859.

53. *St. Louis Democrat* quoted in *National Anti-Slavery Standard*, August 6, 1859.

54. *Marshall Democrat*, July 22, 1859.

55. *Saline County Herald* in *Saturday Morning Visitor*, July 23, 1859.

56. *St. Louis Democrat* quoted in *National Anti-Slavery Standard*, August 6, 1859.

57. *Saturday Morning Visitor*, May 21, 1859.

58. Shackleford sold his farm and left Saline County sometime in early 1860, apparently moving with his wife and five children to Johnson County, approximately fifty miles away. See *Marshall Democrat*, December 9, 1859; Census of the United States, 1860, Johnson County, Missouri.

59. Shackleford's letters were printed in the *Marshall Democrat*, July 22, August 5, 26, September 2, 9, 1859.

60. *Marshall Democrat*, July 22, 1859.

61. Ibid.

62. Ibid.

63. Ibid.

64. *Marshall Democrat*, August 19, 1859; *Saturday Morning Visitor*, September 3, 1859. See also the remarks of "Observer," *Marshall Democrat*, August 5, 1859.

65. *Marshall Democrat*, July 29, 1859.

66. Ibid., August, 19, 26, September 9, 1859. The *Express* files are incomplete and do not contain the issue in which Shackleford's letter was published. Fortunately, the *Democrat* reprinted it.

67. *Saturday Morning Visitor* in *Marshall Democrat*, August 19, 1859.

68. *Saline County Herald* in *Saturday Morning Visitor*, July 23, 1859.

69. Hicks to editors, *Lexington Express*.

70. Ibid.

71. *Marshall Democrat*, August 19, 1859. Judge Hicks was well regarded in Saline County, and his resignation was greeted with general regret. Even James M. Shackleford had kind things to say about him in the wake of the resignation.

72. Ibid., August 26, 1859; Census of the United States, 1860, Saline County, Missouri. In a general way, Shackleford's arguments were tied to the concept of honor which pervaded southern society during the antebellum era. Lynching could take several forms in defense of honor, murder of slaves by mobs being only one and an apparently infrequent one at that. Shackleford's emphasis on the protection of white womanhood as partial justification for the lynching conforms to descriptions of ways in which southern whites behaved within the context of honor. That there was opposition to the actions of the Marshall mob, however, indicates that some residents rejected the notion that law could be suspended for reasons of honor and an understanding that such suspensions would gain little sympathy in a more metropolitan world where the rule of law was a primary value. See Bertram Wyatt-Brown, *Southern Honor: Ethics and Behavior in the Old South* (New York: Oxford University Press, 1982).

73. *Marshall Democrat*, August 5, 1859.

74. Lizzie Marshall to Dear Sis, July 20, 1859, Joseph Marshall Family Papers,

WHMC-Columbia. This is a transcription of the original letter. Internal evidence indicates that the letter was written on July 26.

75. *Marshall Democrat*, July 29, September 2, 16, 1859; *Saturday Morning Visitor*, August 27, 1859; John R. White Slave Record Book, 1846–60, WHMC-Columbia. White's book contains a record of sale of Nathan Hurt during the early autumn of 1859.

76. *Marshall Democrat*, August 26, 1859.

77. *Saline County Herald* in *Saturday Morning Visitor*, July 23, 1859.

78. *National Anti-Slavery Standard*, August 6, 1859.

79. *Annual Report of the American Anti-Slavery Society* (New York: American Anti-Slavery Society, 1861), 205.

80. *History of Saline County*, 262.

81. Eugene Genovese, *Roll, Jordan, Roll: The World the Slaves Made* (New York: Pantheon, 1974), 32. The estimate appears to have come from Cash. See W. J. Cash, *The Mind of the South* (New York: Knopf, 1941), 45. See Clement Eaton, "Mob Violence in the Old South," *Mississippi Valley Historical Review* 29 (December 1942): 351–70.

82. Kenneth M. Stampp, *The Peculiar Institution: Slavery in the Ante-bellum South* (New York: Knopf, 1956), 190–91; Wyatt-Brown, *Southern Honor*, 388–89; Philip J. Schwarz, *Twice Condemned: Slaves and the Criminal Laws of Virginia, 1705–1865* (Baton Rouge: Louisiana State University Press, 1988), 291–92. A sampling of state studies of slavery indicates a somewhat higher frequency of slave lynchings before 1860 than previously thought. Orville W. Taylor, in *Negro Slavery in Arkansas* (Durham: Duke University Press, 1958), implies that lynchings occurred more frequently than they were reported. Taylor includes newspaper accounts of three burnings in two separate incidents in 1849 and a hanging in 1836. Randolph B. Campbell, in *An Empire for Slavery* (Baton Rouge: Louisiana State University Press, 1989), 105, states that Texas slaves who committed serious crimes against whites "often were dealt with by lynch law." Campbell reports that "lynchings were common enough that Texas newspapers reported at least three in 1859 alone." James B. Sellers, in *Slavery in Alabama* (University: University of Alabama Press, 1950), 262–64, makes assertions similar to Campbell's and Taylor's citing "a few [four] typical instances of lynchings," including a hanging in 1856 and burnings in 1854, 1855, and 1860. Ralph Betts Flanders, in *Plantation Slavery in Georgia* (Chapel Hill: University of North Carolina Press, 1933), 268–69, reports four lynchings in Georgia—one in 1851 and three in a single incident in 1857.

83. Trexler, *Slavery in Missouri*, 72n; Hurt, *Agriculture and Slavery*, 248; James Elbert Cutler, *Lynch-Law: An Investigation into the History of Lynching in the United States* (New York: Longmans, Green, 1905), 119. Robert Duffner, in "Slavery in Missouri River Counties," 51, observes that "it was not uncommon for the community to take the law into its own hands," citing one example of a severe beating of a black for attempted rape but pointing to no lynchings.

84. David Grimsted, "Rioting in Its Jacksonian Setting," *American Historical Review* 77 (April 1972): 361–97. "Anarchic hero" is Grimsted's term.

85. Richard Maxwell Brown, *Strain of Violence: Historical Studies of American Violence and Vigilantism* (New York: Oxford University Press, 1975), 21, 100, 104–5, 115–17, 120, 123–24, 145–46, 156. For a useful exploration of vigilantism in Missouri and states to the north, see Patrick B. Nolan, *Vigilantes on the Middle Border: A Study*

of *Self-Appointed Law Enforcement in the States of the Upper Mississippi from 1840 to 1880* (New York: Garland, 1987), 7–10. Nolan argues that a "wave" of vigilantism had occurred in the 1840s in the Mississippi Valley and that the establishment of the San Francisco vigilance committee had "set off a new wave of vigilantism" in the older states to the east.

86. W. Fitzhugh Brundage, *Lynching in the New South: Georgia and Virginia, 1880–1930* (Urbana: University of Illinois Press, 1993), 19, 36–37. There is a vast literature on postbellum lynching, summarized in Brundage's excellent notes. For a useful discussion of postbellum lynching in Missouri, see Michael J. Pfeifer, "The Ritual of Lynching: Extralegal Justice in Missouri, 1890–1942," *Gateway Heritage* 13 (Winter 1993): 22–33.

87. *Marshall Democrat*, September 2, 1859. Benjamin Hinton came from a fairly prominent family and had friends among the independent farmers of Lafayette and Saline counties in addition to younger acquaintances. William Durrett, a prosperous farmer and slave owner, belonged to the elite of Arrow Rock township. Practically nothing is known about Mary Habecot's social or economic position, but it is clear that her husband was a member of the second Marshall mob and that other relatives and neighbors had come to Marshall that day. The first mob in Marshall may have had a narrower base composed mainly of farmers and younger friends of Benjamin Hinton.

88. *Marshall Democrat*, December 21, 1859.

89. Michael Wayne, "An Old South Morality Play: Reconsidering the Social Under-pinnings of the Proslavery Ideology," *Journal of American History* 77 (December 1990): 838–63.

90. Although 6.5 percent of Saline County slave owners could be considered as members of a planting class, based on landholdings (five hundred acres) and numbers of slaves (twenty or more) owned, only one person in the county owned more than one hundred slaves and only sixteen owned twenty-five or more (see Hurt, *Agriculture and Slavery*). In fact, it is not clear that the wealthiest of Saline County's slaveholders even thought of themselves as planters. "Farmer" was the term of preference in the county, and none of the county's slave owners identified themselves as "planters" to census takers.

91. *Marshall Democrat*, July 22, 1859.

A Lynching in
Wartime Carolina
The Death of Saxe Joiner

Joan E. Cashin

O n the night of March 15, 1865, a lynching fraught with horrible symbolism occurred in Unionville, South Carolina. An armed mob of white men wearing disguises and dressed in Confederate uniforms broke into the ground floor of the Union County jail. Most of them were not soldiers anymore, but they dressed in gray to broadcast what they took to be the meaning of the Confederacy, even as it crumbled around them, and to enforce what they understood to be the proper hierarchies between the sexes and the races. Many had been drinking, and all of them were enraged by what they believed to be the lenient treatment the law had accorded Saxe Joiner, a slave man. He was incarcerated in a cell upstairs for allegedly insulting a white woman.

The mob stormed into the jail at around 9:00 P.M. and threatened to kill the sheriff if he interfered, warning him that they had already killed one man that night over the matter. The sheriff handed over the keys, the mob surged into the cell, tied Joiner up, and hauled him outside. They hanged him from a tree in the front yard of Joseph Dogan, a white man who had lived in Unionville for over forty years, and then left Joiner's body there all night, a gruesome symbol of white supremacy.[1] It was the first lynching in the community's history, and it was no accident that it happened in 1865, for the upheavals of the Civil War exacerbated long-standing cultural divisions among the local planter elite and the town professionals. (The only white woman who described Joiner's death disagreed with most of the white men, and there is no record of what local black women may have thought of these events.) This ghastly crime also provides a snapshot of the transition between the slavery regime and the postwar order at a moment when white men were infuriated by transformations in gender and race relations. As we will see, they were ferociously determined to halt or slow those changes if they could.

It is perhaps not surprising that this tale unfolded in South Carolina, for the state had a tortured racial and cultural history. Barbadian planters settled the low country in the late seventeenth century, and they brought thousands of African American slaves with them to cultivate rice. Slavery spread throughout the eighteenth century and the planter elite prospered, and by the antebellum era South Carolina had a large slave population and a flourishing plantation economy, now changing over to cotton. The white men at the top proved to be shrewd and resilient, incorporating up-country planters into their ranks as the slavery regime reached through the state. They kept tight control over the black population and crushed any challenge to white supremacy. Denmark Vesey, a free black carpenter, and thirty-four other men were executed in Charleston in 1822 for planning a rebellion. Lynching was rare, primarily because the planter class would rather let the court system deal with slave crimes. Under antebellum law codes, planters were financially compensated for any slave executed for a crime. On gender relations, men in the planter class enforced patriarchal roles. White men both dominated and cared for white women, who gave up their autonomy in exchange for protection. Dissidents such as Sarah and Angelina Grimké who condemned the inequities of race and gender were banished, while literary iconoclasts like Mary Chesnut were tolerated as long as they did not publicly challenge those hierarchies. The state's politicians engaged in a spirited debate about all other public issues, however, into the late antebellum era.[2]

In the mid-eighteenth century Scotch-Irish immigrants settled Union County, which was located in central South Carolina about sixty miles northwest of Columbia. From the beginning, its farmers raised cotton and worked the land with slave labor. Slave owners struggled through the downturns in the cotton market in 1819 and 1837, but by the 1850s cotton prices were on the rise again. The local slaveholding elite was small but unusually affluent. In 1860, 676 whites in the county owned slaves (8 percent of the white population), and 178 of them were planters (26 percent of the slave owners). By contrast, only about 25 percent of whites in the entire South owned slaves, and approximately 8 percent were planters. Slaves outnumbered whites in the county's population by the mid-1840s and on the eve of the Civil War, 10,801 bondsmen lived in Union, 8,670 whites, and 164 free blacks.[3]

Unionville, the county seat, was founded in 1787. Located in the center of the county, it spilled over fourteen blocks, seven on each side of Main Street, with most of the businesses and homes clustered near the courthouse (see Figure 1). By 1860, its population numbered about five hundred people. Many of its white denizens were related through the multiple, overlapping kinship ties that can develop over several generations in a small community, and its social life resembled that of most small towns, with the attendant rivalries, gossip, and scandals. Joseph Dogan, in whose front yard Saxe Joiner died in 1865, was its oldest and most eminent physician. Dogan was born in North Carolina in 1793 and settled in Unionville in the 1820s after graduating from the University of Pennsylvania. His marriage to Sarah Herndon Rice in 1825 connected him to the up-country planter elite, and he soon purchased slaves and a plantation outside of town. His daughters' marriages in the 1850s solidified his position, for two of his sons-in-law were prosperous lawyers and one was a merchant. William Dogan, his only son, was a lawyer and planter. The Dogan clan was intensely social, hosting gala parties in Unionville for their relatives and friends, and they kept up a friendly rivalry with the country planters. The town also had its share of incongruous marriages. Tongues wagged in 1855 when James Keenan, a law clerk who owned no slaves, bested several other suitors and married a rich widow, thereby entering the planter class. (Ten years later Keenan would play a key role in Saxe Joiner's story.) And Unionville had the occasional deadly crime. In 1851, Phineas Johnson, a poor white laborer, killed Mary Ann Hyatt, the seventeen-year-old daughter of an overseer and the mother of Johnson's illegitimate child. He was tried, found guilty, and executed in a public hanging in 1852.[4]

The class that James Keenan entered by marriage was confident, hard-driving, and prosperous. A number of local planters, some of whom we will revisit below, were very rich even by late antebellum standards: in 1860 William McLure owned 45 slaves, Benjamin Rice owned 96, and William Gist owned 177. Several of them maintained lavish homes in Unionville as well as plantation houses in the country. They also took an active part in state and national politics, such as Benjamin Rice, who served in the state legislature, and Daniel Wallace, who was a member of the United States Congress. In 1851 the county voted overwhelmingly for prosecession delegates to a state convention, and many local planters, including Benjamin Rice and William Gist, openly advocated disunion. At least one, William McLure, may have participated in a filibustering expedition in South America in the mid-1850s, and several other planters traveled to Kansas in 1856 to fight alongside proslavery guerrilla forces in that territory. In their worldview, preserving white supremacy mattered

FIGURE 1. *Unionville, South Carolina*

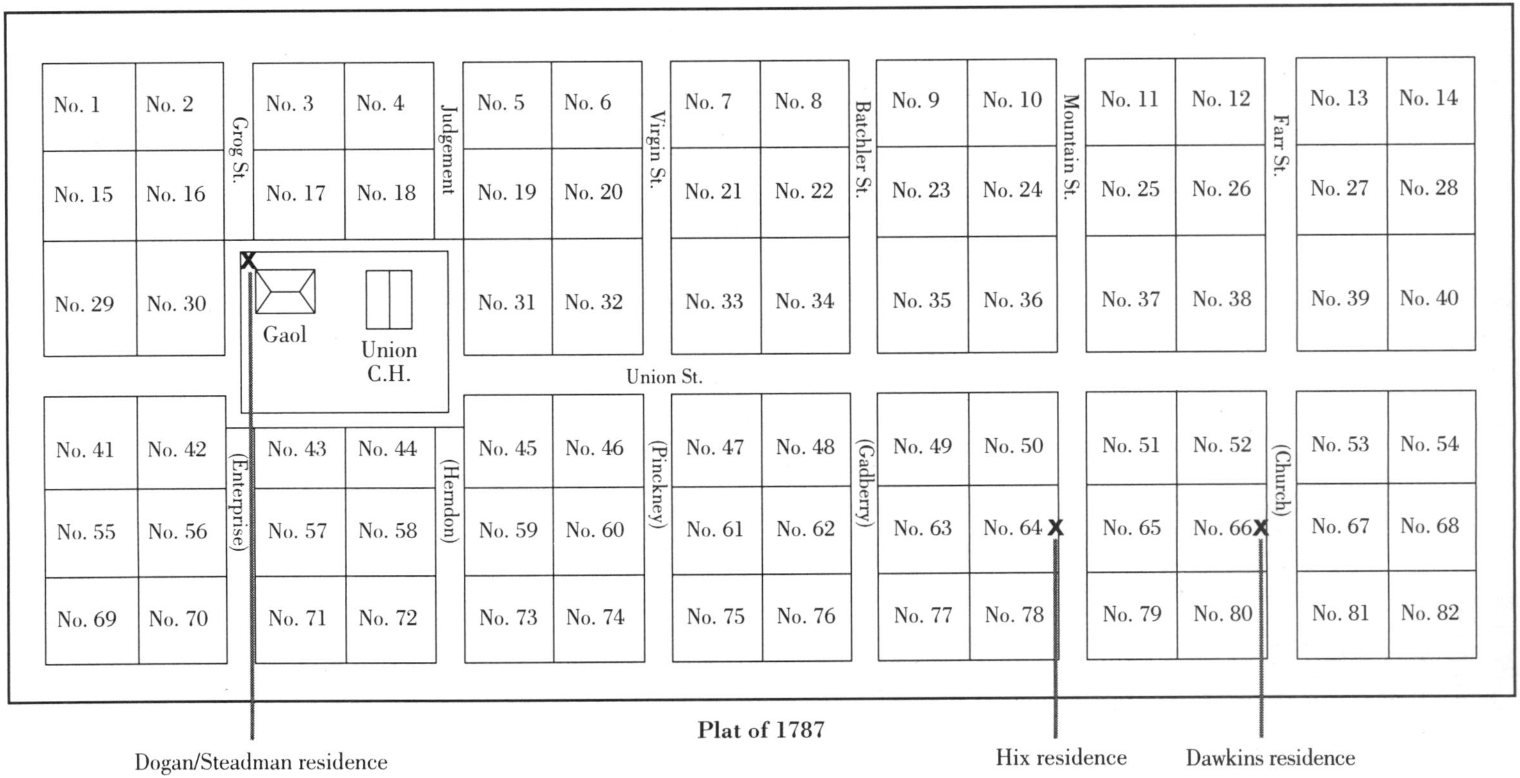

No. 1
No. 2
No. 3
No. 4
No. 5
No. 6
No. 7
No. 8
No. 9
No. 10
No. 11
No. 12
No. 13
No. 14
No. 15
No. 16
No. 17
No. 18
No. 19
No. 20
No. 21
No. 22
No. 23
No. 24
No. 25
No. 26
No. 27
No. 28
No. 29
No. 30
No. 31
No. 32
No. 33
No. 34
No. 35
No. 36
No. 37
No. 38
No. 39
No. 40
No. 41
No. 42
No. 43
No. 44
No. 45
No. 46
No. 47
No. 48
No. 49
No. 50
No. 51
No. 52
No. 53
No. 54
No. 55
No. 56
No. 57
No. 58
No. 59
No. 60
No. 61
No. 62
No. 63
No. 64
No. 65
No. 66
No. 67
No. 68
No. 69
No. 70
No. 71
No. 72
No. 73
No. 74
No. 75
No. 76
No. 77
No. 78
No. 79
No. 80
No. 81
No. 82
Grog St.
Judgement
Virgin St.
Batchler St.
Mountain St.
Farr St.
(Enterprise)
(Herndon)
(Pinckney)
(Gadberry)
(Church)
Union St.
Gaol
Union C.H.
Plat of 1787
Dogan/Steadman residence
Hix residence
Dawkins residence

Source: Adapted from Allan D. Charles, *The Narrative History of Union County, South Carolina* (Greenville, S.C.: A Press Printing Co., 1989), n.p. Map not to scale.

more than the rule of law. Even if most Union County planters did not go to South America or Kansas, they believed in a culture of action. Belligerently anti-intellectual, they drank heavily, gambled recklessly, and settled feuds with pistols.[5]

Unionville also supported a lively group of professionals, mostly doctors and lawyers. They too were active in politics and supported white supremacy, but they focused on the town's civic life. These men served on the board of the local railroad, ran the town academies, and presided over meetings of its temperance society. The village had its own medical society in 1808, and its doctors maintained contacts with professional colleagues throughout the up-country.[6] Many of the town professionals owned bondsmen, but they did not have nearly as much money invested in slavery as the planters did. In 1860, Joseph Dogan's sons-in-law Benjamin Arthur, Jackson Scaife, and James Steadman owned five, three, and no slaves respectively. Moreover, their cultural outlook diverged from that of their planter neighbors. They made a living by their skill with words, they were interested in ideas, and they valued the stimulation that a town could offer. William Wallace, son of Congressman Daniel Wallace, moved to Unionville to edit the newspaper because he grew tired of the countryside's "seclusion." These men would rather form debating societies than fight in duels. Many of them were good friends, and they often socialized together. In 1851, one of the Dogan in-laws threw a dazzling masquerade ball, and the guests came in costume dressed as historical figures.[7]

Other cultural differences separated the planters from the town professionals, probably best represented by the temperance issue. White men all over antebellum America drank a great deal, and men in Union County shared the national thirst. The county had dozens of taverns and distilleries, some located along Unionville's aptly named "Grog Street," and candidates for public office routinely gave out free liquor while campaigning. By the 1850s, many of Unionville's professionals believed that excessive consumption had become a serious problem. Like most supporters of the temperance movement, they deplored heavy drinking for undermining masculine dignity. Propriety and self-restraint ranked high among their values, an outlook that was probably reinforced by their membership in the Presbyterian and Methodist churches. (Most local planters attended the Episcopalian church, when they attended services at all.) Benjamin Arthur, a lawyer and Joseph Dogan's son-in-law, headed the town chapter of the Sons of Temperance. He organized elaborate public ceremonies, parades, and alcohol-free socials, attended by the Dogans and their circle. One of the country planters, William Gist, was a firm supporter of the movement, but most planters were conspicuously absent from the Sons' activities. A cultural divide, subtle, half-submerged, and mediated by family ties, ran through the white male population.[8]

In 1860, however, there was little disagreement on the central political issue of secession. Most of the county's white men supported it, including Joseph Dogan, James Steadman, Benjamin Rice, James Keenan, and William McLure. In fact, some of the state's leading secessionists hailed from this community. Governor William Gist signed the secession ordinance on December 20, 1860; Benjamin Arthur clerked at the secession convention; and William Wallace also signed the convention ordinance. Men from both sides of the town's cultural divide rushed to join up when the Civil War began at Fort Sumter in April 1861, for both camps could enthusiastically support states' rights, slavery, and white supremacy. Union County filled nine companies in the Confederate army before the war ended.[9] Several men rose to high rank during the long, bloody conflict, most notably William Wallace, who joined the Eighteenth South Carolina Volunteers and surrendered at Appomattox Courthouse as a general in Robert E. Lee's army. Dozens of men from Union County died in the war, including William Gist's son. The Dogan clan was more fortunate than most, however, in that none of Joseph Dogan's sons-in-law died, nor did his son William.[10]

No serious fighting took place near Union County, but the war's disruptions nevertheless undercut traditional gender and race relations. Gender roles by necessity began to shift almost immediately, as white women had to take over businesses, plantations, and households in town and in the country. As the war ground on, these women coped with food shortages and skyrocketing prices for household goods. They also cared for the wounded who came home on furlough and buried loved ones who came home in coffins. Some women coped better than others, of course, but they all had to shoulder new responsibilities that had once belonged to men. In the words of one white woman, they "did everything" to keep households functioning. A black man who lived on the Gist plantation made similar comments, recalling years later that the mistress "had to do ev'ything." Even white women whose husbands did not join the military had to contend with hunger and fear. It was a swift transformation, upending the certainties of patriarchal relations in just a few years. White men could no longer protect white women or even provide for their material needs.[11]

Race relations changed almost as rapidly between 1861 and 1865. In the spring of 1861 dozens of male slaves left for the front to serve with their masters, while the black women and men who remained at home followed their routines. But when Northern troops arrived in coastal South Carolina later that year, slaves began to run away, and by 1863, the exodus had swelled into the thousands. Farms and plantations fell into disrepair, and the age-old etiquette of racial deference began to break down. One slave man, for instance, wished aloud that his master, former congressman Daniel Wallace, would stop the war. Whites interpreted this remark as evidence of his loyalty, but it sounds more like a subtle reminder that Wallace could no longer control events. There must have been other moments like this one, as slaves obliquely or directly challenged their once-powerful masters. Slavery was indeed collapsing, and perhaps white supremacy would go with it.[12]

In the last months of the war, one of the most feared of all the Northern commanders, General William T. Sherman, brushed close by Union County. He concluded his March to the Sea at Savannah in December 1864, while hundreds of whites flocked into up-country South Carolina and yet more slaves escaped to federal lines. After Sherman entered South Carolina in January 1865, the refugee population grew to a flood. He arrived in the state capital, Columbia, on February 17 after some of his troops had looted and torched small towns along the way. When his army evacuated the capital the next day, a fire broke out, and within hours much of the city was in ruins. For several days afterward, no one could predict where Sherman and his army, sixty thousand strong, might be headed next, which threw the white population into complete pandemonium. By mid-February, wagons packed the muddy streets of Unionville as thousands of white South Carolinians fled north and west, trying to stay out of Sherman's way. Twenty soldiers detached from a Confederate regiment stood guard in town, trying to maintain a semblance of order, while others scouted the roads on the lookout for Sherman. On February 20, the dreaded cavalry leader Hugh Judson Kilpatrick destroyed a bridge on the Broad River, Union County's eastern boundary, and on February 21 other Northern troops sacked Winnsboro, a village thirty miles southeast of Unionville. Renegade federal soldiers scavenged through the countryside, stealing property and attacking civilians.[13]

In the midst of this rising chaos, the slave Saxe Joiner was arrested. His owner, Dr. James E. Hix, was aged forty-seven and was married to twenty-eight-year-old Martha Hix. The couple lived with their three children in a large house on Mountain Street several blocks from the Unionville courthouse. The son of an affluent physician, Hix graduated from the state medical school in 1841 and put out his shingle in Unionville. In 1850, while he was still unmarried, he boarded with John Joiner, a gin maker who owned nine slaves. Hix may have purchased Saxe Joiner from his landlord in the 1850s, or he may have inherited him along with thirty-seven other slaves from his father. By 1860 Hix had inherited his father's house on Mountain Street as well. He was forty-three years old in 1861, and he did not serve in the Confederate military. The doctor apparently spent the entire war in Unionville.

On Sunday morning, February 19, 1865, his slave Saxe Joiner, in the opening act in this drama, wrote a note to Martha Hix. According to Mary Dawkins, a white woman who lived on the next block, Joiner wrote it himself. He allegedly told Mrs. Hix not to "grieve" about the approaching federal troops because he had a "safe place" for her—perhaps a hideaway in the house, in town, or in the countryside. The note has not survived, and there is no transcript, so that all we know of its contents comes from Mary Dawkins.[14]

In the few weeks left in Saxe Joiner's life, no one disputed his author-ship of the note, so it must have been widely known that he was literate, although it was illegal in South Carolina to teach a slave to read and write. The federal censuses of 1850 and 1860 offer some clues about his identity. If Saxe Joiner acquired his surname from his previous master, a sometime custom in the Old South, then James Hix probably purchased him in the 1850s from his landlord John Joiner, who owned a seventeen-year-old male mulatto in 1850. It follows that Saxe Joiner was probably the twenty-six-year-old mulatto described as a "master carpenter" among the Hix slaves in 1860. Or, to reason backward in time, among the Hix slaves only the carpenter was the right age, being almost ten years older in 1860 than Joiner's slave in 1850. Assuming that Joiner was the carpenter, his skill would have increased his opportunities to become literate and made him more mobile than a field laborer, giving him the chance to find or con-struct a hideaway. In 1865 he was living in the Hix household and evi-dently unmarried. As to why he felt compelled to write this message to his master's wife rather than telling her in person, he left no explanation. Mary Dawkins believed that Joiner was "impertinent" but well meaning, behaving as she thought a devoted slave should behave.[15]

Dawkins was probably one of the more unbiased witnesses to the events preceding Joiner's death, and she knew all the members of the Hix household. Born Mary Poulton in Exeter, England, in 1820, she came to North America with her parents in 1833 and attended Emma Willard's renowned female academy in Troy. After she came to South Carolina to teach school in the early 1840s, she married Thomas Dawkins, an affluent planter and lawyer from Union County. The marriage proved to be child-less, and Mary Dawkins threw her considerable energies into her social life. Her husband maintained a splendidly appointed house in town on Church Street, where she loved to entertain. She was close friends with the Dogans but enjoyed a wide acquaintance, and individuals from both of Unionville's cultural camps attended her parties. (Her many friendships may explain why she knew so much about the Joiner case.) A highly cultivated woman, she was also a devout Episcopalian. She professed great affection for her house slaves and had adopted the "paternalistic" view of slavery.[16]

When abolitionists mounted a direct attack on slavery for the first time in the 1830s, many white southerners responded that it was not a brutal, heinous institution but instead resembled a loving family. Supposedly be-nevolent slave owners cared for their allegedly childish slaves, who were in turn obliged to serve their owners. This argument, which scholars have come to call "paternalism," may have appealed to whites such as Mary Dawkins because it might assuage any guilt they felt over exploiting other human beings. The idea was reified in southern culture from the 1830s onward, to the point that many whites deluded themselves about the vio-lent coercion underlying slavery. Most slaves rejected the paternalistic ethos out of hand, of course, as their long tradition of resistance in South Carolina and elsewhere shows. But a minority of slaves may have accepted it or adopted the rhetoric for their own purposes. It would be hard to ignore, for slaves heard it from masters, mistresses, clergymen, and other white figures throughout their lives. House slaves and craftsmen might have been especially vulnerable to its influence because they were forced into close proximity with whites and often isolated from other blacks. Dur-ing the Civil War a few slaves may have continued to think in this vein, be-lieving that it was their duty to protect white people in a desperate hour.[17]

Although Saxe Joiner expressed himself with unusual directness, his note to Mrs. Hix could still be taken as a sincere gesture from a devoted slave who had adopted the paternalist ideal. Most of Unionville's white men must have interpreted Saxe Joiner's note to Martha Hix in this light, for they allowed it to pass without incident. The legal records do not even mention it, and we would not know of its existence without Mary Daw-kins's remarks. Doctor Hix's silence also indicates that he probably agreed with this interpretation, for he took no public action against his slave for writing it. Because Mr. Hix was his wife's protector, no other white man was likely to trespass upon his role and take action either. But Saxe Joiner also communicated that day with another white woman in the Hix household, eighteen-year-old Susan Baldwin. On the evening of Sunday, February 19, he sent her a separate note, telling her not to worry because he would "protect" her too from the Northern troops. (Again it is unclear why Joiner wrote to her rather than telling her face to face.) The note miscarried, Dr. Hix found it, and somehow it became public.[18]

This second message was more likely to be interpreted as a violation of paternalism's etiquette, even a calculated defiance of it, for the recipient was an unmarried white woman in her teens. Susan Baldwin's father worked as an overseer before the war, and her brother was serving in the Confederate army, so she was probably boarding with the Hixes or working for them. In contrast to Mrs. Hix, she was young and vulnerable, and she had no clearly defined protector; hence she was the charge of all honorable white men. Furthermore, protecting white women had been the sole prerogative of white men in the antebellum South. During the war, it proved almost impossible for them to fulfill this role, which helps explain their hysterical reaction. Joiner's note to Susan Baldwin implied that he was a white man's equal or even his superior. If he was the twenty-six-year-old "master carpenter," his status as a mulatto and a highly skilled slave may have made him appear even more threatening. Dawkins for her part declared that Joiner meant no harm, and decades later, she stated emphatically that slaves committed no violent acts, "especially towards [white] women," at the end of the war.[19]

But in February 1865, Mary Dawkins observed that many white men believed that the note proved Saxe Joiner planned on "assaulting" Baldwin, meaning a sexual assault, which was a capital offense in South Carolina. This conclusion is quite a leap from Dawkins's own view of the matter, so let us pause to consider Saxe Joiner's possible motives. We are inhibited by the note's disappearance and by the author's silence, but several explanations present themselves: possibly Joiner was infatuated with or in love with Baldwin and wanted to initiate a sexual relationship with her; maybe they already had an intimate relationship and a consensual one. (Such relationships did take place in the wartime South, although Unionville's white men seem to have found the idea too awful to put into words.) Or perhaps Joiner really was planning to "assault" Baldwin. He may have harbored a variety of feelings for her at one time or another—love, desire, rage—or she for him. They lived in the same household, thrown together in tumultuous times.[20]

Among all these possibilities, rape seems the most implausible. If Saxe Joiner was plotting a sexual assault, it is unlikely that he would bother to notify his victim in advance and leave written evidence of his intentions in his master's house. He had remained in the household despite many chances to escape to the federal army, which may suggest some regard for members of the Hix household. He may have known about General Sherman's reputation for vengefulness and the fact that Columbia and other towns had gone up in flames. He also may have heard that some federal troops had raped white and black women. He may have even hoped that his status as a black man might shield Baldwin from the Northern soldiers. Given these circumstances, it seems more likely that Mary Dawkins was right: Joiner probably wanted to protect Susan Baldwin, just as he had promised to protect Martha Hix.

If this was true, it suggests a certain heedlessness on Joiner's part as well as a perilous isolation from other African Americans. If Joiner had relatives or close friends nearby, they probably would have advised him not to write a note to an unmarried white woman in a town full of soldiers and panicked civilians. Slaves had learned generations ago to exercise caution in dealing with whites; this too was part of African American culture. With no one to counsel him, Joiner may have been so naive that he did not think that anyone could misinterpret his actions or so headstrong that he did not care if they did.[21]

An oral tradition handed down through the Dawkins family suggests that he may have been both naive and headstrong. Mary Dawkins's greatniece recorded the story in the 1980s, and the essentials conform to what we know about the sequence of events. It concerns a slave *butler* belonging to *Thomas and Mary Dawkins* who declared at the end of the Civil War that *he wanted a white wife.* Some of Mary Dawkins's *nieces* learned of it, and she tried to hush it up because she feared the *Ku Klux Klan* would punish her slave. Word got out anyway, and the slave man was hanged. This appears to be a garbled version of Saxe Joiner's history, and it is easy to see how the facts might have gotten mixed up as the decades passed. A master carpenter could have been confused with a butler; Mary Dawkins's sympathy for the slave might have led her descendants to think that she and her husband owned him; Susan Baldwin, a dependent young woman in another household, may have been transformed over time into Dawkins nieces; Joiner's desire to protect a white woman could have been translated into the desire to marry one; the lynch mob could have been mistaken for the Ku Klux Klan, which was founded in 1866. This man is also described as a "highly prized" slave who was the "envy" of Mary Dawkins's white friends. Finally, he was remembered as a "foolish" man, which would support Mary Dawkins's comment in 1865 that Saxe Joiner was "impertinent." It is a tantalizing story, and it may bring us a step closer to understanding him, yet he remains an enigma at the vortex of so much passion and violence.[22]

After Dr. Hix discovered the note to Susan Baldwin, events moved with brutal swiftness. Saxe Joiner was immediately arrested and spent that night, Sunday, February 19, in the town jail on Main Street, and the following day, Monday, February 20, went on trial at the county courthouse down the block. Joiner did not appear before the local Magistrate's Court, however, which typically handled all cases within the town limits, all cases involving slaves, and all capital crimes, including assault with attempt to rape. Instead he was tried for an unspecified misdemeanor by a "civil authority," a justice of the peace and at least two other white men. According to the South Carolina law codes of 1714, this gathering had the power to try any slave who had committed a misdemeanor, for which the usual punishment was a public flogging, confinement in stocks, or a prison term. It is not clear who set up this meeting or why. The acting magistrate (equivalent to the justice of the peace) was one M. C. Hughes. Nothing is known about him other than his occupation, mechanic, and his age, fifty-three. Because this civil authority was not a court of record, it generated no documents of any kind.

Joiner was found guilty of a misdemeanor, but, in another strange twist, he was sentenced to serve immediately on the front lines with the Confederate army, rather than any of the punishments prescribed by law. Someone in town apparently wanted to get Joiner out of the way as quickly as possible, regardless of procedure. In fact, the proceedings' irregular, clumsy quality suggests that none of the participants were lawyers. The civil authority's actions hint at further divisions within Unionville's white men, or perhaps the brief emergence of a new group, a third force no longer strongly committed to either white supremacy or the rule of law. It is most unfortunate that the historical record is completely silent on the civil authority's membership and motivations.[23]

News of the decision raced through Unionville on the afternoon of Monday, February 20, as sensational news will do in a small town, and this bulletin aggravated its cultural tensions. If the third force ever existed, it collapsed, and the town's white men quickly polarized into two camps. Both groups wished to preserve white supremacy against Joiner's alleged threat, but they disagreed vehemently on how to do it. The earlier gathering's illegitimacy offended most of the lawyers and doctors, who wanted to deal with Joiner in a court of law. The sentence itself outraged many planters, who called it an insult to Southern troops, especially to Susan Baldwin's brother serving in the Confederate army. These men believed in a culture of action; they would quash this perceived challenge to their authority without delay, definitively, and violently. Around 3:00 P.M. that day, an angry, noisy crowd of men boiled out of Sander's Hotel in downtown Unionville and headed for the courthouse, where they suspected Joiner was being held. Obviously anticipating trouble, a handful of militia stood waiting for them, including Dr. J. Park Thomas, his teenaged son William, and his adult nephew Reuben G. Thomas. Many white men from the hotel crowd had been drinking, and men on both sides carried arms. The few Confederate troops stationed in Unionville were suddenly nowhere to be seen.[24]

Out of the milling crowd stepped James Keenan, the law clerk who became a planter when he married widow Sallie Phifer in 1855. Now forty-two years old, he lived with his wife and older brother William on Main Street in Unionville. During the war he occasionally purchased goods for the Confederacy, but he did not serve in uniform. Perhaps because he had married into the planter class and had not been a soldier, Keenan may have felt compelled to prove his loyalty to the slavery regime even as it was disintegrating. If he ever believed in paternalism, he had abandoned the idea by now. Today he was intoxicated and carrying a rifle. After ascertaining that Joiner was imprisoned in the county jail, he called to the hotel crowd to "fall in," and they marched down the block in ragged order. The militia and many onlookers, among them Keenan's brother William, followed right behind them. At the jailhouse door James Keenan again stepped forward, brandished his rifle, and shouted to all present that he would "kill the first damned rascal that tried to protect the negro." Then he burst inside the jailhouse, where Saxe Joiner waited alone in a cell upstairs. The town sheriff, who was never named in the legal records, was conveniently absent.[25]

Park Thomas arrived a moment later at the tail of the crowd, too late to hear Keenan's threat, and followed him into the jail. Thomas had grown up in Unionville and graduated from the state medical college in 1842. There he undoubtedly knew James Hix, who graduated the previous year. Thomas then returned to Union County, married, and fathered three children, but by 1860 he was a widower. The owner of four slaves, he practiced medicine in Unionville. In 1861, he was forty-three years old, and he did not serve in the Confederate military. Nothing in his life was out of the ordinary, but he showed extraordinary courage in the town jail on this February day in 1865.[26]

Inside the jail a furious argument broke out. Give the man a proper trial, Park Thomas demanded, and James Keenan repeated that he would hang Joiner and kill anyone who tried to stop him. Other white men pushed in through the jailhouse door, and Park Thomas insisted that they halt, catching one of them by the wrist to prevent a pistol from discharging. Then he planted himself at the foot of the stairwell, blocking the path to Joiner's cell upstairs. Keenan warned him to get out of the way and raised his rifle. At that instant two onlookers rushed to intervene, William Keenan, who pleaded with his brother to leave the jail, and Reuben Thomas, who begged his uncle to go outside. Park Thomas paused, took a step back, and cried, "Jim, don't shoot me."

James Keenan fired anyway, but he was so intoxicated that he only grazed the doctor a few yards away. The wound drew blood, however, and it enraged Park Thomas. He pulled out his own pistol and fired back. Being "perfectly sober," as his nephew later testified, he hit his mark, shooting Keenan in the chest. Neither Thomas nor any other doctor treated Keenan, and within fifteen minutes he bled to death. His last words to his brother—"I am killed but I am right"—showed no remorse. His death deflated the hotel crowd, for it soon dispersed and left Saxe Joiner upstairs, alive. Meanwhile, William Thomas helped his father outside, and they disappeared into the countryside, not to resurface for three weeks.[27] It was all over in a few seconds, and nothing had turned out as the principals expected. James Keenan entered the jail intending to kill Saxe Joiner but was himself killed; Park Thomas went in attempting to stop a murder and instead committed one. Long-standing cultural tensions between local white men, inflamed by the war's upheavals, now exploded into the open, and the struggle focused on what would happen to Saxe Joiner.

The next day, Tuesday, February 21, one of Unionville's lawyers tried to steer Joiner's case into a legitimate court. James Steadman, thirty-five years old, had moved to town from Charleston in 1857 and soon allied himself with the Dogan clan. In 1858, he married Caroline Dogan, one of Joseph's daughters, and he lived with his bride in the doctor's house for two years. Although he owned no slaves, in January 1861 he joined the Pea Ridge Volunteers, which was reorganized into Company E of the Fifth South Carolina Volunteers. Severely wounded at Second Bull Run in 1862, he was captured and imprisoned in Fort Delaware. He was paroled at the rank of sergeant, although local tradition had it that he gained a battlefield promotion to major. By early 1865 he had returned to Unionville, where his service record must have enhanced his reputation. A sister-in-law once described him as a man of only "fair talents," but he had daring and an iron will. He was also a personal friend of James Hix.

On Tuesday, February 21, James Steadman went to the Unionville courthouse and sought out M. C. Hughes, the acting magistrate. Then Steadman swore that an unnamed person had informed him that Saxe Joiner had written what Hughes recorded as "grossly insulting proposals" to Susan Baldwin on Sunday, the nineteenth. It is not clear if Hughes or Steadman chose this language, but Steadman must have known that it had been a crime in South Carolina since 1796 for slaves to behave with "insolence" toward white people, the definition of which was left up to whites, or, in this case, white men, for neither Steadman nor Hughes quoted Susan Baldwin or mentioned Martha Hix. (This offense, too, was a misdemeanor, punishable by public flogging, confinement in stocks, or a prison term.) Now Steadman treated the case as if he were appealing a decision by the Magistrate's Court and started at the next level, the Court of General Sessions. Hughes promptly issued a warrant for the misdemeanor, so Joiner was arrested again, although he had been languishing in jail for three days and had been in mortal danger the day before.[28]

With breathtaking audacity, Steadman then appointed himself acting coroner. He had no formal medical training, but that was evidently not germane to his purpose. His brand-new position empowered him to take statements from witnesses to James Keenan's death, and he took only one, that of townsman William C. Harris, a merchant in his mid-thirties. Before the war Harris had been a staunch member of the Sons of Temperance, once giving a public address organized by Steadman's brother-in-law Benjamin Arthur. He socialized with the Dogan clan and attended their fancy masquerade ball in 1851. If he joined the Confederate service, there is no record of it. Now, in February 1865, Harris's statement was pointedly hostile to Keenan, for he stated that the planter was in a state of "drunken excitement" and ignored his brother's plea that he leave the jailhouse. James Steadman must have believed that Saxe Joiner had done something wrong, but he was determined to build up documentation for a proper trial. The only combat veteran among the key white men in this drama (Dogan, Hix, Thomas, Keenan), he was nonetheless determined to put an end to the violence.[29]

So in the last weeks of the Civil War, with the Confederacy disintegrating around them, Unionville's professionals tried to force Saxe Joiner's case back into court. At first glance the entire business seems perverse, like rearranging deck chairs on the *Titanic*, but their actions become comprehensible when we recall that many of them were lawyers, that one white man had died over the matter and another had disappeared, and that they had taken one side in what had become a public and very bitter dispute. Now a slave man stood charged with a crime. This time they would do it their way, and they would do it by the book.[30]

James Hix most likely agreed with them. There is no evidence of his part in this drama, one of the many mysteries surrounding it, but his friend James Steadman probably would not have acted without consulting him. The doctor may not have wanted his slave to die, if only out of financial self-interest, and he may have had some paternalistic regard for Joiner. Hix may also have remembered another trial in Unionville, that of murderer Phineas Johnson in 1851. The doctor testified at the inquest for Johnson's victim, Mary Ann Hyatt, another teenaged daughter of an overseer. Johnson shot Hyatt in the head at point-blank range, and Hix may have believed that Saxe Joiner, who was accused of planning a violent act, not committing one, deserved a trial as much as Johnson did.[31]

The next day, Wednesday, February 22, eight white men from Union County received summonses to begin jury deliberations on the case of "State of South Carolina versus, Saxe, a slave." An officer of the court, presumably a district judge, selected the jurors from the county voter list, and they represented a spectrum of its white male population, including one laborer, one carpenter, three yeoman farmers, and one planter. The jury also included two men with ties to the town professionals: Robert Gage, another planter, was one of Joseph Dogan's in-laws, and farmer William Alman raised two orphaned children from the Thomas family before the war. Everything was in place so that the Joiner case could be resolved properly in a legal venue.[32]

But the legal system ground to a halt for several weeks in late February, for reasons unknown. By the end of the month William Sherman's army had veered to the northeast and crossed into North Carolina. No newspaper was published in Unionville during the war, and none of the up-country papers describe what happened in town. There is no indication of Saxe Joiner's whereabouts in the interval, but he apparently remained in jail. The legal records do show that he was there when Park Thomas surrendered to Unionville authorities on March 8. Thomas was lodged in a separate cell in the jail's "inner walls," surely to protect him from a lynch mob. Whether he and his jailmate Saxe Joiner ever conversed about James Keenan's death on February 20 is also unknown. On the night of March 15, Joiner was ensconced in a cell on the second floor when the lynch mob confronted the sheriff. His heart must have frozen with terror as he heard the mob roar up the steps.[33]

The individuals who swarmed upon Saxe Joiner have never been identified, although James Keenan's brother William may well have been among them. On their way to the jail they had already killed a man, whose race and identity have never been discovered. The mob left Park Thomas in his cell but dragged Joiner out and hanged him from a tree in Joseph Dogan's front yard a few doors away, rather than choosing one of the trees surrounding the courthouse or lining Main Street. Thus ended the tragic life of this enigmatic man, who died in the last weeks of the Civil War for penning a note to a white woman. Its vicious work done, the lynch mob melted away, and none of its members were ever indicted or tried for murder. Their crime sent a blazing message to African Americans, that they could pay with their lives if they seemed to challenge white supremacy in any way. It also gave an unmistakable warning to all black men and white women to refrain from even the appearance of intimate relationships. Finally, it was an ugly retort to the Dogan family and its allies for their behavior of the last month.

But the Dogan clan was not yet defeated. The next day, March 16, Joiner's body was cut down and buried in an unmarked grave. The same day Reuben Thomas arrived at the courthouse to give his eyewitness account of what transpired in the town jail on February 20, and six days later, on March 22, William Thomas, Park's son, gave his deposition in preparation for his father's murder trial, both statements of course quite sympathetic to Park Thomas. An unidentified official (most likely Steadman, the acting coroner) planned to launch an "investigation" into Joiner's death.[34]

The inquiry never took place, however, as the Civil War finally shuddered to a close. In April 1865 Robert E. Lee surrendered at Appomattox, Abraham Lincoln was assassinated, and the Confederate government evacuated Richmond. In May 1865, Jefferson Davis was captured and put in prison, federal troops occupied South Carolina, and Republicans took over the state government. By 1866 white vigilante groups sprang up all over the state, and the Ku Klux Klan organized a chapter in Union County. In the meantime, Park Thomas was still under arrest in Unionville for James Keenan's murder.[35]

The legal machinery cranked up again in March 1866, when an unnamed local attorney—the handwriting resembles that of Mary Dawkins's husband, Thomas—charged Park Thomas with murder, and a grand jury met to consider the indictment. Thomas's defense attorneys were none other than Benjamin Arthur and James Steadman (still the acting coroner), and one Mr. Williams, identity unknown. The defense team asked that the charges be dropped, and the grand jury foreman, Benjamin Rice, one of Joseph Dogan's brothers-in-law, obliged them by returning "no bill." Judge Thomas Glover, a college friend of Thomas Dawkins, granted the defense attorneys' request that Park Thomas be freed on his own recognizance, and that was the end of it. The grand jury left no proceedings, but the cast of characters and the outcome suggest that the town professionals, working through the legal system, had moved to protect a white man who had killed in self-defense while attempting to stop a crime.[36]

The figures in the drama then returned to private life and their individual destinies. By 1870 no one in the Hix or Keenan families lived in Union County, and Susan Baldwin had either married or moved away. Park Thomas settled in Columbia, South Carolina, but by 1885 he remarried and was practicing medicine in Santuc, a tiny village in Union County. In 1900 he died there. Joseph Dogan, Benjamin Arthur, and Thomas Dawkins remained in Unionville pursuing their professions until they died within several months of each other in 1870. James Steadman practiced law in town and became more active in the temperance movement. In 1883 he was elected mayor on a prohibitionist ticket, and he served two years before his death in 1885. Steadman was buried in Unionville's Presbyterian cemetery, where Dogan, Arthur, and James Keenan had been laid to rest years before. Mary Dawkins outlived them all, dying in Union County in 1906 at age eighty-six.[37]

The legal struggle between the town's white men at the Civil War's end came to a draw, for Saxe Joiner died without ever standing trial, while Park Thomas was not prosecuted for killing James Keenan. These events all took place during the convulsive transition from the antebellum world to the new order of Reconstruction. Unionville's white men attempted to reassert their power in the face of unprecedented crises in gender and race relations, after white women had taken on a host of new roles and a slave man appeared to challenge their prerogatives, all while the enemy's army was at the door. What were the demands of patriarchy in such a context? What were the obligations of paternalism? Most of the local white men agreed that racial supremacy must be preserved, but they disagreed in the strongest possible terms on the means toward that end. Beyond that, they could not agree on a rank order of cultural values: the restraint and legal propriety advocated by the town professionals versus action and immediate resolution practiced by the planters.

What general conclusions can we draw from this riveting tale? That Saxe Joiner's second note did not remain a domestic matter reflects the extent to which the old order of master-slave relations had broken down. Joiner's fate was catapulted out of the household into the public realm, with the most tragic results. Furthermore, the three-week gap between the first, thwarted attempt in February to kill Saxe Joiner and the second, successful attempt in March demonstrates that lynching was not always the spontaneous act of a frenzied mob. This second crowd acted with deliberate calculation, right down to their choice of Confederate attire. Finally, it suggests that white supremacy was socially constructed, even as slavery was in its death throes in 1865.[38]

NOTES

I wish to thank Michael Les Benedict, John Inscoe, Lee Shepard, and Warren Van Tine for their valuable comments on this article; Marion Chandler, Henry Fulmer, and Carolyn Quickmire Hamby for their kind assistance in tracking down court records; and Steven Stowe for generously providing information about the medical profession in the Old South.

1. Coroner's Inquisition, "Sax [sic], (slave)," March 16, 1865, K–T, 1806–69, Court of General Sessions, Union County, South Carolina, South Carolina Archives, Columbia (hereafter SCA). In the 1870s, Unionville changed its name to Union.

2. Rachel N. Klein, *Unification of a Slave State: The Rise of the Planter Class in the South Carolina Backcountry, 1760–1808* (Chapel Hill: University of North Carolina Press, 1990); Lacy K. Ford Jr., *Origins of Southern Radicalism: The South Carolina Upcountry, 1800–1860* (New York: Oxford University Press, 1988); *Intellectual Life in Antebellum Charleston*, ed. Michael O'Brien and David Moltke-Hansen (Knoxville: University of Tennessee Press, 1986); Peter H. Wood, *Black Majority: Negroes in Colonial South Carolina from 1670 through the Stono Rebellion* (New York: Knopf, 1974); W. Fitzhugh Brundage, *Lynching in the New South: Georgia and Virginia, 1880–1930* (Urbana: University of Illinois Press, 1993), 5–6; C. Vann Woodward, ed., *Mary Chesnut's Civil War* (New Haven: Yale University Press, 1981); Gerda Lerner, *The Grimké Sisters from South Carolina: Pioneers for Woman's Rights and Abolition* (New York: Houghton Mifflin, 1967).

3. Agriculture Schedule, Census of 1860, 237; *Lippincott's Gazeteer of the World* (New York: N.p., 1905), 452; Ford, *Origins of Southern Radicalism*, 46, 260.

4. Allan D. Charles, *The Narrative History of Union County, South Carolina* (Spartanburg, S.C.: Reprint Company, 1987), 55, 103–19; Joseph Ioor Waring, *A History of Medicine in South Carolina, 1670–1825* (Charleston: South Carolina Medical Association, 1964), 391; *South Carolina v. Phineas Johnson*, 1851–52, Court of General Sessions, Union County, SCA, testimony of Jane Davis, n.d. September 1851, copy of sentence, December 15, 1851, bill of court costs, by J. G. McKissick, April 17, 1852; Free Schedule, Census of 1850, South Carolina, Union County, 81; Free Schedule, Census of 1860, South Carolina, Union County, 274. James Keenan shared ownership of forty-five slaves with his brother William; see Slave Schedule, Census of 1860, South Carolina, Union County, 370. Joseph Dogan's son-in-law William Stringfellow lived in Florida, and another son-in-law, Jackson Scaife, served in the Confederate army throughout the war so that neither one participated in these events in Unionville.

5. Slave Schedule, Census of 1860, South Carolina, Union County, n.p.; *Biographical Directory of the American Congress, 1774–1971* (Washington, D.C.: U.S. Government Printing Office, 1971); Joan E. Cashin, " 'Since the War Broke Out': The Marriage of Kate and William McLure," in *Divided Houses: Gender and the Civil War*, ed. Catherine Clinton and Nina Silber (New York: Oxford University Press, 1992), 200–212; Ford, *Origins of Southern Radicalism*, 200–201, 205; Charles, *Union County*, 458, 107–10, 167–68.

6. *Unionville Journal*, June 14, 1851, February 6, 1852, August 9, 1851; Charles, *Union County*, 106; Joseph Dogan to Sarah Rice Dogan, December 4, 1834, Sarah Ann Rice Dogan Papers, Perkins Library, Duke University, Durham N.C.

7. Slave Schedule, Census of 1860, South Carolina, Union County, n.p.; Addie and Caroline Dogan to Caroline Gordon, May 21, 1851, January 6, 1854, Addie Dogan to Caroline Gordon, October 16, 1851, Gordon and Hackett Family Papers, Southern Historical Collection, University of North Carolina, Chapel Hill; *Cyclopedia of Eminent and Representative Men of the Carolinas of the Nineteenth Century* (Spartanburg, S.C.: Reprint Company, 1972), 1:65–66.

8. Addie Dogan to Caroline Gordon, July 16, 1855, Addie and Caroline Dogan to Caroline Gordon, June 7, 1849, Gordon and Hackett Family Papers; Charles, *Union County*, 55, 59, 96–97, 107; Cashin, " 'Since the War Broke Out,' " 202; *Dictionary of American Biography*, ed. Allen Johnson and Dumas Malone (New York: Charles Scribner's Sons, 1957), 4:325.

9. *Dictionary of American Biography*, 4:325; *Cyclopedia*, 1:66; Charles H. Lesser, *Relic of the Lost Cause: The Story of South Carolina's Ordinance of Secession* (Columbia: South Carolina Department of Archives and History, 1990), 21; Charles, *Union County*, 169–71.

10. *Cyclopedia*, 1:66; Ford, *Origins of Southern Radicalism*; *The National Cyclopedia of American Biography* (New York: James T. White, 1904), 12:172–73; Charles, *Union County*, 181–84; Mark Boatner, ed., *The Civil War Dictionary* (New York: David McKay, 1959), 344–45. Benjamin Arthur was exempted from Confederate service for medical reasons but sometimes provided supplies for the army; see Charles, *Union County*, 170.

11. Charles, *Union County*, 194, 90; Cashin, " 'Since the War Broke Out,' " 207–12. On gender relations, see also Reid Mitchell, *The Vacant Chair: The Northern Soldier Leaves Home* (New York: Oxford University Press, 1992); George C. Rable, *Civil Wars: Women and the Crisis of Southern Nationalism* (Urbana: University of Illinois Press, 1989); LeeAnn Whites, *The Civil War as a Crisis in Gender: Augusta, Georgia, 1860–1890* (Athens: University of Georgia Press, 1995).

12. Charles, *Union County*, 192–93; Mary Dawkins, "Recollections of Mary Poulton Dawkins, Widow of Judge Thomas N. Dawkins," n.p., 1902, McLure Papers, South Caroliniana Library, University of South Carolina, Columbia (hereafter USC). On race relations, see also Clarence L. Mohr, *On the Threshold of Freedom: Masters and Slaves in Civil War Georgia* (Athens: University of Georgia Press, 1986).

13. Kate McLure to William McLure, December 10, 1864, Mary Dawkins to Kate McLure, February 21, 1865, McLure Papers; James Moore, *Kilpatrick and Our Cavalry* (New York: Hurst & Co., 1865), 219; John G. Barrett, *Sherman's March through the Carolinas* (Chapel Hill: University of North Carolina Press, 1956), 44–116; Dawkins, "Recollections," n.p.; Joseph T. Glatthaar, *The March to the Sea and Beyond:*

Sherman's Troops in Savannah and Carolinas Campaigns (New York: New York University Press, 1985).

14. Free Schedule, Census of 1860, South Carolina, Union County, 37; Slave Schedule, Census of 1860, South Carolina, Union County, 368; Book of Catalogs, J. E. Hix, Class of 1841, Waring Historical Library, Medical University of South Carolina, Charleston; Charles, *Union County*, 156–57, 161; Dawkins to McLure, February 21, 1865, McLure Papers. There is no other information on Martha Hix.

15. David J. McCord, *The Statutes at Large of South Carolina; Edited, under Authority of the Legislature*, Vol. 7: *Containing the Acts Relating to Charleston, Courts, Slaves, and Rivers* (Columbia: A. S. Johnston, 1840), 413; Dawkins to McLure, February 21, 1865, McLure Papers; Slave Schedule, Census of 1850, South Carolina, Union County, n.p.; Slave Schedule, Census of 1860, South Carolina, Union County, 368. Census marshals were not required to give slave occupations, but this one did so. In 1860 James E. Hix owned three other mulatto men who could have been Saxe Joiner (a nineteen-year-old carpenter, a forty-five-year-old house slave, and a thirty-five-year-old mason), but the master carpenter's age nominates him.

16. Caroline and Addie Dogan to Caroline Gordon, November 26, 1852, M. E. Martin to Caroline Gordon, June 19, 1854, Gordon and Hackett Family Papers; Charles, *Union County*, 163; Dawkins, "Recollections," n.p. Thomas Dawkins owned thirty-seven slaves; see Slave Schedule, Census of 1860, South Carolina, Union County, n.p.

17. For an excellent summary of the literature on paternalism, see Peter Kolchin, *American Slavery, 1619–1877* (New York: Hill & Wang, 1993), 111–32.

18. Dawkins to McLure, February 21, 1865, McLure Papers.

19. Free Schedule, Census of 1850, South Carolina, Union County, 90; Dawkins to McLure, February 21, 1865, McLure Papers; Dawkins, "Recollections," n.p. On race and southern honor, see Bertram Wyatt-Brown, *Southern Honor: Ethics and Behavior in the Old South* (New York: Oxford University Press, 1982), 402–61.

20. Dawkins to McLure, February 21, 1865, McLure Papers; John Belton O'Neall, *The Negro Law of South Carolina* (Columbia: John G. Bowman, 1848), 29, indicates that since 1843 it was a capital crime for a slave to commit "assault and battery on a white woman, with intent to commit a rape." On sexual relationships real and imagined, see Winthrop Jordan, *Tumult and Silence at Second Creek: An Inquiry into a Civil War Slave Conspiracy* (Baton Rouge: Louisiana State University, 1993); and Martha Hodes, "Wartime Dialogues on Illicit Sex: White Women and Black Men," in *Divided Houses*, ed. Clinton and Silber, 230–42.

21. On open and covert resistance among slaves, see Eugene D. Genovese, *Roll, Jordan, Roll: The World the Slaves Made* (New York: Pantheon Books, 1972); John W. Blassingame, *The Slave Community: Plantation Life in the Antebellum South* (New York: Oxford University Press, 1972); Deborah Gray White, *Ar'n't I a Woman? Female Slaves in the Plantation South* (New York: Norton, 1985).

22. Mary Bailey Butt, "The Poultons in America," 3, Poulton Family Manuscript, USC.

23. McCord, *Statutes at Large*, 7:365–66, 400–401; O'Neall, *Negro Law*, 34; Free Schedule, Census of 1860, 274; Charles, *Union County*, 114.

24. James M. McPherson, *Battle Cry of Freedom: The Civil War Era* (New York: Oxford University Press, 1988), 836–37; Coroner's Inquisition, K–T, 1806–69, Testi-

mony of William C. Harris, February 21, 1865, Court of General Sessions, SCA; Affidavit of William K. Thomas, March 22, 1865, *Doctor J. P. Thomas* v. *State of South Carolina*, Court of General Sessions, SCA. Reuben G. Thomas was a yeoman farmer in his early thirties. See Free Schedule, Census of 1860, South Carolina, Union County, 208. Unionville's white men probably did not know that in February 1865 the government in Richmond debated using black troops in the Confederate army. In March the government decided to accept them in exchange for giving them freedom, and two black companies were organized before the war ended.

25. Addie and Caroline Dogan to Caroline Gordon, May 21, August 14, 1851, July 29, 1852, Addie Dogan to Caroline Gordon, July 16, 1855, Gordon and Hachett Family Papers; Affidavits of William K. Thomas, March 22, 1865, R. G. Thomas, March 16, 1865, Record Group 109, War Department Collection of Confederate Records, "Citizens" File, South Carolina, National Archives. In 1860 Joseph Fant served as Unionville's sheriff, but it is not clear whether he remained in office during the war. See Free Schedule, Census of 1860, South Carolina, Union County, 275.

26. Charles, *Union County*, 146; *Centennial Memorial of the Medical College of the State of South Carolina, 1824–1924* (Charleston: N.p., 1924); Free Schedule, Census of 1860, South Carolina, Union County, 265; Slave Schedule, Census of 1860, South Carolina, Union County, 365.

27. Testimony of William C. Harris, February 21, 1865; Affidavits of R. G. Thomas, March 16, 1865, William K. Thomas, March 22, 1865.

28. Charles, *Union County*, 181, 187–88, 190; Caroline Dogan to Caroline Gordon, May 29, 1857, Addie Dogan Scaife to Caroline Gordon, July 28, 1860, Gordon and Hackett Family Papers; Compiled Military Service Records Series, South Carolina, Record Group 109, National Archives; Affidavit of James B. Steadman, Summons of Arrest for "Saxe, a slave," February 21, 1865, Summons to Jurors, February 22, 1865, Papers of Court of General Sessions, SCA; O'Neall, *Negro Law*, 33; *Judicial Cases Concerning American Slavery and the Negro*, Vol. 2: *Cases from the Courts of North Carolina, South Carolina, and Tennessee* (New York: Negro Universities Press, 1926), 403.

29. Addie and Caroline Dogan to Caroline Gordon, May 21, 1851, Addie Dogan to Caroline Gordon, October 16, 1851, Gordon and Hackett Family Papers; Free Schedule, Census of 1860, 268; Testimony of William C. Harris, February 21, 1865. Harris owned no slaves in 1860.

30. For somewhat similar behavior by white southern lawyers, see Melton McLaurin, *Celia, a Slave* (Athens: University of Georgia Press, 1991).

31. Inquest recorded by C. S. Gregory, September 17, 1851, *South Carolina* v. *Phineas Johnson*, 1851–52, Court of General Sessions, SCA.

32. On Gage, see Free Schedule, Census of 1860, South Carolina, Union County, 246; Slave Schedule, Census of 1860, South Carolina, Union County, 353; on Alman, see Free Schedule, Census of 1850, South Carolina, Union County, 105; Free Schedule, Census of 1860, South Carolina, Union County, 232. On other jury members see Free Schedule, Census of 1860, 203, 303, 197, 248, 272, for James Cunningham, Benjamin Hawkins, John Meadon, E. G. Park, J. H. Skelton, and Slave Schedule, n.p., for John Meadon. See Free Schedule, Census of 1850, 38, for John Becknell.

33. Statement of R. Macbeth, March 8, 1865, Court of General Sessions, SCA.

34. "To any Lawful Court," March 16, 1865, Court of General Sessions, SCA. On lynching in the post–Civil War era, see Jacquelyn Dowd Hall, " 'The Mind That Burns

in Each Body': Women, Rape, and Racial Violence," in *Powers of Desire: The Politics of Sexuality*, ed. Ann Snitow, Christine Stansell, and Sharon Thompson (New York: Monthly Review Press, 1983). A careful search of the Union County church and cemetery records did not yield Joiner's burial place or the name of the other man killed by the lynch mob on March 15, 1865.

35. Charles, *Union County*, 220; Allen W. Trelease, *White Terror: The Ku Klux Klan Conspiracy and Southern Reconstruction* (New York: Harper & Row, 1971).

36. *South Carolina* v. *John P. Thomas*, March 6, 1866, Journal of Court of General Sessions, 441, 442, 445, SCA; Dawkins, "Recollections," n.p.

37. Census of 1870, South Carolina, Richland County, 169; *Butler's Medical Register and Directory of the United States* (N.p.: N.p., 1974); Mrs. E. D. Whaley Sr., *Union County Cemeteries: Epitaphs of 18th and 19th Century Settlers in Union County, South Carolina, and Their Descendants* (Greenville, S.C.: A Press, Inc., 1976), 64, 154, 157, 152; Charles, *Union County*, 277.

38. On the construction of white supremacy in the antebellum and postbellum eras, see David R. Roediger, *The Wages of Whiteness: Race and the Making of the American Working Class* (London: Verso, 1991); Alexander Saxton, *The Rise and Fall of the White Republic: Class Politics and Mass Culture in Nineteenth-Century America* (London: Verso, 1990); Brundage, *Lynching in the New South*.

When Race Didn't Matter

Black and White Mob Violence against Their Own Color

E. M. Beck and Stewart E. Tolnay

Between 1880 and 1930 the American South experienced a rising surge of collective violence. Southern newspapers reported almost weekly incidents of mobs hanging, shooting, burning, or drowning hapless victims. African Americans endured the brunt of this wave of savagery, and more than two thousand blacks died at the hands of white lynchers.[1] Although mob violence directed at African Americans has been well documented, intraracial lynchings—those in which the victim and the mob had the same skin color—have received decidedly less scholarly attention. Perhaps the best-known incident of this type of mob violence is the 1915 lynching of Atlanta factory supervisor Leo Frank for the murder of Mary Phagan.[2] This case was sensationalized by the contemporary press and later dramatized for television, but it is only one of the over two hundred incidents of white-on-white collective violence that took place between 1882 and 1930 in the American South.[3]

Concurrent with being subjected to frequent white mob rule, the African American community witnessed the enigmatic spectacle of blacks lynching other blacks. Between 1882 and 1930, 148 southern blacks died at the hands of mobs that were integrated or composed entirely of African Americans. In this essay we examine the phenomenon of same-race lynchings, document trends in the frequency with which blacks and whites employed collective action in their own communities, identify the areas of the South where same-race lynchings were the most numerous, and offer an interpretation for mob violence when race was not the issue.

A reasonable first step toward understanding the phenomenon of same-race lynchings is to describe their distribution through time and space. Were intraracial lynchings more concentrated during some periods of this forty-nine-year era than others? Did some regions of the South experience more than their share of intraracial violence? These are important questions as we search for possible explanations for this type of lethal sanctioning.

Before considering the trends in intraracial lynchings, it will be useful to examine the pattern of conventional white-on-black lynching activity and then use this as a basis for gauging trends in same-race lynchings. Figure 1a graphs the number of casualties of traditional lynchings each year from 1882 to 1930.[4] As this figure demonstrates, conventional antiblack mob violence increased during the 1880s, peaked in 1893, and then began a gradual descent to the Great Depression. This general decline after the mid-1890s was interrupted, however, by three resurgent waves of antiblack violence: during the turn of the century business recession, again during the 1908 economic downturn, and finally after World War I, coinciding with yet another recession, the resurgence of the second Ku Klux Klan, the rise of nativism, and the return of black troops from Europe.[5]

Figure 1b presents the trends over time in intraracial mob violence for the period 1882 to 1930. The annual toll of blacks lynched by other blacks increased unevenly during the decade of the 1880s, reached its maximum in 1892, then entered a decline to 1930, with only one significant reversal in the period between 1900 and 1904.[6]

The trend in white-on-white lynchings shown in Figure 1b has a configuration comparable to that of black-on-black lynchings, with increased lynching activity until the early 1890s followed by a decline and only a small increase during the Ku Klux Klan revival in the early 1920s. Figure 1b shows, however, that before 1900 and after 1914 the annual number of whites killed by white mobs was greater than the number of blacks murdered by black mobs.[7]

In the broad view, the trends in black-on-black and white-on-white lynchings are similar, and both are roughly comparable to the trend in traditional white-on-black lynchings.[8] The number of victims of lynch mobs grew during the 1880s, reached its annual maximum early in the 1890s, then diminished gradually over the next thirty-five years, with only occasional violent resurgences.

This similarity among patterns raises the possibility that the trend of

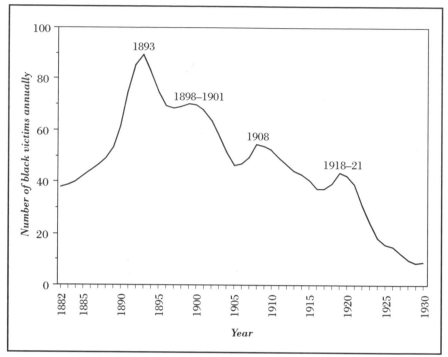

intraracial lynchings simply mimicked the secular trend in mob violence and that there is little unique about these less conventional varieties of lynchings. In other words, the patterns of same-race lynchings in Figure 1b may be confounded with the more general trend in mob violence seen in Figure 1a.

The trends in same-race lynchings in Figure 1b are a mixture of two elements: a pattern resulting from the trend in mob violence in general and a trend unique to same-race lynchings. One way to separate these two components is to use time-series regression to eliminate the general component from the same-race trends reported in Figure 1b.[9] After that is accomplished, the "purified" trends can be reexamined for informative patterns.

Figures 2a and 2b present the smoothed trends in same-race lynchings adjusted for the secular trend in mob violence. The zero line is the overall trend in traditional lynchings, and each point is a deviation away from that baseline trend. Deviations above zero indicate years when the number of same-race lynchings was greater than would have been predicted from the general trend, and deviations less than zero indicate years when the number of same-race lynchings was less than expected.

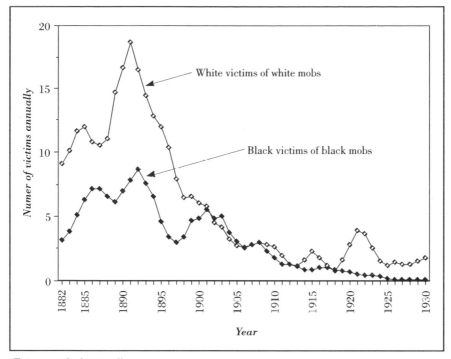

[a]Twice smoothed statiscally

Figure 2a shows that from 1882 through the early 1890s, there were more black-on-black lynching victims than would be expected on the basis of the general trend in conventional mob violence. This is remarkable because, as shown in Figure 1a, the overall lynching trend during this period was increasing dramatically. After the early 1890s, the number of blacks lynching other blacks was generally less than would have been predicted.

The pattern for white-on-white lynchings, Figure 2b, is broadly comparable to that of black-on-black lynchings in Figure 2a. During the 1880s and until the early 1890s, the number of white victims of white mobs exceeded the general trend in mob violence, but after about 1895 the number of white victims was less than would have been predicted based on the general trend.

Figures 2a and 2b demonstrate that during the 1880s, same-race lynchings increased at a rate greater than that of traditional white-on-black lynchings, and after the early 1890s they declined at a steeper rate than

FIGURE 2A. *Adjusted Trend in Black-on-Black Lynching Victims*[a]

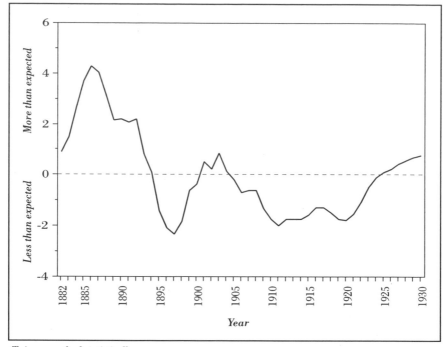

[a]Twice smoothed statistically

that of traditional lynchings. Thus, while the temporal pattern of same-race lynchings follows the broad sweep of mob violence during the lynching era, they differ in one significant way: they were more prevalent during the early years of the 1880s, and they were relatively less frequent after the frenzy of mob violence peaked in the 1890s. Documenting this pattern in a different way, we discovered that 67.4 percent of the incidents of black-on-black lynchings and 70.5 percent of the incidents of white-on-white lynchings occurred before 1900, whereas only 46.4 percent of the traditional white-on-black lynching incidents occurred before that date.[10] This indicates, therefore, that same-race mob violence was primarily, although not exclusively, a nineteenth-century phenomenon and that same-race lynchings became increasingly rare after the turn of the century. This, of course, raises the question, Why were same-race lynchings more common in the early years of the lynching era? One possibility is that intraracial lynchings were a form of "popular justice" in which racial communities punished violators of community norms in the absence of an efficient, formal law enforcement authority.

FIGURE 2B. *Adjusted Trend in White-on-White Lynching Victims[a]*

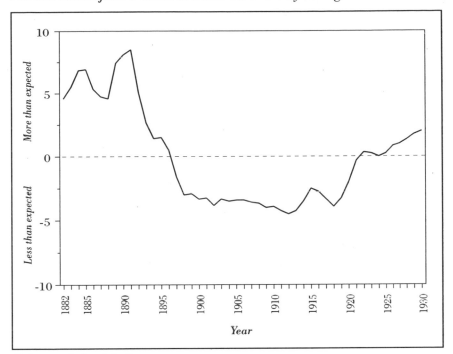

[a]Twice smoothed statistically

BLACK-ON-BLACK MOB VIOLENCE

Spatial Patterns

For additional clues that might point toward an explanation of intra-racial violence we can turn to their geographical distribution across the southern landscape. If same-race lynchings were concentrated in certain areas of the South, then the characteristics of those areas may suggest conditions that gave rise to these incidents.

Map 1 illustrates the distribution of black-on-black lynching incidents across ten southern states during the 1882–1930 period. We have noted elsewhere that intraracial violence within the African American commu-nity was geographically concentrated and that most lynchings occurred in the more recently settled areas of the South.[11] A similar pattern emerges in Map 1, which shows the geographic distribution of the 129 incidents of black-on-black violence. A heavy clustering of intraracial lynchings is

MAP 1. *Incidents of Black or Integrated Mobs Lynching Black Victims*

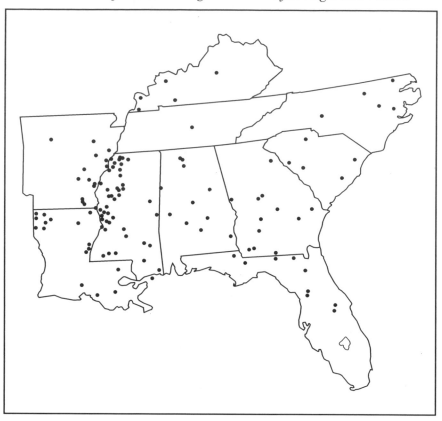

clear along the Mississippi River delta in Arkansas and Mississippi and extending southward into Louisiana. Indeed, these three states alone account for fully 61 percent of all black-on-black lynching incidents.[12] In contrast, Georgia, which compiled one of the bloodiest histories of conventional white-on-black violence (368 incidents, or 17 percent of the total lynching incidents for the South), recorded only 12 incidents of black mob violence (9 percent of the total).[13] To be sure, incidents of black-on-black violence also occurred outside of the Mississippi River delta region, but they account for a relatively small percentage of all such episodes.

An intriguing concentration of black intraracial violence appears in Bossier and Caddo Parishes, both in the extreme northwest corner of Louisiana. With a total of nine incidents, they account for half of Louisiana's eighteen incidents of black-on-black lynching. An even harsher picture emerges, however, if we shift our attention to the number of black victims of intraracial lynching. Both Bossier and Caddo Parishes had incidents in which more than one victim was killed. Indeed, Bossier had five incidents with six victims, and Caddo had four incidents with six victims—mobs in these two parishes were responsible for more than half of Louisiana's twenty-one black victims of intraracial lynching. On October 19, 1893, for instance, two unnamed black men were lynched by an integrated mob in Bossier Parish for being "notorious hog thieves."[14] Three men were lynched in Caddo Parish on November 30, 1903, for attempted murder. Phil Davis, Walter Carter, and Clint Thomas were taken to the bayou, given time to pray, then hanged from a willow tree.[15] These multiple-victim incidents demonstrate the lethality of intraracial violence in these two parishes.

A possible explanation for the geographic distribution of black intraracial violence emphasizes the size and concentration of the African American population. That is, there was greater opportunity for such violence where the black population was larger. Indeed, there is a moderate relationship, across counties, between the absolute size of the black population and the number of black victims of intraracial violence ($r = +0.213$), suggesting that simple availability of potential black victims and mobs partially accounts for the pattern observed in Map 1.[16] A second, related explanation stresses the proportionate, rather than absolute, size of the African American population. Where the black population represented a larger percentage of a county's total population, the African American community may have retained somewhat greater independence in exercising social control—including the punishment of norm violators. Of course, given the importance of the racial caste line in southern society, this independence would have extended only to cases in which blacks were victims of the norm violation. Whenever whites were victimized by blacks, punishment typically was inflicted by white courts or white mobs. There is also empirical evidence supporting this second explanation, with a significant association between the number of black victims of intraracial lynching and the proportionate size of the black population across counties ($r = +0.298$).[17]

To gain greater insight into the social forces that may have been responsible for blacks lynching other blacks we now move beyond the temporal and geographic distributions of such incidents and examine more closely the circumstances surrounding these events.

Interpreting Lynchings by Black Mobs
Elsewhere, we have suggested that the best way to understand the motivation for interracial lynching is to ask the question, How was the

white community threatened, and by whom? For the more typical incident of interracial lynchings, we have argued that whites were more likely to lynch blacks when they felt threatened by the black population, especially economically.[18] The same general approach may be taken to interpret black-on-black violence. Naturally, southern blacks were constrained in their ability to react violently to redress grievances against the white population, by whom they were certainly threatened during this era. So it comes as no surprise that there are extremely few records in our database that document the lynching of a white person by a black mob.[19] Thus interracial tensions must figure only marginally in our consideration of the social forces responsible for the activities of black mobs. Conversely, interaction within the African American community will assume greater prominence.

In a few incidents, representing only a small percentage of all black-on-black lynchings, interracial conflict was indirectly responsible. In every case, the black community punished a fellow member for collaborating with whites in the prosecution, or persecution, of blacks. Two examples will suffice. John Brown was lynched in Talladega County, Alabama, on September 29, 1891, for testifying against other blacks. Apparently Brown had passed along information to the police implicating two black males in a barn burning. According to Brown's wife, a group of blacks visited their home, telling John that they had a warrant for his arrest for killing hogs. Later, Brown was found in the Tallasahatchie creek with his hands and feet tied and a rope around his neck.[20] A similar incident had its origin in events that occurred on June 10, 1899, when a black man was lynched by a white mob in Marion County, Florida, for murdering a police officer. The following day, two black men were lynched in the same county by a mob of angry blacks. The victims were accused of aiding the white mob during the lynching on the previous day.[21] These and similar cases suggest that some members of the black community felt threatened when other blacks aided and abetted efforts by whites to punish African Americans.

Far more common, however, were cases in which black mobs lynched victims accused of serious crimes (e.g., murder, rape, and assault) against other blacks (see Table 1). We have suggested that, unlike the more common lynching of blacks by whites, many black intraracial lynchings were instances of popular justice. Four key pieces of information support this conclusion: the concentration of black-on-black lynchings before the turn of the century; the concentration of black intraracial lynchings in less developed areas of the South; the serious nature of accusations against the lynch victims; and the lack of enthusiasm with which the white-

TABLE 1. *Alleged Offenses of Lynch Victims (in percentages)*

Offense	Black Victims, Black Mobs[a]	White Victims, White Mobs	Black Victims, White Mobs
Rape or incest	25.68	8.45	29.21
Murder	45.95	59.51	37.25
Murder and rape	2.03	2.82	1.86
Miscegenation or other sex offense	4.06	1.76	4.37
Assault	6.08	4.93	9.77
Theft or fraud	4.73	7.04	4.02
Arson	3.38	3.52	4.28
Other and unknown	8.11	11.97	9.25
Total	100.02	100.00	100.01
	(N = 148)	(N = 284)	(N = 2,314)

[a]Black or integrated mobs.

dominated criminal justice system punished black criminals who victimized other blacks. Regarding the last of these points, between 1882 and 1930 the state of Georgia legally executed forty-four black men charged with rape, but only seven of these men were accused of raping a black woman. Over the same time period, Georgia executed only one white man for rape, and his victim was a white women. So, taking sexual assaults as a single example, the formal justice system clearly overlooked or dealt relatively leniently with crimes against black victims. Perhaps black mobs took matters into their own hands because they had little confidence that the white-dominated justice system would mete out punishment that was swift enough or severe enough to satisfy them.[22] If there is merit to this popular justice interpretation, then another reason for black intraracial lynchings is that the black community felt threatened by the criminal activity of some of its members.

Most victims of black mobs were accused of very serious offenses; fully 73.7 percent were alleged to have committed murder, sexual assault, or rape-murders. In this respect, black-on-black lynchings were similar to the more common lynching of blacks by white mobs, in which 68.4 percent of victims were accused of murder or rape. The crimes attributed to Sam Wilson mirrored most of the vile motives usually ascribed to black lynching victims of white mobs. Wilson, who was lynched on December 17, 1885, in Jones County, Mississippi, was accused of murdering a black woman and her son, as well as raping and murdering her daughter. Wilson was half-brother to the two murdered children. Upon learning of the crime, a group of black men ambushed Wilson, "gave him a dose of lead and then hung him to a tree." Interestingly, the white press, in this case the *New Orleans Daily Picayune*, strongly endorsed the lynching of Wilson, as it often did the actions of white lynch mobs. The paper described the lynching as "a fate too good for such a monster" and opined, "It is a good thing to know the villain was captured and that he did not live to see the sun go down on his bloody work."[23]

Not all victims of black mobs stood accused of such heinous crimes as those committed by Sam Wilson. W. J. Jackson, who was lynched on October 15, 1908, in DeSoto County, Mississippi, stood accused of stealing a bale of cotton from a neighboring black man.[24] In another incident a black Baptist preacher, known only as "Lightfoot," was lynched in Jackson County, Arkansas, on December 9, 1892, for committing a "stupendous fraud" upon the black population. Apparently, Lightfoot claimed to be a government agent responsible for preparing African Americans for a trip to Liberia and collected fees for that purpose from over eight hundred local blacks. When his deception was discovered, several contributors demanded that Lightfoot return their money. When he refused, they shot him to death.[25]

A special category of black-on-black lynchings involved the punishment of behavior that may be labeled as "offenses against the black family." Roughly 16 percent of all incidents involving black mobs included victims accused of crimes against other members of their family—more than we find among white-on-white or black-on-white lynchings. These "crimes" included such behavior as murder of a spouse, murder of a father-in-law, getting "too thick" with kinsmen's wives, and nonmarital cohabitation. One of the most common was incest, or the rape of a young family member. A typical example of the latter group of incidents was the lynching of David Scruggs in Jefferson County, Arkansas, on July 23, 1885. After Scruggs was accused of engaging in incestuous acts with his daughter, he was abducted by a black mob and "carved to pieces with knives."[26] Julien Mosely was similarly dispatched by a black mob in Desha County, Arkansas, on July 14, 1892. Mosely, who was accused of raping his seven-year-old stepdaughter, had been arrested and was in custody when a mob of black men overpowered the constable. They "took Mosely to a cotton gin and hanged him with a rope used for drawing up cotton."[27] It is well known that the African American family was under stress during this era. Mortality, desertion, and nonmarital childbearing resulted in more female-headed households and more children living separately from one or both parents than was the case in the white community.[28] Therefore, it would not be surprising if the African American community had mobilized to promote greater stability for families, especially children, even if it meant the lethal and visible punishment of behavior that threatened the family. Of course, this connection between black family patterns and black mobs must remain only speculative until it is investigated further.

The description of black intraracial lynchings as incidents of popular justice may appear to be contradicted by the fact that in roughly one-third (36 percent) of all lynching incidents by black mobs the victim was removed from the custody of a sheriff, jailer, or judge. Labeling black-on-black lynchings as acts of popular justice may appear inappropriate when the formal criminal justice system was already engaged. Justice, after all, might have been done even without the intervention of the mob. To be sure, in some cases the justice system would have meted out punishment that was swift and severe enough to satisfy the black community's desire for retribution. In those cases, mob action was not required to achieve "justice." The record compiled by the southern justice system, however, at least with respect to rape, probably gave African Americans cause to doubt its effectiveness in punishing black-on-black crimes. Furthermore, the frequency with which victims of black mobs were removed from custody falls short of the corresponding frequency for the victims of white-on-white or white-on-black violence. In all southern states 52.5 percent of white victims of white lynch mobs were removed from the custody of authorities, whereas 39.5 percent of black victims of white mobs in Arkansas were so obtained. In sum, we believe that the description of black intraracial lynchings as episodes of popular justice is reasonably accurate. But we also recognize that black mobs, like their white counterparts, lynched victims who would have been punished adequately by legal authorities and sometimes sought to send a message to the larger African American community through their punishment of norm violations.

Black Brutality
Occasionally, black mobs subjected their victims to extreme suffering—possibly to make sure that other potential norm violators received the message. Several lynch victims were burned alive or after they had been killed by other means. More rarely the victim was tortured with more elaborate methods. Anderson Moreland, who was lynched in Monroe County, Georgia, on June 8, 1892, was one of those unfortunate souls. When Moreland was captured by the mob that accused him of raping a

black girl, "he was stripped of his clothes and beaten into insensibility and dropped into a hot tub of salt water."[29] Dan Reynolds of Phillips County, Arkansas, was also tortured by the mob that lynched him on January 13, 1889, for "jilting" a black girl. After whipping Reynolds nearly to death, the mob of nine black men rubbed mud into his wounds and packed his nose and mouth with mud.[30] Although our records suggest that black mobs resorted to torture and mutilation somewhat less than white mobs (with either black or white victims), these cases clearly demonstrate that such methods were also in the repertoire of punishments of black mobs.

WHITE-ON-WHITE MOB VIOLENCE

Spatial Distribution

Turning to the spatial distribution of white-on-white mob violence, Map 2 shows that the 224 incidents of white lynchings were concentrated in the parishes of northern Louisiana, in the counties of central Arkansas, along the Kentucky-Tennessee border, and in the upland areas of eastern Tennessee and Kentucky.[31] There was also a significant cluster of white lynchings along the Mississippi-Alabama border.

A comparison of Map 2 with Map 1 shows that white-on-white lynchings were rarely located in the same areas as black-on-black mob violence. In fact, of the counties that had any intraracial lynchings, only 10 percent experienced both types. White lynchings were somewhat more likely in counties with a high concentration of white population, and 60 percent of white-on-white lynching incidents took place in the least densely populated counties. This indicates that white intraracial lynchings occurred disproportionately in predominantly white, rural counties of the South. Again, in concert with the temporal concentration of white-on-white lynchings, this spatial distribution is consistent with a popular justice interpretation.

Varieties of White-on-White Lynching

The worst single incident of white-on-white mob violence took place in a far different environment. This tragedy occurred in New Orleans, Louisiana, where eleven Italians were lynched in late winter of 1891.[32] David C. Hennessy, police chief of New Orleans, was slated to testify against one of the city's main gang factions. On October 15, 1890, two days before he was scheduled to appear in court, Hennessy was shot down by five gunmen on Rampart Street. A close friend reported that as he lay dying, he implicated

MAP 2. *Incidents of White Mobs Lynching White Victims*

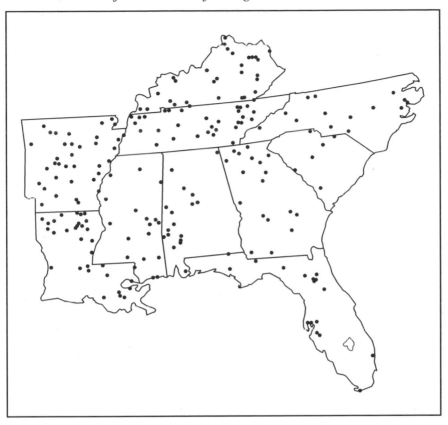

Italians in the assassination. Nine Italians were indicted, and their trial began in late February 1891 for conspiracy to murder. Six of the accused were acquitted, but the jury could not agree on the guilt of three others. Immediately the district attorney speculated that the jury had been bribed. The next morning, March 14, city newspapers carried a notice for a "Mass Meeting," which urged outraged citizens to "Come prepared for action."[33] A throng estimated in the thousands gathered at Canal and Royal Streets to hear three mob leaders goad the crowd into marching to Parish Prison to hang the Italians. After failing to storm the prison's main entrance, the mob assaulted the Treme Street gate of Parish Prison, forced entry, and shot nine Italians and hanged two more. The vigilantes were praised by local and state leaders for their actions, and a subsequent grand jury investigation concluded that the incident was a popular "uprising" of the city's "best and even most law-abiding" citizens.

The second worst incident of white-on-white violence took place in a more typical remote settlement in the rural South. On December 25–26, 1891, citizens of Choctaw County, Alabama, killed seven members of the Sims-Savage outlaw gang. Apparently the Sims-Savage band had terrorized the community for many months and had murdered a family the previous December. Robert Sims, the leader, and the four members of the Savage family had been arrested and were being taken to the jail in Butler when a white mob intervened and killed the five captives. The next evening, a mob captured two more members of the gang and lynched them as well.[34] Almost three years later, a similar incident took place in a neighboring county. Over a three-day interval in August 1893, angry citizens of Clarke County lynched four members of the Meacham gang, a band of rogues accused of moonshining, counterfeiting, and murder.[35] Five other members evaded a posse and escaped into Mississippi. In these cases, some members of the white community felt that the miscreants were either beyond the grasp of the formal system of criminal justice, as was the Meacham gang, or that the judicial system had failed to reach an adequate solution to unacceptable behavior.

Being in the hands of the authorities did not preclude mob violence, as the lynchings of the eleven Italians in New Orleans and of the Sims-Savage gang in Alabama illustrate. In fact, we estimate that over half (52.5 percent) of white victims were seized while in the custody of lawful authorities. Typical of this type of violence was the 1892 lynching of Charles Stewart. Stewart was awaiting trial in the Perry County, Arkansas, jail for criminally assaulting a ten-year-old girl. Not wanting to trust his fate to blind justice, Stewart tried to escape and killed Deputy Sheriff Holmes in the process. On May 21, a mob took Stewart from the jail and hanged him, but before dying he implicated his three uncles, the McArthur brothers, in the abortive jailbreak. Apparently, the McArthurs had encouraged Charles Stewart to kill the jailer and flee Perry County. The local sheriff arrested the three brothers and was delivering them to Little Rock when a mob abducted the brothers and lynched them as well.[36]

Another representative incident took place in Tennessee. A white woman of DeKalb County accused Charley Davis of assault. On Friday, August 2, 1901, friends and relatives of the accuser snatched Davis from the courthouse and hanged him.[37] An Arkansas mob abducted John Coker and Dr. Flood, a dentist, from the Yell County Jail in Danville on the night of September 8, 1883. The mob took the pair to the iron bridge across the Petit Jean River and hanged them from the center span. Coker had been suspected of leading a sheriff's posse into an ambush several weeks before, and Dr. Flood had been accused of sheltering outlaws.[38] As these incidents testify, white lynch mobs were not hesitant to storm jails or seize civil authorities in order to capture accused white offenders.

One might think that after the judicial process was complete, defendants would have little concern for popular justice, but this was not always the case, as W. H. Hardin of Clinton, Arkansas, discovered. Hardin had been found guilty of murder and sentenced to be hanged by state authorities. For reasons that are not clear, the governor commuted his sentence to twenty-one years in prison. Outraged at this turn of events, a mob of fifty well-armed masked men broke into the Van Buren County jail on April 17, 1899, secured the jailer and a guard, then obliterated Hardin's head with shotgun blasts.[39] Also illustrative is the case of J. V. Johnson of Wadesboro, North Carolina. Johnson had been accused of murdering his brother-in-law, but the jury was unable to reach a unanimous decision. At about 2:00 A.M. on May 28, 1906, a mob acted more decisively and hanged Johnson until he was dead.[40] Fellow North Carolinian John Starling did not fare any better. He had been charged and tried for the murder of his mother-in-law and nephew to inherit their property. Although acquitted on those charges, he was still suspected by many in the community, and recently he had made threats against a local citizen. On Saturday night, May 24, 1890, Starling was shot to death by a throng of masked men.[41]

We argued above that a partial explanation of black-on-black lynching was the hesitation of white police, white prosecutors, white judges, and white juries to address (at least to the satisfaction of blacks) crime within the black community. Clearly, the same argument cannot be applied directly to white-on-white lynchings unless we substitute the element of social class for that of color. It is possible that some less advantaged whites perceived the formal judicial system as being nonresponsive or too lenient toward white-on-white violence among the lower class. If there was a class bias in the effectiveness of the formal system of criminal justice, it could have provided a strong motivating factor for mob violence, especially considering that the formal system indulged lynch violence in general.[42]

Within the white community, like the African American community, persons believed to have committed incest, fratricide, spouse abuse, or related offenses against the family were sometimes punished by kin and family confidants. There may have been strong cultural values placed on keeping kinship offenses private and relying on those most immediately involved to sanction the malefactor, rather than depending on some distant judicial body for amends. We estimate that 13 percent of the white victims had been accused of family-related offenses. For example, a man named Barker of Hurricane Creek, Arkansas, was believed to have murdered his daughter because she wanted to marry a young man of whom he disapproved. Barker's neighbors took the law into their own hands and hanged Barker in his front doorway.[43] A similar fate awaited Redden Williams. Williams was en route from Mantua, Alabama, to the jail in Eutaw when he was killed by a mob of vigilantes on May 8, 1896.[44] He had been accused of raping his daughter.[45] William Herring of St. Francis, Arkansas, allegedly murdered his young wife, Julia, and her lover in December 1887. Trying to escape Arkansas, Herring fled north but was captured by a band of vigilantes and hanged.[46]

White Brutality

The NAACP's *Thirty Years of Lynching* documents the ruthlessness with which white mobs treated blacks, but mobs could also be unmerciful with victims of their own color.[47] A case in point is that of George Corvett, a white resident of Crittenden County, Arkansas. Ada Goss of Crawfordsville was raped and murdered, and Corvett stood accused of the foul deed. After being interrogated by a mob, Corvett's wife admitted that her husband was guilty of the outrage against Mrs. Goss. On February 13, 1890, the mob took George Corvett to the scene of the murder, amputated his arms and legs with a barnyard ax, and then summarily decapitated him.[48] The Polk brothers of Pike County, Arkansas, did not die a lenient death either. Having been charged with murder, the two brothers were incarcerated in the iron cage jail of Murphreesboro. On Sunday night, September 6, 1885, a mob attacked the keep, piled wood around the caged men, and "roasted the prisoners alive."[49] A few weeks later, an accused murderer named Churchill was placed in Murphreesboro's old wooden box jail, the previous jail having been destroyed in the lynching of the Polk brothers. On October 20, 1885, a mob soaked the wooden structure with coal oil and set it aflame, burning Churchill to death.[50]

These examples demonstrate that brutality and cruelty were not the special province of white mobs torturing black victims. Although we do not yet understand why some lynchings were particularly horrific, it is safe to say that the dynamics that sometimes led to extreme savagery in conventional lynchings could be present in same-race lynchings as well.

CONCLUSION

We estimate that more than twenty-seven hundred southerners died at the hands of mobs during the lynching era, 1882–1930. Scholars have devoted most attention to episodes of whites brutalizing and murdering African Americans, and rightfully so because eight out of every ten casualties were black victims of white mobs. It is important to remember, however, that mob violence was not always a racist affair—two of every ten victims were killed by mobs of their same color, especially in the early years of the era.

We found that black-on-black mob violence was concentrated along the Mississippi River delta regions of Arkansas and Mississippi and in northwestern Louisiana. There is some evidence that black intraracial lynching was more common in counties where the African American population dominated. This distribution is not entirely surprising because in these "black" counties, the local population may have resorted to popular justice because the white-controlled criminal justice system was notorious for ignoring black-on-black crime.

White intraracial lynchings showed greater geographical dispersion and seemed to be more pronounced in the hinterlands of the South. The most common offense cited by white lynch mobs was murder, and more than half of the victims were abducted from the custody of proper authorities.[51] Like black intraracial lynchings, a significant minority of white lynchings involved offenses against related family members. White-on-white lynching incidents pose a significant problem to explain because whites controlled the formal system of punishment. One interpretation rests on differences in social class within the white community. Possibly some members of the white lower class thought the formal system was too remote or too lax in dealing with deviant behavior in their own community and that the only recourse was the popular justice of the lynch mob, especially when the aggrieved party was kin.[52]

Racial hatred and race-based competition cannot offer plausible explanations for incidents in which mobs lynched victims of their own race. When race did not matter, we must turn to alternative explanations for mob violence. While this portrait of intraracial lynchings is limited in its ability to unearth those alternatives, it does provide intriguing evidence that many same-race lynchings occurred when the white or black communities felt threatened by norm violators in their midst. Either unwilling or unable to rely on legal authorities to punish those violators, whites and blacks got out their ropes and guns.

We have mentioned some differences between intraracial and interracial lynchings, for example, their temporal and spatial distributions. But there were also many similarities. A hypothetical exercise may illustrate this point. Imagine that we know nothing about the race of the lynch victim or the racial composition of the mob—only the circumstances surrounding the event, such as the mob's grievance and behavior. Could we successfully guess whether the incident was interracial or intraracial? We suspect the success rate from a series of such guesses would be greater than 50 percent, but probably not by much. This, we believe, is revealing for it suggests that the black and white communities alike endorsed mob violence as an acceptable method of social control. Vigilantism, then, must have had rather broad legitimacy within southern society.

Was the motivation for intraracial extralegal violence the same within the black and white communities? We believe that it was, but only to a degree. Both communities shared a skepticism that the formal justice system would, or could, punish norm violators to their satisfaction. For whites, this concern may have had origins in their basic suspicion of the southern justice system which also carried over to motivate some interracial lynchings. In addition, less privileged whites may have perceived a special ambivalence by legal authorities toward norm violations within the lower class. For blacks, another layer of explanation is probably required. Formal avenues of social control, where they existed, were controlled by whites who were little concerned about crime within the African American community as long as it victimized only blacks. In both cases, then, blacks and whites perceived a special need to resort to a supplementary variety of punishment that enjoyed wide acceptance in the region.

Why, then, did same-race mob violence decline earlier than the more typical white-on-black lynching? We can suggest an explanation based on two fundamental, and related, factors: increased and improved legal alternatives for punishment and the tight connection between interracial lynchings and the southern "race problem." As the southern region developed, especially after the turn of the twentieth century, the formal avenues of punishment became more widely established. As a rule, disorder and lawlessness, including intraracial crime and extralegal violence, became more serious threats to the social order and those who were empowered to enforce it. That is, lawlessness challenged institutional power and strengthened the incentive for authorities to take intraracial offenses more seriously. As a result, the motivation for intraracial lynchings weakened. Why did not interracial lynchings respond in the same way? Primarily, we suggest, because white-on-black lynchings were so intimately intertwined in the broader race conflict and competition that extended far into the new century. As we have suggested elsewhere, interracial lynchings were linked to maintaining white dominance, socially and economically, rather than to victimization of whites at the hands of black criminals.[53] Because interracial lynchings served this broader southern agenda, they continued to be tolerated by the legal authorities even though the latter were probably perfectly capable of squelching such mob activity.

We offer these speculations about the motivations for intraracial lynchings and their decline for our readers' consideration. And they must be considered only that—speculation. By presenting these ideas, however, we hope to have placed them on the agenda for future research into mob violence.

NOTES

1. See Stewart E. Tolnay and E. M. Beck, *A Festival of Violence: An Analysis of Southern Lynchings, 1882–1930* (Urbana: University of Illinois Press, 1995), for detailed statistics and a description of the data used in this chapter. Classic studies of lynchings include Jessie Daniel Ames, *The Changing Character of Lynching: Review of Lynching, 1931–1941, with a Discussion of Recent Developments in This Field* (Atlanta: Commission on Interracial Cooperation, 1942); James E. Cutler, *Lynch-Law: An Investigation into the History of Lynching in the United States* (New York: Longmans, Green, 1905); Arthur Raper, *The Tragedy of Lynching* (Chapel Hill: University of North Carolina Press, 1933); and Walter White, *Rope and Faggot: A Biography of Judge Lynch* (1929; rpt. New York: Arno Press, 1969). More recent work includes the comparative studies of W. Fitzhugh Brundage, *Lynching in the New South: Georgia and Virginia, 1880–1930* (Urbana: University of Illinois Press, 1993); and George C. Wright, *Racial Violence in Kentucky, 1865–1940: Lynchings, Mob Rule, and "Legal Lynchings"* (Baton Rouge: Louisiana State University Press, 1990), as well as the case studies of Dennis B. Downey and Raymond M. Hyser, *No Crooked Death: Coatesville, Pennsylvania, and the Lynching of Zachariah Walker* (Urbana: University of Illinois Press, 1991); James R. McGovern, *Anatomy of a Lynching: The Killing of Claude Neal* (Baton Rouge: Louisiana State University Press, 1982); and Howard Smead, *Blood Justice: The Lynching of Charles Mack Parker* (New York: Oxford University Press, 1986).

2. See Leonard Dinnerstein, *The Leo Frank Case* (New York: Columbia University Press, 1968); Robert S. Frey and Nancy Thompson-Frey, *The Silent and the Damned: The Murder of Mary Phagan and the Lynching of Leo Frank* (Lanham, Md.: Madison Books, 1988); and Nancy MacLean, "Gender, Sexuality, and the Politics of Lynching: The Leo Frank Case Revisited," in this volume.

3. Although less well known than the Leo Frank incident, the lynching of eleven Italians by a Louisiana mob in 1891 has received some study. See Richard Gambino, *Vendetta: A True Story of the Worst Lynching in America, the Mass Murder of Italian-Americans in New Orleans in 1891* (Garden City, N.Y.: Doubleday, 1977). W. Fitzhugh Brundage devotes a chapter in *Lynching in the New South* to white-on-white lynchings in Virginia and Georgia.

4. The trend has been twice-smoothed statistically to dampen annual variation and more clearly reveal the general trend.

5. See Nancy MacLean, *Behind the Mask of Chivalry: The Making of the Second Ku Klux Klan* (New York: Oxford University Press, 1994); Kathleen M. Blee, *Women of the Klan: Racism and Gender in the 1920's* (Berkeley: University of California Press, 1991); and Kenneth T. Jackson, *The Ku Klux Klan in the City, 1915–1930* (New York: Oxford University Press, 1967), for discussions of the post–World War I Klan revival.

6. Incidents of black-on-black mob violence are those in which blacks were killed by black or racially integrated mobs.

7. The risk of being a lynching victim, however, was about equal. Using 1900 population estimates as a base, there were 2.39 black victims of black mobs per 100,000 black population, as compared to 2.84 white victims of white mobs per 100,000 white population. As a point of comparison, the risk of a black becoming a victim of a white mob was 37.38 per 100,000 black population.

8. The zero-order correlations between the raw, unsmoothed trends are +0.598 between traditional lynchings and black-on-black lynchings, +0.520 between traditional lynchings and white-on-white lynchings, and +0.630 between the trends in black-on-black and white-on-white lynchings.

9. Time-series regression is similar to standard regression except that the units of observation are points in time. See any introductory econometrics textbook for a discussion of the technique and its assumptions. To make this adjustment for the secular trend in traditional lynchings, we regressed each race-specific lynching trend on the smoothed trend in conventional white-on-black lynchings. Then we computed the residuals for each regression. These residuals represent the annual amount each race-specific trend differed from the general pattern of conventional mob violence. The raw residuals were then twice smoothed statistically to reveal the patterns shown in Figure 2.

10. Here we are speaking of incidents or events of lynchings, not necessarily the percentage of victims. Each incident or event may have multiple victims. There were an average of 1.27 white victims per white-on-white incident and 1.15 black victims per black-on-black incident. We will shift between the use of victims and incidents as the discussion requires, but from the context it will be clear whether we are speaking of victims or events.

11. See Tolnay and Beck, *Festival of Violence.*

12. These three states also account for 61 percent of all black victims of black mobs.

13. Georgia's 368 incidents resulted in 423 African American victims of white lynch mobs, 18 percent of the total number of blacks in the South murdered by white mobs.

14. *New Orleans Daily Picayune,* October 25, 1893.

15. *New Orleans Daily Picayune,* December 1, 1903.

16. The correlation between the size of the black population and the number of incidents of black-on-black mob violence is marginally higher, $r = +0.226$.

17. The correlation between the percentage black in the population and the number of black-on-black lynching incidents is $r = +0.313$.

18. Tolnay and Beck, *Festival of Violence.*

19. Brundage cites a case in Virginia (*Lynching in the New South*, 45, 178–79), but in our states there are only three cases in which it is reasonably clear that a black mob

lynched a white victim. All three occurred during the 1880s, one incident each in Mississippi, South Carolina, and Tennessee. In a fourth case, the racial composition of the mob is uncertain. On June 16, 1890, George Swayze was lynched in East Feliciana Parish, Louisiana, for attempting to keep blacks from voting on a lottery issue. Although it might seem safe to infer that the mob was black, it is also possible that other whites were angered by Swayze's effort to keep blacks from supporting their side of the issue.

20. *Montgomery Advertiser*, October 3, 1891.

21. *Jacksonville Times-Union*, June 13, 1899.

22. We have discounted a similar explanation for black lynchings by white mobs because there is little evidence to suggest that the southern criminal justice system was reluctant to punish blacks accused of crimes with alacrity and severity.

23. *New Orleans Times Picayune*, December 18, 1885.

24. *New Orleans Daily Picayune*, October 16, 1908.

25. *Macon Telegraph*, December 11, 1892.

26. *Little Rock Daily Gazette*, July 25, 1885.

27. *Jacksonville Times-Union*, July 21, 1892.

28. Philip Morgan, Antonio McDaniel, Andrew T. Miller, and Samuel H. Preston, "Racial Differences in Household Structure at the Turn of the Century," *American Journal of Sociology* 98 (January 1993): 799–828; Steven Ruggles, "The Origins of African-American Family Structure," *American Sociological Review* 59 (December 1994): 136–51.

29. *Atlanta Journal*, June 8, 1892.

30. *Little Rock Daily Arkansas Gazette*, January 15, 1889.

31. These 224 incidents of white mob violence claimed 284 white lives.

32. See Gambino, *Vendetta*, for a detailed narrative and analysis of this lynching and the general anti-Italian sentiment in New Orleans. This was not the only attack on the Italian population of Louisiana. In 1899, five Italian men in Madison Parish were taken from the sheriff and killed by a mob (*New Orleans Daily Picayune*, July 22, 1899).

33. Gambino, *Vendetta*, 77.

34. *Atlanta Constitution*, December 27, 29, 1891.

35. *Atlanta Constitution*, August 12, 13, 15, 1893.

36. *New Orleans Times Democrat*, May 22, 1892; *New Orleans Daily Picayune*, June 1, 1892.

37. *Memphis Commercial Appeal*, August 3, 1901; *Atlanta Constitution*, August 3, 1901.

38. *New Orleans Daily Picayune*, September 11, 1883.

39. *Memphis Commercial Appeal*, April 19, 1899.

40. *Charleston News and Courier*, May 29, 1906.

41. *Charlotte Chronicle*, May 27, 1890.

42. Unfortunately, we do not have the data necessary to examine this social class thesis empirically.

43. *Memphis Daily Appeal*, August 5, 1883.

44. This victim was listed as Radden H. William in some newspaper accounts.

45. *Columbus Enquirer-Sun*, May 10, 1896.

46. *Memphis Appeal*, December 31, 1887.

47. National Association for the Advancement of Colored People, *Thirty Years of Lynching in the United States, 1889–1918* (1919; rpt. New York: Arno Press, 1969).

48. *New Orleans Times Democrat*, February 14, 1890.

49. *New Orleans Daily Picayune*, September 8, 1885.

50. *Little Rock Daily Arkansas Gazette*, October 22, 1885.

51. As shown in Table 1, 59.5 percent of white victims of white mobs had been accused of murder. White victims were significantly less likely to be accused of rape or incest than were black victims of either black mobs or white mobs.

52. Apologists for antiblack mob violence often alleged that lynchings were instruments of uncontrollable lower-class rabble. We are not advancing the same argument.

53. See Tolnay and Beck, *Festival of Violence*.

Part III

The Cultural Context
of Lynching

When Rebecca West observed in 1947 that white southerners viewed lynching as "a social prophylactic" she
grasped one of the fundamental impulses behind mob
violence.[1] Lynching, she understood, served avowedly
conservative aims by "protecting" white women, racial privileges, and
economic interests—in short, the southern way of life. But despite the
reactionary intent of lynchers, the persistence of lynching across the nineteenth and twentieth centuries demonstrates its adaptability to such profoundly different contexts as, for example, antebellum Missouri and New
South Georgia. The following essays explore some of the diverse cultural
forces that both fueled and gave meaning to collective violence in the
South. The authors of these essays step back from close scrutiny of the
unfolding of specific incidents of violence and instead focus on the sexual
politics, class tensions, political competition, and cultural import of lynching. Taken together, these essays clarify the enduring effects of lynching
on generations of Americans.

Nancy MacLean's essay, a version of her award-winning article, illumi-
nates the central importance of contemporary gender definitions and tensions over sexual politics in the lynching of Leo Frank. In addition to
exploring anew the Leo Frank lynching, one of the most infamous lynchings in American history, her essay deepens our understanding of the
connection between gender, class, extralegal violence, and reactionary
politics in the South. Scholars have long recognized the central role that
anti-Semitism played in the controversy surrounding the Leo Frank case.
But MacLean's nuanced interpretation of the debate over Frank's alleged
crime—the rape of a white factory girl—and of the state's response to it

demonstrates that conceptions of gender fundamentally shaped the motives and behavior of all the parties involved. The Frank case, MacLean explains, was contentious precisely because it became the forum for a heated debate about far-reaching transformations in southern social relations, transformations that extended from the mills of Atlanta to the sharecroppers' cabins of central Georgia. Although her essay focuses on the Frank lynching and its historical context, she implicitly suggests that issues of sexuality and power between the sexes, in conjunction with economic and political inequality, incited generations of southerners to join and sanction lynch mobs and other forms of reactionary violence.

Terence Finnegan's contribution to the collection underscores the relationship between political power and lynching. His essay clarifies the political dimensions of regional variations in collective racist violence by linking the patterns of lynching in Mississippi and South Carolina to the shifting political fortunes of blacks. More important, Finnegan substantiates the arguments of blacks who insisted that lynching was intended to render blacks politically, as well as economically, powerless. The dehumanization of blacks, whether through the savagery of lynch mobs or the rantings of demagogues, was essential to the campaign to deprive blacks of their political voice and rights. While individual lynchings silenced black activists and politicians, the justifications for mob violence simultaneously depicted blacks as unfit for the rights and privileges of full citizenship. Finnegan exposes the absurdity of white claims that extralegal violence against blacks would cease once blacks were rendered politically powerless; in fact, the disfranchisement campaigns of the late nineteenth century provided new pretexts for violence, including violence by newly marginalized whites who vented their frustrations on vulnerable blacks. Finnegan's essay illustrates just how willing whites were to use any means necessary to establish their control over the South and how narrow were the openings for black political opposition to lynching. Generations of southern blacks faced the daunting challenge of devising ways to protest against white violence while denied the most fundamental guarantor of rights in a democracy—the right to vote. Thus Finnegan simultaneously sheds light on the causes of lynching and the conditions that dictated black responses to their oppression.

Bruce Baker's essay uncovers a previously ignored aspect of the culture of lynching—the lynching ballad. As we struggle to understand how southerners explained lynchings to themselves, we should move beyond the printed page and closely study the full array of cultural artifacts of lynching. Along with photographs of lynchings and relics taken from lynching sites, ballads represent one of the enduring folk representations of lynching. Drawing upon the methods of folklore studies, Baker uncovers the origins and describes the stylistic forms of several lynching ballads in North Carolina. His findings are yet another reminder of the myriad ways in which lynching both gave expression to and shaped the folk cultures of the South. For example, while representing a distinctive genre, lynching ballads share important traits with other genres such as execution broadsides and murdered-girl ballads. Baker enriches his account by incorporating recent cultural studies about the role of cultural expression in the creation of a social memory. Just as we cannot understand fully a lynching without a nuanced understanding of the precipitating circumstances and context, so too we cannot understand the repercussions of a lynching without taking into account the power of lynching ballads and other cultural forms to transmit the meaning and passion of the event across generations. Baker's pathbreaking essay should be a catalyst for a search for all cultural texts related to lynching, including ballads and other song forms. Only then will we understand fully how tightly lynching was woven into the culture of the South.

NOTE

1. Rebecca West, *A Train of Powder* (New York: Viking, 1955), 77.

Gender, Sexuality, and
the Politics of Lynching
The Leo Frank Case Revisited

Nancy MacLean

The trial and lynching of Leo Frank have long fascinated historians and popular audiences alike. A Jewish, northern-bred factory supervisor, Frank was accused in 1913 of the murder of Mary Phagan, a thirteen-year-old local white worker in his employ in Atlanta. The killing was grisly; the morning after, Phagan's corpse was found in the factory's basement mangled and caked with blood and grime. Within days, police had arrested Frank, and the lead prosecutor, Hugh Manson Dorsey, soon affirmed his belief in Frank's guilt. Dorsey's certainty persisted throughout the subsequent two years of the case, despite other evidence pointing to the factory's janitor, Jim Conley. A black man with a prior record of arrests for theft and disorderly conduct, Conley might seem the logical target in a society committed to white supremacy and willing to lynch African Americans on the slimmest pretext. Yet for reasons that will become clearer in the course of this essay, a curious reversal of standard southern practice occurred in this case. The prosecutor, the jury, and much of the public not only absolved a black suspect but relied on his testimony to condemn a wealthy white man. As Phagan's minister, who at first believed Frank guilty but changed his mind after the verdict, mused in hindsight, it was as if the death of a black man "would be poor atonement for the life of this innocent little girl." But in Frank, "a Yankee Jew . . . here would be a victim worthy to pay for the crime."[1]

Fostered by sensational press accounts, the case engaged popular interest from the outset. Some ten thousand people turned out to pay homage to Phagan as her body lay in state. Frank's trial, which consumed four months and culminated in a conviction and death sentence, absorbed more attention than any other in the state's history. Over the next year and a half, his attorneys appealed the case all the way through the United States Supreme Court, to no avail. When the last rejection was handed down in April 1915, they shifted to a new strategy: a campaign for executive clemency. This effort inaugurated an impassioned battle—involving hundreds of thousands of people from the state and the nation—over whether the Georgia Prison Commission or the governor, John Marshall Slaton, should commute Frank's death sentence. Ultimately, his supporters won. Citing evidence unavailable to the jurors, Slaton commuted the sentence to life imprisonment shortly before Frank was to hang. This act won the governor accolades from some quarters but produced in others a fury so intense that—as armed masses of people surrounded his home pledging revenge—he became the first state executive in American history to declare martial law for his own protection. Two months later, on August 16, 1915, an assembly of prominent male citizens from Mary Phagan's hometown kidnapped Frank from the State Prison Farm, drove him across the state to the county of her birth, and there carried out the jury's sentence. Their act drew widespread popular acclaim.[2]

That the Frank case aroused such interest among both contemporaries and later scholars is understandable, for in it the central conflicts of early twentieth-century southern history erupted. Some historians, for example, have pointed out that the system of white supremacy and the prevalence of lynching in the New South encouraged the mobs who threatened the governor and murdered Frank. Others have emphasized the anti-Semitism directed against Frank, which made this "an American Dreyfus case." They have argued that this break in the general pattern of lynching—the murder not of a rural African American but of a prominent, metropolitan white—can be explained only in light of the social tensions unleashed by the growth of industry and cities in the turn-of-the-century South. These circumstances made a Jewish employer a more fitting scapegoat for disgruntled whites than the other leading suspect in the case, a black worker. Moreover, in pitting the old Populist leader Tom Watson against the rising urban Progressives who rallied to Frank's defense, the case provided dramatic personae for deep-rooted political conflicts.[3]

Yet one aspect of the Frank case has never received sustained attention: that of gender. Deepening the conflicts other historians have described, gender and sexual themes saturated the outcry against Frank. Although he stood trial on the charge of murder alone, the allegation that he had raped Mary Phagan became the centerpiece of the case against him. The facts, however, were ambiguous. Clear evidence of rape never emerged— but there were indications that Phagan may have been sexually active.

Whatever the facts of her death, the striking point for our purposes here was the determined refusal of wide sections of the state's nonelite adult white population to countenance the latter possibility. Their staunch insistence that Phagan died to preserve her chastity evinced profound concern about changing relations between the sexes and generations and about shifting sexual mores among wage-earning women. The outcry against commutation for Frank can be understood only in light of these contested relations. But these, too, must be viewed in a wider context, for the furor over gender relations and sexuality in turn fueled class hostilities and anti-Semitism.

Indeed, the patterns revealed here have a larger significance. The case constitutes a spectacular instance of a pattern of political mobilization best described as reactionary populism. At first sight, the term appears an oxymoron. Most American historians, after all, associate populism with grass-roots democratic mobilizations and associate reaction with the elite opponents of such initiatives. In most instances, such associations work— but not in all. My purpose is to draw attention to such exceptions: to episodes in which the antielitism characteristic of populism coexists, actually garners mass support for, a political agenda that enforces the subordination of whole groups of people. The mobilization against Frank illustrated this dynamic, which included hostility toward *both* big capital *and* working-class radicalism, the use of extreme racism, nationalism, and religion as alternatives to class explanations and strategies, and, the primary focus of this essay, militant sexual conservatism. My contention is that since changing gender and generational relations contributed so much to the appeal of reactionary populism, sexual conservatism, like class grievances and racial antipathies, should be seen as one of its defining elements.[4]

The concept of reactionary populism also helps make sense of the particular features of the Leo Frank case. First, it highlights the distinction between the elite following of conventional conservatism and the popular basis of the opposition to Frank, which included farmers, small-town merchants and professionals, urban workers, and others who harbored well-founded resentments against large capital and its political representatives, whether liberal or conservative. Second, the depiction evokes both the self-representation of Frank's opponents—who resisted class politics and gathered instead under the mantle of "the people"—and the defensive, restorationist character of their protest. In the end, they sought solutions not in radical change or even substantive reform but rather in anti-Semitism and murder. After describing the context of Mary Phagan's murder, this essay briefly delineates the responses of different groups to the trial and to the subsequent struggle over commutation. It then examines the gender themes of the opposition to Frank and how these contributed to the lynching, the effects of which would shape Georgia politics for years after the murders of Mary Phagan and Leo Frank.

Gender analysis thus opens a new window on the Frank case and the social order that produced it. Through this window, we see more clearly how change and contestation, not stasis and consensus, constituted the very essence of early twentieth-century southern history. Economic development acted as a solvent on older relations of power and authority—between men and women and between parents and children as well as between workers and employers and blacks and whites. The dissolution of the older sexual order produced losses as well as gains. The popular anxieties and resentments thereby created proved multivalent; they made class hostilities at once more volatile and more amenable to reactionary resolution. To observe these operations in the Frank case is to gain insight into the processes by which protean concerns about family and sexuality may help tame and redirect popular opposition to a dominant social order. The inclusion of gender as a category of analysis is thus not an optional flourish but a vital tool to uncover elements upon which both mobilization and outcome hinged.

The setting for the case was, appropriately, Atlanta, the showcase city of the New South. Virtually destroyed during General William T. Sherman's March to the Sea in 1864, Atlanta had resurged as a modern metropolis by the turn of the century. From 1880 to 1910, the number of the city's residents more than quadrupled to almost 155,000. Atlanta's booming and relatively diversified economy fueled this growth. The value of its manufacturing grew by almost ninefold over these years, while the city's position as a major rail center linking the Southeast with the North enhanced its leading role in trade, distribution, insurance, and banking. By 1910, approximately 28 percent of Atlanta's labor force was engaged in manufacturing and mechanical pursuits, 26 percent in commercial activity.[5]

Young women such as Mary Phagan played an important role in this expanding economy, which led the region in the extent and variety of women's labor force participation. The number of female workers aged sixteen and over in the city's manufacturing industries doubled between 1900 and 1919 to more than four thousand, while thousands of others staffed its burgeoning white-collar and service sectors. Atlanta offered only the most accelerated example of developments taking place as legions of young women entered the region's workforce. More than seven in ten of the South's female industrial workers were under the age of nineteen, according to a 1907 United States Senate study of working women. Of the southern families included in the study, 94.5 percent of those with daughters aged sixteen or older had at least one in the labor force. That the earnings of daughters made up from one-quarter to two-fifths of total household income indicates the extent of their families' reliance on their contributions.[6] The spread of youthful female wage earning broadened the ranks of those who might find personal meaning in Phagan's fate.

The release of daughters from the confining household economy of the rural South signified a wider transformation. The relative decline of the agrarian economy threw older relations of power open to question and stimulated organizing by diverse groups with rival visions for the state's future. In the years after its establishment in 1891, for example, the Atlanta Federation of Trades assumed an active role in city and state politics, backing labor candidates for office and proposing legislation to limit exploitation, promote the health and welfare of working people, and enhance popular control over public institutions.[7] Such efforts unnerved Atlanta's rising urban business elite, who in the years after 1901 sought to centralize power and impose their own concepts of order on the tumultuous, expanding city. Their efforts to supplant elective municipal offices with appointive boards in 1911 and again in 1913 met with stiff opposition from trade unionists and working-class voters, forcing compromises that satisfied no one.[8] Such conflicts influenced both groups' perceptions of the Frank case: workers viewed the mobilization to overthrow his conviction as yet more evidence of the ruling class's contempt for democracy; elites read the clamor for his execution as confirmation of the unruliness of the lower classes and of the need to control them with a firm hand.

In addition to class divisions inside Atlanta, tensions between its elite and the agrarian forces that once dominated the state also shaped responses to the case. Although three-quarters of Georgia's population was still rural in 1910, that margin slipped rapidly as the state's urban population grew by 400 percent over the years 1880 to 1920. Atlanta's numerical growth augmented the power of its business and civic elite, whose Progressive vision of an active, development-promoting central state was anathema to the landed classes. Indeed, in the years preceding Phagan's death, Georgia's town and country interests had clashed repeatedly over such issues as the regional apportionment of taxes and legislative representation. In 1908, for example, farm representatives Tom Watson and Joseph Mackey Brown attacked the Progressive governor Hoke Smith for his efforts to overturn an archaic county-unit voting system that favored rural areas. The two later vilified Governor Slaton for his role in the 1913 enactment of a rural-urban tax equalization measure perceived as a "deliberate attack on landowners." These disputes fed into the Frank case, as Watson and Brown ultimately assumed leadership of the anti-Frank forces while Smith and Slaton came to advocate commutation.[9]

In this highly contentious milieu, Mary Phagan became a symbol capable of unifying groups with a wide variety of grievances. In many ways she was perfect for the role in which Frank's opponents cast her. Just approaching her fourteenth birthday when she was murdered, Phagan was described by her mother as "very pretty" with "dimples in her cheeks."[10] And indeed, her widely publicized picture depicted an attractive, engaging young woman, whose appearance contrasted so starkly with her brutal fate that people were moved to outrage. "The killing of Mary Phagan was *horrible*," one Athens, Georgia, woman declared to her brother. "I hope the right man will be found and *not* hung or killed but *tortured to death*."[11]

While Phagan's death produced almost universal horror, particular details of her short life appealed to different audiences. The descendant of an established Piedmont farm family that had lost its land and been reduced first to tenancy and then to wage labor, she emblemized the plight of rural Georgians.[12] Having started factory work at a very young age to help support her widowed mother and five siblings, Phagan also personified the bitter dilemma of the region's emerging industrial proletariat, forced to rely on children's wages to make ends meet. Her reported membership in the First Christian Bible School and her destination the day of the murder, the annual Confederate Memorial Day parade, endeared her as well to rural conservatives none too supportive of landless farmers or organized labor. Indeed, farm employers vexed over the flight of their tenants might find in Phagan's fate ammunition for their efforts to dissuade would-be migrants to the city.[13] Yet not everyone would rally around Phagan. Blacks, Jews, and the urban, white, gentile elite reacted to other aspects of the case of more direct concern to them. For blacks that aspect was racism, for Jews anti-Semitism, and for members of the urban white elite, potential threats to their class power.

The position of African Americans in relation to the case was difficult. The black press later condemned Frank's lynching as it did all lynching. Yet the evolution of the case did little to endear Frank to African Americans. Several black observers voiced resentment at the outpouring of sympathy for him, in sharp contrast with ongoing white indifference to the outrages suffered routinely by African Americans. What proved most decisive in shaping blacks' attitudes toward the case was the strategy of

Frank's defense: a virulent racist offense against the only other suspect, the janitor Jim Conley. Many elite supporters of commutation for Frank expressed outrage that a white employer was indicted, rather than a black worker with a criminal record, and shock that their appeals to white supremacy failed to rally the jury or the public. When Frank's attorneys based their case on the most vicious antiblack stereotypes of the day and on outspoken appeals to white solidarity, blacks rallied around Conley for the same reasons that Jews rallied around Frank.[14] Thus, whereas gentile whites split on class lines in the case, blacks and Jews responded in a cross-class manner to perceived cross-class threats.

Not only Jews supported Leo Frank, however. Both in Georgia and nationwide, the gentile urban elite in general and its Progressive wing in particular came to espouse clemency for Frank. The support he garnered from leading Georgia Progressives is the more notable because some had earlier campaigned against child labor. That they came to the aid of one of its beneficiaries reflects in part the elitist, social-control impulse some historians have described as characteristic of southern Progressivism.[15] In fact, the concern of elites with the Frank case reflected profound fears about the stability of the social order over which they presided. Time and again, they complained about the spread of "anarchy" and "mob rule" as revealed in the case. "Class hatred was played on" by the prosecutors, Frank's attorney complained in court. "They played on the enmity the poor feel against the wealthy" and encouraged "discontent." A prominent liberal supporter of Frank, the Reverend C. B. Wilmer, observed that "class prejudice" "was perfectly obvious" at every stage in the case and warned of the dangers of pandering to it.[16]

Wilmer's fear reflected his constituency's own class prejudice, which became more candid as the case progressed. In true patrician style, Frank's supporters repeatedly asserted that "the best people" were on his side. Often their elitism was less subtle. Frank's attorney Reuben Arnold, for example, described those who believed his client guilty as "ignorant people," referred to the courtroom audience as "that gang of wolves" and "a vicious mob," and characterized one white worker who had testified against Frank as "the ugliest, dirtiest reptile . . . [whose] habitat was in the filth." So oblivious were Frank's backers to the sentiments of those beneath them in the social order that they hired William J. Burns, the most notorious union-busting private detective in the country, to discredit the case against their client. Burns barely escaped alive from his inquiries in Phagan's hometown of Marietta.[17]

That debacle was but one indicator of how actions by representatives of the employing class in the case escalated working people's hostility. Among Georgia trade unionists, the murder heightened the sense of urgency about ending child labor. They expressed revulsion at the way the city's mainstream press sensationalized the dead girl's miserable fate while ignoring the political economy that sent her, like thousands of other youths, out to work in the first place. "Mary Phagan," proclaimed the *Atlanta Journal of Labor*, was "a martyr to the greed for gain" in American society, "which sees in girls and children merely a source of exploitation in the shape of cheap labor that more money may be made or the product may be disposed at a cheaper price." The unionists' anger was understandable. For almost two decades, the Atlanta Federation of Trades and the Georgia Federation of Labor had made abolition of child labor their preeminent political demand. Yet with the state's planters and industrialists solidly arrayed against them and with scarcely any support from other quarters, they could not secure even the miserable standards achieved in other southern textile states. Indeed, at the time of Mary Phagan's death, Georgia alone among the states allowed factory owners to hire ten-year-old children and to work them eleven-hour days.[18]

If other elements of the Frank case determined the reactions of African Americans and the urban elite, its gender themes appealed to an audience much wider than the ranks of wage earners, a class still in the process of formation and deeply tied to the countryside. Indeed, although historians of the case have assumed that most of the opposition to Frank came from urban workers, research on those who signed petitions against commutation reveals a diverse coalition. Opposition was expressed in all areas of the state, the rural black belt as well as the industrial Piedmont. Of the 36 percent of signers whose occupations could be determined, the overwhelming majority were landholding farmers, followed by renting farmers, merchants, and lower-level white-collar workers. The data no doubt understate the presence of industrial workers and landless farmers, who were more likely to be mobile or uncounted in the census. Nevertheless, they show that the case had meaning not only, perhaps not even primarily, for the dispossessed but also, perhaps especially, for people of small property. And whether they were farmers, shopkeepers, clerks, or wage earners, those most concerned with the gender and sexual issues of the Frank case were gentile whites who had or could anticipate having family ties to female workers. Since relatively few immigrants settled in the South, the families of such working women made up an unusually homogenous group. Most were native southerners, and if they did not work the land, their parents or grandparents had. Through their letters about the Frank case to the governor, the Georgia Prison Commission, and the press, their testimony in court, and their collective public actions, these people left a record of their perceptions of gender, class, and state power. The concerns revealed therein were distinct from those of blacks, Jews, or the white elite.[19]

First, there were the "working girls" themselves. We can sense the vulnerability they felt—and perhaps their anger, too—from the fear and nervousness over Phagan's murder that so disrupted the factory it had to be shut down for the week. In the trial itself, a few female employees took the unpopular step of vouching for Frank's character from the stand. But a score of their peers used the trial as an opportunity to vent grievances and settle old scores by testifying against their former manager.[20] Some women and children, presumably from the working and lower middle classes, participated in the demonstrations against commutation, which pitted them against the prominent women who came to Frank's defense. By and large, however, women's voices were few in the public chorus raised against Frank. Perhaps hesitant to make demands on the state in their own right, they wrote only a handful of the myriad letters against him and rarely signed the many petitions.[21]

The relative silence of women, particularly the young women presumably most directly touched by Phagan's murder, provides a clue as to the nature of the uproar over the case. The compelling issues at stake involved not simply female victimization in a static sense but shifts in the power different groups of men wielded over young women in the new circumstances created by their employment. Older male opponents of Frank exhibited love and concern for their daughters' welfare mingled with anger at having lost control of them. In his agitation against Frank, Tom Watson spoke of female employees as being in the "possession" of their bosses, implicitly equating access to women's labor with ownership of their persons. Some male peers of working girls were likewise inclined to view them as property, albeit of a different kind. This sense of proprietorship was apparent in the common ritual among young men in southern factory neighborhoods of "rocking" or beating up wealthier outsiders who came to poach "their" women. Antipathy toward Frank thus fed on earlier rivalry among men of different classes over access to working-class women.[22]

Indeed, paternalistic outlooks dominated the campaign against Frank. The circular for a mass meeting to oppose commutation billed the event as "a citizen's meeting in the interest of our mothers, sisters, and daughters," presuming an audience of outraged men. One man who warned the governor not to commute the sentence invoked "the citizens of Ga. who have girls" as a distinct political constituency, announcing that "the parents of girls are provoked."[23] These people identified with the victim's family. They implored Slaton, as one forty-nine-year-old farm father put it, to "think of Mary Phagan and her people." "Suppose you had a little girl murdered by such a fiend," another man demanded. He urged the governor to prove himself "a friend and protector to the Little girls of Georgia" by refusing to "let money or anything offered defeat Justice." These men begged the governor to let the sentence stand because, according to one, "our wives and daughter[s] are at stake."[24]

Some spoke as parents who had entrusted their children to employers' custody in exchange for the wages their labor could bring. They were furious at Frank's alleged betrayal of that trust. "A little girl of tender years," fumed Churchill P. Coree, "attacked and murdered by the man to whom she had a perfect right to look for protection." Whereas these fathers saw their own paternalism as benevolent and protective, they saw that of their daughters' employers as exploitative and deeply resented it. Indeed, their inability to protect their daughters signaled their own loss of power, authority, and status in the New South since dominion over one's dependents was the most basic prerequisite of male independence and honor in the yeoman world from which their culture derived.[25]

Frank's alleged use of his class power to gain sexual access to women in his employ further infuriated them. It added humiliation and guilt to their loss of power. Fathers familiar with factories must have known that male supervisory employees could use their control of job assignments to pressure female subordinates into dates and sexual favors. "The factory was a great place for a man with lust and without conscience," one of the prosecuting attorneys reminded the jury. Few needed to be told. One female petitioner for Frank, however, who had taught among mill workers for eighteen years, turned this common sense to unorthodox ends. She urged the governor to commute Frank's sentence on the reasoning that if he *had* assaulted Mary, "the mill boys would have known it to a man, and lynched him before he reached jail." "They have strong class feeling," she explained, "and I know the bitter resentment they feel towards the 'super' who abuses his position in regard to the mill woman." Indeed, in the view of one enraged writer, Frank was a "low skunk white livered hell hound defiler and murderer of infants"![26]

Such anxieties about the sexual prerogatives of class power were rife, in the courtroom and out. Mary Phagan died, the lead prosecutor told the jury, "because she wouldn't yield her virtue to the demands of her superintendent." Another man later drew out the logic of this allegation. Commutation of Frank's sentence, he maintained, would send the "brutes . . . who commit rape on poor girls" the message "that money can do anything." Sexual control of men over women and of parents over daughters thus became the object of class conflict in the case, as nonelite white men acted out their anger at their inability to safeguard the women of their families and class from the predations of the richer and more powerful.[27]

The extraordinary depth of that anger may reflect the fact that the Frank case came on the heels of a massive evangelical campaign against "white slavery." Conducted by the Men and Religion Forward movement, the campaign aimed to abolish the city's protected vice district. One of the leaders of the crusade was Mary Phagan's minister, the Reverend L. O. Bricker. In mass meetings, public visits to the brothel district by ministers and their parishioners, and a dramatic series of more than two hundred newspaper advertisements that ran regularly between 1912 and 1915, the campaign drove home the message that Atlanta's widespread child prostitution industry was the awful fruit of the low wages paid working girls. Promoting an image of prostitutes as naive victims of cunning men, the reformers implored adult residents to take action on behalf of "the fallen girls in their virtual slavery."[28]

The trial itself aggravated concerns about female industrial employment. Testimony about working conditions in the National Pencil Factory—the workplace of Frank and Phagan and the site of the crime—revealed pitifully low pay and precarious employment. More striking, though, were the casual but repeated references to the factory's excruciating filth. Witness after witness described floors that had gone unwashed for years, now steeped not only in oil and dirt but also in blood from the accidents that took place "almost every two weeks," as when the "girls . . . mash their fingers on the machines" or when a machinist "had his head bursted open."[29] Few could remain dispassionate while imagining their own children in this environment.

Other testimony revealed working conditions that degraded women specifically. Operatives described numerous bloodstains near the dressing rooms from "girls whose sickness was upon them." Management assertions that such stains were common "in establishments where a large number of ladies work" no doubt inflamed the anger they sought to allay. Witnesses also reported that only a makeshift divider separated the women's dressing room from the men's. Such conditions outraged those schooled in the myth that southern gender conventions applied to all white women. Even more appalling to them, however, was supervisors' practice of peeking into the women's dressing room to see if any of the women were shirking work.[30]

Frank's alleged involvement in such snooping contributed materially to his downfall. It gave force to the charge of "perversion" that ensured his conviction. Indeed, it was a key piece of circumstantial evidence buttressing the prosecution's case that the murder was an attempt to cover up a premeditated attempted rape.[31] Other such evidence included operatives' testimony that Leo Frank had a "lascivious" character, as well as innuendos about other sexual improprieties: clandestine trysts with prostitutes, homosexual liaisons, and even the bizarre anti-Semitic fantasy that Frank engaged in sexual acts with his nose. The prosecution and press discussed these accusations in titillating detail, producing a kind of folk pornography that aggravated the popular outrage the testimony itself elicited.[32] In a society in which such "unnatural acts" as sodomy and cunnilingus were capital crimes, those who gave credence to the charges saw Frank as a moral pariah.[33]

The allegations of perversion carried weight because the concerns they evoked were so tangible and the symbols they involved so potent among those with ties to female workers. The language of sexuality also offered compelling metaphors for nonsexual aspects of the case, for it best expressed the speakers' feelings of loss of control and impending chaos in their world. References to the "rape of justice" and the "prostitution of the courts" abounded, signifying the sense of intimate, personal violation that changing power relations in society aroused among the losers.[34]

The charge of perversion did not resonate with Frank's opponents as simply a metaphor for social disorder. It also encapsulated class and gender conflicts over the very definition of propriety in the new circumstances of female employment. These conflicts surfaced from the testimony of women workers about perceived sexual harassment by Frank. Their reports that he touched them, called them by their first names, spied on them, and met with them behind closed doors constituted ample proof of his dishonorable character in the view of ordinary working people. Frank's defenders, in contrast, who shared his notions of employers' prerogatives and did not have to endure the unwanted familiarity that communicated inferior status and powerlessness, seemed unable to comprehend the girls' interpretation, much less to counter it convincingly. The closing speech to the jury by Frank's attorney Reuben Arnold was a model of this insensitivity. He expressed astonishment at the charges of sexual misconduct made by the prosecution and annoyance at their "prudish" failure to catch up with the times and be more "broad-minded" about practices such as an employer putting his hand on a female employee's shoulder. He also made a rhetorical effort to belittle the complaints that Frank violated the privacy of the women's dressing room: "Surely a woman isn't so absolutely sacred that you can't ask her to perform her contract . . . and if she isn't doing it, ask her why, and find out why."[35] Arnold's incredulity was the measure of the vast social distance separating him from Leo Frank's opponents.

Yet the gender meanings of the case involved far more than a conflict among men over control of women. In addition to stirring up resentment about the potential sexual power of employers, the case dramatized common adult concerns about the implications of employment for young women's *own* behavior and sexual activity. Among Frank's opponents, the intense, nearly universal insistence that Mary Phagan died "in defense of her virtue" barely camouflaged their anxiety about young women's—perhaps increasingly—active sexual agency. Then as now, it was frequently difficult to separate agency from victimization in that women often experienced men's disproportionate social power most painfully and intimately in sexual relations.[36] This was particularly the case for dependent adolescents like Mary Phagan, not yet fourteen at the time of her death. Their vulnerability notwithstanding, there was nevertheless a liberating potential for these young women in paid labor outside the home, and the sparse evidence available indicates that they themselves perceived and acted upon it, much as their parents feared it.

Unfortunately, historians have been slow to recognize this potential in the South; as a result, our knowledge of its manifestations is limited. The northern bias of women's history and labor history and the male, agrarian bias of southern history have produced—through neglect—the impression of static gender and generational relations in the South. An impressive body of literature now documents the ways young working women transformed gender roles and claimed once-taboo pleasures for themselves in the North and Midwest in the early twentieth century. "But these 'modern' workers, pioneers of a new heterosocial subculture," as Jacquelyn Hall aptly observed, "disappear below the Mason-Dixon line. Here feminist historians find no Sister Carries, no 'women adrift,' no 'charity girls,' only the familiar figures of a reactionary sexual mythology: the promiscuous black woman and the passionless white lady." Hall's pioneering studies show, however, that relations between women and men in southern cities and small towns were indeed changing in these years, in good part because of the spread of female wage earning. This background can help account for the conflicts within and between classes over gender roles and female sexual behavior that surged into view when women workers went out on strike.[37]

Indeed, while the form of women's labor force participation and responses to it may have been different in the South, there seems no reason to doubt that the basic processes were analogous to those in the North. Certainly contemporary southern observers recognized that a transformation was afoot. "The business girl," wrote William J. Robertson in his 1927 survey of the changes that had swept the South since 1900, "is almost as prevalent in the South as she is in the North." Robertson's remark was as much a lament as an observation, for he attributed to "the women themselves," no longer sheltered by "their fathers and brothers," a veritable revolution in relations between the sexes among the younger generation. Female modesty and male chivalry were giving way to a new "frankness and lack of convention," Victorian morality to widely practiced casual sex. Whether or not they sympathized with the developments they witnessed, informed commentators at the time believed that young working women throughout the country were claiming new independence and employing it in pursuit of male companionship and sexual adventure. Evangelist Billy Sunday delivered the same sermons on the sexual transgressions of "working girls" to audiences North and South in the 1910s, confident that Atlantans engaged in the same sins as Yankees.[38]

So the issue of young women's labor was not specific to the Frank controversy. On the contrary, the responses of participants echoed earlier reactions toward female labor voiced by middle-class reformers and male craft unionists. As early as 1891, in a sensational and widely debated article, the journalist Clare de Graffenried portrayed southern mill communities as places that turned the natural order upside down: idle fathers lost their manhood as wives and daughters, their modesty and chastity gone, toiled in the mills. It was not until the turn of the century, however, as the campaign against child labor gained momentum, that contention over gender roles began in earnest. Fear that enforced early adulthood, freedom from parental supervision, and close association with the opposite sex were leading young women astray pervaded the discourse over youthful female labor North and South, particularly after the massive 1907 Senate investigation of female wage earning reported that it did indeed contribute to "immorality" among young working women. In 1910 the Georgia Federation of Labor urged women to stay out of industry; their proper place was in the home and not competing with male breadwinners. At the same time, however, the federation endorsed woman suffrage and equal pay and the Atlanta *Journal of Labor* published regular columns by Ola D. Smith, a labor organizer and working-class feminist, who insisted on women's right to labor and to participate in public life.[39]

These varied, often ambivalent, reactions suggest that female employment acutely tested earlier patterns of paternal authority. Even if she continued to live with her family, a daughter going out to work still had opportunities to assert her autonomy and to make choices about her relations with men that would have been difficult for her grandmother to imagine. By keeping all or part of her wages, by courting or marrying against her parent's wishes, she might not only defy her father's sense of his own prerogatives but also endanger his strategy for family survival. In the classes from which Frank's opponents came, paternal authority was integral to organizing a household's subsistence. Farmers, tenants, wage earners, and small-business people alike had a material stake in control of their children's behavior in this period. Youths made vital contributions to their households' maintenance, whether plowing the family's land, tending its store or garden, supervising younger children while parents worked, or bringing in cash from mill or factory work. Moreover, in the absence of elementary social security provisions from the state, parents had to look to their children for support in old age. Wage-earning daughters threatened not only to affront the cultural values of their parents but also to disrupt patterns of household economy. Such practical concerns informed fathers' desires to regulate their children's behavior.[40] In these new circumstances, the boundaries of male dominance and the methods of its enforcement became open to renegotiation. The Leo Frank case was an episode in that process.

The testimony of women workers during the trial gave cause for parental alarm in this regard. Several witnesses, for example, told of "girls" in the factory "flirting" with male passersby out the dressing room window. Despite orders from management to stop and efforts by disapproving older female employees to prevent the practice, the girls persisted. Reports of the flirtations led at least one father to make his daughter quit the job against her will. Other testimony showed that by bringing young women and men together in daily interaction, the National Pencil Factory, like other factories in the South, became a site of courtship as well as production. Indeed, reports indicated that a few of Mary Phagan's male coworkers had taken a shine to her and that their antipathy to Frank flowed in part from jealousy. Evidence of unwed motherhood and prostitution among some former employees of the National Pencil Factory also came to light. Some young women workers evidently engaged in forms of self-assertion and interaction with men that threatened prevailing gender codes. Revelations of their activities during the trial confirmed common adult fears about the implications of wage labor for the sexual purity of Atlanta's "working girls."[41]

This context helps make sense of an otherwise mysterious aspect of the case: although the sexual accusations leveled against Frank were widely accepted by those who believed him guilty, they lacked foundation. Medical examiners, for example, never found clear evidence of rape. The case initially made by Frank's defense—that Conley had killed Mary in an attempt to rob her—was as plausible as the prosecution's case; indeed, her handbag was never found. By the time of Frank's commutation, moreover, some of the testimony against him had been discredited, and new evidence pointed toward Conley. Nevertheless, the popular desire to believe the rape charge was so great that even Frank's own attorneys ultimately altered their strategy and argued as if a rape had accompanied the robbery they initially alleged as the motive for the crime.[42] For the historian, the question is why the charge of rape won so much credence.

The answer reflects the central role of sexual conservatism in the mobilization against Frank. The belief that Mary Phagan was raped by Leo Frank rather than robbed by Jim Conley can be read in part as a massive exercise in denial on the part of people unwilling to acknowledge youthful female sexual agency. For although there was no compelling evidence of recent or forcible intercourse, there were physical signs that Phagan might not have been a virgin.[43] Once her body had been found and examined, there were two choices: to believe that she had been murdered to cover up a perverse sexual assault that failed to leave the normal evidence or to admit that perhaps she had been sexually active before the day she was murdered and come to terms with the new social reality this scenario represented. Frank's opponents refused to do the latter; their gender code did not allow for such ambiguities. Either a woman was chaste and worthy of protection or she shamed herself and her people, thereby relinquishing her claim to protection.

The mere innuendo that Phagan was unchaste drew howls from Frank's opponents. "Shame upon those white men who desecrate the murdered child's grave, *and who add to the torture of the mother who lost her,*" bellowed Tom Watson, "by saying Mary was an unclean little wanton." Another man condemned Frank's supporters for what he described as their efforts "to portray her character as a strumpet." For all the speakers' sympathy for Mary Phagan as a young virgin struggling against an employer's lust, they would have nothing but contempt for a sexually active Mary Phagan, even as the victim of brutal robbery and murder. Like the scores of young women workers who became unwed mothers or prostitutes, without the halo of innocence and purity Phagan could not have served their purposes.[44]

Frank's accusers' response to the case reflected a longing to ward off the change in sexual behavior that a nonvirgin Mary would have represented. They actively promoted a mythology of Phagan as a sexual innocent who died in a noble effort to defend her "virtue."[45] This mythology registered grievances about contemporary class relations while it harkened back to an ideology of gender relations developed in an agrarian household economy. As a graphic morality play, it offered a way of coping with social change that avoided the complex reality of female sexual agency. And in so doing, it helped old gender and class ideology survive in a new age.

For in death, Phagan became a role model for her peers in a moral tale of epic proportions. She became, in the words of a resolution by an Atlanta union, an example of the girl who, despite her poverty, "yet holds pure the priceless jewel of virtue and surrenders her life rather than yield to the demands of lustful force." The editor of the city's labor paper applauded the union's call for a "shrine of a martyr to virtue's protection." A local minister made even more explicit the instructive power her example was to have. He solicited contributions for a monument depicting "the little factory girl who recently laid down her life for her honor" shown "in the agonies of death." He wanted the statue to stand "on the State Capitol grounds . . . as a lesson to the working womanhood of Georgia who are having to battle their way alone." It was left to the United Confederate Veterans of her hometown, however, with the support of the United Daughters of the Confederacy, actually to build such a monument as "a symbol of the purity of the little virgin." They hoped that in rewarding Mary, "who surrendered her sweet young life to save her honor," they would teach others high esteem for chastity, "that Christian attribute—the crown, glory and honor of true womanhood."[46]

That two organizations devoted to the glorification of the Old South, with its roots in slavery and racist, patrician values, should rally against a white employer rather than a black worker indicates the complexity of the conflicts in the case. And, in fact, although the case raised issues concerning the susceptibility of working-class women to economic and sexual exploitation that a radical labor or women's movement might address, these issues were resolved in a thoroughly reactionary way. Not only did the leaders of the agitation against Frank make a fetish of virginity and deny women's sexual agency; they also demanded "protection" for women by men rather than measures that might enable young women to protect themselves, thus reinforcing the paternalism of male supremacy.[47]

The most graphic illustration of this paternalism was the lynching of Frank by twenty-five men calling themselves "the Knights of Mary Phagan." The name was an obvious appeal to the chivalric tradition that the lynching acted out, a tradition in which, as Jacquelyn Hall put it, "the right of the Southern lady to protection presupposed her obligation to obey." The mob that killed Frank included some of the leading citizens of Phagan's hometown, who had pledged themselves at the time of the commutation to avenge her family's honor. Their act evoked plaudits from many quarters; "no finer piece of Ku-Kluxing was ever known in Georgia," the official state historian later exulted.[48] Most telling was the behavior of the crowd that gathered around Frank's suspended body. One reporter described the scene as being "like some religious rite"; the participants exhibited a "curiously reverent manner" and an air of "grave satisfaction." Phagan's family also endorsed the paternalistic settlement. Indeed, her mother's first public statement after the lynching was that "she was satisfied with the manner of ending the case." Popular sanction for the lynching was further evident in the way it became enshrined in the folk culture of the South. The "Ballad of Mary Phagan," composed during the trial and performed for anticommutation crowds by the popular musician Fiddlin' John Carson, was later updated to glorify her avengers. It was sung for decades afterward in mill communities throughout the region.[49] Frank's lynching thus scored a symbolic triumph for Old South gender ideology, as represented by the Knights of Mary Phagan, over the emerging power of industrial capitalism, as represented by Frank, while the way of life associated with that earlier culture was rapidly losing ground.

In the end, this "chivalrous" resolution of the gender concerns not only expressed the popular malaise that the case revealed. It also helped submerge the radical potential in the popular mood. The paternalistic reaction to the gender issues constituted an integral element of a more general reactionary populist response. The conservative dynamics of this populism were most obvious in the way class antagonisms ultimately were channeled into anti-Semitism and in the way the lynching assuaged popular hostility to the state. But in each case, the power of gender issues contributed to the outcome.

That the Frank case served as a forum for the expression of class enmity has already been demonstrated. Yet as the commutation struggle unfolded, the hostilities of the popular classes toward large capital and its representatives more and more took on an anti-Semitic cast. "Our country has been bartered to the shylocks of high finance," declared one pro-Watson editor, for example, while other Frank opponents denounced "Dirty Jews with thir [sic] Dirty Dollars" and "big Hebrew money."[50] If not all of Frank's opponents shared this approach, none condemned anti-Semitism in forthright terms. As a result, through the active efforts of some and the passive default of others, Jews became the foil for all capitalism's evils, while Georgia's and the nation's most powerful capitalists escaped notice or blame.[51]

To view the anti-Semitic trajectory of the case as a conscious, cynical sleight of hand on the part of leading Frank opponents would be simplistic. Politicians such as Tom Watson and Joseph Mackey Brown, themselves men of substantial property who stood to lose should a genuinely anticapitalist labor movement develop, *did* energetically promote anti-Semitic interpretations of class hostilities. Yet their inclination to view the case in this way came from the petty producer–based political culture they shared with their followers. Indeed, given the antipathy of Populism and producerist ideology more generally to "unproductive" finance capital, with which Jews were particularly associated in the minds of many contemporaries, the potential for anti-Semitic responses to the case existed without the machinations of men like Watson and Brown.[52]

What is most interesting for our purposes here, however, is not the source of this potential but the role gender issues played in its realization. Just as sexual anxieties infused prejudices against African Americans in southern society, so fears about changing gender roles and sexual jealousies combined with class hostilities in the anti-Semitism of the Frank case. Popular associations of Jews with the vice trade and stereotypes about the alleged lust of Jewish men for gentile women made Frank vulnerable as a suspect in the first place.[53] One opponent of commutation for Frank informed the Prison Commission that "there is two things most of them [Jews] will do. One is they will steal or make or have money [and] the other is this[:] do every thing posible [*sic*] all through life to seduce our Gentile Girls and Women." Tom Watson, who had recently added anti-Catholicism to his arsenal, implied that Jewish employers had a penchant for taking sexual advantage of women akin to that he alleged against papal priests. He described the factory as " 'a Jewish convent as lascivious as a Catholic monastery,' " a belief some of his readers endorsed. Years later a Ku Klux Klan writer, complaining of supposed "outrages inflicted upon innocent girls by Hebrew libertines," referred back to the Frank case as evidence.[54] Anti-Semitism thus provided simple answers for the complicated questions of changing patterns of class power and female sexuality. Capitalism was a good social system, unless manipulated and deformed by Jews; young women were pure, asexual beings, unless lured into depravity by treacherous racial others.

While anti-Semitism deflected economic class hostilities, the lynching itself defused political class hostilities. Popular distrust of the state apparatus and suspicion that it was becoming a tool of the wealthy emerged early on in the controversy over commutation. Over and over again, Frank's opponents decried the elite's control of political affairs and denounced class injustice in the court system. Governor Slaton's commutation of Frank's sentence confirmed these beliefs. "As usual," one writer put it, "the rich have triumphed over the poor, the strong over the weak, those who neither toil or spin over the working people. . . . God help the poor; the rich take care of themselves."[55] And Frank's opponents were right that immense amounts of money and power, resources to which Mary Phagan's people had no access, were marshaled on his behalf, and the governor did yield to this power and override the authority of a duly constituted jury. Georgians could readily interpret Slaton's disregard for the decisions of the jury and the appeals judges as reflecting a larger pattern in which the state in Georgia by the early twentieth century served capital, usually to the detriment of other classes. Not only did the government exclude all women, most blacks, and many poor whites from the electorate and deny them all but rudimentary education and welfare. It also bolstered the power of wealth through violent opposition to strikes, through class and race privilege in the court system, and through vagrancy, contract and lien laws that limited workers' and tenants' freedom of movement.[56]

Yet rather than proposing substantive measures to redress class injustice, Frank's opponents instead sought solutions in a political ideology developed under conditions that no longer existed. They directed their hopes toward the restoration of a now-mythical republican state in which "the people"—white, male heads of household in the producing classes—controlled a government of limited powers. The rationale for the lynching expressed this reactionary populist ideology. Frank's opponents viewed vigilante activity as a legitimate exercise of popular sovereignty when state policy no longer reflected the citizenry's will. They equated the killing of Frank with a tradition of popular mobilization against the powerful in the service of "justice." The Knights of Mary Phagan were but the latest in a line that included Christ driving the money changers from the temple, Martin Luther and the early Protestants, the *sans culottes* of the French Revolution, and the Boston Tea Party. "*All power is in the people*," explained Tom Watson in a paean to the "righteous wrath" of the "Vigilance Committee" that murdered Frank. "When the constituted authorities are unable, or unwilling to protect life, liberty, and property," he averred, "*the People must assert their right to do so*."[57] Many Frank opponents defended the lynching on the grounds that by "rob[bing] the law of part of its terror," as one petition put it, the commutation of his sentence encouraged disrespect for the law and promoted "anarchy" and "mob rule." In other words, the act of the mob, in administering the stern punishment prescribed by the courts, would achieve the *conservative* goal of preserving fear of the law. Taking Frank's life would ensure order, stability, and respect for property.[58]

Here again, though, conceptions of gender contributed to the motives and the rationale. They influenced the sanction given to the lynching and to the model of state power it represented. Punishment for alleged rape served as the ultimate justification for lynchings in southern society in general and for this lynching in particular. "Any man," explained one writer after the commutation, "who has very much family pride in their hearts, would be in favor of mob law, under the circumstances." Another wrote that if Frank's sentence were commuted, "if there shall be left in Georgia, men who love their wives, their daughters, and their state, they will wipe out, with gun-powder and leaden bull, the stain on Georgia's name, that she didn't have men enough to protect her courts and her women." Indeed, the editor of one up-country newspaper insisted, fear of lynching was all that kept would-be rapists at bay.[59] Defending the Knights of Mary Phagan, James G. Woodward, the labor-backed mayor of Atlanta, voiced the factually inaccurate but eminently useful white apologia for lynching: "When it comes to a woman's honor, there is no limit we will not go to avenge and protect it." This culture of "honor" had material roots in the historical role of patriarchal authority in the household economies of plantation slavery and yeoman farming in the preindustrial South. It drew its emotional power from the intersection of white supremacy and female subordination. It was a profoundly reactionary creed in that it aimed to buttress both hierarchies against the leveling potential of social change. Through the lynching of Frank, it scored a symbolic triumph over the emerging culture of "Mammon" associated with industrial capitalism by meting out honor's "ultimate punishment" (death) for honor's "ultimate offense" (rape).[60]

The reactionary populist resolution of the case also had a more tangible impact on the state's public life, sparking turmoil reminiscent of the 1890s. Criticism of Frank's lynching thus led one small-town editor to explode that "the common people" were "tired of having orders dished out to them by a bunch of kid glove politicians and city editors." He denounced Frank's supporters as "the same gang that has practiced gag-rule for so long . . . that has ridden roughshod over the people . . . that stole the election from Watson" in 1894 and crushed the Populist movement for which he then campaigned. The scale of such rage, which involved not merely polemical attacks but also crowds threatening Jewish businesses and burning the governor in effigy, terrified elite Georgians. "You can have no conception of the situation [here]," Frank's attorney Luther Z. Rosser informed an associate after the lynching. "Public opinion has never been so wild, so unreasonable, and so savage"; "the hatred and bitterness here now is inconceivable." The unrest unleashed by the commutation and the lynching upset the state's economy and endangered its prospects for outside investment. It also delivered a severe blow to the ambitions of the urban political elite with which Rosser, like Slaton, was associated. This group had no doubt about the source of their predicament. "The real cause of all the present trouble is Tom Watson," as Rosser summed up the consensus. The conclusion appeared simple: "Georgia [has] to put her foot down on Watson. . . . [She has to] crush him as a political power for all time in this state."[61]

The state's leaders failed utterly in this endeavor, their inability to reestablish hegemony a measure of the potency of the conflicts unleashed by the Frank case. Rather than destroying Watson, they themselves suffered stinging reverses. Slaton's commutation of Frank's sentence proved the end of a once promising political career. Watson's candidate for governor, Leo Frank's prosecutor Hugh Manson Dorsey, swept the polls in the primaries after Frank was lynched, trouncing his establishment-backed rivals in one of the largest electoral victories in Georgia's history. Although the results stunned elite observers, no one doubted that the Frank case had made Dorsey governor. Rebuffed at the polls, Watson's opponents fell back on more circuitous strategies to undermine his influence, including having him prosecuted by the federal government on charges of obscenity for his political journalism and trying to expel him from the state Democratic Party. These behind-the-scenes efforts, too, yielded only humiliating defeats for their orchestrators, as Watson tapped an undreamed-of reservoir of popular support that shielded him from their power and within a few years catapulted him to a seat in the United States Senate. From this august post, he would defend the second Ku Klux Klan from its critics. In fact, this organization, whose might by the mid-1920s surpassed that of any other right-wing movement in American history, gained direct impetus from Watson's agitation in the Frank case. In short, although the victory proved Pyrrhic—in the long run tragic—for many of their supporters, the forces of reactionary populism had scored a significant triumph over their establishment adversaries, the consequences of which would resound for years.[62]

There were many reasons why the potent conflicts involved in the murder of Mary Phagan and the uproar over Leo Frank took the direction they ultimately did. Cases of female sexual victimization, in part because of the reality of women's vulnerability in our society, may be particularly prone to conservative manipulation and repressive panaceas. Then, too, other features of contemporary southern life made a reactionary outcome likely: the region's repressive political economy, the racial divisions that undermined coherent class loyalties, and not least, the sway of the demagogic politicians that the one-party South produced in abundance, who used populist rhetoric to gain support but opposed militant trade unionism and political radicalism.[63] The key point for this essay, however, is that the Frank case could never have incited the passions it did without changes in female behavior and family relations as the context and without the charged issues of sexuality and power between the sexes and generations as the trigger.

NOTES

A slightly different form of this essay, with fuller citations, appeared as "The Leo Frank Case Reconsidered: Gender and Sexual Politics in the Making of Reactionary Populism," *Journal of American History* 77 (December 1991): 917–48. For their helpful comments on that work, I thank Edward Ayers, Leonard Dinnerstein, Maureen Fitzgerald, Joyce Follet, Jacquelyn Hall, Jackson Lears, Gerda Lerner, Leisa Meyer, David Thelen, and especially Linda Gordon.

1. L. O. Bricker, "A Great American Tragedy," *Shane Quarterly* 4 (April 1943): 90. For other reasons many whites believed Jim Conley, see Leonard Dinnerstein, *The Leo Frank Case* (New York: Columbia University Press, 1968), 45–46, 53. Illustrating how live the Frank case remains, in 1983 Alonzo Mann came forward to swear that seventy years before, while an office boy at the National Pencil Factory, he had seen Jim Conley toting Mary Phagan's lifeless body to the basement. Terrified by Conley's threats and silenced by his parents' fears, he said, he never came forward until his own death seemed imminent. Mann's statement encouraged the Anti-Defamation League to file for a posthumous pardon for Frank. For these developments, see Steve Oney, "The Lynching of Leo Frank," *Esquire*, September 1985, 90–104.

2. For details of the case, see Dinnerstein, *Leo Frank Case*; and Clement Charlton Moseley, "The Case of Leo M. Frank, 1913–1915," *Georgia Historical Quarterly* 51 (March 1967): 42–62.

3. On the episode's anti-Semitic content against the backdrop of the industrialization of the South, see Dinnerstein, *Leo Frank Case*; and Steven Hertzberg, *Strangers within the Gate City: The Jews of Atlanta, 1845–1915* (Philadelphia: Jewish Publication Society of America, 1978), 202–15. On its connection to the defeated Populist

movement of the 1890s, see C. Vann Woodward, *Tom Watson: Agrarian Rebel* (New York: Macmillan, 1938). On the response of blacks, see Eugene Levy, " 'Is the Jew a White Man?': Press Reaction to the Leo Frank Case, 1913–1915," *Phylon* 35 (June 1974): 212–22. For popular treatments, see Harry Lewis Golden, *A Little Girl Is Dead* (New York: World, 1965); and Charles Samuels and Louise Samuels, *Night Fell on Georgia* (New York: Dell, 1956).

4. I develop this argument at greater length in a study of a related movement, the Ku Klux Klan of the 1920s, which was spurred by the Leo Frank case. See Nancy MacLean, *Behind the Mask of Chivalry: The Making of the Second Ku Klux Klan* (New York: Oxford University Press, 1994).

5. Hertzberg, *Strangers within the Gate City*, 28, 98; Blaine A. Brownell, *The Urban Ethos in the South, 1920–1930* (Baton Rouge: Louisiana State University Press, 1975), 5, 11–17; Kenneth Coleman, ed., *A History of Georgia* (Athens: University of Georgia Press, 1977), 233; Thomas M. Deaton, "Atlanta during the Progressive Era" (Ph.D. diss., University of Georgia, 1969), 1–2, 15–18.

6. Julia Kirk Blackwelder, "Mop and Typewriter: Women's Work in Early Twentieth-Century Atlanta," *Atlanta Historical Journal* 27 (Fall 1983): 21; U.S. Department of Commerce, Bureau of the Census, *Fourteenth Census of the United States Taken in the Year 1920*, Vol. 9: *Manufactures, 1919: Reports for States* (Washington, D.C.: U.S. Government Printing Office, 1923), 268–69; U.S. Department of Labor, Bureau of Labor Statistics, Bulletin 175, *Summary of the Report on Condition of Woman and Child Wage Earners in the United States* (Washington, D.C.: U.S. Government Printing Office, 1916), 16–17, 19–20.

7. For contemporary perceptions of the transformation of the region, see William J. Robertson, *The Changing South* (New York: Boni and Liveright, 1927). For such perceptions in Georgia, see Steven Wayne Wrigley, "The Triumph of Provincialism: Public Life in Georgia, 1898–1917" (Ph.D. diss., Northwestern University, 1986), 30–40. On labor's response, see Mercer Griffin Evans, "The History of Organized Labor in Georgia" (Ph.D. diss., University of Chicago, 1929).

8. Deaton, "Atlanta during the Progressive Era," 386, 399; Franklin M. Garrett, *Atlanta and Environs: A Chronicle of Its People and Events*, 3 vols. (1906; rpt. Athens: University of Georgia Press, 1954), 2:602, 611; Eugene J. Watts, *The Social Bases of City Politics: Atlanta, 1865–1903* (Westport, Conn.: Greenwood Press, 1978), 21; Evans, "History of Organized Labor in Georgia," 276. On Atlanta's "commercial-civic elite," see Brownell, *Urban Ethos in the South*.

9. Wrigley, "Triumph of Provincialism," 31, 40 (on population), 230. See also ibid., 107, 122, 178, 212–17, 232–35, 250.

10. Brief of Evidence at 1, *Leo M. Frank v. State of Georgia*, Fulton County Superior Court at the July Term 1913, Atlanta Miscellany, Special Collections Department, Robert W. Woodruff Library, Emory University, Atlanta. The original transcript has not survived, but both the prosecution and the defense accepted the Brief of Evidence as a correct account and relied on it in subsequent appeals, beginning with the Supreme Court of Georgia, Fall Term 1913. See Dinnerstein, *Leo Frank Case*, 222–23.

11. Helen Newton to Edwin D. Newton, May 2, 1913, Box 5, Carlton-Newton-Mell Collection, Special Collections Department, University of Georgia Libraries, Athens.

12. Mary Phagan's family's roots in Cobb County were emphasized in a petition against commutation from a mass meeting there to the governor. See "Hearing before

Gov. John M. Slaton re: Commutation of the Death Sentence of Leo Frank, Atlanta, Ga., June 12–16, 1915," 41, Atlanta Miscellany.

13. Thomas Watson, "The Official Record in the Case of Leo Frank, a Jew Pervert," *Watson's Magazine* 21 (September 1915): 256. For farmers' complaints about the rural labor shortage, see Wrigley, "Triumph of Provincialism," 128–30, 249–51.

14. On blacks and the Frank case, see Eugene Levy, " 'Is the Jew a White Man?' " See also Hertzberg, *Strangers within the Gate City*, 207–8. For examples of the racism of Frank's defense, see Reuben Arnold, *The Trial of Leo Frank: Reuben Arnold's Address to the Court on His Behalf*, ed. Alvin V. Sellers (Baxley: Classic, 1915), 51–52, 64, 67; "Hearing before Gov. John Slaton," 141–43; C. P. Connolly, *The Truth about the Frank Case* (New York: Vail-Ballou, 1915), 88, 93; *The Frank Case: Inside Story of Georgia's Greatest Murder Mystery* (Atlanta: Atlanta Publishing Co., 1913), 132. For the response of Jews to the anti-Semitism directed against Frank, see Dinnerstein, *Leo Frank Case*; Golden, *A Little Girl Is Dead*; and Hertzberg, *Strangers within the Gate City*.

15. For a list of Frank supporters in Georgia, see "Georgia Letters and Petitions for Commutation of Sentence for Leo M. Frank to Life Imprisonment," Box 5, John Marshall Slaton Collection, Manuscripts Division, Georgia Department of Archives and History, Atlanta.

16. Arnold, *Trial of Leo Frank*, 35. See also *Atlanta Constitution*, October 26, 1913, reel 2822, A. D. Lasker to Jacob Billikopf, December 28, 1914, reel 1069, and Louis Marshall to Herbert Haas, December 24, 1914, reel 1069, Leo Frank Collection, American Jewish Archives, Cincinnati, Ohio. For Wilmer's statement, see "Hearing before Gov. John Slaton," 75. For a similar pattern, see David L. Carlton, *Mill and Town in South Carolina, 1880–1920* (Baton Rouge: Louisiana State University Press, 1982), 246.

17. For a reference to the "best people," see *Forsyth Advertiser*, July 9, 1915, reel 2824, Frank Collection. For a listing of Frank supporters headed "Names That Count for Much," see *Augusta Chronicle*, December 18, 1915, supplement, 29–30. Arnold, *Trial of Leo Frank*, 12, 21, 30, 42–43. On the episode of William J. Burns, see Dinnerstein, *Leo Frank Case*, 100–101; Jacquelyn D. Hall, "Private Eyes, Public Women: Images of Class and Sex in the Urban South, Atlanta, Georgia, 1913–1915," in *Work Engendered: Toward a New History of American Labor*, ed. Ava Baron (Ithaca, N.Y.: Cornell University Press, 1991).

18. *Atlanta Journal of Labor*, August 1, 1913, 6, May 2, 1913, 4; Evans, "History of Organized Labor in Georgia," 229; Elizabeth H. Davidson, *Child Labor Legislation in the Southern Textile States* (Chapel Hill: University of North Carolina Press, 1939), 69–88, 194–214; A. J. McKelway, "Child Labor in Georgia," *Child Labor Bulletin* 2 (August 1913): 54–55. Interestingly, a recent study of a major Atlanta labor dispute that coincided with the Frank case concluded that "the Atlanta labor movement remained remarkably free of anti-Semitism" through these events. See Gary M. Fink, *The Fulton Bag and Cotton Mills Strike of 1914–1915: Espionage, Labor Conflict, and New South Industrial Relations* (Ithaca, N.Y.: ILR Press, 1993), 88.

19. For a portrayal of Frank's opponents as ignorant, fanatical workers, see Dinnerstein, *Leo Frank Case*; and Leonard Dinnerstein, "Atlanta in the Progressive Era: A Dreyfus Affair in Georgia," in *The Age of Industrialism in America*, ed. Frederic Cople Jaher (New York: Free Press, 1968), 127–59. The generalization in the text is based on

information in the 1910 federal manuscript census population schedules about signers of petitions against commutation (now in the Slaton Collection). For counties and
breakdowns, see MacLean, "Leo Frank Case Reconsidered."

20. Brief of Evidence at 39, *Leo M. Frank* v. *State of Georgia*; Arnold, *Trial of Leo
Frank*, 35.

21. For glimpses of women's participation on both sides, see *Augusta Chronicle*,
June 23, 1915, 1; *American Israelite*, March 26, 1914, reel 2822, Frank Collection;
Nathaniel E. Harris, *Autobiography* (Macon: J. W. Burke, 1925), 361. Almost all the
women who wrote letters against commutation did so as mothers of female workers.
See Mrs. Henry L. Ozburn to John M. Slaton, June 22, [1915], reel 2, Leo Frank
Correspondence, Special Collections, Brandeis University Library, Waltham, Mass.;
"A Mother" to Mr. Davidson, n.d., and "A Mother" to John M. Slaton, November 23,
1914, Box 35, Slaton Collection; Esther Gerald to Slaton, May 26, 1915, Box 45, ibid.

22. Watson, "Official Record," 284. See Delores Janiewski, *Sisterhood Denied:
Race, Gender, and Class in a New South Community* (Philadelphia: Temple University
Press, 1985), 128; Jacquelyn Dowd Hall, James Leloudis, Robert Korstad, Mary Mur-
phy, Lu Ann Jones, and Christopher B. Daly, *Like a Family: The Making of a Southern
Cotton Mill World* (Chapel Hill: University of North Carolina Press, 1987), 223–24. On
other forms of class rivalry among southern men over women, see Victoria Byerly,
*Hard Times Cotton Mill Girls: Personal Testimonies of Womanhood and Poverty in the
South* (Ithaca, N.Y.: ILR Press, 1986), 114; and the richly evocative short story "The
Old Forest," in Peter Hillsman Taylor, *The Old Forest and Other Stories* (Garden City,
N.Y.: Dial Press, 1985). For an excellent overview of the sexual politics of labor history,
see Ava Baron, "Gender and Labor History: Learning from the Past, Looking to the
Future," in *Work Engendered*, ed. Baron, 1–46.

23. *Augusta Chronicle*, June, 11, 1915, 1; A. J. Cash to Slaton, June 14, 1915, Box 45,
Slaton Collection; *New York Times*, June 25, 1915, reel 2822, Frank Collection. For
explicit appeals to readers' concerns for their daughters' sexual vulnerability, see
Thomas E. Watson, "The Celebrated Case of the State of Georgia v. Leo M. Frank,"
Watson's Magazine 21 (August 1915): 196, 230.

24. See, e.g., W. S. Lancaster to Slaton, December 29, 1914, Box 45, Slaton Collec-
tion; T. B. Hogan to Slaton, R. J. Smith to "Prison commissioners," April 29, 1915, and
W. L. Dubberly to Slaton, Box 35, ibid.; A. J. Cash to Slaton, June 14, 1915, and R. C.
Wilson to Slaton, Box 45, ibid.

25. Churchill P. Goree to Slaton, June 1, 1915, Box 45, Slaton Collection. See also
"A mother" to Mr. Davidson, n.d., Box 35, ibid.; Mrs. H. Bolton to Prison Commis-
sioners, May 31, 1915, Box 45, ibid. On the culture of "honor," see Edward L. Ayers,
*Vengeance and Justice: Crime and Punishment in the Nineteenth-Century American
South* (New York: Oxford University Press, 1984), 10–29, 274–75.

26. Frank A. Hooper, quoted in *Frank Case*, 109. On sexual harassment in the
mills, see Byerly, *Hard Times*, 121; and Hall et al., *Like a Family*, 253, 314–15.
Louise A. Lane to Slaton, May 15, 1915, Box 35, Slaton Collection; "A Georgian" to
Slaton, June 23, 1915, reel 2, Frank Correspondence.

27. *Argument of Hugh M. Dorsey, Solicitor-General, at the Trial of Leo M. Frank*
(Macon: N. Christophulos, 1914), 145. See also Minnie Weldon to editor, *Watson's
Magazine* 21 (December 1915): 108–9; W. R. Pearson to Slaton, May 27, 1915, Box 45,
Slaton Collection.

28. "An Advertising Campaign against Segregated Vice," *American City* 9 (July 1913): 4; "How Atlanta Cleaned Up," *Literary Digest* 46 (May 3, 1913): 1012–13; Harry G. Lefever, "Prostitution, Politics and Religion: The Crusade against Vice in Atlanta in 1912," *Atlanta Historical Journal* 24 (Spring 1980): 7–29. For the nationwide agitation over "white slavery," see Joanne Meyerowitz, *Women Adrift: Independent Wage-Earners in Chicago, 1880–1930* (Chicago: University of Chicago Press, 1988), esp. 61, 64; Egal Feldman, "Prostitution, the Alien Woman, and the Progressive Imagination, 1900–1915," *American Quarterly* 19 (1967): 192–206.

29. Brief of Evidence at 16, 30, 77, 80, 105–7, 119, 131, *Leo M. Frank* v. *State of Georgia.*

30. Brief of Evidence at 15–16, 30, 35, 119, 172–73, 222, ibid. For similar grievances among other female industrial workers in the South, see Jacquelyn Dowd Hall, "Disorderly Women: Gender and Labor Militancy in the Appalachian South," *Journal of American History* 73 (September 1986): 364.

31. See *Argument of Hugh Dorsey*, 25–27, 139; "Hearing before Gov. John M. Slaton," 87–89; Thomas E. Watson, "A Full Review of the Leo Frank Case," *Watson's Magazine* 21 (March 1915): 238–40; Watson, "Celebrated Case," 184–85; Lucian Lamar Knight, *A Standard History of Georgia and Georgians*, 2 vols. (Chicago: Lewis, 1917), 2:1121–22; Harris, *Autobiography*, 350; and Dinnerstein, *Leo Frank Case*, 19.

32. Brief of Evidence at 50–51, 55–62, 165, 222, 223, *Leo M. Frank* v. *State of Georgia*; "Hearing before Gov. John M. Slaton," 146, 148, 187–91; W. E. Thompson, *A Short Review of the Frank Case* (Atlanta: N.p., 1914), 24–25; Watson, "Official Record," 271–73. On reports of rapes and lynchings serving as "folk pornography," see Jacquelyn Dowd Hall, *Revolt against Chivalry: Jessie Daniel Ames and the Women's Campaign against Lynching* (New York: Columbia University Press, 1979), 150–51.

33. Golden, *A Little Girl Is Dead*, 133. One of Frank's lawyers maintained that the charge of perversion was "the very pith and marrow of the case against Frank," for "the minute they said he was a pervert . . . then nothing was too bad" for him ("Hearing before Gov. John M. Slaton," 189–90, also 185–86).

34. See, e.g., Watson, "Official Record," 267, 268, 293.

35. *Atlanta Journal*, August 21, 1913, 1, 7, 9, 11, reel 2822, Frank Collection. See also Arnold, *Trial of Leo Frank*, 36.

36. For discussion of this point, see Ellen Carol DuBois and Linda Gordon, "Seeking Ecstasy on the Battlefield: Danger and Pleasure in Nineteenth-Century Feminist Thought," *Feminist Studies* 9 (Spring 1983): 7–25.

37. Hall, "Private Eyes, Public Women," 245. See also Hall, "Disorderly Women"; and Hall et al., *Like a Family*, 184–236.

38. Robertson, *Changing South*, 126–29; Orie Latham Hatcher, *Rural Girls in the City for Work* (Richmond, Va.: Garrett and Massie, 1930), 41, 83–84; Robert A. Woods and Albert J. Kennedy, eds., *Young Working Girls: A Summary of Evidence from Two Thousand Social Workers* (Boston: Houghton Mifflin, 1913), esp. xiii, 1, 7–8; Ben B. Lindsey and Wainwright Evans, *The Revolt of Modern Youth* (New York: Boni and Liveright, 1925); Mark K. Bauman, "Hitting the Sawdust Trail: Billy Sunday's Atlanta Campaign of 1917," *Southern Studies* 19 (1980): 385–99; William G. McLoughlin, "Billy Sunday and the Working Girl of 1915," *Journal of Presbyterian History* 54 (Fall 1976): 385–99.

39. Clare de Graffenried, "The Georgia Cracker in the Cotton Mills," *Century*

Magazine 51 (February 1891): 483–98. On the ensuing debate, see LeeAnn Whites, "The De Graffenried Controversy: Class, Race, and Gender in the New South," *Journal of Southern History* 54 (August 1983): 449–78. For contemporary perceptions of young working women's immorality, see U.S. Department of Labor, *Summary of the Report*, 273–74, 380–82; Fred S. Hall, "Child Labor and Delinquency," *Child Labor Bulletin* 3 (November 1914): 37–51; and Felix Adler, "Child Labor in the United States and Its Great Attendant Evils," in National Child Labor Committee, *Child Labor* (New York: National Child Labor Committee, 1905), 15. On Smith and on southern craft unionists' uneasiness with unskilled women workers' sexuality, see Jacquelyn Dowd Hall, "O. Delight Smith's Progressive Era: Labor, Feminism, and Reform in the Urban South," in *Visible Women: New Essays on American Activism*, ed. Nancy A. Hewitt and Suzanne Lebsock (Urbana: University of Illinois Press, 1993), 166–98; and Hall, "Disorderly Women."

40. On southerners' reliance on the labor and services of family members, see, e.g., Margaret Jarman Hagood, *Mothers of the South: Portraiture of White Tenant Farm Women* (1939; rpt. New York: Norton, 1977); Allison Davis, Burleigh Gardner, and Mary B. Gardner, *Deep South: A Social Anthropological Study of Caste and Class* (Chicago: University of Chicago Press, 1941), esp. 327–28, 409–10, 413; Herbert G. Gutman, *The Black Family in Slavery and Freedom, 1750–1925* (New York: Pantheon, 1976); John Kenneth Morland, *Millways of Kent* (Chapel Hill: University of North Carolina Press, 1958), esp. 84, 95; Lois MacDonald, *Southern Mill Hills: A Study of Social and Economic Forces in Certain Mill Villages* (New York: A. L. Hillman, 1928), esp. 131; Jennings J. Rhyne, *Some Southern Cotton Mill Workers and Their Villages* (Chapel Hill: University of North Carolina Press, 1930).

41. Brief of Evidence at 20, 23, 173–74, 135, 223, 224, *Leo M. Frank* v. *State of Georgia*; Watson, "Celebrated Case," 200; "Hearing before Gov. John M. Slaton," 94. On workplace-based courting elsewhere in the South, see Byerly, *Hard Times*, 131, 156; Janiewski, *Sisterhood Denied*, 98; Hall et al., *Like a Family*, 86, 140–41.

42. Brief of Evidence at 45–50, 159, 161–64, *Leo M. Frank* v. *State of Georgia*; "Hearing before Gov. John M. Slaton," 11–12. For the change in the case made by Frank's lawyers, see ibid., 10–13.

43. See, e.g., Brief of Evidence at 15–16, 46–50, *Leo M. Frank* v. *State of Georgia*.

44. Watson, "Full Review," 266. See also Watson, "Official Record," 190; J. D. Chason to Slaton, May 31, 1915, Box 45, Slaton Collection. One former Augusta resident pointed out that the red-light districts there were "filled with mill girls"; prostitution was "organized and wide open" with "not the smallest protest on the part of anybody there." "The trouble with Georgia," he concluded, "is that she thinks too little of Mary Phagan alive and too much of Mary Phagan dead" (Edwin W. Walker to editor, *New York Sun*, September 10, 1915, reel 221, Lynching File, 1899–1919, Tuskegee Institute News Clippings File, Tuskegee, Ala.).

45. This is not to deny that Phagan may have been a virgin but to underscore the intensity of the will to *believe* that she was among Frank's opponents and their agency in constructing the meaning of her death. Nor am I using the word "mythology" loosely: as icon, Phagan became part of the folk culture of the South and of mill workers in particular. Her ordeal was recounted in the "Ballad of Mary Phagan," which in several versions circulated through the mill regions of the South in ensuing decades. See Gene Wiggins, "The Socio-Political Works of Fiddlin' John and Moon-

shine Kate," *Southern Folklore Quarterly* 40 (1977): esp. 100–104; Stephen R. Wiley, "Songs of the Gastonia Textile Strike of 1929: Models of and for Southern Working-Class Women's Militancy," *North Carolina Folklore Journal* 30 (Fall–Winter 1982): 94–95.

46. *Atlanta Journal of Labor*, September 12, 1913, 4; J. C. Parrott to editor, *Atlanta Journal of Labor*, September 15, 1913, 4. For similar homilies on Phagan, see Watson, "Official Record," 275, 279, 280; Watson, "Full Review," 257, 266; *Argument of Hugh M. Dorsey*, 76; *Marietta Journal and Courier*, July 16, 1915, 1, 6.

47. "Perhaps if Georgia were more ready to protect by law the honor of young girls," the suffragist Anna Howard Shaw quipped at the time, "and to better the working conditions that menace it, lynch law might not so often be invoked to mend morals by murder" (*Dekalb* [Ill.] *Chronicle*, August 26, 1915, reel 2822, Frank Collection).

48. Hall, *Revolt against Chivalry*, 151; Knight, *Standard History of Georgia and Georgians*, 2:1182–96. On popular support for the lynching, see Dinnerstein, *Leo Frank Case*, 139–46; Harris, *Autobiography*, 368, 371; and L. Z. Rosser to Slaton, September 1, 1915, Box 49, Slaton Collection. Although the identity of the lynchers was said to be known to many, they were never indicted.

49. *Atlanta Georgian*, August 17, 1915, reel 2824, Frank Collection; *Newnan* (Ga.) *Herald*, August 20, 1915, 2; *Atlanta Constitution*, August 21, 1915, 2; Wiggins, "The Socio-Political Works of Fiddlin' John"; Wiley, "Songs of the Gastonia Textile Strike of 1929," 94–95; Olive W. Burt, ed., *American Murder Ballads and Their Stories* (New York: Oxford University Press, 1958), 61–64.

50. *La Grange* (Ga.) *Graphic*, February 14, 1916, and J. M. Gassaway to Slaton, June 6, 1915, Box 45, Slaton Collection; H. O. Durham to R. E. Davison, June 1, 1915, Box 35, ibid. Virtually all of the crowd actions (boycotts, warnings out of town, arson, and so on) after Frank's commutation not aimed at the governor were aimed at Jewish merchants or employers. See the leaflet *Carry Me in Your Purse* ([Marietta] ca. late June 1915) and accompanying letter "To the Citizens of Marietta" and *New Orleans American*, June 23, 1915, 1, 9, reel 2825, Frank Collection; *Augusta Chronicle*, August 29, 1915, 7; *Athens Daily Herald*, October 20, 1915, 1; B. H. Meadows to Nathaniel E. Harris, July 1, 7, 1915, Box 228, Nathaniel E. Harris Papers, Executive Department Correspondence, Georgia Department of Archives and History, Atlanta.

51. Watson, "Full Review," 242; Watson, "Official Record," 262, 267, 292–97; Watson, "Celebrated Case," 222; *Southern Ruralist*, March 15, 1914, reel 2822, Frank Collection.

52. For earlier tensions, see Hertzberg, *Strangers within the Gate City*, 184, 152–53, 163; Thomas D. Clark, "The Post–Civil War Economy in the South," in *Jews in the South*, ed. Leonard Dinnerstein and Mary Dale Palsson (Baton Rouge: Louisiana State University Press, 1973), 160–67; John Higham, "American Anti-Semitism Historically Reconsidered," in *Jews in the Mind of America*, ed. Charles H. Stember et al. (New York: Basic Books, 1966).

53. On these associations, see Hertzberg, *Strangers within the Gate City*, 161–62, 186–87, 214; and Feldman, "Prostitution, the Alien Woman, and the Progressive Imagination," 192–206. Many writers have noted the importance of sexual themes and anxieties in racism, including Lillian Smith, *Killers of the Dream* (New York: Norton, 1978), 27–28, 83–84, 111, 121–22, 124; Hall, *Revolt against Chivalry*, esp. 145; Davis, Gardner, and Gardner, *Deep South*, 24–25; James Weldon Johnson, *Along*

This Way (New York: Viking, 1968), 170, 311–13, 391; Charles Herbert Stember, *Sexual Racism* (New York: Elsevier, 1976).

54. M. M. Parker to Prison Commission, May 31, 1915, Box 35, Slaton Collection. See also G. M. Wilson to Prison Commissioners, n.d., Box 45, ibid.; Jno. H. Wellington to Slaton, June 24, 1915, reel 2, Frank Correspondence. For Watson's statement, see Golden, *A Little Girl Is Dead*, 23. Blaine Mast, *K.K.K., Friend or Foe: Which?* (N.p.: Blaine Mast, 1924), 22, 19.

55. [Name illegible] to Watson, June 25, 1915, reel 2, Frank Correspondence. See also "A Friend of the Just" to Slaton, June 22, 1915, H. L. Williamson to Slaton, June 21, 1915, and H. G. Williams to Slaton, June 24, [1915], ibid.; B. H. Hatfield to Slaton, May 11, 1915, Box 45, Slaton Collection.

56. On the lobbying effort for Frank, see Dinnerstein, *Leo Frank Case*, 117–35; and the correspondence between A. D. Lasker, Julius Rosenwald, and Jacob Billikopf, reel 1069, Frank Collection. For protest against Slaton's usurpation of the jury's role, see, e.g., "General Public" to Slaton, June 22, 1915, W. L. Sikes to Slaton, June 24, 1915, and "The Life Takers" to Slaton, June 24, 1915, reel 2, ibid.

57. Watson, "Official Record," 254, 290–91. For other defenses of the lynching couched in a restorationist, populist idiom, see A. Morgan to editor, *North American Review*, August 1, 1915, reel 2824, Frank Collection; *Marietta Journal and Courier*, August 20, 1915, 6; *Madisonian*, July 16, 1915, 4, August 20, 1915, 4; *Newnan Herald*, August 27, 1915, 1.

58. Omega, Georgia petition, n.d., Box 35, Slaton Collection. See also "Citizens of Troup County" to Slaton, telegram, June 24, 1915, reel 2, Frank Collection; J. D. Chason to Slaton, May 31, 1915, Box 45, Slaton Collection; L. D. McGregor to Prison Commissioners, June 1, 1915, Box 49, ibid.

59. T. B. Hogan to editor, *Augusta Chronicle*, July 28, 1915, 4; Donald Clark to Slaton, May 25, 1915, Box 45, Slaton Collection; *Madisonian*, September 13, 1915, 4. Despite evidence that only a small fraction of lynchings involved allegations of rape, the apologia endured that lynching occurred in retribution for rape. See Ida B. Wells-Barnett, *On Lynchings* (rpt. New York: Arno Press, 1969), 87–88; Walter F. White, *Rope and Faggot: A Biography of Judge Lynch* (New York: Knopf, 1929), 16–17, 54–55, 65–66, 82, 170; Arthur F. Raper, *The Tragedy of Lynching* (1933; rpt. New York: Arno Press, 1969), 9, 20, 50; Johnson, *Along This Way*, 329–30, 365–66; Hall, *Revolt against Chivalry*, 146–49; Ayers, *Vengeance and Justice*, 237.

60. For Woodward's remarks, see *Atlanta Constitution*, August 19, 1915, reel 2824, Frank Collection. For echoes from the incoming governor, Nathaniel Harris, see *New York Times*, August 20, 1915, 5, reel 2825, ibid.

61. *La Grange Graphic*, February 24, 1916, Box 45, Slaton Collection; Rosser to B. Z. Phillips, August 21, 25, 1915, Box 49, ibid.; *Augusta Chronicle*, September 30, 1915, 7, June 22, 1915, 1; Harris, *Autobiography*, 356–61; Dinnerstein, *Leo Frank Case*, 131–33; Rosser to Slaton, September 1, 1915, Rosser to Phillips, September 15, 1915, Box 49, Slaton Collection.

62. *Augusta Chronicle*, October 3, 1915, sec. C, p. 6, September 14, 1916, 1, September 16, 1916, 4. See also Phillips to Jacob Schiff, May 17, 1916, Box 49, Slaton Collection; E. F. Dumas to Brown, May 4, 1914, Box 3, Joseph Mackey Brown Papers, Atlanta Historical Society, Atlanta; Dinnerstein, *Leo Frank Case*, 159. Ironically, once in office, Dorsey became the most forthright critic of lynching ever to occupy the

governor's chair in Georgia. On his latter-day liberalism, see MacLean, *Behind the Mask of Chivalry*, 125–28. For examples of the efforts against Watson and his support, see *Augusta Chronicle*, February 4, 1916, 5; Rosser to Slaton, September 1, 1915, Box 49, Slaton Collection. On the obscenity prosecution, see Fred D. Ragan, "Obscenity or Politics? Tom Watson, Anti-Catholicism, and the Department of Justice," *Georgia Historical Quarterly* 70 (Spring 1986): 17–46. For Watson's encouragement to the second Ku Klux Klan and his campaign and conduct in the Senate, see Woodward, *Tom Watson*, 446, 451–86.

63. On the availability of cases of women's sexual victimization for conservative manipulation, see Judith R. Walkowitz, *Prostitution and Victorian Society: Women, Class, and the State* (Cambridge, Eng.: Cambridge University Press, 1980); and Judith R. Walkowitz, "Jack the Ripper and the Myth of Male Violence," *Feminist Studies* 8 (Fall 1982): 543–76; DuBois and Gordon, "Seeking Ecstasy on the Battlefield." On southern politicians' use of populist rhetoric for conservative ends, see J. Morgan Kousser, *The Shaping of Southern Politics: Suffrage Restriction and the Establishment of the One-Party South, 1880–1910* (New Haven: Yale University Press, 1974), 80, 233–37; Tom Watson, *Socialists and Socialism* (Thomson, Ga.: Press of the Jeffersonians, 1910); Hugh M. Dorsey, *The Record: Upon Which Governor Hugh M. Dorsey Asks Your Support for U.S. Senator* (Atlanta: N.p., 1920), esp. 8–9, in Hugh Manson Dorsey folder, File II, Names Section, General Library, Georgia Department of Archives and History, Atlanta; and the many diatribes against organized labor, framed in racist, populist terms, by Joseph Mackey Brown, Brown Papers.

Lynching and Political Power in Mississippi and South Carolina

Terence Finnegan

I n the last year of his life Frederick Douglass, the great nineteenth-century African American leader, excoriated the white suprema-cist South for using lynching as a means of disfranchising African Americans of their political rights. Douglass dismissed as incredu-lous the claims of white southerners that black males had suddenly be-come menacing rapists. Whites had made no such charge during the Civil War, Douglass noted, when white women were left with black men while white men served in the Confederate army. Given the political climate of the United States in the 1890s, Douglass charged that the old shibboleths concerning black supremacy were no longer believable; so whites created a myth of black criminality to inflict terror on African Americans and to deny them their constitutional rights.[1]

Other black leaders agreed that lynching was inseparably intertwined with the concerns of whites about African American political power. David Augustus Straker, a former candidate for lieutenant governor of South Carolina, first dean of law at Allen University in Columbia, South Car-olina, and an accomplished criminal defense lawyer, claimed that south-ern disfranchisers fabricated the rape complex to "destroy Northern senti-ment in the favor of the Negro by charging him with committing, as a class, the most heinous offense, next to murder." Straker offered no apology for rapes when actually committed but argued that the "true purpose" of lynching was not punishment but to "cast odium upon ... [blacks] ... and thus show unfitness for political suffrage."[2] Black lawyer and newspaper editor Robert C. O. Benjamin insisted that the charge of rape resulted from the "pretended and baseless fear of Negro supremacy" and was nothing less than "an effort to divest the Negro of his friends by giving him a revolting and hateful reputation."[3]

Lynching and violence were, in the words of one scholar, "a sort of final solution" to the problem of black political participation in the South.[4] Of course, whites lynched for a variety of transgressions, both real and imagined, but the unprecedented wave of lynchings that beset the South in the last quarter of the nineteenth century was nothing if not a consequence of emancipation. Emancipation enabled African Americans to strive for social and political equality in the South, a prospect that many white southerners found inherently threatening. Although whites frequently claimed that they tolerated lynching only for the unspeakable crime of rape, in calmer moments they often admitted that racial violence was basically an outgrowth of the social competition among blacks and whites. Former Alabama supreme court justice Henderson Somerville, for instance, claimed that lynchings (and alleged rapes) were few in sections where "the negro vote has been eliminated as a controlling political factor" but numerous where blacks held "the balance of political power."[5] To many white southerners the "negro problem" was essentially a political one, for as one white Mississippian put it, "If the Negro is permitted to engage in politics his usefulness as a laborer is at an end. He can no longer be controlled or utilized." Because the economic well-being of many whites was built on the coercion of black laborers, the white South was "forced to assert its control over him [the black laborer] in sheer self-defense."[6]

The psychological, social, economic, and political elements of white racism merged in lynching, which whites used brutally to subjugate African Americans to white caste conventions and to dehumanize black males so that whites could deny them any semblance of political power. African American leaders bitterly resented the hypocrisy of whites who preached that if rape stopped so too would lynching, even while black men were lynched "for murder, arson, burglary, attempt at murder, impertinence, and also on suspicion of having committed a murder, on suspicion of knowing where a criminal is concealed, and for being a United [S]tates postmaster. Yet the cry goes forth: 'Stop the crime and lynching will stop.'" The political ramifications of lynching were all too apparent to black leaders, who repeatedly claimed that "the lynching habit was simply an expression of . . . race prejudice . . . that it was simply designed to be used against the negro."[7]

Although every lynching was a political statement about the social inferiority of blacks, scholars have been unable to arrive at a satisfactory political interpretation of lynching because they have focused their investigative efforts too narrowly on the so-called power-threat hypothesis. According to this theory, the rate of lynching should have been higher in counties with a higher percentage of black population because the greater the percentage of blacks, the greater the potential for black political dominance. Following this logic, several scholars have tried to prove that disfranchisement had a negative impact on lynching but have found the evidence wanting.[8]

Lynching was political terrorism, but it was predicated primarily upon social rather than political competition. Three years after South Carolina had disfranchised blacks, for instance, the *Saluda Advocate* lamented that it was becoming increasingly difficult for blacks and whites to live with one another in the South. Since the Civil War, the newspaper noted, blacks had been busy educating themselves, expanding their minds, capabilities, and ambitions. Not only were blacks competing with whites for jobs and resources, but the political equality that blacks had received under the Reconstruction amendments had made it even more difficult to keep them in their "place." The *Advocate* concluded that when blacks refused to accept the subservient "place" that whites accorded them, whites readily took "to the shot gun, a primitive remedy but the final and supreme one, and so [did blacks]." The bloodshed and brutality that plagued the South after the Civil War would not dissipate, said the *Advocate*, "while we continue the experiment of trying to hold together in one body of citizenship a race which will always hold itself to be the superior and a race which is less and less inclined each year to accept a place as the inferior."[9]

Efforts to prove that disfranchisement had a uniform negative effect on patterns of lynching are futile because whites never understood the threat that blacks posed exclusively in electoral terms. Furthermore, the notion that disfranchisement would necessarily cause a decrease in lynching ignores the considerable political power that blacks wielded in some areas of the South before disfranchisement and excludes the possibility that disfranchisement could make blacks more, rather than less, susceptible to lynching. Indeed, in parts of both Mississippi and South Carolina lynching became worse after disfranchisement because it constricted the autonomy and independence of blacks, aggravated tensions within the white community, and encouraged whites to use extralegal violence with impunity.[10]

Lynching was one measure of the racial and political conflict in a given region. Before disfranchisement in Mississippi, for instance, whites applied the lessons of lynching most severely in the Republican counties and regions of the state. Tables 1 and 2 show that Republican counties in Mississippi (as measured by the presence of black state legislators) had a higher incidence of lynching than their non-Republican counterparts and

TABLE 1. *Lynching and African American Political Power in Mississippi and South Carolina*

	MISSISSIPPI		
	No. of Counties	Lynching Incidents per County, 1882–90[a]	Lynching Incidents per County, 1891–1900[a]
One or more black state legislators, 1881–90	15	2.1	2.27
No black state legislators, 1881–90	60	1.34[b]	1.9
All counties	75	1.49	1.59
	SOUTH CAROLINA		
	No. of Counties	Lynching Incidents per County, 1881–95[a]	Lynching Incidents per County, 1896–1910[a]
One or more black state legislators, 1881–90	6	.5	1.67
No black state legislators, 1881–90	38	1.6[c]	1.58
All counties	44	1.37	1.59

[a]Excludes lynching incidents known to have been committed by an African American mob.
[b]One county in this category was formed after 1890.
[c]Three counties in this category were formed after 1895.

that Republican regions had over 60 percent more lynchings than non-Republican regions before disfranchisement.[11] Black political power in Mississippi was strongest in the state's richest agricultural region, which intensified white concerns about the possibility of a resurgence of the Republican Party. In South Carolina, conversely, Republican regions experienced fewer than 40 percent of the lynchings committed in non-Republican regions before disfranchisement. Black political power in South Carolina was located in regions of declining economic importance, hence the need to use violence was less apparent than in Mississippi.[12]

The political position of African Americans in Mississippi was more tenuous than in South Carolina, partly because the black population in Mississippi was more concentrated than in South Carolina. Although Mississippi had a higher percentage of black population than South Car-

TABLE 2. *Lynching Incidents in Mississippi and South Carolina Regions*[a]

MISSISSIPPI

Regions with Black State Legislators, 1881–90	Lynching Incidents, 1882–90	Lynching Incidents, 1891–1900	Regions with No Black State Legislators, 1881–90	Lynching Incidents, 1882–90	Lynching Incidents, 1891–1900
Bluff Hills	18	11	Black Prairie	10	13
Old Natchez	24	11	Pine Hills	7	22
Yazoo Delta	26	37	Pontotoc Hills	5	8
Piney Woods	6	12	Red Hills	14	20
Totals	68	72	Totals	42	75

SOUTH CAROLINA

Regions with Black State Legislators, 1881–95	Lynching Incidents, 1881–95	Lynching Incidents, 1896–1910	Regions with No Black State Legislators, 1881–95	Lynching Incidents, 1881–95	Lynching Incidents, 1896–1910
Inner Coastal	5	5	E. Piedmont	13	5
Outer Coastal	7	14	Midlands	6	7
S. Pee Dee	3	5	N. Pee Dee	1	5
			Upper Piedmont	9	7
			W. Piedmont	12	22
Totals	15	24	Totals	41	46

[a]Excludes lynching incidents known to have been committed by an African American mob.

olina, it had only four predominantly black regions compared to seven in South Carolina. The most important of these regions was the Yazoo Delta, which was the center of the postbellum cotton kingdom and was also the bastion of the Republican Party. Unlike the western Piedmont in South Carolina or the Black Prairie in Mississippi, which were rich agricultural regions where minority white populations had quashed black political aspirations during an orgy of Reconstruction violence, the Yazoo Delta had been an undeveloped frontier during the 1870s. Hence chronic violence was unnecessary during Reconstruction.

Racial tension and violence in Republican regions of Mississippi stemmed in large part from demographic changes that occurred after the Civil War. In the years after Reconstruction, a huge influx of black agricultural workers provided the small minority of white planters in the Yazoo Delta with a statewide political influence that greatly exceeded their numbers. Hill farmers from white regions resented this and other inequities and began to demand the exclusion of African Americans from the political process to diminish the power of delta planters. In an attempt to remain in power, conservative Democrats emphasized that if whites divided, blacks would conquer, and thereby revived the specter of "negro domination."[13] Sectional conflict among whites caused racial politics to resurface much earlier in Mississippi than in South Carolina, where the creation of a low-country "black district" in 1882 in combination with the relatively benevolent practices of "tolerant white supremacists" largely defused racial politics until the early 1890s.[14]

The Yazoo Delta was the worst lynching region in Mississippi during the 1880s, but contrary to the protestations of southern apologists, alleged murder rather than the "usual crime" of rape was the driving force behind lynching in the delta. The frontierlike conditions of the delta produced a fluid social structure that enabled some blacks to buy their own land, and thousands of others came to the region with similar aspirations. The heavily black populations of the delta translated into a modicum of black political power as well, and not surprisingly the delta produced more black legislators than any other Mississippi region. Delta whites were keenly cognizant of the overwhelming demographic presence of blacks and often conducted brutal reprisals for race incidents, especially attacks on landlords, that appeared to threaten the prevailing order.[15] Important, too, were the black mobs that lynched with some regularity during the 1880s and made the precarious political and social predicament of delta whites painfully apparent.[16]

In September 1889 the Yazoo Delta experienced its worst violence ever when whites massacred about twenty-five blacks in Leflore County. The outrages in Leflore County grew out of black farmers' attempts to overcome their "peasant status."[17] Under the leadership of Oliver Cromwell, a dynamic black organizer, the Colored Farmers' Alliance in Leflore County became a force for independence among delta blacks. Through personal contact and charismatic speeches, Cromwell convinced many African American farmers to join the Alliance and to trade with a cooperative store some thirty miles south of Leflore County instead of with local white merchants, on whom blacks had traditionally relied for credit and supplies.

Because Cromwell's activities threatened white hegemony, Leflore

County whites worked quickly to undermine his leadership. In August 1889 rumors began circulating that Cromwell had used Alliance membership dues for personal enjoyment. Shortly thereafter Cromwell was threatened with physical harm if he did not leave Leflore County immediately. When black Alliance members resolved to defend Cromwell against aggression, whites feared a race war and Governor Robert Lowry sent the militia to maintain order. Before sending off the troops, Lowry gave a rousing speech in which he told the men that "he was from the crown of his head to the soles of his feet a white man's man, and should always uphold the superiority of the Anglo-Saxon race." Nevertheless, Lowry insisted that he wanted African Americans to have a "fair showing" and justice done.[18]

In apprehending some forty black Alliance leaders, the militia and white posses killed approximately twenty-five blacks, although white authorities never acknowledged the deaths. Whites specifically targeted four prominent leaders of the Alliance, whom they shot and killed. Days after the initial massacre, whites continued to search for other African American leaders and lynched those who resisted. When some blacks burned a white merchant's store to the ground after the merchant refused to sell them ammunition, whites retaliated and hanged four blacks at Shell Mound, ending the African Americans' efforts at resistance. The massacre and lynchings decimated the leadership of the Alliance, and soon thereafter the movement collapsed. Whites brutally crushed the organizational efforts of black tenants to protect their own economic and political interests. But the hopes and dreams of African Americans died hard, and not even the extraordinary bloodshed of the massacre could quell the conflict between whites and blacks for long. A little over a year after the massacre, Leflore County whites found it necessary to lynch two more African Americans: one for killing a merchant in an argument and another for attempting to organize blacks to avenge the first lynching.[19] Despite all the violence, blacks were not cowed back into slavery and refused to submit obsequiously to the will of whites.

Not all Republican regions in Mississippi and South Carolina were as prone to lynching as the delta, however, demonstrating that different historical experiences and precedents resulted in different patterns of lynching. Republican regions and counties in South Carolina, for instance, had relatively few lynchings before the passage of the 1895 disfranchising constitution because African Americans in these locales were relatively independent of whites both economically and politically and because of the declining economic importance of these areas. Republican

Party strength in South Carolina was confined primarily to the low-country regions, which had the highest percentage of black population in the state. Here, especially in the outer coastal plain, African Americans had a strong and well-developed political organization that remained unchallenged until the mid-1880s. These regions had experienced little violence during Reconstruction, partly because of their large black populations but also because they were no longer prime agricultural areas. Many blacks in the low country were able to purchase land, which made them less susceptible to the attacks of whites if for no other reason than that an independent black farmer did not have to deal regularly with a white landowner.[20]

In addition, black majorities in the South Carolina low country were well organized and effectively resisted white aggression on several occasions.[21] In 1883, for example, a mob of one thousand Colleton County blacks threatened to lynch a white store clerk who had killed a twenty-eight-year-old black man of bad reputation in an argument. The standoff was not resolved until a coroner's jury of eight blacks and four whites was impaneled and ruled that the deceased had been murdered by the white man, who came from a prominent family and was a graduate of the Citadel.[22] Such a situation, in which blacks dictated to whites the outcome of a racial confrontation, was unthinkable in the up-country regions of the state and helps explain why low-country regions experienced relatively few lynching incidents before the passage of the 1895 South Carolina constitution that disfranchised black males.

Before disfranchisement in South Carolina, whites were most likely to lynch blacks in non-Republican, tenant-filled regions. Although South Carolina had only one majority white region, the Republican Party did not fare well outside of the low country, particularly in the best agricultural regions such as the western Piedmont. In much of the up-country, whites had vigorously contested black political power during Reconstruction and continued to subject blacks to periodic pogroms for the rest of the century. The high black tenancy rates in up-country regions ensured that the brunt of lynching in South Carolina would always occur there, primarily because of the violent conflict that was a habitual part of white landlord–black tenant relations. In the fifteen years before disfranchisement, nearly three-quarters of all South Carolina lynchings occurred in up-country regions; the corresponding figure for the fifteen years after disfranchisement was about 66 percent.

A series of three lynching incidents in Barnwell County, South Carolina, demonstrates how lynching, even for alleged murder or rape, had political ramifications and eventually encouraged whites to use lynching as a means to instill abject terror among the black population. Barnwell County was within South Carolina's inner coastal plain, a region of moderate Republican strength. On December 28, 1889, a mob of one hundred masked white men broke into the Barnwell County jail during the pre-dawn hours, removed eight black prisoners, tied them to trees, and shot them to death. Two of the victims, Ripley Johnson and Mitchell Adams, were accused of murdering their landlord, James Heffernan, in late October 1889. The other six victims were charged with murdering the son of a plantation owner for whom they worked. In the weeks following the Heffernan killing, three other white men had been either shot or killed by black men, which had aroused "a state of indignant resentment among our [white] people that can be better imagined than described, but cannot be imagined by any one not present in our midst."[23] Rural whites were utterly fearful of black-on-white violence and felt that these racial affronts merited a swift and deadly response.

In the aftermath of the massacre, whites maintained that local blacks had been completely demoralized, but blacks appeared indignant at the funeral of Johnson and Adams a day or so later. Barnwell African Americans regarded the two lynched men as martyrs and had even raised funds to pay for their defense. At the funeral some 550 blacks lined the streets of Barnwell in a demonstration of solidarity. Black women were conspicuous in their rage, shouting and gesticulating wildly and asking "that God should burn Barnwell to the ground." Although Johnson and Adams were buried in the African American cemetery, African Americans refused to bury the other men, claiming that whites had killed them and that whites should bury them. Whites eventually buried the other victims in a potter's field.[24]

Both blacks and whites understood the massacre in political terms. Governor John P. Richardson believed that the massacre proved that the two races must be separated. "Unquestionably the two races cannot live together in peace while both are aspiring to supremacy," he told a reporter. The appeals of African Americans "to Congress to give them [political] control of the South," Richardson insisted, had aggravated the racial antagonisms that were the underlying cause of lynching.[25]

In early January 1890, African American leaders from all over the state assembled at the Bethel Methodist Episcopal Church in Columbia to discuss the Barnwell massacre. A committee consisting of representatives from three-quarters of South Carolina's counties drafted a statement charging that the lynching stemmed not from black-on-white crime but from the pervasive notion "that there are no rights for the negro which a white man, whether worthy or unworthy, is bound to respect, when the observance of these rights is judged by a white man as in any way contrary to his personal views or prejudices."[26] A few weeks later, Barnwell blacks gathered at the county courthouse and passed resolutions recommending that African Americans leave Barnwell for safer locales.

Some three years later, Barnwell County was the scene of another controversial lynching after the fourteen-year-old daughter of prominent white farmer J. D. Baxter was allegedly assaulted on April 14, 1893, by a black man named Henry Williams. Captured in Orangeburg County, Williams was returned to Denmark, where Mamie Baxter identified him on two separate occasions. On April 20, 1893, a mob of several hundred men, including many prominent citizens, broke down the doors to the jail and removed Williams to lynch him. But state senator S. G. Mayfield intervened on Williams's behalf and somehow convinced the mob to allow Williams to spend the night in his office until positive proof was available.

The next morning people began flooding into Denmark from all directions, prompting the mayor to ban the sale of liquor. Some of the crowd took Williams from Mayfield's office and paraded him through the streets for all to see. It was understood that the mob would hang Williams at noon, despite doubts about his guilt. One "hard-featured, horny-handed old farmer" expressed the sentiments of many when he declared, "Gentlemen, Barnwell's reputation is at stake, and by [God] somebody has got to die." About an hour before Williams was scheduled to be lynched, however, "four reputable and well-to-do farmers" arrived from Orangeburg County with an alibi for Williams. When the news about an alibi spread, the mob assembled in front of the jail and demanded that the farmers and Williams be interrogated in their presence. Williams appeared with a broad smile on his face, and he quickly called each of the white farmers by name. Each farmer claimed that he had seen Williams on his land on the day of the crime, and two of them said that Williams had helped them load phosphate on the morning of the attempted rape. After Mayfield and some of the others present conducted a spirited cross-examination, Mayfield asked the crowd for its verdict. Although some still wanted to hang Williams, the general opinion was that he was innocent but should be kept in jail.[27]

The desire among whites to punish African Americans for the alleged crime resulted in the arrest of more than twenty black men in the days following the alleged rape. Mobs assembled daily for over a week in the hope of lynching someone. Consequently, when John Peterson, a local black man who was known to frequent gambling dens and prostitutes, learned that a warrant was out for his arrest, he fled to Columbia and arranged a meeting with Governor Benjamin Tillman. Peterson hoped that Tillman would protect him and hold him in Columbia until his trial occurred. After all, in Tillman's inaugural address of 1890, he had called lynching "a blot on our civilization" and noted that since whites controlled every aspect of the criminal justice system it was "simply infamous that resort should be had to lynch law." After his first term, however, Tillman's views regarding lynching changed. Using antiblack rhetoric for political gain, Tillman gave his unequivocal support to lynching during the 1892 election campaign, saying, "Governor as I am, I'd lead a mob to lynch a man who had ravished a white woman. . . . I justify lynching for rape, and, before Almighty God, I'm not ashamed of it."[28]

When Henry Williams had been threatened with lynching, Tillman sent a private letter to Senator Mayfield intimating that he would do nothing to prevent the crime. After a brief meeting with Peterson, Tillman turned him over to the Columbia police. During his interrogation, Peterson convinced the police of his innocence, but Tillman decided to return Peterson to Denmark anyway. Fully aware of the potential for violence, Tillman sacrificed Peterson for political expediency.

When Peterson arrived in Denmark, a crowd of hundreds met his train at the depot. An impromptu trial was held at the offices of Senator Mayfield, who apparently did what he could to save Peterson. When a committee of prominent citizens brought Peterson before Mamie Baxter, she said that he was not her attacker. After hearing the news of yet another unidentified suspect, the mob became greatly excited, especially when Baxter's father broke down and sobbed that she would never be able to identify her attacker. Despite the tension, Mayfield again convinced the mob to disperse and to return home after promising to have the evidence against Peterson transcribed and read to them.

But some in the mob were unwilling to wait any longer. Shortly after dark, about twenty-five men battered down the jail door and removed Peterson to the scene of the attack on Baxter. Along the way, people jeered and taunted him. At the lynching scene, about two miles from Denmark, a large crowd of citizens, including farmers, laborers, and professionals, gathered around a fire. Some talked of burning Peterson; others wanted to mutilate him. When Mayfield learned that the mob had Peterson, he rushed to the scene and pleaded with them not to lynch the black man. Mayfield's insistence that Peterson was innocent may have persuaded the mob that he should only hang. Six or eight men put a plow line around Peterson's neck and pulled him up over a tree limb. Someone then ordered all present to retreat to the railroad tracks, from where hundreds of men took shots at Peterson's body.[29]

That no evidence existed against Peterson mattered little to those in the lynch mob. They acted not because they wanted to purge the community of a known evildoer but to send a message to African Americans that their lives were outside the pale of the law. Few if any of those present believed that Peterson was guilty, but as one reporter commented, "Barnwell realized that it had to preach a sermon to its negroes and use unmistakable illustrations." The message preached was, in the opinion of one black minister, that the lives of blacks were not their own. Unwilling to accept the consequences of emancipation, which accorded black men the same rights as whites, white men lynched to reaffirm the notion that no black man could challenge the authority, honor, or property of a white man without fearing for his life.

The African American community responded vociferously to the Denmark lynching. On April 26, 1893, five hundred blacks gathered at the Columbia courthouse to denounce Governor Tillman for his complicity in the lynching and to exhort blacks to resist. Resolutions passed at the meeting called Tillman's actions "unwarranted, unprecedented, and inhuman" and charged that the lynching of blacks proved that the state could not protect African Americans, whether guilty of a crime or not. A predominant theme at the rally was that the time for speaking was over and that blacks could no longer wait for a "higher court" to intervene on their behalf. The last speaker to appear, a black mail agent named Shelton, seethed that blacks were "too submissive" and were too dependent on whites for protection. With the blood of Peterson dripping "from the fingers of the Governor," Shelton urged those gathered to "rise up and defend ourselves against mob law and lynchers." Some blacks responded to lynching with political action. After a mob of York County whites lynched Jefferson Crawford in June 1894, for instance, African Americans registered to vote in the "greatest numbers of the past ten years."[30]

The race-based terror that bedeviled Barnwell County culminated in the June 1895 lynching of a sixty-year-old black fisherman named John Barnwell. Barnwell lived alone in a shanty about a mile from Branchville. One Saturday night four white youths came to Barnwell's house, broke down his door, and shot him for no apparent reason. The next morning a constable took Barnwell's dying statement, in which he identified two of the youths involved. The lynching process in Barnwell had reached its natural conclusion. Although whites justified lynching as avenging crime, its larger meaning was always directed at the black community as a whole. That four white youths should murder a lonely and defenseless old black man in his home was entirely reasonable under such circumstances. The four boys involved had, in the opinion of the *Charleston News and Cou-rier*, "learned only too well" the lessons that were taught at the "lynching school in which all boys of the State are being educated."[31]

Ironically, lynching, which was a violent rejection of the concept of black equality, became worse after disfranchisement in both Mississippi and South Carolina. To be sure, lynching activity resulted from a boiling cauldron of social tensions, not just political ones, but in Mississippi lynching incidents increased by a third in the ten years following the passage of the 1890 constitution as compared to the preceding nine years. In South Carolina the situation was similar: lynching incidents increased by 25 percent in the fifteen years following adoption of the new constitution.

One reason why lynching grew worse after disfranchisement was that the court system became one of the last spheres of public life in which blacks had at least theoretical equality with whites. Southern courts were far from benevolent toward black defendants and no doubt became harsher after Jim Crow, but the southern judicial system did not always adhere to the rigid precepts of white supremacy.[32] Even when a case involved the inflammatory charge of rape, the courts (or the state) sometimes acted against the presumed will of the white community. In 1890, for instance, Willie Leaphart was sentenced to death for rape in Lexington, South Carolina, but after evidence surfaced about the veracity of the charge, Governor John Richardson granted Leaphart a reprieve. When the presiding judge ordered Leaphart jailed in Columbia for safekeeping, the local white community became so outraged that they sent a committee of fifteen prominent citizens to request that the governor return the accused to Lexington. After the men pledged their "law-abiding" reputations as a guarantee for Leaphart's safety, the governor agreed to return him but ordered an undercover detective to remain in Leaphart's cell as a precaution. Shortly after Leaphart was returned to Lexington, a mob broke into the jail and shot him in his cell (the detective was wounded in the fracas). The mob adorned the jail with a sign that blamed Richardson and the judge for the lynching. The next day a drunken mob threatened Leaphart's white attorney and his family with violence, apparently in anger over the attorney's defense of Leaphart.[33]

After the removal of blacks from politics, whites began to doubt the wisdom of having courts enact "justice" for other interracial crimes besides rape. Disfranchisement had boldly rebuffed the federal Constitution's claim that blacks and whites were equal, and yet courts still operated under a theoretical premise of equality. Disfranchisement was a salve for the wounded patriarchal authority of white males, but it could do little

TABLE 3. *Most Frequent Alleged Causes of Lynching in South Carolina*[a]

	Regions with Black State Legislators, 1881–95		Regions with No Black State Legislators, 1881–95	
	1881–95	1896–1910	1881–95	1896–1910
Rape-related	46.7%	20.8%	39.0%	21.7%
Murder/assault	–	41.7	29.3	34.7
Murder-related	13.3	–	–	–
Property crimes	20.0	12.5	9.8	8.7
Crimes against women	6.7	4.2	4.9	–
Community crimes	–	–	4.9	4.3
Murder and rape	–	4.2	2.4	–
Racial crimes	–	–	–	4.3
Moral crimes	–	–	–	2.2
Absence of crime	13.3	12.5	–	15.2
Unknown	–	4.2	–	8.7

[a]Excludes lynching incidents known to have been committed by an African American mob.

to prevent intractable blacks from continuing to resist the demands of their alleged superiors. Lynching violently repudiated any notion of black-white equality and served notice that blacks who challenged white hegemony were beyond the pale of the law. It is not without significance that following disfranchisement, which was intended to shore up the power of white males, the primary cause of lynching changed from the purported defense of white female virtue to direct attacks on the persons or interests of white males themselves. This was especially apparent in Republican regions, where disfranchisement had eliminated the need to cry rape. Before disfranchisement whites frequently resorted to lynching for alleged sexual crimes to demonize black males and to show that they were unfit for the franchise. Before 1895 nearly half of all lynching incidents in Republican regions of South Carolina, for example, resulted from alleged sexual assaults, but after disfranchisement only slightly more than a fifth of lynching incidents in these same regions stemmed from alleged sexual crimes (see Table 3). Lynching in retaliation for murder- or assault-related crimes, conversely, increased dramatically from approximately 13 percent of all lynching incidents in the decade and a half before 1896 to nearly 42 percent of all lynching incidents from 1896 to 1910. In Republican

TABLE 4. *Most Frequent Alleged Causes of Lynching in Mississippi*

	Regions with Black State Legislators, 1881–90		Regions with No Black State Legislators, 1881–90	
	1882–90	1891–1900	1882–90	1891–1900
Rape-related	35.3%	22.2%	33.4%	28.0%
Murder/assault	36.8	45.9	28.5	32.0
Property crimes	10.3	9.7	14.3	6.7
Crimes against women	2.9	2.8	2.4	6.7
Community crimes	1.5	–	4.8	5.3
Murder and rape	1.5	1.4	7.1	2.7
Racial crimes	5.9	6.9	–	5.3
Moral crimes	1.5	–	–	1.3
Absence of crime	4.4	5.6	–	12.0
Unknown	–	4.2	9.5	–

regions of Mississippi the same pattern is evident: rape-related lynching declined substantially while lynching for murder or assault-related crimes increased from about 37 percent of all lynching incidents from 1882 to 1890, to approximately 46 percent of all lynching incidents in the decade following disfranchisement (see Table 4).

The removal of black males from politics did not end the "negro question" as whites had hoped and instead sometimes made it more likely that interpersonal confrontations between blacks and whites would end in lynching. The lynching of Cairo Williams is one example of how the conflict between caste and justice, which had always plagued southern courts, became exacerbated after disfranchisement. In February 1904, Williams shot and killed Thurston McGhee, a white farmer, during an argument over an animal trade. McGhee apparently had his eye on Williams's mule and tried to browbeat him into trading the animal for a horse. Williams refused the "offer," but McGhee ordered a companion to take the mule from Williams anyway. When Williams attempted to take his mule back, McGhee hit him several times, knocking him down repeatedly. Terrified, Williams attempted to flee but tripped over a buggy shaft, only to see McGhee charging at him, gun in hand. By this time a crowd had gathered at the scene and had started chanting, "shoot him, shoot him!" Fearing for his life, Williams continued to run, but a group of whites cut him off. In desperation, Williams fired two shots in the direction of McGhee, mortally wounding him. Williams probably would have been lynched on the spot had it not been for the local sheriff, who that night surreptitiously removed him to Kingstree for safekeeping.

Williams was held in Columbia until April, when his trial was scheduled to open at Lake City. In a decision that shocked local white sensibilities, the presiding judge decided that the case should be continued because he claimed that Williams could not obtain "anything even remotely resembling justice" in Lake City. In defending his decision, the judge argued that the courts guaranteed every person equal protection under the law, and, despite feelings in the community to the contrary, it was his duty to "see that substantial justice is done, be the party on trial white or black." The judge admonished the white people in Lake City that they were "doing themselves and their community a great wrong when they allow their feelings to crop out in the presence of the Court and of jurors who must unconsciously be influenced by their neighbors." Under such circumstances, the judge said that it was the fault of the community that a speedy trial was not held. Adding insult to injury, he appointed two of the best lawyers from the Kingstree bar as Williams's defense attorneys and continued the case until the June term of court.

When Williams's four-day trial began in late June 1904, black and white spectators, who for different reasons were intensely interested in the outcome of the case, packed the courtroom. To the disbelief of the white population, the jury was unable to reach a verdict, not because they believed that Williams was innocent but because they could not agree whether he was guilty of murder or manslaughter. A mistrial was simply too much for local whites to bear, and that evening Williams was removed from the custody of officers and shot dozens of times. The court had accorded Cairo Williams the appearance of impartiality and fairness and had thereby affirmed that whites and blacks were equal, at least in the eyes of the law. This notion was obviously antithetical to Thurston McGhee and other whites who used violence to coerce and control the behavior of blacks. A black man who resisted the violent intimidation of a white man was a threat to white ascendancy, and whites responded by lynching not only Cairo Williams but the law as well.

Disfranchisement could also intensify divisions within the white community, providing the impetus for a new wave of lynching. Most of the growth in lynching activity in Mississippi after disfranchisement, for example, occurred in white regions of the state. In regions with no black legislators, lynching nearly doubled from a total of forty-two incidents during the period from 1882 to 1890 to a total of seventy-five incidents between 1891 and 1900. Table 2 demonstrates that in the Piney Woods, the Pine Hills, and the Red Hills, all of which were predominantly white, lynching increased dramatically after the adoption of the constitution of 1890. In these regions the disfranchising constitution helped trigger an unprecedented outbreak of lynching, no doubt made worse by the knowledge that whites could now lynch blacks with impunity. John Tommas, a black tenant farmer from Mississippi, for instance, wrote the Justice Department in 1899 lamenting that because whites had "all the advantage of us We are Shot down for nothing We are killed by the white people in the State of Miss. just like were . . . some . . . pherocious [sic] beast."[34]

Although the severe economic depression of the 1890s undoubtedly contributed to the increase in lynching, political considerations were also important. The suffrage restrictions of the new constitution disfranchised not only blacks but also poor whites, which meant certain defeat for the Populist Party in Mississippi.[35] Denied any legitimate role in the political process, disfranchised whites lashed back by destroying property and terrorizing black tenants, who worked for absentee landlords or upper-class whites. The two white regions that had the most lynching activity in the decade after disfranchisement, the Pine Hills and the Red Hills, also experienced the largest decline in the number of voters between the presidential elections of 1896 and 1900. Disfranchisement exacerbated class tensions that not only sparked an increase in lynching in white regions but also changed the nature of lynching there.

Table 4 details the alleged causes of lynching in political regions of Mississippi both before and after the constitutional convention of 1890. After 1890, the importance of sexual crimes as a supposed cause of lynching declined throughout Mississippi. But in regions where blacks had previously been politically impotent, whites began lynching blacks for no crime whatsoever at an alarming rate. The blatant brutality of mobs that lynched for no apparent reason gave even white Mississippians cause for concern. At long last sensing the threat that terroristic lynching posed to the prevailing order, establishment whites began to condemn lynchings of all types. In the mid-1890s the *Natchez Democrat* decried the number of lynchings occurring in the state and "hoped that some means may soon be derived by which these extra judicial methods may have a stop put to them." The *Jackson Evening News* described lynching as "wrong from beginning to end" and, reflecting its own racist attitudes, commented that the recent increase in brutality "would disgrace the center of Africa." By early 1897 the *Vicksburg Commercial-Herald* counseled African Americans not to feel vengeful over lynching but to "watch and wait" because time would prove Shakespeare's dictum that "'bloody instructions, being taught, return to plague the inventors.'" Until then a black man could console himself, the paper said, "with the thought that for the crime of taking life without warrant or process of law, for the reproach and stain it brings upon the state, he and his race are blameless."[36]

In no white region of Mississippi did the lynching plague prove more deadly during the 1890s than in the Pine Hills. Here bands of white terrorists, known as Whitecaps, wreaked havoc on the lives of African Americans for over a decade. The Pine Hills region was in the southwest portion of the state, immediately to the east of the more fertile Old Natchez lands. Before the great timber boom of the late nineteenth century, much of the land in the region was filled with long-leaf yellow pine trees. Because of the sandy soil, whites with capital considered most of the region nearly worthless for farming, which allowed many African Americans to obtain land in the area.[37] As late as the turn of the century, over 18 percent of all farmers in the Pine Hills were black landowners, the highest percentage in the state.

When northern timber interests began harvesting the region, land values increased by over 40 percent from 1880 to 1890.[38] Higher land values improved the financial position of African American landowners, which earned them the enmity of their Whitecap neighbors. In addition to the relative prosperity of some blacks, whites resented the labor practices of sawmill owners and merchants, both of whom preferred cheap black labor over white.[39]

Merchants also found African Americans more amenable to their needs than white "Cane Hill Billies." Merchants often employed blacks to work farms foreclosed on whites for supplies furnished. Many of the Jewish merchants in the region, moreover, preferred black tenants, who did not usually share the anti-Semitic sentiments of whites. Whites begrudged the good reputation that black tenants had among white merchants, which often made it easier for black farmers to obtain credit than their white counterparts.[40] The relative independence of black tenants who worked for absentee landlords prompted further malevolence among some whites.[41]

Whitecaps threatened and destroyed not only the lives of blacks but also the property of whites, which caused white authorities to respond vigorously to Whitecap terrorism. In early 1893, for instance, Hiller & Co., a Jewish firm in Pike County, Mississippi, claimed that within the previous two months twenty-seven of its houses had been burned and $50,000 in property was destroyed. The company threatened to sue the county for its losses. But even after whites formed "Law and Order" clubs to elimi-nate the Whitecaps, their depredations continued unabated.[42]

From 1891 to 1895 no less than sixteen lynchings occurred in the eight counties that composed the Pine Hills region. After a one-year hiatus in 1896, at least six more lynchings occurred in the region before 1901. Although Whitecaps were not responsible for all the lynchings, they com-mitted at least eleven (50 percent of the total) and possibly more. A typical incident involved Jesse Pittman, an "inoffensive" black man from Marion County, who was shot by ten Whitecaps in the middle of the night while he was sleeping. Authorities charged the men involved with Pittman's mur-der, but a grand jury failed to return an indictment.[43] Historian William F. Holmes has concluded that Whitecaps embodied the "dark side" of Popu-lism, but they should not be separated from other terroristic mobs that operated in the region, especially since Whitecaps reappeared in the early twentieth century, years after Populism ceased to be a viable movement.[44] Terroristic mobs continued to lynch well after the South was politically "solid," often out of a sense of frustration with the prevailing economic and social order.

White mobs often directed their dissatisfaction at African Americans who advocated black equality or at black institutions of advancement. In July 1894, for instance, a group of seventy-three whites from Amite County, among them "some of the coolest of the law-abiding element," lynched a black schoolteacher named Hood, whom whites claimed had insulted the local school superintendent by accusing him of "showing particularity in his appointments[,] discriminating between whites and blacks." Similar to Whitecaps, the mob appointed a small committee to confront the man at a local schoolhouse.[45] The mob claimed that they only wanted to tell Hood to leave the county. Hood apparently thought otherwise and killed the committee spokesman, Nolan Hanks, who was a young man with a wife and three children. After the mob had riddled Hood with bullets, whites held a mass meeting to exonerate themselves and to establish a relief fund for Hanks's widow and their children.

A few weeks later, the terror began anew when whites burned two black schoolhouses.[46] The local white paper blamed the atrocities on "a low down set of whites who are taking advantage of the present state of af-fairs." The paper regretted the violence but said that such incidents could not be helped because God had decreed that "the sons of Ham should be the servants unto their brethren, and it is flying in the face of Providence to disobey a Biblical injunction." The paper claimed that whites as a rule had no hatred for blacks but warned "the negro to respect the white man always and to so live that the white man will respect him." As a final tribute to the violence, Amite County whites established July 2, the day of the lynching, as Nolan Hanks memorial day.[47]

In South Carolina disfranchisement also helped to create a "racialized" social context in which whites increasingly vented their anger and frustrations on blacks. Table 2 shows that total lynching incidents in South Carolina increased by one-fourth in the decade and a half after disfranchisement as compared to the fifteen years before. Over 70 percent of this increase occurred in what had been Republican regions, especially the outer coastal plain. After disfranchisement in South Carolina, lynching became more wanton and terroristic in nature. "No-crime" lynching, for instance, increased from only 3.5 percent of lynching incidents in the years before 1896 to over 14 percent in subsequent years, becoming the third leading cause of lynching in the state.[48]

The lynching of Postmaster Frazier Baker and his young daughter at Lake City, South Carolina, in February 1898 is a striking example of the new realities that disfranchisement created. Lake City was a "white man's town" that had fewer than a dozen black residents, none of whom owned "a foot of land" within the corporate limits of the city. Hence white residents were shocked in September 1897 when Baker, a forty-year-old "coal black" schoolteacher and Colored Farmer's Alliance man from Florence County, was appointed postmaster of Lake City. E. H. Deas, the black deputy collector of internal revenue for South Carolina, had recommended Baker for the job, but trouble began almost immediately after Baker assumed office. Whites complained that Baker was "uncivil, ignorant, and lazy," and they noted that under the previous white postmaster there had been three mail deliveries per day but that Baker managed only one.[49]

Baker did reduce service, but only after whites repeatedly tried to mob him. In December 1897 a postal inspector was sent to investigate the trouble. When the inspector recommended that the office be closed, whites burned the post office to the ground in January 1898, hoping that Baker would be forced to resign because no white person would rent the government space in town. Seeking to ensure Baker's safety, the U.S. postmaster general ordered Baker to restrict mail delivery to daylight hours. After the government acquired an old schoolhouse in the "suburbs," however, some of the racial tension evidently dissipated and Baker felt safe enough to send for his wife and six children in early February 1898. But local whites remained determined to remove Baker from office at any cost, and a week or so after his family arrived they resolved to kill him. A few days before his death, Baker had received new threats on his life, which he had reported to Washington.[50]

On the night of February 21, 1898, Baker awoke to find the post office (which doubled as the family's residence) in flames. He leaped from his bed and tried unsuccessfully to douse the flames lapping at his door with some jugs of water. As he gathered his family, Baker told his son Lincoln to raise the alarm, but as soon as the boy opened the door shots rang out. Realizing the danger, Baker dragged his son back from the door, screamed at the lynchers, and ran back and forth in the small room praying for God's deliverance. When the flames became unbearable, Baker told his wife, Lavinia, that the family "might as well die running as to die standing still." With his family behind him, Baker again started for the door, but before he opened it a bullet struck his two-year-old daughter Julia, who was in his wife's arms, and killed her. After seeing that his youngest child was dead, Baker told the rest of his family to follow him. When Baker opened the door, a barrage of bullets greeted him, and he fell backward on his wife's lap, dead. Lavinia Baker was shot in the arm, but she somehow managed to gather her panicked family, and they crawled out of the house and hid in some nearby bushes. Two of the children, Sarah and Millie, who were seven and five respectively, managed to escape unharmed; but eighteen-year-old Rosa had her left arm broken by a gunshot; fourteen-year-old Cora had a bullet lodged in her right hand; and eleven-year-old Lincoln received a severe abdominal wound and both bones of his right forearm were broken. The family remained in Lake City for three days after the lynching, during which time local whites offered them no medical treatment for their injuries.[51]

National attention surrounding the Baker case prompted some uncommon candor, even among South Carolina newspapers. In a March 1898 editorial, for instance, the *Charleston News and Courier* admitted that the *New York Evening Post* had been correct in asserting that the sole cause of the lynching was that Baker was black. "We do not plead the color of the victims of the mob as an excuse for mob violence," said the paper, "but we simply state the fact as an explanation of such outbreaks of lawlessness." Racism rather than a desire for retributive justice was now at the heart of lynching, according to the *News and Courier*, for it was not "the enormity of the crime, but the color of the victims that controls in such matters." Two days later, the same paper acknowledged that it had been an "easy step" from the tacit and open approval that many "law-abiding men" had given to rape-related lynching to the "lynching of a colored man for no offence whatsoever, except that he had been appointed to the place of postmaster."[52]

Other whites were more recalcitrant, however. The *Saluda Advocate*, for instance, blamed the lynching on the McKinley administration for appointing Baker and said that "we need not expect anything else when black negroes are put in office over white men. . . . We in the South have never stood it, and never will."[53] Although progressive voices like the *News and Courier* could not understand why white mobs would lynch and treat the law with contempt, a more frank appraisal of lynching came, ironically, from the racist editor of the *Abbeville Scimitar*, W. P. Beard. Beard claimed that lynching stemmed from the desire of whites to maintain their "racial integrity," which had been threatened by "a non enforceable constitutional guarantee of equality." Beard dismissed public calls for "law and order" and excuses that "the best people" did not approve of lynching as hollow drivel for northern consumption. "The 'best people' of South Carolina," wrote Beard, "know that when white men cease to whip, or kill negroes who become obnoxious, that they will take advantage of the laxity, and soon make this state untenable for whites of ALL kinds, and that under such conditions the 'best' will be 'like the worst, and the worst like the best.' " Lynching, in Beard's opinion, was the "law of the survival of the fittest," which was higher than any constitutional law and demanded that the "black must submit to the white or the white will destroy."[54] The upsurge in murder- and assault-related lynchings and no-crime lynchings that occurred after disfranchisement confirms Beard's supposition that the primary cause of lynching was the attitude of blacks who refused to acknowledge their inferiority to whites.

Frenzied political racism was also responsible for South Carolina's worst postdisfranchisement lynching incident, the Phoenix election riot, which occurred in the western Piedmont in November 1898. Phoenix was a small hamlet that lay in newly formed Greenwood County, bordering Edgefield and Abbeville Counties. Living in the area since the 1820s was a wealthy family of white Republicans, headed by the sixty-three-year-old patriarch Colonel John R. Tolbert, who farmed over twenty-eight hundred acres of land with the assistance of numerous black tenants. Before the war, Tolbert had not supported secession, but he nevertheless fought for the Confederacy, rising to the rank of colonel. After the war the Tolberts supported Ulysses S. Grant for president, much to the disgust of their neighbors, who reacted so violently that the legislature closed the Phoenix polls in 1868 and did not reopen them until 1897.

Republican administrations in Washington liberally rewarded the Tolberts for their loyalty with patronage plums. In 1898 the elder Tolbert was collector of customs at Charleston, one of Tolbert's sons, Robert "Red" Tolbert, was state Republican chairman, one of his nephews was Republican township leader in Phoenix, and the wife of another of Tolbert's nephews was in charge of the post office at McCormick. The Tolberts' preference for black tenants combined with their "egalitarian beliefs," Republican politics, and privileged status elicited enmity among many whites in the area, especially landless whites struggling against poverty.[55]

The "Ben Tillman Constitution," as African Americans derisively referred to it, had severely weakened the political clout of the Tolberts but not their spirit of independence. In 1898 Red Tolbert united the Republicans behind his candidacy for the Third District congressional seat, which he hoped to contest before the Republican Congress. For weeks before the election Tolbert encouraged all eligible Republicans to go to the polls and tender a ballot. Tolbert prepared blank affidavits for those Republicans denied the right to vote at the polling place, which he intended to use in his case before the House of Representatives. When Democrats learned of the plan, they threatened violence, saying they would rather kill two or three white men "than let the niggers vote and have to kill a whole lot of people later."[56]

Nevertheless, on election day Tom Tolbert, along with an African American bodyguard named Joe Circuit, was at the Phoenix polling place collecting the affidavits of black Republicans who were not allowed to vote. Early in the morning two Democratic enforcers, J. Giles "Bose" Etheridge and Robert G. "Bob" Cheatham, came to the polling place (a dry goods store) to prevent Tolbert from collecting the affidavits. After Etheridge struck Tolbert on the head with a piece of wood, Circuit hit Etheridge with an iron rod. Shooting then broke out, and Etheridge was killed with a bullet through the head. When the crowd of heavily armed whites at the polling place began firing, those blacks present fled in all directions. Tolbert was severely wounded during the shoot-out, but relatives rescued him. Although it was unclear who killed Etheridge (some thought it was Cheatham), whites predictably blamed Circuit for the killing, which precipitated a pogrom against the African American community.

The next day white men from Newberry, Edgefield, Abbeville, and Saluda Counties responded to the call of "Color and Country" emanating from Greenwood. Mobs rounded up eleven blacks accused of wounding three whites in an ambush that occurred the night of the riot at Rehoboth Methodist Church, the church that the Tolbert family had helped establish after being expelled from a Baptist congregation for opposing secession before the war. In the churchyard the mob of three hundred extracted confessions from some of the accused through "such persuasions as a pistol at the ear or a rope around the neck." The mob then ordered the men to sit on a log and opened fire on them. Four of the men were perforated from head to foot with bullets, two others were mortally wounded, but the other five somehow escaped with their lives. One of the men killed was named, ironically, Wade Hampton McKinney, after Wade Hampton, the hero of the "redemption" movement and the patriarch of the South Carolina Democratic Party. The next day whites brought McKinney's father, "Old Uncle" Loudon McKinney, to the church to identify the bodies. Although Loudon McKinney was considered an "old school darkey" and a good Democrat, some of the mob wanted to lynch him simply because "his skin was black." Reporter August Kohn noted that this "anti-negro expression was characteristic of the mob" and pointed out that it was "just such expressions and the final whoops and breaking away of the hotheads that are accountable for the dead and dying in the county."[57]

Earlier that day Kohn had witnessed another lynching at Rehoboth Church. About the time that Kohn had arrived to view the bodies of the first victims, a mob of fifteen or twenty white men came marching down the road with a black man, Essex Harrison, in front of them. The mob ordered the trembling Harrison to stand in front of the stiffened corpses and face them; when Harrison began to move, the mob killed him in an instant, his body falling on top of the others. When Kohn questioned the mob about why they killed Harrison, one member responded that Harrison had gone to Phoenix and voted.

Terror reigned over the area for four days. Bands of whites scoured the countryside in search of African Americans allegedly involved in the riot. Ben Collins and Jeff Darling were lynched in separate incidents on the evening of November 10, 1898, for allegedly firing shots at the Phoenix polling place (Collins was the tenant of a white man who had been elected captain of the Democratic forces at Phoenix). Red Tolbert claimed that two black tenants who worked for his brother Tom were found dead in a pasture, killed by unknown parties. On November 13, 1898, a black woman named Eliza Goode was killed by a shot to the abdomen after a mob fired indiscriminately into her cabin. Black institutions also were singled out for destruction, including one black church that was badly damaged and desecrated.

Although the mobs were motivated primarily by the belief that "an occasional clearing up of the race atmosphere by a killing does good and makes the negro remember his place," class tensions were also evident. A white mob nearly lynched a wealthy white planter named Andrew Stockman, for instance, after Stockman refused to join his neighbors in the pogrom. The mob accused Stockman of renting land to blacks, which he admitted, claiming that black tenants "gave less trouble and were more easily satisfied with their homes." Stockman was apparently saved by the intervention of his wife, who shamed the mob by insisting that they would have to kill her before they killed her husband. Stockman's tenants, however, were not so fortunate. The mob drove them from their homes and in all likelihood lynched some of them.

The threat of class warfare and the fear of losing black labor finally convinced elite whites to end the violence. "Conservative" citizens formed a Committee of Safety, which insisted that the indiscriminate killings must stop. At mass meetings held in Greenwood and Ninety-Six, resolutions passed that agreed "that there must be a turning in the tide, not only because [of] the brutality and shamefulness of further killings, but because . . . further killings will only result in driving away colored labor."[58]

Not even Senator Tillman could deny that the Phoenix lynchings were the result of "race antagonism." In an interview Tillman claimed that under "ordinary circumstances" Tolbert's farcical election campaign would have merited only derision but that the Wilmington, North Carolina, race riot had heightened race tensions. Tillman insisted that the race question was dormant in other parts of the state and added that the disfranchisement of blacks in South Carolina had ensured "as far as possible, a cessation of angry race feeling." But the aftermath of the Phoenix massacre proved otherwise. For a year after the riot, Whitecaps routinely whipped black men and sexually assaulted black women in the hope of driving black families from their lands and securing lower rents. Whites accused blacks who struggled to make a living and to educate their children of promoting the "diabolical doctrine" of social equality. Although Tillman blamed the Phoenix melee on selfish white men like the Tolberts, who interjected race prejudice into politics, he eventually had to visit Greenwood and threaten federal intervention to put an end to the class-based violence that was directed against "poor Negroes who have nothing to do with the Tolberts."[59]

The connection between disfranchisement and lynching escaped Tillman's myopic vision, but it was more than apparent to the *Charleston News and Courier*. The newspaper observed that the white man's constitution gave whites license to kill blacks against whom "no offence was proved or even charged." The paper perceived that a new mob, which no longer rode in the night and wore masks while carrying out its bloody work, had arrived on the scene. Mobs now organized as troops "in full light of day" and not only killed innocent men in churchyards but, even worse, killed women and children. The state was impotent against mobs, which, the paper proclaimed, were "stronger than constitutional authorities." In Reconstruction days, the *News and Courier* reminded its readers, whites had justified lynching "because we were living under what we called 'an alien form of government.'" Now the paper wondered whether whites would continue killing blacks "under our own constitution without let or hindrance."[60]

After 1890 African Americans in the South entered the second stage, as one historian has described it, of their "dark journey," one necessarily concerned more with economic than political advancement. But white supremacy demanded the subservience of African Americans in all phases of life. Now that blacks and many poor whites were excluded from political participation, lynching assumed a new character of indiscriminate violence and increased dramatically in parts of Mississippi and South Carolina that had been relatively free of lynching before disfranchisement. Disfranchisement was not the only cause of this orgy of violence, but it was the most public manifestation of the social and economic tensions that engendered lynching. Whites disfranchised blacks to confirm in law their status as second-class citizens and the alleged "uneradicable differences" between the races.[61] When blacks refused to acquiesce to the dictates of white hegemony, whites would sometimes lynch to sear the sentiments of racial superiority into the consciousness of southern society.

The insidious effects of disfranchisement on lynching were recounted by no less an observer than the African American civil rights activist Ida B. Wells-Barnett, who explained:

> With no sacredness of the ballot there can be no sacredness of human life itself. For if the strong can take the weak man's ballot, when it suits his purposes to do so, he will take his life also. Having successfully swept aside the constitutional safeguards to the ballot, it is the smallest of small matters for the South to sweep aside its own safeguards to human life. Thus "trial by jury" for the black man in that section has become a mockery, a plaything of the ruling classes and the rabble alike. The mob says: "This people has no vote with which to punish us or the consenting officers of the law, therefore we indulge our brutal instincts, give free reign to race prejudice and lynch, hang, burn them when we please." Therefore, the more complete the disfranchisement, the more frequent and horrible has been the hangings, shootings, and burnings.[62]

The disfranchising constitutions were but a part of the hardening of racism that occurred during the Jim Crow years. But the constitutions enshrined the color line in the highest law of the state and thereby strengthened the notion that whites could treat African Americans as they pleased. The removal of many poor whites from the political process, moreover, unleashed a reaction of terroristic violence that was aimed not only at African Americans but also at the privileged whites for whom they worked. Whites disfranchised African Americans because of their supposed inferiority, but they lynched when African Americans challenged the myths that sustained white supremacy and refused to accept the social, economic, and political constraints that white racism demanded.

NOTES

1. Philip S. Foner, *The Life and Writings of Frederick Douglass* (New York: International Publishers, 1955), 491–524; also see Herbert Shapiro, *White Violence and Black Response: From Reconstruction to Montgomery* (Amherst: University of Massachusetts Press, 1988), 37–38.

2. D. Augustus Straker, *Negro Suffrage in the South* (Detroit: The Author, 1906), 35. On Straker's accomplishments in South Carolina, see George Brown Tindall, *South Carolina Negroes, 1877–1900* (Columbia: University of South Carolina Press, 1952), 43, 48, 145–47, 232; also see J. Clay Smith Jr., *Emancipation: The Making of the Black Lawyer, 1844–1944* (Philadelphia: University of Pennsylvania Press, 1993), 218.

3. Quoted in George Wright, *Racial Violence in Kentucky, 1865–1940: Lynchings, Mob Rule, and "Legal Lynchings"* (Baton Rouge: Louisiana State University Press, 1990), 67. For a similar interpretation, see Oliver C. Cox, *Caste, Class and Race* (1948; rpt. New York: Modern Reader Press, 1970), 559–60. In 1887 Robert Charles O'Hara Benjamin was the first black admitted to the bar in California, and he reportedly had practiced law in twelve other states, including Virginia and Alabama. In San Francisco Benjamin was editor of the *Sentinel*, a black paper that advocated "political conciliation" with whites. See Smith, *Emancipation*, 232, 272, 485, 522 n. 15.

4. Cox, *Caste, Class and Race*, 555. See, e.g., Frederick D. Wright, "The History of Black Political Participation to 1965," in *Blacks in Southern Politics*, ed. Laurence W. Moreland, Robert P. Steed, and Tod A. Baker (New York: Praeger, 1987), 9–30; and David C. Colby, "White Violence and the Civil Rights Movement," ibid., 31–48.

5. Henderson M. Somerville, "Some Cooperating Causes of Negro Lynching," *North American Review* 177 (October 1903): 509–10. Somerville was a Democrat who served on the Alabama Supreme Court from 1880 to 1890. In 1873 he founded the law school at the University of Alabama. See *National Cyclopaedia of American Biography* (New York: James T. White, 1898–1984), 18:220.

6. Quoted in John L. Love, "The Disfranchisement of the Negro," in American Negro Academy, *Occasional Papers No. 6* (Washington, D.C.: American Negro Academy, 1899), 23.

7. George Wright has written about the debilitating effect of lynching on black political activity in Reconstruction Kentucky; see Wright, *Racial Violence in Kentucky*, 48–52.

8. For an able summary of the power-threat hypothesis and the problems associated with it, see Stewart E. Tolnay and E. M. Beck, *A Festival of Violence: An Analysis of Southern Lynchings, 1882–1930* (Urbana: University of Illinois Press, 1995), chap. 3.

9. *Saluda Advocate*, November 2, 1898.

10. This essay posits in part that the relationship between lynching and political power must be considered from a regional perspective. To replicate this study for the other southern states, one would have to construct sociopolitical regions for each state and then analyze a given state's lynching record in accord with those regions. The time and effort required for such an analysis was beyond the scope of this study.

11. Because complete records of black voter registration during the period do not exist, I used the election of blacks to the state legislature as a substitute measure for black political participation. The record of African American service in the state legislatures of Mississippi and South Carolina during the post-Reconstruction period can be found in Mrs. Charles C. Mosely, *The Negro in Mississippi History* (Jackson, Miss.: Hederman Brothers, 1969), 65–69, and Tindall, *South Carolina Negroes*, appendix.

12. From 1880 to 1890 Republican regions in Mississippi had approximately 61.5 percent of the state's black population and 64.1 percent of black lynching incidents. From 1890 to 1900 the same regions had approximately 63 percent of the black population but only 49 percent of black lynching incidents. From 1880 to 1895 in South Carolina, Republican regions constituted about 43.5 percent of the state's black population but had only 26.8 percent of black lynching incidents. From 1896 to 1910 the Republican regions had about the same percentage of the black population, but black lynching incidents increased to 34.3 percent of the state's total.

13. John Ray Skates, *Mississippi: A Bicentennial History* (New York: Norton, 1979), 122.

14. William J. Cooper Jr., *The Conservative Regime: South Carolina, 1877–1890*, 2d ed. (Baton Rouge: Louisiana State University Press, 1991), 105–15.

15. See Terence Finnegan, "'At the Hands of Parties Unknown': Lynching in Mississippi and South Carolina, 1881–1940" (Ph.D. diss., University of Illinois, 1993), chap. 2.

16. In one instance a black mob even lynched a white convict guard, which was a particularly unsettling precedent for delta whites. See *New Orleans Daily Picayune*, April 29, 1884. On black-on-black mob violence in the Mississippi Delta region, also see E. M. Beck and Stewart E. Tolnay, "When Race Didn't Matter: Black and White Mob Violence against Their Own Color," in this volume.

17. William F. Holmes, "The Leflore County Massacre and the Demise of the Colored Farmers' Alliance," *Phylon* 34 (September 1973): 273, 271.

18. *New Orleans Daily Picayune*, September 2, 1889.

19. Holmes, "Leflore County Massacre," 270–74; *New Orleans Daily Picayune*, September 5, 6, December 8, 10, 1889.

20. W. Fitzhugh Brundage, *Lynching in the New South: Georgia and Virginia, 1880–1930* (Urbana: University of Illinois Press, 1993), 132, 153.

21. Shapiro, *White Violence and Black Response*, 13, 21–22; W. McKee Evans, *Ballots and Fence Rails* (Chapel Hill: University of North Carolina Press, 1969), 101–2; Joel Williamson, *After Slavery: The Negro in South Carolina during Reconstruction, 1861–1877* (Chapel Hill: University of North Carolina Press, 1965), 265–66; for a

similar argument about coastal Georgia, see Brundage, *Lynching in the New South*, 133–35.

22. *Charleston News and Courier*, November 6, 1883.

23. *Charleston News and Courier*, December 29, 1889; also see Tindall, *South Carolina Negroes*, 239–40.

24. *Charleston News and Courier*, December 29, 1889.

25. *Charleston News and Courier*, December 31, 1889.

26. *Charleston News and Courier*, January 3, 1890; also see Tindall, *South Carolina Negroes*, 248–49.

27. *Charleston News and Courier*, April 15, 19, 21, 22, 1893.

28. *Charleston News and Courier*, July 11, 1892, quoted in Tindall, *South Carolina Negroes*, 251–52.

29. *Charleston News and Courier*, April 25–27, 1893.

30. *Charleston News and Courier*, April 27, 1893, June 8, 1894.

31. *Charleston News and Courier*, June 26–27, 1895.

32. On the nature of the Jim Crow court system in Mississippi, see Neil McMillen, *Dark Journey: Black Mississippians in the Age of Jim Crow* (Urbana: University of Illinois Press, 1989), 201–4.

33. Information on the Willie Leaphart case can be found in Lexington County Coroner Inquisition Book, 1890–97, 22–44, South Carolina Department of Archives and History, Columbia; and *Charleston News and Courier*, May 6–11, 14, June 14, 1890. Also see Tindall, *South Carolina Negroes*, 240–44, 249.

34. Department of Justice year file 17743-1898, Department of Justice, Record Group 60, Folder 3, National Archives.

35. J. Morgan Kousser, *The Shaping of Southern Politics: Suffrage Restriction and the Establishment of the One-Party South, 1880–1910* (New Haven: Yale University Press, 1974), 144.

36. Quoted in *New Orleans Daily Picayune*, July 7, 1894, November 29, 1895, March 22, 1897.

37. William F. Holmes, "Whitecapping in Mississippi: Agrarian Violence in the Populist Era," *Mid-America* 55 (April 1973): 134.

38. Bureau of the Census, *Eleventh U.S. Census of Population, 1890* (Washington, D.C.: U.S. Government Printing Office, 1895), 1:417–18, 427; *Twelfth U.S. Census of Population, 1900* (Washington, D.C.: U.S. Government Printing Office, 1901), 1:545, 555. Information on land values was obtained from Thomas J. Pressly and William H. Scofield, eds., *Farm Real Estate Values in the United States by Counties, 1850–1959* (Seattle: University of Washington Press, 1965).

39. *New Orleans Daily Picayune*, May 6, 1893.

40. See Philip Foner, "Black-Jewish Relations in the Opening Years of the Twentieth Century," *Phylon* 36 (Winter 1975): 369–70.

41. Holmes, "Whitecapping in Mississippi," 136.

42. *New Orleans Daily Picayune*, January 12, 1893.

43. *New Orleans Daily Picayune*, May 5, 6, 12, June 16, 1894.

44. Holmes, "Whitecapping in Mississippi," 147–48. Holmes has also written on the reappearance of Whitecaps. See William F. Holmes, "Whitecapping: Agrarian Violence in Mississippi, 1902–1906," *Journal of Southern History* 35 (May 1969): 165–85.

45. On the organization of Whitecaps see *New Orleans Daily Picayune*, May 6, 1893, and Holmes, "Whitecapping in Mississippi," 136–37.

46. Roger Ransom and Richard Sutch have noted that whites routinely targeted black schools and teachers for violence so as to circumscribe the economic opportunities available to black laborers. See Ransom and Sutch, *One Kind of Freedom: The Economic Consequences of Emancipation* (London: Cambridge University Press, 1977), 27–31.

47. *New Orleans Daily Picayune*, July 3, 4, 5, 14, 16, 1894.

48. A "no-crime" lynching occurred when whites killed a black for no alleged crime or affront against racial etiquette. Such incidents are distinct from "unknown" lynchings, in which the alleged cause could not be determined.

49. *Charleston News and Courier*, February 22–28, 1898, April 12, 1899.

50. *Charleston News and Courier*, April 14, 1899.

51. *Charleston News and Courier*, February 27, July 2, 1898.

52. *Charleston News and Courier*, March 1, 3, 1898.

53. *Saluda Advocate*, April 11, 1900.

54. *Abbeville Scimitar*, February 1, 1917.

55. The account of the Phoenix massacre is drawn from H. Leon Prather Sr., "The Origins of the Phoenix Racial Massacre of 1898," in *Developing Dixie: Modernization in a Traditional Society*, ed. Winfred B. Moore Jr., Joseph F. Tripp, and Lyon G. Tyler Jr. (New York: Greenwood Press, 1988), 62–93; Tindall, *South Carolina Negroes*, 256–58; and primarily from the *Charleston News and Courier*, November 9–18, 22, 24, 26, 28, 1898, April 23, 25, 29, May 2, 1899.

56. *Charleston News and Courier*, November 28, 1898.

57. *Charleston News and Courier*, November 11, 1898.

58. *Charleston News and Courier*, November 16, 1898.

59. *Charleston News and Courier*, November 14, 1898; Tindall, *South Carolina Negroes*, 258.

60. *Charleston News and Courier*, November 14, 1898.

61. McMillen, *Dark Journey*, 297, 43.

62. Quoted in Shapiro, *White Violence and Black Response*, 121.

North Carolina
Lynching Ballads

Bruce E. Baker

I f, as is often claimed, lynchings have had profound effects on the communities in which they happened, those effects should be evident in the cultural productions of those communities. Although scholarship has begun to look at cultural productions concerning lynching, this attention to date has focused on "high culture" such as novels and poetry. These productions are rich, but they typically reflect sensibilities that may be distinct from those of communities in which lynchings occurred. To study cultural productions directly shaped by lynching, we need to concentrate on those which, although created by an individual, have been widely accepted in and have become part of the folklore of the community in which the lynching occurred. With this aim in mind, this essay focuses on ballads associated with three lynchings that occurred in the lower Piedmont of North Carolina just north and east of Charlotte between 1892 and 1906. These ballads were a vital part of the communities' own construction of the meanings of these lynchings, and without understanding their role within the folk culture of lynching, we cannot fully appreciate the cultural context in which the lynchings occurred.[1]

Ballads have long been an important area of study within American folklore scholarship. Francis J. Child's monumental collection *English and Scottish Popular Ballads*, published between 1882 and 1888, is often regarded as the birth of American folkloristics. Later, Cecil Sharp's discovery of English ballads still being sung in the southern Appalachians paved the way for still more collecting and study. By mid-century, the trend was toward classification and study of themes within ballads. G. Malcolm Laws helped bring the focus of ballad studies from Britain to America with his 1950 book *Native American Balladry*. In the past two decades, there have been important studies of railroad songs and murdered-girl ballads. But to date, only scanty attention has been given to ballads about lynchings. Aside from a couple of articles in the *North Carolina Folklore Journal* on two of the ballads discussed in this essay and a passing mention in Alan Lomax's memoir, *The Land Where the Blues Began*, folklorists have left preservation of lynching ballads and commenting on them to journalists and historians.[2]

Lynching ballads are one important part of what I call the "folk culture of lynching." By this I mean expressive texts broadly conceived in traditional forms which have as their subject a specific lynching or lynchings in general and which become traditional within a given group or region. The folk culture of lynching encompasses a wide variety of texts. The forms of these texts among any given group depend on the forms traditional to it. Thus legendary accounts of lynchings are part of the folk culture of lynching in nearly every area where lynchings occurred, but fiddle tunes commemorating lynchings, for example, may be found only where there already exists a tradition of fiddle playing. In addition to legendary accounts and fiddle tunes, we can include haunt tales, place names, customary behavior, souvenirs, and ballads among the forms of the folk culture of lynching.[3]

Studying lynching ballads is important because it offers a glimpse into the process by which the social memory of a lynching is constructed. Since these ballads tended to be local in composition and circulation, local social hierarchies and local aesthetics influenced the form the composition took and the style in which it was written. Once written, the ballad and the values expressed in it would have been compared to the values held by the majority of the members of the community. Obviously, ballads that espoused widely held values would stand a greater chance of being sung and remembered over longer periods of time. Lynching ballads, then, provide the opportunity to listen to the voices of those who were directly involved in the social structures that gave rise to lynchings, the people who knew both the mob and the victim and felt compelled to sing that knowledge in ballads. Although use of folkloric sources is more methodologically problematic than use of traditional historical scholarship based on newspaper accounts or court documents, the insights yielded by study of folk material overshadow any hesitancy over its validity.

The existence of a folk culture of lynching reminds us that when we conceive of a lynching we need to think of more than just a sequence of events in which a mob puts a person or persons to death. We need to think of lynching as a cultural text made up of many elements operating on different levels. The event sequence, like the other elements, is a stylized action laden with meaning which is intended to convey a message to various audiences. This metaphor of the lynching as a text, that is, of many different elements each contributing to the propagation of messages, allows us to see the cultural expressions about lynchings, whether in novels, newspapers, or ballads, as a part of the lynching.

One feature of lynching ballads is that, like most other American ballads, they tend to be "accurate enough in detail to permit an investigator to demonstrate positively their factual basis." This characteristic is most evident in the nearly universal use of accurate personal names, a trait shared by the North Carolina lynching ballads as well as such other lynching ballads as "In a Little Country Schoolyard," "Emmet Till," "The Ashland Tragedy," and "The Strayhorn Mob." This documentary quality serves to maintain the memory of the event and the participants in the folk culture of the community in which the ballad was composed and sung. The use of specific names in lynching ballads, moreover, serves as a marker of the power relationships involved. The victim's name reminds listeners of the crime and warns them to avoid a similar fate. Since the mob is nameless, using the name of the victim while not mentioning the names of the mob reinforces the power conferred by anonymity. Lynch law, while applied at a specific point, draws its power to terrorize in large part from the uncertainty of the identity of mob members: anyone could be a potential lyncher, just as anyone could be a potential lynching victim. This representational function of lynching ballads is evident in four lynching ballads from North Carolina.[4]

EMMA HARTSELL

One extant North Carolina ballad recounts events that follow the archetypal pattern for a southern lynching: a white girl was raped and murdered, and suspicion fell on two black men, with lethal results. The murder of Emma Hartsell, a twelve-year-old white girl, and the subsequent lynching of Tom Johnson and Joe Kizer in Concord, North Carolina, in 1898 inspired a ballad, "The Death of Emma Hartsell," which has circulated among singers, journalists, and folklorists for nearly a century.

The outlines of the murder and lynching that became the basis for the ballad may be quickly sketched. On May 29, 1898, the Hartsell family went to church, leaving an infant daughter at home in Emma's care. When they returned around five o'clock, they found Emma dead on the kitchen floor, "her head nearly severed from her body." A local doctor examined the corpse and declared that she had been raped. A search party formed to hunt down the killers, and suspicion came to rest on two black men, Tom Johnson and Joe Kizer. When the sheriff placed them in the Concord jail around seven o'clock, the search party followed him to the jail and demanded that he turn the prisoners over. The sheriff refused, and the mob assaulted the jail, knocking in the front door and seizing Johnson and Kizer. The mob took the pair down the Mt. Pleasant road about a mile and a half out of town before finding a dogwood tree suitable for the hanging. A minister who had tried to convince the mob of two thousand people not to lynch Johnson and Kizer spoke to the prisoners, and then they were hanged. After the hanging, the mob fired several hundred rounds into the corpses. Spectators took souvenirs, including the rope, parts of the tree limbs, and various articles of clothing (but not body parts). The next morning, a court of inquest visited the scene, and "their verdict, of course, was nothing more than a formal report as is required."[5]

The ballad, "The Death of Emma Hartsell," which has been collected in several variants, preserved an oral record of these events.

(1)   In eighteen hundred and ninety eight
        Sweet Emma met with an awful fate.
        'Twas on the holy Sabbath day
        When her sweet life was snatched away.

(2)   It set my brain all in a whirl
        To think of that poor little girl.
        Who rose that morning fair and bright,
        And before five was a mangled sight.

(3)   It caused many a heart to bleed
        To think and hear of such deed.
        Her friends, they shed many a tear.
        Her throat was cut from ear to ear.

(4)   Just as the wind did cease to blow,
        They caught the men, 'twas Tom and Joe.
        The sheriff he drove in such a dash
        The howling mob could scarcely pass.

(5)   They got to town by half past seven
        Their necks were broken before eleven.
        The people there were a sight to see.
        They hung them to a dogwood tree.

(6)   Fathers and mothers a warning take
          Never leave your children for God's sake
          But take them with you wherever you go
          And always think of Tom and Joe.

(7)   Kind friends we all must bear in mind
          They caught the men who did the crime.
          There's not a doubt around the lurk
          Tom said he held her while Joe did the work

(8)   Sweet Emma has gone to a world of love
          Where Tom and Joe dare not to go.
          We think they've gone to hell below
          For treating poor little Emma so.

(9)   Dear friends we all remember this
          That Emma will be sadly missed.
          And one thing more I also know
          This world is rid of Tom and Joe.

(10)   As they stood on death's cold brink
          Joe Kizzer [sic] begged the man for drink
          No drink no drink the man replied.
          To Hell to Hell your soul must fly.

(11)   And one thing more my song does lack
          I forgot to say the men were black.
          Her friends and neighbors will say the same
          And Emma Hartsell was her name.

Certain features of the text of "The Death of Emma Hartsell" shed light on the way people in the eastern Cabarrus and western Stanly area recalled this event. Some of these features are common throughout the genre of lynching ballads. The last line of verse 7, "Tom said he held her while Joe did the work," is reminiscent of the stories and "rumors of rape" which Jacquelyn Dowd Hall claims "became a kind of acceptable folk pornography . . . a public fantasy that implies a kind of group participation in the rape of the woman almost as cathartic as the subsequent lynching of the alleged attacker." Interestingly, none of the contemporary newspaper accounts of the lynching include the "begging for water" scene from verse 10. The only mentions of it in print are long after the fact. In the *Concord Daily Standard*, however, the correspondent reported that the lynch mob with their prisoners turned off the main road at Big Cold Water Hill, suggesting that perhaps the name of the location of the hanging got incorporated into the lore of the lynching as an event rather than a name.[6]

Anne Cohen observed in her study of "Poor Pearl," a murder ballad, that although both ballads and newspaper accounts of the murder of Pearl Bryan drew on certain set formulas for characterization and other features, "there can be little doubt that composers of Pearl Bryan ballads got their information about the case from news stories," and there is strong textual evidence to suggest a similar influence in "The Death of Emma Hartsell." In the account of the murder and lynching that appeared in the *Concord Daily Standard*, we read that Tom Johnson confessed that "he held the girl, but that Kizer did the work," just as verse 7 states. The sheriff had to drive through a "howling mob" in both the newspaper account and the ballad. Describing Emma's body, the newspaper writes, "It was soon found that the back of her neck was cut from ear to ear." In the ballad, "Her throat was cut from ear to ear." Thus the ballad recorded for subsequent audiences and generations details that would form the folk memory of the lynching.[7]

Surprisingly, race is not explicitly discussed in the ballad until the last verse. Almost certainly, this is because of the popular conception of rape and lynching at the turn of the century: all rape victims were white, pure, and frail, and all rapists were big and black. When race is mentioned in the last verse, it is as an afterthought: "And one thing more my song does lack / I forgot to say the men were black." Since "The Death of Emma Hartsell" was originally composed as a poem and later set to music, its identification as a "song" in this verse suggests that the final verse was added later, perhaps by the same person who set the poem to music. If this was the case, it seems plausible that the author of the final verse chose to designate the race of Tom and Joe and include Emma's surname for listeners who may not have been familiar with the details of the incident. The poem's original local audience, of course, would have known these essential details.

"The Death of Emma Hartsell" has a plot device common to lynching ballads: a request by the lynching victim followed by the rejection of that request by the mob. The tenth verse of "The Death of Emma Hartsell" involve a request and its denial, in this case for water:

As they stood on death's cold brink
Joe Kizzer [*sic*] begged the man for drink.
No drink no drink the man replied.
To Hell to Hell your soul must fly.

The request/denial device is also used in the ballad "J. V. Johnson," in which Johnson asks, "Oh, just give me one moment to pray," but is answered, "You did not give Guinn time to pray. / ... / We will not give you time to pray." Subsequently, his request for mercy is refused as well. The motif of a request for mercy is also found in the Mississippi lynching ballad "Emmet Till." The request and its denial convey graphically the power of the mob to make life-and-death decisions about the victim as well as to control minute details.

In the text of "The Death of Emma Hartsell," we find much sentiment and sensationalism but little sympathy. This characteristic is typical of most lynching ballads. They tend to sentimentalize the victim of the precipitating crime and demonize the lynching victim but extend true sympathy to no one. Although the influence of sentimental parlor songs on the composers of lynching ballads may partially explain this trait, it is also rooted in attitudes toward the social relationships that led to lynchings. Emma is sentimentalized as "a poor little girl ... bright and fair," but she is portrayed more as an object than as a person. The second verse, after describing Emma, concludes by calling her "a mangled sight." Similarly, the next verse focuses less on Emma's experience than on the external perception of that experience as spectacle. After discussing the reaction of Emma's friends and family to the "mangled sight," the poem gives another snapshot of the corpse, in this case reminding us that "her throat was cut from ear to ear." Unlike many murdered-girl ballads in which the victim carries on a dialogue with her assailant, Emma never speaks, never cries, and exists only as a mute victim, an object to be either assaulted, protected, or avenged. Tom and Joe, likewise, are portrayed in a sensational manner. Verse 6 presents them as bogeymen, warning parents to "always think of Tom and Joe." The judgment expressed in verse 8, "We think they've gone to hell below," portrays them as beyond the pale of Christian sympathy and presumes to judge their souls. This banishment to hell is repeated in verse 10, when a man tells Joe, "To Hell to Hell your soul must fly." Like Emma, Tom and Joe are mute, except for Joe's request for a drink, which is not expressed as a direct quotation.

Another feature of some of the lynching ballads is a concern with the eternal judgment upon the lynching victim. In "The Death of Emma Hartsell," this judgment is explicit:

Sweet Emma has gone to a world of love
Where Tom and Joe dare not to go.
We think they've gone to hell below
For treating poor little Emma so.

The mob has removed the victim from this world, and the ballad claims to know where the victim is going afterward. By contrast, the question of judgment is left open in "J. V. Johnson," where he wonders in each of the last two verses, "My soul, what will become of thee?" Likewise, "In a Little Country Churchyard" ends with a general admonition to "Pray to get right with your master / Before it is too late."[8]

In many ways, "The Death of Emma Hartsell" is the most typical lynching ballad. It provides a representational account of the lynching of two black men for the rape and murder of a white girl, and the way the account is rendered reinforces the attitudes about the social relationships that gave rise to the lynching. Significantly, the ballad presents none of the factors affecting race relations in Concord at that time—the Spanish-American War, the emergence of the first textile mill owned and operated by blacks, and the racially charged white supremacy campaign of 1898 that culminated in the Wilmington riots of October. This simplified version of events is to some extent an effect of the ballad form itself. Whereas other oral accounts of the lynching may be modified by the speaker according to changing performance situations, the ballad, with its constraints of rhyme and meter, must be related in a more stable form, making it more difficult to adapt it to different performance contexts. Likewise, the stable form aids memory by giving the singer a framework for the details of the story. Thus lynching ballads like "The Death of Emma Hartsell" tend to resist changes in content over time more than other oral accounts less constrained by form.[9]

ALEC WHITLEY

The story of the lynching of Alec Whitley differs substantially from the lynching in Concord in 1898, and the ballads about the lynchings differ as well. Alec Whitley, unlike Joe Kizer and Tom Johnson, was white and a member of an established family. He had, however, a reputation and record of violent crime when a mob lynched him in Albemarle, Stanly County, in 1892. The ballads about Alec Whitley express not racial conflict but a communal sense of outrage and satisfaction that a dangerous element had been removed from society.[10]

Whitley was the illegitimate son of Christian Burris, a Confederate veteran, and Susanna Whitley, a member of a prominent local family. Alec grew from a troubled boy into a troublesome man, drinking, fighting, and stealing. He was tried for larceny in 1883 and 1885. Whitley's brother-in-law Bud Cagle was indicted along with him and turned state's evidence in the 1883 trial. Cagle disappeared, and there were suspicions that Whitley either killed him or chased him out of the area. Whitley's history becomes vague at this point, but after the death of his wife, Mary, and their children from natural causes, Whitley migrated to Arkansas in 1888 with his half-sister, Judy Burris, accompanying him as his wife. Another Stanly County native, Burt Tucker, followed in 1890.

In early 1892, Whitley argued with Tucker and killed him, dismembering the body and throwing it in a nearby creek. Accounts of the murder vary, attributing its cause to either a gambling dispute, jealousy over Burris, or Tucker's threat to tell the authorities about an earlier killing committed by Whitley. Whitley apparently tried to hide the murder by making it look as though Tucker had merely moved away. Two months passed before the discovery of Tucker's body. Meanwhile, Whitley and Burris traveled east toward North Carolina, parting company in Georgia. The sheriff in Arkansas put out a reward for Whitley, and the Stanly County sheriff was on the lookout for him.

Whitley arrived in Stanly County early in June and met his death less than two weeks later. A posse captured Whitley while he was hiding on his cousin's farm. The sheriff placed Whitley in jail to await the arrival of the sheriff from Arkansas, who would escort him back to stand trial there. Early on the morning of June 9, 1892, a mob of seventy-five to one hundred "disguised bloody shirt men" overpowered the sheriff and carried Whitley from the jail. The mob took him to the edge of town and hanged him from a red oak tree. Even impending death failed to rattle Whitley, who refused to confess to Tucker's murder and claimed that Bud Cagle was still living somewhere in South Carolina.

The powerful emotions provoked by Whitley and his lynching have been remembered by some area residents in song.[11] One of these was a ballad composed by a Baptist minister, Rev. Edmond P. Harrington.

LINES WRITTEN ON THE ASSASSINATION OF D. B. TUCKER

(1) Come, young man of the present age, and listen to my call,
     And don't be overtaken by strong alcohol,
       There was a man both young and gay, his name to you I'll tell,
     It was Burton Tucker, of whom you know so well.
       Chorus
       They dumped him in water,
       The fish swam o'er his breast,
       The water in gentle motion,
       We hope his soul's at rest.

(2)   Times were financially hard, and money coming slow,
       He went to the West where many young men go.
       He went to his employment which was teaching school,
       His scholars, they all loved him, and all obeyed his rules.

(3)   He only taught eight months instead of teaching ten,
       When he met with Aleck Whitley, who brought him to his end.
       Yes, he met with Aleck Whitley, all in a smile you see,
       "Go home with me Cousin Burton, and get your lodging free."

(4)   And after long persuading with him he did agree.
       He went along home with him where murder was to be.
       Alex says to Wilson, "We've got him now you see,
       We will take his life and his money will ours be."

(5)   Yes, Aleck watched him close to see that he was not seen.
       He raised the fatal weapon and the blood ran down in a stream.
       Judy said to Aleck, "Don't this take the lead."
       They took him in the back room and laid him on the cotton seed.

(6)   The like in old Arkansas had never yet been seen,
       They cut his body in pieces, the number of seventeen.
       Aleck says to Judy, "This secret you must keep."
       They cut his body in pieces and dumped it in the creek.

(7)   Judy says, "Oh, Aleck, you'll die in public sure,
       For murdering Cousin Burton, and mangling his body so.
       You'll be arrested for this, and in the jail you'll go
       And on the fatal hangman's tree, you'll pay the debt you owe."

(8)   His wife in North Carolina she could not take her rest.
       She felt that there was trouble with her husband in the West.
       Oftimes she had looked for him, and oftimes seen him come,
       But now he is gone from her to never more return.

The textual genealogy of "Lines" demonstrates how folk cultural forms were adapted to create a folk culture of lynching. In composing "Lines," Harrington drew upon styles of sentimental balladry then current to adapt an older Anglo-American ballad to recount an event of great local interest. Folklorists Roger D. Abrahams and George Foss suggest that "the addition of a chorus" is "a tendency discernible in sentimental songs" and that typically "a song which has a chorus-verse arrangement uses the chorus as the most extreme expression of the emotional involvement of the situation." Such is certainly the case in "Lines," where the chorus reminds the listener of the gruesome fact of Tucker's dismemberment after each verse. The chorus itself is clearly modeled on a verse from "Young Edwin in the Lowlands Low," a Child ballad that circulated widely in North Carolina. Harrington, who was a preacher, storyteller, and composer and singer of ballads, found an apt model for his composition in "Young Edwin in the Lowlands Low." In that ballad, Edwin gets drunk and is murdered for his money by the father of his lover, Emily. In "Lines," Tucker, succumbing to "strong alcohol," is murdered by Whitley for his money and possibly out of jealousy over Judy, setting up a familiar triangular relationship among the protagonists. Like Emily, Judy is pressured to be an accomplice and hush up the affair. The ballad closes with a conversation between Emily and her father. She tells him, "you'll die a public show," leading Harrington to have Judy warn Alec, "you'll die in public sure." "Young Edwin in the Lowlands Low" is more moralistic than most other Child ballads, making it more appropriate as a model for the sort of sentimental song warning against the dangers of alcohol that Harrington was writing.[12]

One of the most prominent details in this case is the dismemberment of Tucker. Every account, especially oral ones, mentions this fact.[13] Dismemberment seems to hold a morbid fascination. While a corpse is still human, dismemberment violates the integrity of the body, questioning whether the corpse is actually human or only disassembled flesh. "Lines" also highlights this concern with dismemberment. The sixth verse says, "They cut his body in pieces, the number of seventeen," and then repeats, "They cut his body in pieces and dumped it in the creek." In the next verse, when Judy panics, she indicates that Whitley's punishment will be as much for this dehumanizing act as for the murder itself, saying, "Oh, Aleck, you'll die in public sure, / For murdering Cousin Burton, and mangling his body so."[14]

Curiously, this ballad about the murder made no mention of the eventual fate of Alec Whitley other than to predict that "on the fatal hangman's tree, you'll pay the debt you owe." The fact that the ballad focuses on the murder of Tucker and only alludes to the equally sensational lynching of Whitley leads me to believe that Harrington wrote this ballad between the time news of Tucker's death reached North Carolina newspapers and June 9, 1892, when a mob lynched Whitley.

The ballad, if Harrington composed it during this time, was probably written for distribution at Whitley's execution. John Harrington Cox in *Folk-Songs of the South* describes this custom in his discussion of a

Kentucky ballad, "The Ashland Tragedy." Elijah Adams had composed this ballad about a murder, lynching, and execution in 1884 in Ashland, Kentucky. According to a witness at the execution, "Lige Adams had a *stack* of ballads on the day of the hanging, stood on a big rock, and sold them as fast as three men could hand them out." Similarly, James A. Turpin writes that verses of the ballad "Frankie Silver" "were printed on a strip of paper and sold to people who assembled at Morganton to see Frances Silver executed." There is evidence that "Lines Written on the Assassination of D. B. Tucker" had a similar use. Broadsides served as aids to singers' memories and also as a means of distributing and preserving information about events. Hangings particularly had been accompanied by broadside ballads for several hundred years in England, the crowd of spectators providing an accessible and interested market for the ballad seller.[15]

The last stanza of "Lines" bears closer examination, for it holds an important clue to the development of the other ballad about Alec Whitley.

His wife in North Carolina she could not take her rest.
She felt that there was trouble with her husband in the West.
Oftimes she had looked for him, and oftimes seen him come,
But now he is gone from her to never more return.

The supernatural element of Tucker's wife presciently knowing of her husband's trouble is unusual in American balladry. What makes the supernatural element especially interesting in this case is that the first verse of the ballad dealing with the lynching, "Alec Whitley," echoes this motif in a condensed form.

He murdered Bert Tucker in the West,
He murdered Bert Tucker in the West,
He murdered Bert Tucker in the West,
And he knocked a widder out of rest.

In a sense, the first verse of "Alec Whitley" provides a synopsis of "Lines" before continuing the story. Because of the general rarity of supernatural elements in American balladry and the similarity between the two verses, it appears that the composer of "Alec Whitley" was familiar with "Lines" and used the idea of its last verse as a starting point for a ballad memorializing the lynching.[16]

This second ballad about Alec Whitley, focusing on his lynching, exists in the form of two fragments and one complete variant collected by Heath Thomas, a journalist writing for the *Salisbury* (N.C.) *Post*.

(1)   He murdered Bert Tucker in the West,
He murdered Bert Tucker in the West
He murdered Bert Tucker in the West
And he knocked a widder out of rest.

(2)   So they carried Alec Whitley to Albemarle,
So they carried Alec Whitley to Albemarle,
So they carried Alec Whitley to Albemarle,
And they made a prisoner of him there.

(3)   He stayed there three days and two nights,
He stayed there three days and two nights,
He stayed there three days and two nights,
And they hung Alec Whitley to a red oak limb.

(4)   They hung Alec Whitley to a red oak limb,
They hung Alec Whitley to a red oak limb,
They hung Alec Whitley to a red oak limb,
Just to show the world what they'd do for him.

(5)   It was about the tenth of June,
It was about the tenth of June,
It was about the tenth of June,
When they hung that cunning old coon.

"Alec Whitley" is a fairly straightforward narrative account of the lynching. The structure of the verse form, based on the camp-meeting song "Were You There When They Crucified My Lord," limited the creativity of the ballad because there were only two lines per stanza, and these lines had to rhyme. The constraints of rhyme help explain the ballad's most puzzling line, in which Whitley is described as a "cunning old coon." The word "coon" could refer to Whitley's race, but it is more likely that the composer, eager to preserve the date of the lynching in his ballad, merely grabbed for a handy rhyme to "June."

The two ballads about Alec Whitley's crime and lynching evince an active representation of lynching in folk culture. Along with legends, these ballads allowed the residents of Stanly County to preserve a readily accessible account of these terrible events and, more than just the events, the emotions they evoked. The ballads, composed around the time of the lynching, display horror and hatred over Tucker's murder and a smug satisfaction at Whitley's lynching. Today, however, the whole affair provokes mostly embarrassment and shame in Stanly County residents. The ballads, then, leave us a trace of the original emotional climate surrounding Whitley's lynching. Without condoning the lynching, by hearing the ballads we are nevertheless able to understand the power of the emotions of community members which led to the lynching.

J. V. JOHNSON

Sharp class differences separated J. V. Johnson and his brother-in-law, Guinn Johnson, the man for whose murder he was lynched. The story of Guinn Johnson begins with his father, Hugh Johnson, "a large landowner of Morven township," whose lands were described as a "plantation." J. V. Johnson's father, Daniel P. Johnson, in contrast, could be characterized as one of the "yeomen" who "owned only modest amounts of land." In 1896, J. V. Johnson married Marcia Johnson, the daughter of Hugh Johnson, and settled in Morven, in southern Anson County, where he worked on Hugh's plantation.[17]

It is not clear just when the trouble arose between J. V. Johnson and his wife's family which would eventually lead to two deaths. Sometime in the spring of 1905, J. V., who had been drinking, assaulted Hugh and Tom Johnson, Hugh's eldest son, with a pistol and spent two months in a "private hospital at Morganton to be cured of the drink habit." Court records show that on May 9, 1905, two doctors committed J. V. to the state hospital in Morganton, writing that he was "dangerous to himself and the community." Tom Johnson swore out a peace warrant against J. V. when he returned from Morganton, and J. V. decided to move out of North Carolina. But he apparently changed his mind and stayed.[18]

Relations between J. V. and Guinn worsened during the summer and fall of 1905, culminating in Guinn's death at J. V.'s hands on December 27, 1905. J. V. Johnson was arraigned on the charge of first-degree murder on January 15, 1906, and his trial began on April 18, 1906. The final vote of the jury was eleven for second-degree murder and one for acquittal. The presiding judge declared a mistrial, and the trial was rescheduled for July 16, 1906. This turn of events heightened feelings that justice was neither swift nor certain enough.

Frustration over the slow pace and uncertain outcome of justice in Johnson's case led to his lynching on the night of Sunday, May 27, 1906. According to a farmer from Morven who later turned state's evidence, a mob, numbering between 75 and 125, made its way through Morven to the jail at Wadesboro. Johnson was taken out of town toward Morven and hanged from a pine tree on the right side of the road. After hanging him, the mob fired well over a hundred rounds into Johnson's corpse.

Reaction to the lynching was swift and strong but ultimately ineffective. The next morning the coroner impaneled a jury and investigated the lynching. The solicitor began an investigation immediately and telephoned Governor Robert Glenn to request that a special term of court be held to try the lynchers, although no convictions were made. The lynching was noted in the regional *Biblical Recorder* and two decades later made a brief appearance on the national scene in the form of an article in *World's Work*, which used the Wadesboro lynching as a point of departure for a commentary on lynching in general. But Johnson's lynching was soon lost among a flurry of other lynchings that summer and, in September, race riots in Atlanta. Around Wadesboro, however, J. V. Johnson's lynching was remembered and its story incorporated into a ballad, probably written by a Wadesboro merchant, which survived at least sixty years in oral tradition and is different in some important ways from the other lynching ballads discussed in this essay.[19]

J. V. JOHNSON

(1) 'Twas on a gloomy Sunday night
     When Johnson thought he was alright
     A hundred hearts of an angry mob
     Did disobey the laws of God

(2) 'Twas on land[?] at half past two.
     The great fair[?] doors the men broke through.
     They scarcely [——?] for this poor man.
     The cell was opened at their command.

(3) Into the cell they boldly went,
     And only there a moment spent.
     "Come out, come out, your time has come
     When you'll repay the deed you've done."

(4) "Don't hurt me boys," he sadly said.
     "Hush, hush your mouth—you'll soon be dead."
     "Oh, just give me one moment to pray,
     And do not kill a man who prays."

(5) "You did not give Guinn time to pray.
     You took his dear sweet life away.

We will not give you time to pray,
But for his life your life shall pay."

(6)   That was a sad and awful time.
      Just as they reached the fatal time.
      A rope around his neck they tied,
      And hung the man until he died.

(7)   "I know the crime is awful black.
      I wish that I could call it back.
      It is so dark I cannot see.
      My soul, what will become of thee?"

(8)   "Farewell, this world, my friends, my wife.
      This mob will surely take my life.
      It is so dark I cannot see.
      My soul, what will become of thee?"

The most striking thing about the melody to which "J. V. Johnson" was sung is that it is nearly identical to the melody of "The Death of Emma Hartsell." The first phrase is identical; the second phrase differs in only two notes; the third phrase shares the same cadence tones; the fourth phrase is identical. These similarities, added to the fact that both ballads deal with a similar event, strongly indicate that the composer of "J. V. Johnson" modeled his song on "The Death of Emma Hartsell." This is not surprising, if we consider that Marshville, where the likely composer of "J. V. Johnson" had friends, is within nineteen miles of Oakboro, where "The Death of Emma Hartsell" circulated until at least the late 1920s. This transmission is further evidence for the rich folk culture of lynching in the North Carolina Piedmont at this time.[20]

"J. V. Johnson" carefully criticizes the lynching through use of religious references, diction, and the distribution of voice among the characters in the ballad. Verses 4 and 5 use the plot device of a request and its denial. While this suggests the mob's merciless attitude toward Johnson, it is references to religion that give "J. V. Johnson" much of its affective power as a statement against lynching. The first verse claims that the mob "did disobey the laws of God." In addition to disobeying God's laws, the mob refuses Johnson even the comfort of prayer before death. This refusal leads to Johnson's concern with the disposition of his soul expressed in the last two verses. The narrator is clearly against the lynching, as demonstrated by his diction. He describes Johnson as a "poor man" who addresses his assailants "sadly," and the moment of his death is a "sad and awful time." Finally, and most surprising in a lynching ballad, Johnson, not the narrator or the mob, is given the final word. The ballad could logically end after the sixth verse; Johnson's two-verse coda, repeating its pitiful refrain, leaves the listener with the voice of the condemned man, the voice the lynching tried to silence.

The practice of lynching existed on a social landscape in which power and social relationships were being contested on a variety of fronts, and the folklore of lynchings offers a unique perspective on the meanings and functions of lynching ballads. Like other forms of expression, ballads became part of a struggle for power over the representation of lynchings. In a New South concerned with progress, condemnations of lynching are not hard to find; governors' speeches, religious publications, newspaper editorials, and many other voices called for an end to the practice. Likewise, contemporary justifications for lynching abound and in many of the same forms. What distinguishes folkloric forms, such as the lynching ballads discussed here, is that they were part of the discourse of the very communities in which the lynchings occurred. Rather than defending a lynching from outsiders' attacks or condemning those who took part in a lynching, these ballads express the feelings and observations of the people most directly affected by a particular lynching and preserve an account of the event giving their point of view.

INTERPRETING LYNCHING BALLADS

When interpreting lynching ballads, we do well to begin with G. Malcolm Laws's concise definition of a ballad as "*a narrative folksong which dramatizes a memorable event.*" First, there is a bounded event which is a matter of historical record. Second, there is a representation of that event which, by means of language, presents that which is absent, the event itself. Hence, to answer the question, What does this ballad mean? we must interrogate the relationship between the event and the representation. We might interpret lynching ballads in the so-called New Critical mode, considering only their technical and formal perfection. Or, by analyzing both the event and the representation, we might view "the ballad as a record of fact." In this approach, the event is construed as containing objective truth, and it is the task of the representation to reflect this truth as accurately as possible.[21]

Problems arise, however, when ballads are narrowly conceived as records of facts. All too often, the subject matter of balladry, the "facts" themselves, are a matter of contestation. The ballad often has a tactical function which is at least as important as its representational or documentary task.[22] Rather than reflecting a static event, the ballad engages the event, becoming an active factor in an ongoing attempt to define the "facts" of the event. The difference and distance between representation and event are collapsed when the representation attempts to affect the event. This is most clearly seen when the event involves a factionalized society, as does a battle or a lynching.

Familiar traditions of balladry in the southern labor movement and the Irish rebellion of the nineteenth century are conspicuous examples of the role of the tactical folksong. In the early days of the Southern Tenant Farmers Union (STFU) in the Arkansas delta, a union member named Frank Weems was beaten and left for dead. John Handcox, the troubadour of the STFU, composed a ballad, "The Man Frank Weems," about the incident, and it was used along with many others as part of organizing campaigns, strikes, and other forms of protest. Looking at this situation schematically, we see that a given social order (the plantation system of cotton production in the 1930s Arkansas delta and resistance to it led by the STFU) led to an event (the beating of Frank Weems) that was represented in Handcox's ballad, and the representation was used tactically to affect the social order (in strikes). Likewise, the singing of seditious ballads in mid-nineteenth-century Ireland blurred the edges of event and representation in the ballad. Maura Murphy, writing about "the ballad-singing problem," claims that "the popular ballad was both cause and effect of much political and social unrest among the populace, and whether contemporaries approved or disapproved of its influence, all were agreed on its power."[23]

Thus Irish rebel songs, labor songs, and lynching ballads are all tactical rather than merely representational. To say that "The Man Frank Weems" is a song *about* the labor movement does not adequately describe its function; it is *a part of* the labor movement in much the same way that a strike or a government policy or a contract is. Whereas Irish rebel songs and labor songs are revolutionary, seeking to change the social order, most lynching ballads are reactionary, seeking to protect the existing social order from potential change.[24] Lynching ballads, therefore, are neither forms divorced from fact nor merely "records of fact" but tactical representations that merge to a great extent with the events they represent. They are statements in the discourse by which society is constructed.[25] Lynching ballads are about lynching, but, even more important, they are a part of the phenomenon of lynching.

Discourse, however, is but one side of the construction of society. Bruce Lincoln contends, in *Discourse and the Construction of Society*, that "no consideration of discourse is complete that does not also take account of force." Although discourse is a useful tool for fusing the "complex amalgam of multiple subunits . . . that are only imperfectly bonded together to form the social unit," its dual modes of "ideological persuasion" and "sentiment evocation" are not always sufficient. Sometimes direct force is required to establish or maintain the social order. "Together," writes Lincoln, "discourse and force are the chief means whereby social borders, hierarchies, institutional formations, and habituated patterns of behavior are both maintained and modified."[26]

Lincoln's discussion of force and discourse is enlightening, but his separation of the two concepts overlooks an important aspect of their relationship: the discursive value of force. Just as statements, legislation, scripture, literature, and institutional practices figure into a discursive economy, acts of violence have an effect on discourse in addition to their direct effects on society. If we accept that discourse affects action, that is, that people often do what they talk about, as in the case of the Concord lynching that was preceded by racist statements in the editorials of local newspapers, it is not too much to suppose that the acts of violence become the occasion for further statements that affect the shape of the discourse. For example, the lynching of J. V. Johnson, an act of violence, produced a variety of contributions to this discourse in the form of a speech by Governor Robert Glenn, a letter to the newspaper denouncing Johnson's character, and the presiding judge's actions. In this sense, the lynching itself, the act of communal murder, is neither the beginning nor the end of the event of the lynching. The lynching proper and the ballad about it join the newspaper editorials, legends, rumors, court records, and so forth to constitute what we might term a "discursive event" in which each of the above forms acts as a statement within a larger discourse that continually constructs and reconstructs social relationships and structures. Thus to understand lynchings, we must understand how they contribute to such a discourse and how meaning is crafted in the variety of statements produced by the discursive event of a lynching.[27]

When the discursive value of an individual's actions threatened the existing social order, a lynching might result. The case of Alec Whitley is one example. As a young man, he had been involved in a variety of crimes, from larceny to barn burning and possibly murder. None of these crimes upset the social order to any great extent. They could be absorbed or contained within normal procedures. Whitley was brought to trial, found innocent or guilty, and life went on as usual. When he murdered Burt Tucker in such a gruesome manner, however, Whitley flagrantly transgressed his community's sense of how people ought to relate to one another (for example, that we ought not dismember one another). As Bruce Lincoln notes, "When an individual has been branded as a dangerous deviant for one reason or another, society excludes him or her from its midst." The line for blacks was even finer. "Talking back to a white man," writes Jacquelyn Dowd Hall, "seeking employment 'out of place,' refusing to obey an order—the transgression of a whole range of nebulous taboos could lead to a verbal rebuke, a beating, or a lynching."[28]

When the social order had been disturbed, the response of the community was to reestablish it by silencing the action or statement that had caused the disturbance. Jean-François Lyotard defines this as "terror," "the efficiency gained by eliminating, or threatening to eliminate, a player from the language game one shares with him." Merely silencing the voice of the transgressor, however, fails to reestablish the social order because the statement or action is already a part of the discursive event, and subsequent statements may overlay but not entirely efface the original one. The metaphor of the text becomes useful at this point. We may view the corporeal body of the "criminal" as a text, an embodiment of the discursive value of his actions. J. V. Johnson was, in addition to other things, the site of origin for a powerful challenge to the established social order of Morven. His body had effected the death of a wealthy landowner's son, and the challenge of that action to the social order was as salient a feature of his person as the color of his hair.[29]

Since the transgressor was himself a text of resistance, he had to be remade as a text of submission and compliance. The traces of the previous text, however, could not be totally effaced. Joe Kizer, even after his lynching made him into a text displaying the power relationships that existed in the community, was still in part the alleged rapist and murderer of Emma Hartsell, still a challenge to that social order. Like the blood on Lady Macbeth's hands that could not be washed away, Joe Kizer's embodiment of a disruption in the social order remained. It is this problem of the body of the transgressor as palimpsest that accounts for the extraordinary levels of violence used in lynching. To view the violence of lynching simply as an indication of the depravity and barbarism of the lynchers is to beg the question. Why do lynchers commit such horrible acts of violence? Because they are savage and barbaric. How do we know they are savage and barbaric? Because they commit these horrible acts of violence. Rather, the extravagant levels of violence were a stylistic technique used to foreground the text created by the lynching and overwhelm the previous text of transgression.

The stylistics of some lynchings are very similar to the stylistics of public execution in classical France as analyzed by Michel Foucault in *Discipline and Punish*. Like those public executions, lynching "belongs . . . to the ceremonies by which power is manifested." "The public execution," Foucault suggests, "belongs to a whole series of great rituals in which power is eclipsed and restored." The ritual elements of a lynching are, in this paradigm, less a static reflection of belief than a repertoire of techniques for the creation of meaning in a particular text, like the literary devices of imagery or meter. The lynching becomes the vehicle for the conveyance of meaning, not the expression of some sense of justice, however twisted. "Its aim," like that of public execution, "is not so much to reestablish a balance as to bring into play, as its extreme point, the dissymmetry between the subject who has dared to violate the law and the all-powerful sovereign who displays his strength." It is this surfeit of power which is inscribed as the new message in the text of the body of the lynched man.[30]

The very act of the lynching is the principal text, but powerful though the text of the lynching itself is, there are certain limitations inherent in it. For one thing, the audience for the text is limited to those actually present at the lynching, whether participating, resisting, or observing. Also, the event itself is ephemeral. If the text is to continue to disseminate its message, it must be made more enduring. The body of the lynched man serves as the site of several different kinds of attempts to sustain the text of the lynching. The most obvious of these is the viewing of the corpse by the public. Mutilation of the corpse, in the form of wounds, missing fingers or genitalia, bullet holes, and other signs of the mob's work, becomes part of the text which is to be viewed the next day by the public. Another way in which a particular message was inscribed on the corpse was by placing a sign or placard on it. Even though the general outlines of the message inscribed in the text of the lynched man must already be fairly clear, the mob verbalizes its message and leaves a text upon a text. The taking of souvenirs was another way of preserving the text of a lynching. A button, an ear, a finger, or some other personal effect constitutes a locus of memory and a site for the future recounting of the story of the lynching. Finally, photographs were yet another means of preserving the spectacle of the lynching.

It is in ballads and oral accounts, however, that the messages of the lynching are perhaps best preserved. In all of the lynching ballads in

North Carolina, both the transgression and its punishment are described, thus continuing the message of the lynching: transgression and reinscription. Long after the corpse is cut down, after the newspapers that recount the event are thrown away, a ballad, if it survives, will tell the story of the lynching. "J. V. Johnson" was in oral tradition as late as 60 years after the event it describes. "Alec Whitley" is known at least 102 years after the lynching. Every time the ballad is sung, the meaning of the lynching is repeated and its effect on the social order reasserted. An inert text of a lynching, such as a photograph or printed account, may be passed over lightly, but an aural text, such as a legendary account or a ballad, grasps the listener with the immediacy of the spoken word, demanding the active participation of both the listener and the speaker in the communicative process.

Lyotard, in *The Postmodern Condition*, explains this capacity of narration to unify separate performances. Although "the narratives' reference may seem to belong to the past," writes Lyotard, "in reality it is always contemporaneous with the act of recitation." He continues, "It is the present act that on each of its occurrences marshals in the ephemeral temporality inhabiting the space between the 'I have heard' and the 'you will hear.' The important thing about the pragmatic protocol of this kind of narration is that it betokens a theoretical identity between each of the narrative's occurrences." A similar phenomenon, I would argue, happens with ballads, particularly ballads recounting local history. Each singing of "Alec Whitley," for instance, becomes a link in a chain of performances by particular singers stretching back to the first performance of the ballad, each performance not only recounting the event but also reasserting the social values of the ballad.[31]

We can perhaps learn as much from the decline and slow disappearance of lynching ballads as we can from close study of the ballads themselves. Since the lynching ballad was in important ways part of the larger cultural text of the lynching—as befits a tactical representation rather than a static representation—we might expect the fate of these ballads to be more closely connected to the circumstances from which they arose than is the case with other ballads. A ballad like "The Wreck of the Old 97," about a train wreck in Danville, Virginia, in 1903, is not an integral part of the event it represents in the same way a lynching ballad is part of the lynching. Thus "The Wreck of the Old 97" remains popular even though railroads are no longer such a prominent part of American life as they were in 1903. "J. V. Johnson," in contrast, fades away not only because lynching is no longer a major facet of life in the South but also, and more important, because the ballad's tactical function no longer operates in contemporary social circumstances.[32]

Lynching ballads, consequently, are disappearing from oral tradition. With two exceptions, all the lynchings with associated ballads occurred before 1920. Of the lynching ballads discussed in this essay, only "Alec Whitley" and "Lines Written on the Assassination of D. B. Tucker" remain in oral tradition and then only as one-verse fragments. To some extent, we must consider this as part of the overall decline in the past several decades of ballad-singing as a widespread form of folk culture.

Yet even if ballads in general have been in decline, lynching ballads are declining more quickly than others because social change has disrupted the symbiotic relationship between them and the communities in which they were sung. At one time, the memory of the lynching in Concord was still fresh enough in the minds of many local residents for "The Death of Emma Hartsell" to be pertinent. The ballad provided an artfully rendered synopsis of the event and made comments on social facts that were still highly relevant. Lynchings were still a real possibility, as demonstrated by the 1906 lynching of three men in nearby Salisbury. Later, as those who could recall the Concord lynching firsthand began to pass and as lynching was succeeded by other techniques of social control of unruly behavior, "The Death of Emma Hartsell" lost its point of reference.

And yet two final examples show the surprising endurance of two North Carolina lynching ballads and suggest the tenacity of the genre. The murder of Gladys Kincaid in Morganton in 1927 led to the death of Broadus Miller, a black construction worker, at the hands of a posse. Miller's body was dragged through the streets of Morganton and put on view at the courthouse, making this an event with many of the trademarks of a lynching. Of the four texts about Gladys Kincaid's death, one, a ballad by Morganton singer and fiddler Tim Poteat called "The Fate of Gladys Kincaid," was recorded for RCA, although the record was never released. Some thirty years later, however, Poteat's son, Britt Poteat, sang the ballad in Louisiana juke joints where it became popular for a time. Likewise, "The Death of Emma Hartsell" was recorded on a 45rpm record in the 1960s by pioneer hillbilly fiddler J. E. Mainer, who lived in Concord. This record and "a picture of the hanging of Tom and Joe" was included as a bonus to anyone who purchased one of Mainer's LP albums. The text of the ballad along with the photograph was eventually included in Mainer's 1966 songbook. The continuing popularity of these ballads against the backdrop of the civil rights movement poses intriguing questions. Were the listeners drawn to the ballads for their depiction of an earlier time with stricter racial barriers? Or had the social meanings of the ballads become so distant from the folk culture that once informed them that audiences heard only tragic ballads, not tales of violent retribution? These are questions historians and folklorists can answer by studying lynching ballads.[33]

NOTES

1. Trudier Harris, *Exorcising Blackness: Historical and Literary Lynchings and Burning Rituals* (Bloomington: University of Indiana Press, 1984).

2. Any overview of ballad scholarship in this country should start with D. K. Wilgus's indispensable volume, *American Ballad Scholarship since 1898* (New Brunswick, N.J.: Rutgers University Press, 1959). A few key works are Francis James Child, *The English and Scottish Popular Ballads*, 5 vols. (Boston: Houghton Mifflin, 1882–98); Olive Dame Campbell and Cecil Sharp, *English Folksongs from the Southern Appalachians* (New York: Oxford University Press, 1917); Bertrand Bronson, *The Traditional Tunes of the Child Ballads* (Princeton: Princeton University Press, 1959); Tristram Coffin, *The British Traditional Ballad in America* (Philadelphia: American Folklore Society, 1950); G. Malcolm Laws, *American Balladry from British Broadsides: A Guide for Students and Collectors* (Philadelphia: American Folklore Society, 1957) and *Native American Balladry* (Philadelphia: American Folklore Society, 1964); and Roger D. Abrahams and George Foss, *Anglo-American Folksong Style* (Englewood Cliffs, N.J.: Prentice-Hall, 1968). A specific ballad genre is discussed by Anne Cohen, *Poor Pearl, Poor Girl!: The Murdered-Girl Stereotype in Ballad and Newspaper* (Austin: University of Texas Press, 1973). The two articles in *North Carolina Folklore* are Heath Thomas, "Alec Whitley: The Man and the Ballad," *North Carolina Folklore* 8 (December 1960): 16–21; and Jan A. Herlocker, "The Tragic Ballad of Miss Emma Hartsell," *North Carolina Folklore Journal* 23 (August 1975): 82–88. Lomax gives the text of "The Strayhorn Mob," composed by Sid Hemphill of Panola County, Mississippi, and some of its story in *The Land Where the Blues Began* (New York: Pantheon, 1993), 323.

3. Since traditions of narrative ballads were stronger among whites than African Americans, it is not surprising that all the lynching ballads in this essay, indeed, the majority of lynching ballads I have found, come from white communities and present their perspective. For folk cultural expression of lynchings from an African American perspective, we must look to forms other than the ballad. Legendary accounts of lynchings are too numerous to cite here, but one good example would be Heath Thomas's article. For a note on a fiddle tune commemorating a lynching, see my "Lynching Ballads in North Carolina" (M.A. thesis, University of North Carolina, 1995). A haunt tale, or ghost story, about a lynching is exemplified by the story of the lynching of Willie Earle in Greenville, South Carolina, recounted in Nancy Roberts, *South Carolina Ghosts: From the Coast to the Mountains* (Columbia: University of South Carolina Press, 1983), 81–92. Places where lynchings occur tend to become traditional, as W. Fitzhugh Brundage notes in *Lynching in the New South: Georgia and Virginia, 1880–1930* (Urbana: University of Illinois Press, 1993), 41. They are also

named, as in the case of J. V. Johnson to be discussed below and the lynching of Jim Rhodes in Charlottesville, Virginia, mentioned in a 1963 term paper by Ormonde Deane in the A. P. Hudson Collection, Southern Folklife Collection, Library of the University of North Carolina, Chapel Hill. Customary behavior covers a wide range and is discussed in Brundage, *Lynching in the New South*, chap. 1, and my "Lynching Ballads in North Carolina," chap. 1. African American folk culture of lynching is expressed, I believe, in legends such as those collected by folklorist Martha Nelson in North Carolina, possibly blues songs such as one by Sam Price mentioned in Paul Oliver, *Conversation with the Blues* (New York: Horizon Press, 1965), 34, and oral poetry such as "A Black Man Talks to God," composed by National Heritage Award winner Horace "Spoons" Williams in the 1930s.

4. Sid Hemphill's ballad "The Strayhorn Mob," commissioned by the leader of the Mississippi mob, is an exception to this rule; it names the mob leaders. "In a Little Country Schoolyard" is found in Martha L. Cooper, *Life, Liberty, and the Pursuit of Happiness: Nodaway County, Missouri, a Black History, 1840–1940* (Maryville, Mo.: N.p., 1986). Information on "Emmet Till" is in the song file of the Southern Folklife Collection. "The Ashland Tragedy" was collected by John Harrington Cox in his *Folk-Songs of the South* (Hatboro, Pa.: Folklore Associates, 1963).

5. I compiled this account of the murder and lynching from articles in the *Concord Times*, June 2, 1898, and the *Concord Daily Standard*, May 30, 1898.

6. Jacquelyn Dowd Hall, *Revolt against Chivalry: Jessie Daniel Ames and the Women's Campaign against Lynching* (New York: Columbia University Press, 1979), 150. The victim's appeal for water is mentioned by E. J. Linker in Randolph S. Hancock, "Sweet Emma Met an Awful Fate," a newspaper article from 1955, and in Ned Cline, "Even Negroes Took Part in Cabarrus's Last Lynching," *Salisbury Post*, November 29, 1964, in which "Kiser begged for a final drink of whiskey."

7. Cohen, *Poor Pearl, Poor Girl!*, 40.

8. Cooper, *Life, Liberty, and the Pursuit of Happiness*, 285.

9. For more details on the historical context of "The Death of Emma Hartsell" see chapter 2 of my "Lynching Ballads in North Carolina." Just as a ballad has a historical context, a specific performance is conditioned by contextual factors. The manifesto of the performance-based approach to folklore is Richard Bauman, *Verbal Art as Performance* (Rowley, Mass.: Newbury House, 1977).

10. The best account of Alec Whitley's life and death, drawing on court documents and newspaper accounts, is David D. Almond Jr.'s *The Lynching of Alec Whitley* (Albemarle, N.C.: David D. Almond Jr., 1978). This work also includes the ballad by Rev. E. P. Harrington discussed later in this essay as an appendix.

11. In 1927, some kinspeople exhumed his body from beneath the red oak tree and reinterred it in the cemetery of Smith Grove Baptist Church near Big Lick. The tombstone lists his date of death incorrectly as 1894, perhaps to confuse those who would recall his history. According to David Deese of the *Stanly News and Press*, whenever journalist Fred Morgan wrote about the subject for the *News and Press* in the early 1950s, he received angry and even threatening telephone calls. David Deese wrote a column on Whitley as late as 1990, and, a week later, added, "The response to last week's column about the 1892 lynching of Alec Whitley in Albemarle has been encouraging. My home phone began ringing within hours after the newspaper hit the streets. Everyone had a bit of lore to offer me." Deese did not receive any threats in

response to this article. While inquiring about this subject in Stanly County in 1994, I was warned twice by individuals who made sure that I knew that some people still held strong feelings about the subject.

12. Abrahams and Foss, *Anglo-American Folksong Style*, 67; H. M. Belden and A. P. Hudson, eds., *The Frank C. Brown Collection of North Carolina Folklore*, Vol. 2 (Durham, N.C.: Duke University Press, 1952). A very good recent study of "Young Edwin in the Lowlands Low" and the ballad tradition of a particular North Carolina community is Adrienne Hollifield's "Family, Tradition, Orality, and Cultural Intervention in Sodom Laurel Ballad Singing," *North Carolina Folklore Journal* 42 (Winter– Spring 1995): 1–34.

13. Two informants told me that Whitley first cut off Tucker's feet and then forced him to walk.

14. The connection between dismemberment and lynching in folk culture may be stronger than I indicate here. An anonymous informant, talking about the murder of Emma Hartsell, told me that her killers "chopped her up and put the pieces in a dishpan behind the stove." This detail is clearly an exaggeration based on her slashed throat, but it was related as justification for the lynching of Kizer and Johnson.

15. Its size and shape indicate that Harrington's ballad was printed as a broadside. According to Laws in *American Balladry from British Broadsides*, 40, "Many late 18th and early 19th century ballads are to be found on narrow sheets or slips about one-fourth the size of a folio sheet." Typographical clues also support the supposition that it was a broadside. George F. Hahn of Mt. Pleasant, Cabarrus County, found a copy of the broadside in the bottom of a trunk that had belonged to his great-grandmother, Tabitha Hunneycutt Roland, who lived in Big Lick, the Stanly County community where Whitley was from, in 1892. According to Hahn, the broadside was widely distributed around the time of the lynching.

16. For the role of the supernatural in native American balladry, see Laws, *Native American Balladry*, 35. Thomas's article on Whitley was a reprint of a newspaper story Thomas first researched and wrote in 1949. For a full discussion of the history of this article, which contains the only full text of the ballad, see my "Lynching Ballads in North Carolina," 68–70.

17. My account of the murder, trial, and lynching is condensed from several articles in the *Wadesboro Messenger and Intelligencer* dated December 28, 1905, April 26, 1906, and May 30, 1906. There were also articles about the lynching in the *Charlotte Daily Observer* on May 29, 1906, and the *Raleigh News and Observer* on May 29, 1906. Dates of the arraignment and trial are given in the Minutes of North Carolina Superior Court, Vol. H, Anson County, North Carolina State Archives in Raleigh. See also Paul D. Escott, *Many Excellent People: Power and Privilege in North Carolina, 1850– 1900* (Chapel Hill: University of North Carolina Press, 1992), 5.

18. Record of Lunacy, Office of the Clerk of Court, Wadesboro, Anson County, N.C.

19. "The Anson County Lynching," *Biblical Recorder* [Raleigh, N.C.] 71 (June 6, 1906): 8; R. L. Gray, "Winning the War on Lynching," *World's Work*, September 1925, 508–11. This ballad has been collected only once. Novella Caudle Carpenter of Peachland, Union County, sang it for Douglas Helms, then a student in Daniel W. Patterson's class, on December 30, 1966. Patterson transcribed the words and tune, and I corrected them.

20. The melody of "J. V. Johnson" also bears an affinity to "The Drunkard's Hell,"

in *The Frank C. Brown Collection of North Carolina Folklore*, ed. Jan P. Schinhan, Vol. 5 (Durham, N.C.: Duke University Press, 1962), 23.

21. Laws, *Native American Balladry*, 2, 27, 55.

22. In addition to employing the definition in the *Oxford English Dictionary*, 2d ed. (1989), for "tactical"—"of or relating to arrangement, esp. the arrangement of procedure with a view to ends"—I wish to use the term "tactical" in the technical sense employed by philosopher Todd May in his notion of tactical political philosophy discussed in *The Political Philosophy of Poststructuralist Anarchism* (University Park: Pennsylvania State University Press, 1994), 11. He writes: "For tactical political philosophy, there is no center within which power is to be located. Otherwise put, power, and consequently politics, are irreducible. There are many different sites from which it arises, and there is an interplay among these various sites in the creation of the social world."

23. John Greenway, *American Folksongs of Protest* (Philadelphia: University of Pennsylvania Press, 1953), 220–21; Maura Murphy, "The Ballad Singer and the Role of the Seditious Ballad in Nineteenth-Century Ireland: Dublin Castle's View," *Ulster Folklife* 25 (1979): 84.

24. In a few exceptions such as "J. V. Johnson" and "In a Quiet Country Churchyard," the lynching is condemned.

25. A better term may be "phrase," as Jean-François Lyotard uses it in *The Differend* (Minneapolis: University of Minnesota Press, 1988).

26. Bruce Lincoln, *Discourse and the Construction of Society: Comparative Studies of Myth, Ritual, and Classification* (New York: Oxford University Press, 1989), 3, 89.

27. A particularly inflammatory editorial about a local African American politician appeared in the *Concord Daily Standard* on May 4, 1898, three weeks before the lynching there. The letter about J. V. Johnson, signed by most of Morven's prominent citizens, is found in the *Wadesboro Messenger and Intelligencer*, July 5, 1906.

28. Lincoln, *Discourse and the Construction of Society*, 99; Hall, *Revolt against Chivalry*, 141.

29. Jean-François Lyotard, *The Postmodern Condition: A Report on Knowledge* (Minneapolis: University of Minnesota Press, 1984), 63.

30. Michel Foucault, *Discipline and Punish: The Birth of the Prison* (New York: Vintage, 1977), 47–48.

31. Lyotard, *Postmodern Condition*, 22.

32. Norm Cohen, "Robert W. Gordon and the Second Wreck of 'Old 97,'" *Journal of American Folklore* 87 (1974): 12–38.

33. For a fuller account of Gladys Kincaid's murder and the ballads it inspired, see the second chapter of my "Lynching Ballads in North Carolina." I am indebted to Wayne Martin of the Folklife Office of the North Carolina Arts Council for the information on J. E. Mainer's recording and publication of "The Death of Emma Hartsell."

Part IV

Black Responses and
the Legacy of Lynching

Writing in 1892, Anna Julia Cooper observed that "there are two kinds of peace in this world; the one produced by suppression, which is the passivity of death; the other brought about by a proper adjustment of living acting forces." As long as lynching and racial oppression persisted, there was little likelihood that either black or white Americans would enjoy "the secret of true harmony" that Cooper hoped for.[1] Instead, the peace that existed between the races was violent, intended to cow and demoralize African Americans into accepting their less-than-equal status. But despite the "suppression" that so troubled Cooper, blacks never did surrender to "the passivity of death." The final three essays in this collection, which focus both on traditions of suppression that endured long after lynching abated and on the response of African Americans to mob violence, reveal some of the contradictory legacies of lynching. The struggle by blacks against white violence fostered rich traditions of protest that would undergird black activism throughout the twentieth century. Yet even as lynching waned in the South, brutal manifestations of institutional racism persisted and continued to challenge activists already seasoned by the campaign against lynching.

George C. Wright offers a chilling essay on the persistence of gross violations of the legal rights of blacks in Kentucky at the hands of the law. His conclusions confirm the folk wisdom of a South Carolina black in 1928, who summed up a lifetime of close observation of the white man's justice: "It seems to me when it come to trouble, de law an' a nigger is de white man's sport, an' justice is a stranger in them precincts, an' mercy is unknown. An' de Bible say we must pray for we enemy. Drap on your knee, brothers, an' pray to God for all de crackers an' de judges an' de courts an' solicitors, sheriffs an' police in de land, for we must er been all er we livin' in sin."[2] In addition to reminding us that the decline of extra-legal violence against blacks during the twentieth century did not diminish the threat of legal oppression, the essay also has broad implications for our understanding of the effects of racism on the modern criminal justice system. While conceding that violence by state authorities, in the form of public executions and "legal lynchings," differed in fundamental ways from lynchings, Wright insists that executions, especially when held in public, were intended to convey many of the lessons in civil and social order that lynchings did. And those lessons were sanctioned time and time again by the highest courts and officials of Kentucky. Wright exposes the reasons why generations of blacks have understood that when they enter the courts they become "de white man's sport."

It is tempting to assume that fear of repression alone was sufficient to prevent blacks in the South from carrying out effective agitation against white violence. But, in fact, blacks devised various subterfuges and techniques to resist white violence. Writing in the 1960s, Julius Lester observed, "It is not an exaggeration to say that the history of blacks in America is one of resistance." Lester conceded that black resistance "has remained, for the most part, unorganized, and thus the difficulty in recognizing the struggle that has been constantly taking place."[3]

Nowhere in the South did blacks have the effective means to suppress lynching, but they could, as Brundage's essay explains, play an important and complex role in restraining white violence. Deeply resentful of each failure of local authorities to prevent mob violence, some southern blacks turned to their own race for protection and devised diverse strategies of resistance. Brundage provides a glimpse of some of those "hidden" traditions of black resistance to white violence, traditions which underscore that even during the nadir of race relations during the late nineteenth century, blacks were not simply sullen, powerless victims of mob violence. Very little is known about the actual response of southern black communities either to threatened or accomplished lynchings, and until more is known, our understanding of lynching in the South will remain incomplete.

Patricia Schechter recounts the more familiar campaign of black women against lynching. Precisely because lynching was rife with both gender and racial significance, black women activists recognized the social and political stakes involved in protesting against mob violence. Her essay concentrates on the evolving role of women in the antilynching campaign during the 1890s and explains Ida Wells's signal contribution to that effort. Her account provides a new and fuller understanding of how Wells recast the debate over lynchings in ways that compelled whites to address at least some of the social realities of lynching. By repudiating whites' justifications for lynching, Wells and other black women asserted their will and agency to define themselves outside the parameters of the prevailing racist discourse. Schechter's essay also reveals just how difficult was the task that black women like Wells assumed. They could not refute the logic behind either lynching or their subordination as black women without challenging entrenched and unflattering images of black women that circulated in both the black and white communities. Thus, Schechter explains, the antilynching campaign became a forum in which some black women articulated a public discourse critical of both racial and sexual subordination. Finally, by prodding us to recognize the shifting contexts that framed black women's antilynching activism, Schechter clarifies the extent to which black women activists were able to overcome the limits of their strategies, gender, race, and age.

NOTES

1. Anna Julia Cooper, *A Voice from the South* (1892; rpt. New York: Oxford University Press, 1988), 149.

2. Edward C. L. Adams, *Tales of the Congaree*, ed. Robert G. O'Meally (1927; rpt. Chapel Hill: University of North Carolina Press, 1987), 188.

3. He went on to add that "Ol' Aunt Jemima was always spitting in massa's soup, while ol' John out in the field couldn't pick up the hoe without it just seeming to break in his hands" (Julius Lester, *Look Out, Whitey! Black Power's Gon' Get Your Mama* [New York: Dial Press, 1968], 35–36).

By the Book

The Legal Executions
of Kentucky Blacks

George C. Wright

B y the turn of the century, racial violence had become one of the
defining characteristics of the American South. Newspapers
carried accounts of white mobs in Georgia, Mississippi, Texas,
and elsewhere seizing and lynching blacks, often in a highly
ritualized manner. From the end of the Civil War until 1940, Kentucky, a
border state, witnessed racial violence that mirrored that of the Deep
South. At least 353 people died at the hands of lynch mobs, and 75
percent of the victims were black. Tragically, 353 victims is a conservative
estimate, since scholars have found it all but impossible to determine the
exact number of lynchings. This was especially true from 1865 to 1875
because whites, fearful of intervention by the federal government, often
buried or burned the bodies of lynch victims. Indeed, although 117 lynchings have been documented for that ten-year period, perhaps as many as
300 occurred during those years.[1]

Kentucky, like Georgia, Mississippi, and Texas, had its share of lynchings that both fascinated and offended the public: the 1893 mutilation and
burning of C. J. Miller, the victim of a false charge of rape; the 1899
torture-burning of Richard Coleman in Maysville that was witnessed by
ten thousand whites, many of whom—from young children to senior citizens—actively participated by contributing wood to the fire; the lynching
of David Walker in Fulton County in 1908 for swearing at a white woman
and the slaughter of his wife and five children as they fled their burning
house; and the 1908 hanging of four blacks in Logan County. In the latter
instance, the mob penned a note to one of the victims warning other
blacks to leave white people alone. This multiple lynching so enthralled
many whites in western Kentucky that photographs of the dangling bodies

can still be found in their homes today. Although it might be an overstatement to label as unique any one of the more than five thousand lynchings that have occurred in the United States, the Opera House lynching in Livermore, Kentucky, in 1911 may fit that description. Will Porter, who was accused of shooting a white man, was carried by a mob from the jail to the theater. Armed men paid an admission fee that entitled them not only to witness the lynching but to riddle Porter's body with bullets. This lynching made national and international news and embarrassed state officials in a manner that previous mob murders had not.

Whites often justified lynchings by proclaiming that mobs were compelled to act because the states failed to punish criminals. This claim may have been true when whites committed crimes; but for blacks, an accusation, no matter how absurd, meant almost certain conviction. In actuality, lynching was a primary way of extracting revenge quickly and upholding southern virtue, especially that of white women. As the killing of the four young men in Logan County demonstrated, whites often lynched blacks as a warning to other blacks not to challenge the status quo in any manner. It is no coincidence that a primary way that Kentucky whites, regardless of their wealth or education, rallied support for their causes was by proclaiming the threat of "Negro Domination." In reality, because whites firmly controlled the police, the state militia, the courts, and the political system, there was no threat of black domination anywhere in the South or the nation. This most surely was the case in Kentucky, where the black population relative to that of whites declined from 1870 onward.[2]

An especially pernicious extension of lynchings was the practice of manipulating the legal system to ensure that blacks accused of rape or murder received the death penalty, the same punishment that would have been meted out by the lynch mob. This practice—often called "legal lynching"—proved to be effective, and the number of death sentences carried out by the state grew in number and significance after 1900. As historian Jacquelyn Hall explained, "The thwarted lynch mob frequently demanded that public officials impose the death sentence in a hasty mockery of a trial. If these 'legal lynchings' were included in the statistics, the death toll would be much higher."[3]

Professor Hall makes a significant point when writing that lynchings and legal lynchings should be listed together. On numerous occasions in Kentucky, judges and prosecuting attorneys negotiated with leaders of a mob to allow blacks accused of rape or murder to have a trial before their executions. These trials never lasted a full day, and many were completed within an hour. The distinction between legal lynchings and mob lynchings was blurred by instances when the court assumed the role of the mob by holding a "trial" even though the defendant stood no chance of being found innocent, as well as instances when the mob assumed the role of the court and gave the victim a "trial" and allowed members of the lynch mob to render a verdict and select the method of execution. In both instances, the outcome—the death of the black person—was a foregone conclusion. There was, however, a crucial distinction: executions carried out by the state were legal because they had the blessing—the sanction—of the state,

Ultimately, it is important to distinguish between legal lynchings and extralegal mob murders because nothing should obscure the fact that legal lynchings were the most brutal form of racial violence. Undoubtedly, being put to death under any circumstances, whether by the state or the mob, was painful. Moreover, I realize that it is highly subjective to argue that a legal lynching was the most brutal form of execution because dying on the gallows or in the electric chair probably seemed like an act of compassion when compared to the slow, torturous burnings that mobs extracted on some of their victims. Regardless of the method used in putting a person to death, it was the role of the state, which in theory was committed to establishing and preserving an ethical system of justice, that made legal lynching especially hideous. Whites rationalized lynchings, saying that some acts were so reprehensible that they demanded quick punishment and that the offender was not worthy of due process. But whites still had to concede that lynchings violated their own laws. White Kentuckians boasted of having controlled their natural instinct for revenge by allowing the legal system to apprehend, convict, and punish the guilty. Kentucky's governors, its civic and religious leaders, and even the most humble of white citizens seemed blind to the injustices committed against African Americans in the name of the law. Whites stacked the deck against black defendants yet maintained a belief in the fairness of the legal system. They refused to believe that trials for black men accused of rape or murder were held in an environment identical to that of a lynching. Simply stated, whites believed that death sentences handed down to African Americans were fair and legal and had been done "by the book," upholding the laws of the state and the nation.

The state of Kentucky carried out at least 229 executions between 1872 and 1940, and African Americans, approximately 10 percent of the population, accounted for 57 percent of the people put to death. Of the 229 people legally executed, 197 were for murder, 31 for rape, and 1 for armed robbery. Given the white racist belief that rape was a "Negro crime," it is a wonder that only 80 percent (25 of 31) of the men put to death for rape were African American. No one—black or white—died for raping a black woman. Furthermore, only a few of the 130 blacks who died on the gallows or in the electric chair were convicted of killing African Americans. Since no blacks served on juries during these years, all of the blacks put to death were convicted and sentenced by all-white juries.[4]

Kentucky whites, when meting out "justice" to blacks, consistently ignored their most sacred beliefs about the legal system. The safeguards that existed to ensure fair trials for whites simply did not apply to black defendants. A review of the cases in which blacks were sentenced to death or long prison terms reveals that discretion rarely worked in their favor. The discretionary decisions made by prosecutors in Kentucky, which ranged from decisions on whether to try cases, the charges to be leveled against the defendants, and the strategies to be used in seeking convictions, are very revealing about the state's legal system. There were numerous instances in which the facts, as presented in white—not black—newspapers, suggested that blacks who killed whites during confrontations acted in self-defense. Prosecuting attorneys and juries most surely refused to use discretion when a black was charged with rape. In some cases, the white woman personally knew her alleged black attacker, and on cross-examination it was clear that they had been romantically involved. When a black was accused of raping a white, nothing else mattered, not even if he and the alleged victim were both teenagers and the offense was his first. Courts refused to consider the mental state of black defendants and whether they understood the charges leveled against them. By contrast, in every reported case in which a white was accused of raping a black woman, prosecutors, judges, and juries used discretion either to drop all the charges or to convict the alleged rapist on a lesser charge, such as detaining a female against her will. For instance, in April 1926, a Lexington court agreed with the attorney for Charles Merchant that he was insane and sentenced him to a mental institution for raping and beating two young black girls. The city's black leaders were outraged over this decision, especially because the prosecuting attorney had promised to treat Merchant, a member of a prominent white family, just like black rapists and seek the death penalty.[5]

One glaring instance of judicial racism occurred after Robert Charles O'Hara Benjamin, a black lawyer in Lexington, was murdered by Michael Moynahan in October 1900. On the surface it seemed as if Moynahan, unlike other whites accused of killing African Americans, would be prevented from claiming self-defense because he shot Benjamin in the back.

Moynahan faced an additional hurdle: he had been arrested earlier in the day for striking Benjamin in the face with a pistol. Several days after Benjamin's death, however, the judge at the examining trial, using his discretion, dismissed the case on the grounds that Moynahan had acted in self-defense. Furthermore, in the eyes of whites, Benjamin's death made the original assault charge against Moynahan moot as well.[6] Black leaders, especially in Louisville and Lexington, consistently denounced the courts for being lenient toward white offenders who committed crimes against blacks. Considering that in only a handful of cases in Kentucky between 1900 and 1940 were whites charged with the murders or rapes of whites and actually held over to trials, one has to wonder how many other instances like Moynahan's shooting of Benjamin occurred in which grand juries used their discretion and refused to charge the whites. This question is especially relevant for cases in rural counties and small towns where charging a white with an offense was as likely to result in additional problems for blacks as to the possible prosecution of the accused white. In addition, in the few instances in which the white offender was brought to trial, juries of their peers routinely refused to convict whites of offenses against blacks.

In contrast, when whites charged and brought African Americans to trial, they systematically worked to exclude other blacks from serving on juries. Whites relied on state law and federal court rulings to prohibit blacks from jury duty. A blatantly racist Kentucky law, enacted in December 1873, disqualified blacks from serving as petit jurors and also "provided that no person shall be qualified as grand juryman unless he be a white citizen." Four years later, another law reaffirmed the exclusion of blacks from juries. It "provided that the selection, summoning, and impaneling of a grand jury shall be as prescribed in the General statutes," which limited service to white men.[7]

Given the overt racism of the two exclusionary laws regarding juries, the Kentucky Court of Appeals, even though it had few scruples where blacks were concerned, had no choice but to rule these laws unconstitutional. In June 1880, in the case of *Commonwealth* v. *Johnson*, the court ruled, "We therefore hold that so much of our statute as excludes all persons other than white men from service on juries is unconstitutional, and that no person can be lawfully excluded from any jury on account of his race or color."[8] Kentucky's highest court was guided by two 1879 United States Supreme Court decisions. In *Strauder* v. *West Virginia*, the court concluded that West Virginia had denied due process and equal protection of the law to blacks when proclaiming that jury duty was limited to white men. The Kentucky legislature, of course, had used similar language. Yet in *Virginia* v. *Rives*, the justices of the U.S. Supreme Court declared that because Virginia law did not limit jury duty to whites, the absence of blacks from a jury did not represent discrimination. Just as in many cases of alleged discrimination brought before the Supreme Court, the justices ruled in *Rives* that the burden of proving discrimination by an all-white jury rested with blacks.[9]

Virginia v. *Rives* provided the loophole for Kentucky whites to continue excluding African Americans from jury duty. The Kentucky Court of Appeals, after concluding that limiting jury duty to whites was unconstitutional, explained that the presence of an all-white jury was still legal. "We do not mean, however, to be understood to say that a Negro cannot be lawfully indicted and tried unless the jury is composed in part of persons of his own race. All we decide is, that such persons must not be excluded because of their race."[10] Kentucky's highest court reinforced this ruling a decade later by upholding, in *Smith* v. *Commonwealth*, the death sentence of a black man even though the three jury commissioners who had selected potential jurors failed to include any African Americans in the jury pool.[11]

The efforts of the legislature and the courts and the determination of local whites effectively excluded blacks from juries in the Bluegrass State until the late 1930s. White Kentuckians steadfastly defended the practice and fairness of all-white juries. A reporter who expressed his satisfaction with the death sentence of an African American reflected the view of most whites: all-white juries "were made up of our best citizens [who were] not likely to be so unanimous in their opinion unless convinced of his [the black defendant's] guilt."[12]

Not until 1938 was the exclusion of blacks from jury duty overturned. In that year, when reviewing the murder conviction and death sentence of James Hale, the Kentucky Court of Appeals acknowledged that no blacks had served on juries in McCracken County, where the case originated. But according to the justices, the failure to consider blacks for jury service did not prove that they were systematically excluded. After Hale's appeal was rejected before the Kentucky court, the National Association for the Advancement of Colored People carried it to the U.S. Supreme Court. Charles H. Houston, the lead attorney for the NAACP, submitted documents showing that one-sixth of the county's residents were African Americans, yet of the six hundred people selected for jury duty in the previous year, none had been black. He demonstrated that the pattern of all-white jury pools was typical of previous years as well. Indeed, another affidavit revealed that no black had ever served on a jury in McCracken

County. In a unanimous ruling, the Supreme Court noted, "We are of the opinion that the affidavits, which by the stipulation of the State were to be taken as proof, and were uncontroverted, sufficed to show a systematic and arbitrary exclusion of Negroes from the jury lists solely because of their race or color, constituting a denial of the equal protection of the laws guaranteed to petitioner by the Fourteenth Amendment." Hale received a new trial, and, with blacks serving on the jury, was found guilty but sentenced to life in prison instead of death.[13]

Whites ignored their sacred beliefs about the legal system by having African Americans stand trial in courtrooms where the mob, not the judge, dominated the proceedings and were ready to act if the "wrong" verdict was reached. Throughout Kentucky there were mob-dominated trials that seem almost surreal. White Kentuckians, in their haste to hang blacks as quickly as possible after their trials, even constructed the gallows before the trials started. Hoping to avoid a mob lynching in 1909, a judge in Williamstown promised that the black teenager accused of rape would be convicted and sentenced to death.[14] Almost twenty years later, while deliberating the fate of a black accused of rape in Covington, the jury informed the judge that they needed additional information before they could reach a decision. Fearful of the mob, the judge admonished the jury for having already taken too long—more than four hours—and instructed them to reach a verdict within ten minutes. With the mandate from the judge ringing in their ears, the jury returned within a matter of minutes with a guilty verdict and the death sentence.[15] On several occasions the governor sent troops to protect the life of a black who was being returned to an area to stand trial for rape or murder. But even the presence of armed soldiers failed to prevent mobs from making known their intentions to lynch the defendant if he was given any sentence short of death.

The speed with which many trials were concluded makes it difficult to distinguish between them and mob lynchings. Blacks, who had been taken from rural areas to Lexington or Louisville for safekeeping, were routinely returned and put on trial immediately to satisfy a community's desire to resolve quickly alleged murders and rapes—with a guilty verdict, of course. Sometimes only hours passed between the appointment of an attorney for the accused, the entire trial, the jury deliberation, sentencing, and the carrying out of the death sentence. In an obvious concession to the mob, trials were often held on Saturday when people from rural areas could leave their jobs and come to town.

Of all such trials, it was the one of Allen Mathias of Mayfield that set a standard for quick justice in Kentucky. Charged in July 1906 with the rape of a white woman, Mathias was carried first to Paducah and then to Louisville for protection. To appease the large number of whites demanding a speedy trial, local officials brought him back to Mayfield within days of his arrest to stand trial. The train returning Mathias and the sheriff to Mayfield was met by ten thousand whites, and, because the scaffold was already assembled, it was obvious that he would die either at the hands of the state or the mob. His entire trial and execution took an hour and two minutes. Therefore, he was prevented from appealing to a higher court or seeking clemency from the governor. The legal lynching of Mathias ended in the same manner as other mob lynchings, with his body being carried through the streets as a warning to other blacks to abide by the law. In addition, following the execution of Mathias, a group of whites forced four blacks to leave town, another form of violence that often accompanied mob lynchings.[16]

White newspaper editors condoned the actions of Mayfield's officials just as they did mob lynchings, which in fact the Mathias trial had been. "Long drawn-out trials followed by appeal with repeated re-trials do much to weaken the popular confidence in the law as a remedy for crime," rationalized the *Louisville Courier-Journal*, the state's leading newspaper. Mayfield was to be applauded for avoiding a lynching, the newspaper concluded. Surprisingly, this view was not shared by the state legislature, where lawmakers responded to the legal lynching of Mathias by enacting a thirty-day "cooling off" period between sentencing and carrying out an execution. This law, however, simply led to executions occurring exactly thirty days after convictions.[17]

In addition to legal technicalities, prevailing mores ensured that blacks seldom encountered justice at the hands of white courts. Under oath, the word of a black man meant nothing when his accusers were white. In murder cases, the claim that an African American killed a white to avoid being attacked rarely proved persuasive to all-white juries. Black men had no defenses that whites found plausible when white women accused them of rape. In Madisonville in the mid-1920s, two black men, Nathan Bard and Bunyan Fleming, were executed for the rape of Neil Breithaupt, even though she could not identify them as her attackers, and, in all likelihood, her accusation of rape was a figment of her imagination. Bard and Fleming, however, had engaged in sexual intercourse with white prostitutes. After Breithaupt claimed to have been raped, the authorities reasoned that since the men were already having sex with whites, they attacked other white women to satisfy their lust. In Covington a decade later, John Pete Montjoy was executed for rape. His "crime" clearly was having an ongoing relationship with the white woman who brought charges of rape against him for revenge. Mary Brite, the secretary of the Cincinnati chapter of the American Civil Liberties Union, tried desperately to save Montjoy's life. After it was obvious that Montjoy would be executed, Brite wrote an essay decrying the form of justice blacks received when accused by whites.

Reduced to its simplest elements, the Montjoy case was an instance in which the unsupported statement of a white woman linked with bitter prejudice to condemn a black man to death. From a legal point of view, it contradicted every principle of administering justice in criminal cases. From a social point of view, the case illustrated the myriad ways in which race hatred and ill will were fostered and fomented. It appears that officers of the law and officers of the court closed their eyes to principles of fair play and simple justice so as to conform to traditions of race hatred.[18]

In contrast, Kentucky's white newspapers contain numerous accounts of court cases in which, to the dismay of the general public, a white charged with a crime was found not guilty because of reasonable doubt. In some cases, white defendants escaped conviction because they provided alibis. There are instances of cases being dismissed because the prosecution failed to establish a motive linking the defendant to the crime. But when African Americans were on trial, rarely if ever was reasonable doubt sufficient to prevent conviction. Without question, given the weak evidence presented by the prosecution against Bard and Fleming in the Madisonville rape trial, reasonable doubt would have been a logical decision if they had been white. No alibi put forward in defense of a black person meant anything if any white offered contradictory testimony. And because the vast majority of whites believed that blacks were natural-born criminals, the prosecution often chose not to establish motives for alleged crimes. Instead, merely reminding whites that blacks were depraved was enough to bring about convictions of black defendants.

Blacks were especially vulnerable to legal injustice when on trial for murdering whites. Blacks seldom were able to claim a recognized defense within the American legal tradition: the right to self-defense. During a time when whites avoided conviction by testifying that they had acted in self-defense (such as when Moynahan shot Benjamin in the back), denying African Americans the same right was the height of hypocrisy. It is difficult to conceive of George Dinning and Rufus Browder having been arrested, charged with murder, and convicted in court had they been white. Dinning, a Simpson County farmer whose property and cattle were the envy of whites, killed a member of a mob that attempted to seize his property and force his removal from the area. Before killing Jodie Cohn, Dinning was wounded twice. A reporter for the *New York Times* speculated that even though Dinning was on trial for the murder of a white, his case would be one rare instance in which a black would be found innocent: "The interesting feature of the case is that Dinning, on the face of the facts, cannot be convicted as he was defending himself. . . . No witness can appear against him without admitting that they were members of the Kuklux band." The evidence showed that after Browder was struck and cut with a whip and shot in the chest, he returned the gunfire and killed James Cunningham, the white man on whose Logan County farm he labored as a sharecropper. The Logan County jury, composed of neighbors and friends of Cunningham, ignored the physician's testimony concerning Browder's wounds and Browder's own claim of self-defense and sentenced him to death. Dinning's murder conviction was such an outrage that the governor gave him a full and complete pardon within ten days of his arrival in state prison.[19]

To understand fully legal lynchings, it is important to assess the actions of Kentucky's governors and justices of the state's highest court. Their role in legal lynchings was comparable to that of the law officers and elected officials who condoned the mob violence that occurred in their communities. Several governors and state judges displayed an awareness of and distaste for some of the most extreme forms of legal lynchings by commuting sentences or ordering new trials for African Americans. Occasionally state officials and judges seemingly overcame the racist conventions of the day. Nevertheless, even the most principled white state officials and judges willingly tolerated procedures that contravened the intent if not the appearance of legal justice. In the overwhelming majority of instances, the governors and justices consistently supported the convictions of African Americans in mob-dominated courts.

Republican governors expressed far more concern about mob violence against blacks than did their Democratic counterparts. This concern was owing in part to the Republican Party's sensitivity to black voters, who overwhelmingly supported the party. The governors had other reasons as well, however. Several governors said that mob violence ruined Kentucky's good name and was like an epidemic, leading to additional outbreaks of lawlessness. In 1895, William O. Bradley became the first Republican elected governor in the state. More than any elected official of that day, he deserved the title "friend of the Negro." Bradley denounced local officials for refusing to take steps to prevent lynchings, offered rewards for the apprehension of members of lynch mobs, and enacted the state's first antilynching law. His sending of troops to the trials of George Dinning and other blacks saved their lives and became a practice adopted by other governors. Bradley, in short, was a symbol of the fight to end mob rule in Kentucky. Yet, although he denounced mob violence, Bradley did not seriously question the convictions, including death sentences, handed down by mob-dominated juries to African Americans.

Augustus E. Willson and Edwin Morrow, both Republican governors, continued Bradley's efforts by designating the ending of mob violence a high priority in their administrations. Willson sent troops to western Kentucky to help end the violence of the night riders. During his administration, a shoot-out occurred in Dixon when twelve blacks attempted to prevent a lynching. During the exchange of gunfire, one white was killed and another wounded. Ignoring the attack of the whites on the blacks and the attempted lynching, the Webster County court gave each black defendant a "light sentence" of seven years in prison for participating in a "race riot." Willson intervened and released all of them from state prison. He explained his decision laconically: "All men of ordinary sense know that Negroes do not band together in such a county as this to mob white men." On another occasion—when commuting the death sentence of Robert Hocker—he stated plainly that "all lawyers realize that there is a lack of care in the trial of blacks."[20] As governor in 1920, Morrow received national acclaim for ordering the state militia to fire on members of a white mob that attempted to seize and lynch a black man on trial. Five members of the mob were killed. Responding to the praise he received, Morrow replied, "What else was I to do? Don't people expect governors to do their duty?"[21]

The justices of the Kentucky Court of Appeals also saved the lives of black men on several occasions. In November 1904, a fight between blacks and whites in a saloon resulted in the fatal shooting of a white man. The prosecutor, using his discretion, brought charges of murder against three blacks but no whites. The men were tried separately, convicted, and sentenced to death. The Court of Appeals concluded that several errors were made by the Lexington court. First, the prosecutor had been unable to determine who had fired the fatal shot and had simply charged the three black men with murder. Second, the court noted, the judge failed to instruct the jury to consider the possibility that the victim had been killed by accident. The appeals court ordered a new trial for the men. They were again found guilty but instead of being condemned to die, they were given life sentences, which, in the context of early twentieth-century Kentucky, was a light sentence for blacks convicted of killing whites.[22]

A few years later, the Kentucky Court of Appeals reviewed the death sentence of Rufus Browder. In overturning his conviction and ordering a change of venue for his new trial, the court established a precedent that should have been applied to the trials of other Kentucky blacks.

> If the defendant had killed a Negro, or if he were a white man, and had killed a white man, we might look at the case differently; but we can not shut our eyes to the fact that here was a case of race prejudice excited to the white heat. A prominent white man had been shot by a Negro laborer working for him. The mob wished to execute the Negro summarily the night he was placed in jail. Being balked in that attempt . . . they wreaked their vengeance on four innocent Negroes whose only offense was that they were friends of his. . . . To say the defendant could have a fair trial in Russellville under such circumstances is to shut our eyes to the conditions which must have prevailed when such things as we have detailed took place.[23]

The justices concluded by making a statement about blacks accused of crimes against whites: "When the public mind is excited by race hostility the feeling may smolder, but though not apparent on the surface, it does not soon die out, on the contrary often the sentiment spreads and strengthens." Browder's second trial took place in Simpson County. He was again found guilty, but he avoided execution, receiving a life sentence instead. A year after Browder's conviction, the governor reduced his sentence to ten years. Again, within the context of the time and the place, for a black man to serve ten years in prison for killing a white—even in self-defense—represented a legal milestone.[24]

In 1918, the justices of the Kentucky Court of Appeals at last addressed the issue of speedy trials. Claiming self-defense, Bradley McDaniel, a black teenager, shot and killed Dee Spears in Warren County. To prevent a lynching, the authorities transferred McDaniel to Louisville. Three weeks later, Bradley was brought back to the area; two days later, he was indicted by the grand jury, made to stand trial, convicted, and sentenced to death within the span of a few hours. A major error had been committed, the justices of the appeals court ruled, when Bradley's motion for delaying the start of his trial immediately after his indictment was denied. Then, in a startling statement, the justices condemned the whites of Warren County for their actions during the trial. The justices explained that a mob had controlled the court proceedings. It was predictable that the black youth was found guilty because the mob had "presented a petition to the county attorney demanding that the defendant be placed upon trial immediately at a special term of the court, and unless he was given the death sentence they would take the law into their own hands and see that he was executed." The justices concluded by acknowledging that unnecessary delays in bringing alleged criminals to trial weakened public confidence in the judicial system. But they stressed, "Notwithstanding the clamor for speedy trials, we believe that trials may be too speedy, and thus do more harm than good to the body politic by lessening in place of increasing respect for the law." Although the ultimate outcome of the new trial is not known, it is clear that the appeals court's decision saved him from death in Kentucky's electric chair.[25]

But if Kentucky's Republican governors and justices of the Court of Appeals on occasion made bold statements and took steps that prevented gross violations of the rights of black defendants, they also displayed conspicuous blind spots regarding issues of race and justice. Though eventually denouncing hasty trials, the justices still refused to comment on the proceedings of the trials in which black men were convicted of rape and sentenced to death. For instance, in upholding the death sentence of Robert Blanks, the justices of Kentucky's highest court chose to ignore the fact that for decades a rumor that a black was accused of raping a white female led to mob-dominated courts in which sentences of death were automatically handed down. Kentucky's justices never denounced the absence of blacks from all-white juries and in fact upheld the practice in 1937 in the case of *Hale* v. *Commonwealth*. Simply stated, the justices' interpretations where blacks were concerned were so narrow that any statement they made, such as denouncing the mob-dominated trial of Rufus Browder or the speedy conviction of Bradley McDaniel, established no enduring precedent. The justices were unwilling substantially to revise the legal traditions that deprived countless Kentucky blacks of their lives.

Far more than state judges, the governors knew that local authorities and community leaders routinely pleaded with mobs to allow a trial to take place with the understanding that the accused black would be severely punished at its conclusion. Despite his concern for black rights, Governor Bradley allowed numerous questionable convictions to stand, especially of blacks tried and convicted in hostile environments. In May 1898, Robert Blanks, a Mayfield black who had fled the area after being accused of rape, was arrested in Cairo, Illinois. The governor of Illinois approved his extradition, but, to the shock of Mayfield authorities, Bradley denied the request. In a widely reported statement, he explained, "The wholesale slaughter of Negroes by mobs in Graves County and the failure to punish their murderers satisfies me that to have this man sent back there would be to have him sent to his death, and that he could not obtain even a semblance of a fair trial. If guilty he deserves death, but punishment should be inflicted by law and not by mob. I decline to issue the requisition."[26]

Bradley informed Mayfield officials that instead of returning Blanks immediately, he would wait at least a month, hoping that the passage of time would ease racial tensions. Accompanied by fifty heavily armed soldiers, Blanks arrived by train in Mayfield on July 5. The local press captured the sentiment of the people: "Several hundred people were at the depot to witness the strange spectacle of a company of soldiers coming to Mayfield to save the neck of a brutal Negro from a mob." Despite the governor's intentions and the presence of the soldiers, the mob controlled events in Mayfield: they not only met the train at the depot but also followed the soldiers to the jail, surrounded the jail until Blanks went to court, crammed the courtroom, and made known their opinion of the defendant's testimony with loud, angry outbursts. Although allowing the trial to take place in Mayfield, Bradley had insisted that the jury be made up of citizens from Hickman County. But as Augustus E. Willson, who served as one of Blanks's three attorneys, noted, having the jury come from Hickman County or from any adjacent counties made little difference; whites living in the surrounding areas almost universally agreed, even before hearing any testimony, that Blanks was guilty of raping a white woman. It took the jury only a few minutes to return with a guilty verdict and a sentence of death.[27]

Willson subsequently appeared before the Kentucky Court of Appeals to have the verdict overturned. In great detail, he informed the justices of how the mob had dominated the trial. Moreover, he explained that from the start the trial had been tainted by the highly inflammatory newspaper coverage of the alleged rape. Finally, the attorney asserted that the conviction should be overturned because of the refusal of the court to grant a change of venue from western Kentucky. After the justices quickly dismissed the appeal, Willson turned to Governor Bradley, a fellow Republican, to save Blanks. Desperately trying to have the sentence commuted to ten years in prison (because, Willson explained, Blanks had admitted to having sex with the white female), he told the governor that he was defending Blanks "without fee or reward" through a sincere belief that justice had to be served in cases such as this one. Unless the governor acted, Willson argued, mob justice would continue to prevail in Kentucky. "This Bob Blanks case is a case in which Providence tests the soundness of our whole system with the wager of an utterly unimportant human cipher. Bob Blanks is the cipher, whose case tests the soundness and the justice of our institutions, as much as if he were the most precious life that ever was thrown in the scale. . . . Bob Blanks' case seems to establish by the lightest possible evidence that the scale of justice is not held evenly in our state."[28]

Though moved by Willson's argument, Bradley felt compelled to contact several prominent citizens of Mayfield before making a decision. Not surprisingly, they reminded the governor of the outrageous crime Blanks allegedly had committed. According to Mayfield whites, they had allowed Blanks to be duly tried by the law rather than resorting to a lynching even though his crime merited swift punishment. The judge who presided over the trial made a telling point with Bradley by explaining that the execution of Blanks would benefit blacks the most since they were the victims of mob violence: "If Bob Blanks should not be executed but have his punishment commuted, or be pardoned, the effect on the colored race in this state would be dreadful. If such action be taken, the life of any colored person who hereafter commits any kind of crime will be very little value to him, for no amount of vigilance on the part of judges and other officers of the law can further restrain the infuriated masses from acts of violence against the colored race." The governor refused to block the execution of Blanks. On April 18, 1899, before thousands of whites who traveled great distances to witness the event, Blanks was executed.[29]

Blanks surely would have been lynched had Bradley not ordered state troops to guard him on his return to Mayfield. Yet, significantly, Bradley somehow believed that allowing Blanks to stand trial before an all-white jury, with thousands of angry whites ready to lynch the defendant, was justice. Perhaps his rationale for allowing Blanks to be executed was a belief that to do so was the only way to convince mobs that justice would be served in court. Even so, Bradley had given in to the will of the mob and sanctioned a legal lynching.

Willson, during his tenure as governor from 1907 to 1911, was often in the same predicament as Bradley. Like Bradley, Willson did a great deal to bring about equality for African Americans, yet, in my view, he still failed to stop the most tragic incident that occurred in the state's deplorable history of racial violence against African Americans. To be sure, this is a highly subjective view; undoubtedly all of Kentucky's 353 mob lynchings (which included women and children) and the 229 supposedly legal executions were tragic. But of all of these incidents, the one above all that cried out for compassion, and most surely the use of discretion to save a life, was the case of James White, a retarded black youth.

In 1909, then sixteen-year-old White was charged in Middlesboro with the rape of a fourteen-year-old white girl. White's court-appointed attorney entered a guilty plea on his behalf, reasoning that this was the only defense that might save his client's life. As was the custom, many of the people attending the trial were prepared to lynch the defendant if he escaped the death sentence. The jury, in finding the black youth guilty and sentencing him to death, ignored White's mental condition—that he was incapable of understanding the charges against him—and evidence that consensual sex, not rape, might have occurred. Significantly, the attorney general, who always argued in support of the death sentence, expressed reservations about the conviction and sentence, and especially the strategy of the defense in White's behalf. That White did not understand the charges also troubled the attorney general. He urged Governor Willson to commute White's death sentence to life in prison. (This sentence also was harsh because the attorney general believed White incapable of standing trial. Yet it affirmed the white viewpoint that blacks must be punished for having sex with whites, whether or not rape had occurred.)[30]

That Willson agreed to review White's case must have seemed like a replay of Bradley being asked by Willson to reconsider the death penalty of Robert Blanks. Years earlier Willson had challenged Bradley that allowing the black man to die "tests the soundness and justice of our institutions." Now, however, as governor, he had a different perspective. Even though he received information confirming that White was mentally retarded and was abnormally small, Willson showed no sympathy for him. In making known his ruling, Governor Willson resorted to language that is remarkable in its lack of compassion toward a fellow human being, even for the time. Imperfect people like White, the governor explained, are a burden to the state and their lives are full of want and suffering. "Our system is wickedly wrong," he continued, for having allowed people like White's parents, both of whom were handicapped, to reproduce. "Such people should be by law prohibited from marriage or subjected to any operation which would prevent offspring. This boy is one of the victims of that system, but he is none the less dangerous to society, and his case if not punished by death, is dangerous to the whole state." Maybe the fact that White was, to use the governor's words, "mentally imperfect," a person of little value and a charge on society, made it easier for Willson to allow his execution. Like Bradley before him, it is possible that Willson believed that sacrificing White would in the long run help bring an end to mob lynchings, especially of blacks accused of rape. Willson, again like Bradley, clearly did not want to be viewed as "soft" on crime. But in sanctioning White's execution, he, like other Kentucky governors, gave in to the will of the mob. On January 30, 1911, James White, most likely unaware of the reason why, died on the gallows in Middlesboro before a crowd that numbered in the thousands."[31]

In Kentucky, early in this century, blatant miscarriages of justice were common against African Americans because whites used the law as a tool to oppress and punish blacks. Not surprisingly, therefore, while whites claimed to believe in and have respect for their own legal system, they believed just as strongly that legal concepts such as reasonable doubt, the right of self-defense, and the right of a trial free of mob intimidation did not apply to blacks.

These conclusions are highly condemning of white Kentuckians. Scholars are correct when cautioning against judging the past and our ancestors and their actions by the standards and values of the present. Yet when documenting the position of women and children in society at the turn of the century and earlier, scholars have correctly condemned family violence and other abuses that powerless people endured. Few observers are restrained in labeling Adolf Hitler and Joseph Stalin as evil, sadistic, and wicked men. So too, we should not hesitate, in the face of abundant evidence, to conclude that white Kentuckians, southerners, and Americans willfully violated fundamental principles whenever blacks were part of the equation. Joel Williamson's highly influential book *The Crucible of Race* documents how deeply embedded racism was in the psyche of white people. In many circumstances, whites were logical, reasonable, and caring. But with chilling frequency, they ignored their professed notions of right and wrong when blacks were involved.

The enduring legacy of legal lynchings in Kentucky's courts persisted long after lynch mobs disappeared. Though tragic, this is not surprising because of the widely held belief among whites that they were acting legally by conducting trials before handing down harsh sentences to blacks. The Supreme Court's ruling in *Hale* v. *Paducah* resulted in Kentucky blacks serving on juries periodically, but significantly, white judges and prosecutors systematically excluded African Americans as jurors from racially sensitive cases. Fifteen of the twenty-four men executed between 1940 and 1962 were black, and in every instance the condemned person was found guilty of committing offenses against whites and convicted by all-white juries.[32] In 1986, just as it had almost fifty years earlier, the Supreme Court ruled on the composition of juries in Kentucky. In the case of *Batson* v. *Kentucky*, the Court, finding that prosecutors excluded blacks from juries, ruled that prosecutors could no longer use their preemptive challenges to bar potential jurors because of their race.[33] Yet this ruling has had little effect because prosecutors are astute enough to resort to other tactics, such as the manner of questioning black potential jurors, to accomplish the same goal of all-white juries for highly sensitive cases.

Furthermore, rulings by the United States Supreme Court on the validity of the death penalty have reinforced the view that legal lynchings continue in American society. In *McCleskey* v. *Kemp*, the Supreme Court affirmed the principle of the death penalty. In upholding (by the narrow margin of five to four) the death sentence for Warren McCleskey, a black convicted of killing a white police officer during the course of a robbery, the Court also dealt a blow to those who argued that the handing down of death sentences was racially biased. Justice Lewis Powell, the author of the majority opinion, critiqued the statistical data produced by Professor David C. Baldus and others claiming that a disparity existed when imposing the death penalty based on the race of the murder victim and the race of the defendant. Simply stated, a black faced the greatest likelihood of receiving the death penalty when charged with killing a white. While admitting the thoroughness of Baldus's work, Powell nevertheless rejected the thesis that the imposition of the death penalty was racially motivated. "For this claim to prevail," Powell reasoned, "McCleskey would have to prove that the Georgia Legislature enacted or maintained the death penalty statute because of an anticipated racially discriminatory effect."[34]

In reaching the conclusion that death sentences were handed down on a color-blind basis, Powell relied on two major points: the importance of discretion within judicial system and the assumption that defendants received fair trials. As we have seen, in Kentucky the discretion exercised by the jury and the prosecution most surely worked to the disadvantage of African Americans. Justice Powell had a different perspective. Each jury, Powell noted, made its decision based on factors that varied according to the characteristics of an individual defendant and the facts of a particular capital offense. "Because discretion is essential to the criminal justice process, we would demand exceptionally clear proof before we would infer that the discretion has been abused." Going further, Powell noted that a jury had the right to reject the death penalty and impose a lesser, milder sentence. "Whereas decisions against a defendant's interest may be reversed by the trial judge or on appeal, these discretionary exercises of leniences are final and unreviewable."[35]

Finally, Powell simply dismissed the argument put forth on behalf of McCleskey by explaining that the primary obligation of the courts was to ensure the fair application of the law in each individual case. "Despite McCleskey's wide-ranging arguments that basically challenge the validity of capital punishment in our multiracial society, the only question before us is whether in his case . . . the law of Georgia was properly applied."[36]

Justice William J. Brennan, in his dissent, reminded the Court that in the decade since the death penalty had been restored, Georgia had executed seven people, six of whom were black, convicted of killing whites. This was striking, he noted, because only 9.2 percent of the murders involved black defendants and white victims whereas 60.7 percent involved black victims. Brennan then touched upon the racist past in Georgia, where black life had meant little before the mob or the law. Between 1930 and 1977, he noted, fifty-eight blacks and four whites were executed for rape. "Citation of past practices does not justify the automatic condemnation of current ones. But it would be unrealistic to ignore the influence of history in assessing the plausible implications of McCleskey's evidence."[37]

Justice Harry A. Blackmun, while agreeing in general with Brennan's dissent, offered a crucial thought of his own. In sharp contrast to the majority on the Court, Blackmun believed that discretion favored whites while ensuring punishment for blacks. "The establishment of guidelines for Assistant District Attorneys as to the appropriate basis for exercising their discretion at the various steps in the prosecution of a case would provide at least a measure of consistency."[38]

It is possible that the greatest area of injustice in the legal system is not that blacks are sentenced harshly but that whites are not being charged or, when convicted, are given much milder sentences. The majority on the Supreme Court admitted that juries exercising their "discretion may reach different results from exact duplicates," but the fact that a white might be given a lesser sentence and a black the death penalty did not mean that discrimination had occurred in either instance. In short, the Supreme Court in 1987 reached the same conclusion that Kentucky whites had reached many decades earlier, that the whites serving on juries that sentenced blacks to death abided by the law and had done it by the book.

NOTES

1. For a complete discussion of these and other Kentucky lynchings, see George C. Wright, *Racial Violence in Kentucky, 1865–1940: Lynchings, Mob Rule, and "Legal Lynchings"* (Baton Rouge: Louisiana State University Press, 1990).

2. Except for Kentucky, the ten states with the highest number of lynchings had

black populations that exceeded 20 percent. In Georgia, the state with the largest number of lynchings, blacks constituted 46.7 percent of the population in 1900, and in Mississippi, which was second in lynchings, almost 60 percent of its citizens were African Americans. Viewing blacks as a threat, whites in these states stripped them of the right to vote because of their almost certain impact on elections. Kentucky black voters, even in Louisville and Lexington, at best could be a swing vote if whites were evenly divided on an issue. In short, in no way were Kentucky blacks a threat to the status quo of white supremacy. See the following sources: National Association for the Advancement of Colored People, *Thirty Years of Lynchings in the United States, 1889–1918* (New York: NAACP, 1919); U.S. Census Bureau, *Negro Population, 1790–1915* (Washington, D.C.: U.S. Government Printing Office, 1918), Table 13, p. 43; U.S. Census Bureau, *A Century of Population Growth: From the First Census of the United States to the Twelfth, 1790–1915* (Washington, D.C.: U.S. Government Printing Office, 1909).

3. Jacquelyn Dowd Hall, *Revolt against Chivalry: Jessie Daniel Ames and the Women's Campaign against Lynching* (New York: Columbia University Press, 1979), 223; see also two earlier works: James H. Chadbourn, *Lynching and the Law* (Chapel Hill: University of North Carolina Press, 1933), 23; Arthur F. Raper, *The Tragedy of Lynching* (Chapel Hill: University of North Carolina Press, 1933), 10.

4. Wright, *Racial Violence in Kentucky*, 226–31.

5. See Lexington's white newspapers, the *Leader* and the *Herald*, and the *Louisville Leader*, a black weekly newspaper, for March and April 1926.

6. *Lexington Morning Herald*, October 3–10, 1900.

7. *Commonwealth v. Johnson*, 78 Kentucky Reports, 509–13 (1880); see also *Haggard v. Commonwealth*, 79 Kentucky Reports, 366–67 (1881).

8. *Commonwealth v. Johnson*.

9. *Strauder v. West Virginia*, 100 U.S. 303 (1879); *Virginia v. Rives*, 100 U.S. 313 (1879).

10. *Commonwealth v. Johnson*.

11. *Smith v. Commonwealth*, 37 Southwestern Reporter, 825–26 (1896).

12. *Lexington Morning Transcript*, November 22, 1884.

13. *Hale v. Commonwealth*, 108 Southwestern Reporter, 2d Ser., 716–20 (1937); *Hale v. Kentucky* 303 U.S., 613–15 (1938).

14. *Boston Guardian*, December 18, 1909; *Louisville Courier-Journal*, December 8, 1909, January 8, 1910.

15. Mary D. Brite, memorandum, "The Case of John Montjoy: A Sample of Justice for a Negro" (written in February 1936). This document can be found in the NAACP Papers, Manuscript Division, Library of Congress.

16. *Louisville Courier-Journal*, July 31–August 2, 1906; *Paducah Weekly News Democrat*, August 2, 1906.

17. *Acts of the General Assembly of the Commonwealth of Kentucky* (Louisville: Courier-Journal Press, 1910), 111–13. Given the hysteria of the mob and its domination of court proceedings, this new law almost certainly was violated on occasion, and the state continued to execute black people immediately after their trials in the name of justice and peace in the community.

18. Information on the Madisonville rape case can be found in the *Madisonville Daily Messenger* from January 1, 1926, through May 1927. See also the records of the

Louisville NAACP, NAACP Papers; Brite, "The Case of John Montjoy"; *Crisis* 43 (April 1936): 105, 114.

19. *New York Times*, June 27, 1897. Information on the Dinning case can be found in the William O. Bradley Papers, Kentucky Governors' Papers, 1792–1926, Pardons and Rejected Petitions, Kentucky Department for Libraries and Archives, Frankfort. See, e.g., the governor's statement, dated July 17, 1897, on Dinning's pardon. On Browder, see *Commonwealth of Kentucky* v. *Rufus Browder*, Logan Circuit Court (1909). The only known copy of this trial transcript is in the Governor Willson Papers, Kentucky Governors' Papers.

20. The pardon can be found in a letter dated November 21, 1910, Governor Willson Papers; *Madisonville Hustler*, April 24, July 21, 1908; *Crisis* 1 (February 1911): 6; *Louisville Courier-Journal*, November 26, 1910. Willson's comments in commuting Hocker's sentence can be found in the *Lexington Herald*, December 6, 1908.

21. *Crisis* 19 (April 1920): 298; Tuskegee Clippings, microfilm, Reel 222, Frame 109.

22. *John Taylor* v. *Commonwealth*, 90 Southwestern Reporter, 581–84 (1906); *Ed Taylor* v. *Commonwealth*, 90 Southwestern Reporter, 584–85 (1906).

23. *Browder* v. *Commonwealth*, 136 Kentucky Reports, 45–54 (1909).

24. Ibid. See also Wright, *Racial Violence in Kentucky*, 280–83, for a longer version of this incident.

25. *McDaniel* v. *Commonwealth*, 181 Kentucky Reports, 766–81 (1918).

26. *Kentucky Standard*, May 28, 1898; *Louisville Courier-Journal*, January 13, May 21, 1898. A longer, more detailed discussion of this event can be found in Wright, *Racial Violence in Kentucky*, 215–18.

27. *Mayfield Monitor*, July 6, 13, August 24, 1898; *Blanks* v. *Commonwealth*, 48 Southwestern Reporter, 161–64 (1898).

28. Augustus E. Willson to William O. Bradley, November 2, December 8, 1898, Bradley Papers.

29. See the many letters to Bradley from Mayfield whites urging him to allow Blanks to be executed, Bradley Papers.

30. *White* v. *Commonwealth*, 140 Kentucky Reports, 9–11 (1910); *Louisville Courier-Journal*, January 19, 1910, January 21, 1911.

31. "Respite of James White," January 14, 1911, Governor Willson Papers. The Willson Collection contains newspaper clippings regarding the case.

32. Wright, *Racial Violence in Kentucky*, 289.

33. *James Kirland Batson* v. *Kentucky*, 106A United States, 1712–45 (1986).

34. See *McCleskey* v. *Kemp*, U.S. Reports, 279–367 (1987); and David C. Baldus, George Woodworth, and Charles A. Pulaski Jr., *Equal Justice and the Death Penalty: A Legal and Empirical Analysis* (Boston: Little, Brown, 1990).

35. *McCleskey* v. *Kemp*, 294–97, 311.

36. Ibid., 298, 313.

37. Ibid., 327, 332.

38. Ibid., 362–65.

The Roar on the
Other Side of Silence
Black Resistance and White
Violence in the American
South, 1880–1940

W. Fitzhugh Brundage

cholars have long recognized that a thread of violence is woven into southern race relations. Lynchings, race riots, and all manner of violence defined the boundaries of black life. Historians have charted the efforts of black organizations, especially the National Association for the Advancement of Colored People, to secure antilynching laws and to mobilize sentiment against violence.[1] But left unexplored, at least until recently, have been the breadth and character of informal, unorganized resistance by blacks during the era of Jim Crow.[2] Except in slavery studies and some recent labor history, the full tradition of furtive dissent, or what Michel de Certeau called the "guerilla warfare of everyday life," has escaped the attention of historians.[3] As important as the responses of black institutions and black elites to white violence were, the resistance of unorganized and seemingly powerless blacks is of equal significance, especially in a region and at a time when only a small minority of blacks were either members of reform groups or participants in organized protest.

The long history of white violence and black resistance poses a question central to any discussion of social justice or civil rights in the United States: how have aggrieved communities maintained cultures of opposition during periods of apparent quiescence? A partial answer to this question can be gleaned from the record of black opposition to white violence in the Jim Crow South. The range of black resistance, including both highly public forms of dissent and what Zora Neale Hurston had in mind when she spoke of the black strategy of "featherbed resistance," suggests some of the ways that a subtle dialectic of accommodation and confrontation, of restraint and militancy, contravened fundamentally the "visible" record of black consent, silence, and apathy.[4] Even this cursory survey of black resistance should demonstrate that black protest was something more than a tactical sleight of hand, something more than merely seizing the possibilities that a moment offered. Black protest flowed from, as George Lipsitz puts it, "underground streams of resistance from the past."[5] These various forms of protest had important implications for the institutions and traditions that oppressed blacks. They represented an ethic of tenacity that ensured that the history of southern African Americans was, in the words of Cornel West, "inseparable from though not reducible to victimization."[6]

Let us begin with two simple propositions. First, southern race relations were a form of systematic subordination. Second, systematic subordination inevitably elicits a desire among the victims of that subordination to speak back to or strike out against their oppressors. If followed to their logical conclusion, these elementary principles have profound implications for an understanding of black responses to white violence. We can take for granted that in some manner, perhaps heavily disguised, blacks carried on a campaign of defiance against white violence. And if there is an apparent absence of resistance by blacks to white violence in the historical record, we must rethink our preconceived expectations about the ways their protest may have been expressed.

Given the ruthlessness of whites and the vigor with which they championed white supremacy, we should hardly be surprised that some blacks concluded that the social order in which they were trapped was both natural and inevitable. Perhaps a few came close to internalizing the values that explained and justified their subordination. The observations of Amzie Moore, a former sharecropper and civil rights activist in Mississippi, are poignant on this point. Moore confessed: "Listen. For a long time I had the idea that a man with white skin was superior because it appeared to me that he had everything. And I figured if God would justify the white man having everything that God had put him in a position to be the best."[7] The response of some blacks to white violence would seem to suggest that they, like Moore, were resigned to their thralldom. That some blacks went to great lengths to divorce themselves from any appearance of protest against white violence implies as much. When, for example, George Bowen heard that he was accused of being in sympathy with Jesse Williams, a black man lynched in Dodge County, Georgia, in 1892, he contacted the local white newspaper "to set himself right in public." He explained that he was "heartily in favor of the lynching and that all the negroes he had talked to are the same way."[8] Similarly, following the lynching of Obe Cox in Oglethorpe County, Georgia, in 1919, a committee of blacks commended the mob. In a thinly disguised plea for whites not to use the lynching as a pretext to terrorize blacks, the letter announced: "We certainly thank you for handling this case so nice, for it could have been worse for us. . . . Our white people fought no one but the brute, Obe Cox, which was right and we thank them for it."9

These examples seemingly bolster one historian's recent claim that "most blacks responded [to lynchings] by fearfully staying within pre- scribed social boundaries" and by trying "even more to placate the dom- inant caste."10 Similar examples may also explain historian Lester C. Lamon's observation that blacks during the Jim Crow era "remained silent . . . taking the line of least resistance."11 But historians make a grave error when they take these endorsements of lynching at face value and fail to recognize the combination of fear, deception, and pragmatic deference that lay behind them. Ample evidence underscores that the periodic pub- lic gestures of submission by blacks should not be misconstrued as accep- tance of the legitimacy of white repression. Indeed, black responses call to mind nothing so much as George Eliot's poignant image of "the roar that lies on the other side of silence."

By broadening our understanding of resistance by all marginalized groups, including African Americans, the work of political anthropologist James C. Scott helps to make the roar of black resistance audible. Scott argues that oppressed groups, despite appearances of consent, challenge their oppressors by adopting an array of forms of resistance. A culture of opposition, to borrow George Lipsitz's phrase, may promote diverse expressions of resistance, including cultural dissent such as songs, as well as theft and vandalism.12 Only rarely does resistance become visible in open attacks on ruling elites or their institutions. These daily acts of insubordination and the culture that sustains them constitute what Scott calls "infrapolitics" (or what Evelyn Brooks Higginbotham labels "micropolitics").13

In the American South, the battleground between whites and blacks over the economic, political, and social order extended from the realm of infra- to formal politics. Unlike antebellum slaves, blacks in the postbel- lum South were never entirely silenced or excluded from public life. Even so, race relations rested not on negotiation or consensus but rather on domination, whenever possible without overt conflict and when necessary through violence and coercion. Blacks were vulnerable in every sense of the word and could seldom risk the luxury of direct confrontation with whites. Their resistance, and resistance to violence in particular, consequently fell on a continuum somewhere between the poles of outright compliance with white values and brazen rebellion against them.

At one end of the continuum of resistance were oblique and symbolic gestures of defiance. Resistance, in its most basic form, assumed the guise of what may be called discursive insubordination. This language of dissent emerged in the rich catalog of humor with which blacks rebelliously jested about mob violence. John Dollard, a witness to such humor during the 1930s, observed, "To take cheerfully a matter of such terrible moment is really to turn the joke back on the white man; some fun is squeezed even out of his warning."[14] On other occasions, blacks denied the prescriptive power of lynching by taunting whites or by dismissing any fear of white authority. For instance, in 1894 Abe Smalls, a black fugitive accused of killing a white policeman in Savannah, boasted to the local white newspaper that "he don't care when he dies, just so he is not taken alive and that he is game enough to die with his boots on."[15] Beyond humor and taunts, the language of dissent sometimes surfaced during the funeral ceremonies for lynching victims when the families of mob victims vented their pain and bitterness by denouncing lynching. In other instances, they protested the mob's actions by refusing to accept the responsibility and cost of burial. In 1897, for example, the aunt of a black lynched in Alexandria, Virginia, raged, "As the [white] people killed him, they will have to bury him."[16]

Blacks developed an arsenal of techniques that allowed them to protest white dominance while shielding their identities. Traditional forms of retaliation, extending from vandalism to arson, served, as William Faulkner noted, as "one weapon for the preservation of dignity."[17] Blacks responded to white violence with threats of arson on many occasions; how often those threats were acted upon is of course impossible to determine.[18] Although blacks were understandably cautious about violent retribution against white lynchers, they were more forthright in punishing fellow blacks who aided white mobs. John Brown, who implicated two blacks in a barn burning in Alabama in 1891, and the black who revealed Davis Harris's hiding place to the lynch mob in Bolivar County, Mississippi, in 1930 are just two examples of blacks who were punished for indefensible subservience to the etiquette of Jim Crow.[19] Most blacks probably did not need the threat of communal punishment to discourage them from abetting white mobs. Instead, blacks perpetuated the tradition of protecting and aiding blacks in flight that extended back through centuries of slavery. By shielding alleged black criminals and speeding their flight to safety, black communities at once prevented possible lynchings and reaffirmed their contempt for white justice.

The flight of large numbers of blacks following eruptions of mob violence, another common response, sometimes took on the traits of cryptic protest, as sociologists E. M. Beck and Stewart Tolnay have demonstrated.[20] News of threatened or actual mob violence often prompted blacks to go into hiding. For blacks who lacked, or refused to depend upon, white protectors, flight was one of the few responses to white violence which at once was independent of whites and yet typically did not inspire retaliation. These actions did not prevent whites from storming jails or running down black victims, but they did protect some blacks from indiscriminate violence.[21]

Whites understood that flight was more than just a supine response; the exodus of black farmhands could pose a genuine economic threat. In 1904, following the lynching of Paul Reed and William Cato near Statesboro, Georgia, roving bands of whites attacked blacks throughout the surrounding countryside. The violence precipitated an exodus of blacks from the area and threatened to create a labor shortage at the beginning of the cotton-picking season. Concerned white citizens and local officials responded by issuing a public statement calling for a halt on attacks against blacks and appointed extra marshals to discourage further violence.[22] In at least one instance, blacks so conspicuously withheld their labor that their action could only be construed as a protest. In 1917, after a mob lynched a black in Northumberland County, Virginia, blacks refused to work for the leader of the mob even though he offered them double wages. The *Norfolk Journal and Guide* warned that future lynchings in the area would depopulate the county.[23]

In another technique of veiled protest, blacks invoked a language of dissemblance or, to use Russian literary critic M. M. Bakhtin's term, "a double-voiced discourse" to undermine the legitimacy of white rule.[24] Central to the struggle between dominant and subordinate groups has been the contest over the production of and limits on social meaning. In the South, whites labored to constrain blacks from voicing conflicting or subversive alternatives to white supremacy. But the hegemony of white supremacy was never complete. As Evelyn Brooks Higginbotham has observed, whites and blacks did not internalize the language and ideology of white domination in the same way.[25] Even while seemingly parroting the slogans of white supremacy, African Americans found ways to code them with political meaning. This disguised form of protest, and its limits, were evident in the Brooks County "race war" of 1894.

At the outset of Christmas celebrations in Brooks County, Georgia, in 1894, the traditionally rowdy festivities were interrupted by violence. A white posse, under the pretext of searching for alleged black murderers, indiscriminately tortured and murdered blacks. Blacks in Quitman, the county seat, wired the governor and pleaded: "We . . . are imposed upon by mobbers and we are trying to obtain by the laws of Georgia. What should we do?" Blacks elsewhere in the county, who were less sanguine about relying on white authorities for protection, sought safety in dense swamps.

Whites took no meaningful steps to curb the violence until it reached the plantation of Mitchell Brice, one of the county's richest planters. Outraged by the mob's beating of an elderly black woman, Brice warned that further mob violence would be suppressed and even announced that he planned to prosecute members of the mob. The planter's intercession, in conjunction with the arrival of state militia and the arrest of the remaining black murder suspects, at last brought an end to the slaughter.[26]

That Brice responded to the appeal of his black farmhands for protection is evidence of his relative power and their vulnerability. Of greatest concern to Brice was the defense of his authority over his workers from the reckless actions of other whites. He was not offended in principle by either mob violence or extralegal punishment but rather was angry that the mob had mistreated *his* hands. As one of Brice's neighbors explained: "[His blacks] are just as much his slaves as they were before the war. If one steals from him the old man will whip him just like he used to. He don't send them to the chain gang and the negroes are better pleased."[27]

The events in Brooks County unmask both the consequences for blacks of accepting white guardianship and the openings that such guardianship offered for protest. By not contradicting the self-definition of the white elite, by behaving publicly as if they accepted paternalism, blacks contributed—wittingly—to the balance of racial power in Brooks County. By acquiescing to whippings at the hands of planters or by appealing to them for protection, blacks risked surrendering any claim on legal institutions to recognize their rights. The necessity of relying on whites provided a strong impetus to remain in their good graces. In such a climate, as sociologist Oliver Cox explained, no black could escape the lessons of deference.[28]

But here again it is worthwhile to return to the idea of a double-voiced discourse of race relations. Deprived of realistic alternatives and having virtually no political resources, blacks in Brooks County nevertheless attempted to turn the rhetoric of white supremacy to their advantage. In other words, blacks at once subverted and reconstructed the language of their oppression. By stressing the tenets of white supremacy—that "good blacks" who "stayed in their place" would enjoy security of life and property—blacks protested that whites who participated in or condoned mob violence violated the norms by which they justified their own authority.

Blacks often wrapped their appeals in morality; it was the white vigilantes, not blacks, they protested, who were deviating from proper codes of behavior. The telegram from blacks in Brooks County to the governor in 1894 is instructive on this point. It pleaded: "We . . . are imposed upon by mobbers and we are trying to obtain by the laws of Georgia. What should we do?" By attempting to manipulate whites by upholding the norms that defined black subordination, blacks in Brooks County protested against white transgressions in a fashion that was awkward for whites to suppress. The deference the blacks exhibited did not imply a denial of the injustice of their situation. Indeed, as Richard Couto has astutely argued, black deference combined both resignation and indignation.[29] Thus the tactic of public deference almost certainly stands as testimony to the subtlety, cunning, and ongoing refusal of Brooks County blacks to internalize white ideology, not their craven obedience to it.

Although blacks' appeals for protection may have been couched in the language of deference, they almost certainly were disingenuous. Blacks publicly performed in ways that conveyed submission even while they sustained an ongoing dialogue of protest. Outside the intimidating gaze of whites, blacks gathered and voiced the words of anger, revenge, and self-assertion that they normally had to choke back when in the presence of whites. In black social spaces, ranging from churches, fraternal lodges, and social clubs to barbershops, a rich culture of opposition flourished.[30] White uneasiness grew in proportion to the degree that blacks successfully carved out an independent social life; it is no coincidence that when racial violence erupted, white arsonists and mobs frequently targeted such symbols of black strivings as schools, churches, and club buildings.[31]

The best evidence of a discourse of dissent that contradicted the public appearance of black conformity can be found in the antilynching files of the NAACP. The organization reached deep into the hinterland and became a conduit for the rage of rural blacks angered by racial violence. Its exposés enabled blacks to compile their own collective history of white repression. The important point is that the black community always had maintained its own memory of white atrocities. The NAACP simply brought that history into public view. It is all too easy to underestimate, or even dismiss, the radical character of these tactics. By straddling the threshold between infrapolitics and formal protest, the NAACP and its campaign against white violence removed the disguise from previously masked dissent. Whites across the South, who well understood the sub versive implications of the NAACP's activities, lashed out violently at the organization and its informers throughout the twentieth century.[32]

At no time during the era of Jim Crow did African Americans limit themselves solely to furtive protest. When the opportunity arose and circumstances warranted, blacks adopted overt tactics as well. In Jacksonville, Florida, in 1920, outraged blacks canceled their policies with a white life insurance company after some of its agents led a lynch mob. Despite the urgent efforts of the firm, sixteen thousand black customers shifted their business to a newly organized black life insurance company.[33] Even during the late nineteenth century, when mob violence peaked, blacks on occasion rebuffed white attacks. In Kemper County, Mississippi, in 1888, in Paducah, Kentucky, in 1892, and elsewhere, blacks organized to fight off white attackers or to protect alleged black criminals while they were in jail.[34] In other cases, blacks publicly protested incidents of racial violence. In 1904, for example, following the murder of a black man at the hands of whites, aroused blacks near Norfolk, Virginia, took to the streets and protested both the lynching and the apparent complicity of the local police. Local authorities, who failed to silence the crowd, requested state militia to restore order. Only after several tense days and numerous melees between blacks and troops did a semblance of calm return to the community.[35]

One compelling example of the potential for defiant public protest is the Darien "Insurrection," which exemplifies the protean, unorganized character of such collective actions. Without either visible organization or leadership, blacks in McIntosh County, Georgia, turned to apparently spontaneous collective action. In August 1899, Henry Denegal was charged with the rape of a white woman. A crowd of blacks soon gathered around the jail, intending to protect Denegal from the threat of mob violence. During the next two days the sheriff made repeated attempts to move the black man to Savannah, allegedly for safekeeping. The assembled blacks, who believed that the move was a subterfuge to turn Denegal over to a mob, refused to allow his removal. Each time the sheriff made an attempt to move Denegal, a sentry rang the bell of a nearby black church as a signal, and in short order hundreds of blacks, many armed, surrounded the jail. Finally, nervous white authorities telegraphed the governor and urgently requested the protection of the state militia.

When soldiers arrived in Darien and began patrolling the streets, the blacks surrounding the jail made no effort to interfere. Indeed, they cheered when the militia placed Denegal on a Savannah-bound train. But the situation threatened to deteriorate after two white men were shot while attempting to arrest several alleged ringleaders of the crowd. Black community leaders then met with the white commander of the militia and worked out a plan that eased the tensions.[36] Of course, such incidents of resistance often met with severe consequences. Although Denegal, whose arrest had precipitated the turmoil, was acquitted of all charges, twenty-three of the alleged insurrectionists were convicted of rioting and received harsh prison terms and stiff fines.[37]

We might dismiss the events in Darien as little more than localized and ephemeral opposition to white violence. After all, local black leaders did not provoke, lead, or control the "Insurrection"; their role was limited to ending the confrontation and regaining the trust of local whites. But on closer inspection, the adoption of fleeting, direct action in Darien reveals both the existence of what Scott calls an "enabling popular tradition" of protest and the dialectical relationship between disguised and public protest.[38] The actions of the Darien blacks illustrate Antonio Gramsci's maxim that "spontaneity is the history of the subaltern classes."[39] The crowd action in Darien may not have required formal organization, but it most certainly did require a degree of coordination, as demonstrated by the posting of sentries to watch the jail. This coordination rested on the informal networks, rooted in church, family, and community, that made resistance possible. What is important for our purposes is that these networks, which were indispensable to collective action, were at once deeply rooted in the black community and yet largely invisible to white authorities. The commander of the militia had to negotiate with local black officials, who apparently had no role in the action around the jail, precisely because of the anonymity of the actual "Insurrectionists." Although the defiant blacks who took over Darien in August 1899 appear to have acted spontaneously, they in fact made manifest traditions that had facilitated direct action during Reconstruction and would survive long after the conclusion of the "Insurrection."

Careful scrutiny of the myriad forms of protest reveals the vital role that black women played in extending the tradition of resistance and the collective memory of it into private as well as public spaces, from the cabin table to the church pew. Numerous accounts suggest that rural black women far removed from the genteel parlors of black women's clubs were the foot soldiers of informal, unorganized resistance. For instance, during the Darien "Insurrection" black women protesters outnumbered black men and, if newspaper accounts can be trusted, were the most vociferous and dogged sentinels at the jail. Likewise, black women in Barnwell, South Carolina, in 1889 were conspicuous in their outrage following the massacre of eight black prisoners. In other incidents, including the protests in Norfolk in 1904, black women cursed and intentionally antagonized whites in the aftermath of white violence.[40]

These black women, working independently from but parallel to the efforts of Ida B. Wells, Mary Church Terrell, and other middle-class black clubwomen, devised a range of strategies of resistance that manipulated gender differences in power relations to contest racial etiquette. Black women from all walks of life knew that they could commit acts of insubordination that whites would not allow if committed by black men. However dehumanizing prevailing racist stereotypes of black women were, whites still did not assume that black women posed the same threat to white women or men that black men did. Therefore, whites tolerated blatant protests by black women that would have drawn very severe penalties had they been made by black men.[41] Black women who probed the boundaries of white tolerance of insubordination, of course, sometimes suffered severe consequences; five women were among the "rioters" arrested following the Darien "Insurrection," and in countless instances whites resorted to forms of violence only slightly less drastic than lynching to silence outspoken black women.[42] But the measure of the significance of resistance by black women is less the white response than the myriad ways that protests by black women, whether through evasive or confrontational tactics, contributed to the collective solidarity that undergirded all forms of black dissent.

Finally, the crusades against lynching conducted by Ida B. Wells, editor of the *Memphis Free Speech*, and John Mitchell, editor of the *Richmond Planet*, reveal the opportunities for highly visible forms of black protest even during the "highest stage of white supremacy." Their antilynching activities, which ranged from gathering information on individual lynchings to denouncing mob violence in print and from the lecture podium, are suggestive of the central role of southern black editors in the leadership of the formal struggle against lynching.[43] As the black press and black editors so often did, Mitchell and Wells became a "safety-valve for the boiling black protest."[44] Against the backdrop of the furtive or spontaneous forms of black protest, it is tempting and perhaps appropriate to assume that the activities of Wells, Mitchell, and others represented a more advanced, more effective, and more important form of protest. Not only were their protests and those of other southern black editors public, but they also were couched in overtly political language. No translation or interpretation was needed for whites to understand Wells and Mitchell when they denounced white violence and the values that bred it.

Mitchell and Wells, however, recognized that their campaigns of public resistance should not be isolated from the tradition of black protest against white violence. Both editors endorsed black self-defense and even condoned retaliation for white violence. Wells's militancy extended from advising that "a Winchester rifle should have a place of honor in every black house" to praising blacks who set fire to Georgetown, Kentucky, following a lynching. "Not until the Negro rises in his might," she admonished, "and takes a hand in resenting such cold-blooded murders, if he has to burn up whole towns, will a halt be called in wholesale lynchings."[45] According to Mitchell, "The best way to secure protection in the South is to own a repeating rifle and a shot-gun and know how and when to use it."[46] Both editors encouraged organized efforts to protect blacks threatened by mob violence and on occasion even actively marshaled community outrage against white violence. After the lynching of three friends in 1892, for instance, Wells promoted acts of communal insubordination, including a black boycott of the Memphis streetcars and the emigration of thousands of blacks from the city.[47]

And yet some of the tactics of Wells and Mitchell reveal a gulf that separated many turn-of-the-century black leaders from the communities for which they claimed to speak.[48] For Wells and Mitchell alike, the rising tide of racial violence in the late nineteenth century demanded a vigorous counterattack that would mobilize middle-class blacks and whites to mold "the public sentiment" and to restrain the white masses. Wells's efforts to mobilize British public sentiment during her controversial tours of Great Britain in 1892 and 1894 were a manifestation of this strategy conducted on an international scale. Her success in redirecting public discussion of lynching by creatively manipulating prevailing white notions of masculinity, femininity, and civilization reveals the common ground that she shared with her white audiences. Both Wells and Mitchell worked with white allies to suppress mob violence because to do so meshed with their notion of reform flowing from a shared sense of justice as much as from the directed power of blacks. Mitchell played on the concern for social order and the preservation of the sanctity of legal institutions which was at the heart of conservative whites' opposition to lynching in Virginia. Mitchell never conceived of local institutionalized opposition to either lynching or white violence in general. And Mitchell and Wells, despite their inflammatory rhetoric, eventually adopted tactics that relied more on the manipulation of powerful whites than on their fitful attempts to organize blacks.[49]

Many other turn-of-the-century black editors in the South, perhaps because of their sense of their own importance as black leaders, virtually ignored everyday resistance. At best, they condoned acts of self-defense even while placing little emphasis upon them. Committed as they were to formal and public modes of protest, many editors were little inclined to acknowledge popular forms of protest. For example, the able editor of the *Savannah Tribune*, one of the South's best black newspapers, virtually ignored the Darien "Insurrection." Indeed, even Mitchell eventually seems to have lost interest in celebrating the tradition of informal resistance that had once been so prominent in his newspaper. Although there can be no doubt about the courage or devotion of such southern black leaders, there is reason to believe that their methods neither articulated nor incorporated the full range of black opposition to white violence.

In time the gap that separated expressions of protest by the black elites and the black masses narrowed. During the 1930s and early 1940s, as Adam Fairclough's study of Louisiana vividly demonstrates, the NAACP forged cross-class alliances that encouraged new expressions of black dissent. Local leaders pioneered innovative techniques of protest which mobilized far more blacks than previous campaigns. Communists and radical labor activists simultaneously carried their attack on the American class and racial hierarchy into the southern hinterland. Their creative tactics in the Scottsboro case and elsewhere focused unwelcome national attention on antiblack violence and also spurred the NAACP to adopt bolder measures. Thus, by the beginning of World War II, blacks could tap the resources of a growing array of organizations dedicated to abolishing white supremacy and the violence that undergirded it. Class and ideological divisions among blacks surfaced in subsequent campaigns, but the diversity of participants ensured that organized and ongoing public protest was never again monopolized by the black elites.[50]

To understand properly black protest against white violence, then, we must begin with the simple fact that blacks labored under tremendous constraints and had limited economic and political resources. That blacks often adopted furtive methods reflected a tactical choice born of their prudent awareness of the balance of power between whites and blacks. Protest therefore assumed a wide variety of forms that may, in a contemporary America reshaped by the protest of the 1960s, appear timid and ineffective.

When the full tradition of resistance to white violence is unveiled, the complexities of power relations in the Jim Crow South and of the struggle by blacks to place limits on white domination also appear more clearly. Care must be taken to avoid the assumption that white dominance preceded black resistance. White supremacy was not a given; rather, it was something continuously struggled for in an ongoing process of subordination. White domination did not spring fully formed into being to be followed by black resistance. Nor did black resistance operate merely within confines predetermined by white domination. Just as black resistance was constructed and refracted through practice, so too white domination and its mystifying conceits were constantly contested and reasserted. Thus white domination and black resistance had contemporaneous origins; even while white power worked to condition and mediate black resistance, black dissent in turn contested and constrained white power.[51]

Blacks and whites were bound together in a ceaseless struggle by whites seeking to maintain and extend their domination and blacks endeavoring to deny and thwart that domination. By taking into account this ongoing contest and the role of black resistance in it, we can replace the image of the black masses cowed by white violence with a more nuanced portrait of an oppressed people who creatively experimented with all manner of dissent, from furtive to public. Rather than concentrating solely on the familiar arena of public protest, we need to explore the full spectrum of black resistance. Beyond recording instances of black resistance, scholars need to explain why resistance took one form rather than another, why it occurred in one place rather than another, and why at a particular time rather than earlier or later. The task is not so much to discover a heroic past, although the record of black resistance is rife with acts of heroism, but rather to chart the resources for dissent and the limits of the possible.

In light of the grisly record of lynchings, race riots, beatings, intimidation, and inhumanity inflicted upon blacks in the Jim Crow South, we may legitimately wonder about the efficacy of black resistance. Furtive forms of dissent—jokes, flight, arson—would seem to have been, at worst, an inconsequential challenge to white power, at best, a substitute for more meaningful dissent. Indeed, some of the unobtrusive methods of resistance may well have been imperceptible to whites as protest. Whites could not easily recognize acts of dissent without at the same time recognizing the hidden culture of opposition. Like other dominant groups, southern whites were intent on creating the appearance that approximated what, ideally, they wanted others, and blacks specifically, to see. White southerners urgently wanted to keep the social fact of black resistance out of public sight. As James Scott explains, "The importance of avoiding any public display of insubordination is not simply derived from a strategy of divide and rule; open insubordination represents a dramatic contradiction of the smooth surface of ephemeral power."[52]

Yet even oblique and disguised resistance, though at first glance primitive and fleeting, testified to the ongoing refusal of blacks to accept the legitimacy or inevitability of their oppression. Rather than a safety valve, black resistance represented a continuing and veiled renegotiation of power relations. Small dramas of resistance to violence by blacks which were not rebuked or punished pressed the boundaries of the permissible and served to encourage other blacks to exploit that breach, to test white resolve. Admittedly, it is often impossible to determine whether anger, unguarded risk-taking, or conscious strategy prompted blacks to break publicly with the rituals of subordination. For Isaac Flowers, a black man in Wayne County, Georgia, the moment of rebellion came when he refused to retract his praise for a notorious black "desperado" whose flaunting of racial norms had provoked a mass lynching several years earlier. Flowers's refusal to denounce the black outlaw so infuriated his white audience that they later murdered him and placed his body on the railroad tracks, where passing trains ran over and mangled it.[53] His murder can be read in two different ways. It reminds us of the narrow limits of white tolerance. It also vividly demonstrates that blacks like Flowers were willing to test those limits despite the possible consequences.

In ways only incompletely understood, the tradition of black resistance shaped institutions and social relations. Blacks, on occasion, did wrest concessions from whites or impose limits on white violence. John Mitchell played an essential role in creating a climate conducive to tentative but important efforts to suppress mob violence in the Old Dominion. If anyone gave direction to the unorganized opposition to white violence during the 1890s, it was Mitchell. He prodded elected officials and concerned whites to assume responsibility for the protection of black prisoners and to use state authority to halt lynching. His activism may not have ushered in a new era of racial harmony, but it did temper the character and the intensity of white domination in Virginia. Similarly, Ida B. Wells, as Gail Bederman and Patricia Schechter have demonstrated, recast the debate over lynchings in ways that compelled whites to address at least some of the social realities of lynching. By repudiating whites' justifications for lynching, she asserted the will and agency of blacks, and especially black women, to define themselves outside the parameters of the prevailing racist discourse. Wells's contributions set a tone for the antilynching campaign and ensured that it became a forum in which black women denounced both racial and sexual subordination.

The protest of blacks in McIntosh County, Georgia, also intruded upon white domination. The militancy of coastal blacks warned whites that they would not suffer mob violence without protest. Coastal whites, who were no less vigorous supporters of white supremacy than whites elsewhere, recognized that violence against blacks could have unintended and, more important, troublesome consequences. Eager to restore at least the perception of tranquil race relations, white newspapers stressed the importance of maintaining interracial cooperation. As one Savannah newspaper noted, the efforts of prominent blacks in Darien helped "to cement the peace and harmony which in the past has so signally blessed the relationship between the races in McIntosh County."[54] The lesson another newspaper drew from the episode was that the two races had to work together to ensure that "misapprehensions" of either race did not produce similar outbursts in the future.[55]

These and other episodes of resistance undoubtedly had important effects on the consciousness of southern blacks. Robin Kelley, who has taken the first step in exploring the complex relationship between organized protest movements and informal modes of resistance, has observed that the process of resistance revealed "the vulnerability of the powerful," "the potential strength of the weak," and "the terrible consequences of failed struggles."[56] The memory of resistance, which informed the self-definition of blacks and their willingness to take risks, created the social and individual preconditions for future resistance. Each time blacks rebuilt a church, a fraternal lodge, or a school burned down by white arsonists, buried a lynching victim with dignity, gave money or information on a lynching to the NAACP, sheltered a black threatened with mob violence, and vented resentment against white violence around the kitchen table, they built up a reservoir of shared indignation and collective self-definition that was essential to all forms of black protest.[57] For much of the era of Jim Crow, blacks wisely limited their public efforts at emancipation and instead retreated into private spaces and engaged in forms of resistance that carried the fewest risks of reprisal. As the political and legal underpinnings of white domination in the South eroded across the twentieth century, blacks increasingly complemented everyday informal resistance with organized dissent. Almost certainly, civil rights activists enjoyed success in mobilizing communities across the South precisely because they tapped into the reservoir of moral anger and power that had been created and sustained by the long history of resistance, both clandestine and public. And it was these traditions of dissent that enabled southern African Americans, though victims of brutal oppression to be, in the words of Ralph Ellison, "more than the sum of [their] brutalization."[58]

I would like to thank audiences at the 1990 Organization of American Historians Convention (especially Howard Rabinowitz), the Georgia Historical Society in Savannah and Darien, Georgia, the College of Charleston (especially Randy Sparks), and the 1994 Conference on American Civil Rights at the University of Helsinki for listening to and commenting on earlier versions of this essay. I am also grateful to Gail O'Brien for inspiration and to Michael Honey for his suggestions.

1. Claudine L. Ferrell, *Nightmare and Dream: Antilynching in Congress, 1917–1921* (New York: Garland, 1986); Charles Flint Kellogg, *NAACP: A History of the National Association for the Advancement of Colored People, 1909–1920* (Baltimore: Johns Hopkins University Press, 1967), 209–46; Herbert Shapiro, *White Violence and Black Response: From Reconstruction to Montgomery* (Amherst: University of Massachusetts Press, 1988); and Robert L. Zangrando, *The NAACP Crusade against Lynching, 1909–1950* (Philadelphia: Temple University Press, 1980).

2. See especially Robin D. G. Kelley, "'We Are Not What We Seem': Rethinking Black Working-Class Opposition in the Jim Crow South," *Journal of American History* 80 (June 1993): 75–112; Kelley, *Race Rebels: Culture, Politics, and the Black Working Class* (New York: Free Press, 1994), chaps. 1–3. We also know little about the opposition of northern white women to lynching; for one interesting exception, see Roger K. Hux, "Lillian Clayton Jewett and the Rescue of the Baker Family, 1899–1900," *Historical Journal of Massachusetts* 19 (1991): 13–23.

3. Michel de Certeau, "On the Oppositional Practices of Everyday Life," *Social Text* 3 (Fall 1980): 7. The literature on slave resistance is vast. For an overview, see Peter Kolchin, *Unfree Labor: American Slavery and Russian Serfdom* (Cambridge, Mass.: Harvard University Press, 1987), chap. 5. On labor history, see Kelley, "'We Are Not What We Seem,'" 89–95.

4. Zora Neale Hurston, *Mules and Men* (1935; rpt. New York: Harper Perennial, 1990), 2.

5. George Lipsitz, *A Life of Struggle: Ivory Perry and the Culture of Opposition* (Philadelphia: Temple University Press, 1988), 229. Similarly, Richard A. Couto suggests that "resistance continually emerges because it never stops" (*Lifting the Veil: A Political History of Struggles for Emancipation* [Knoxville: University of Tennessee Press, 1993], 253).

6. Cornel West, *Race Matters* (Boston: Beacon Press, 1993), 14.

7. Amzie Moore Interview; transcript of "Eyes on the Prize [videorecording]: America's Civil Rights Years, 1954–1965" (Alexandria, Va.: PBS Video, 1986–87), Reel 1, "Awakenings, 1954–1955."

8. *Eastman Times-Journal*, September 9, 1892.

9. *Atlanta Constitution*, September 9, 1919; *Chicago Defender*, November 1, 1919; *New York Times*, September 11, 1919; *Lexington Oglethorpe Echo*, September 12, 1919; *Albany Supreme Circle News*, September 13, 1919; *Cordele Dispatch*, September 24, 1919.

10. James R. McGovern, *Anatomy of a Lynching: The Killing of Claude Neal* (Baton Rouge: Louisiana State University Press, 1982), 11.

11. Lester C. Lamon, *Black Tennesseans, 1900–1930* (Knoxville: University of Ten-

nessee Press, 1977), 18. For similar conclusions, see Neil McMillen, *Dark Journey: Black Mississippians in the Age of Jim Crow* (Urbana: University of Illinois Press, 1989), 227.

12. Lipsitz, *A Life of Struggle*, esp. 11–14, 232–47.

13. James C. Scott, "Everyday Forms of Resistance," in *Everyday Forms of Resistance*, ed. Forrest D. Colburn (Armonk, N.Y.: M. E. Sharpe, 1989); Scott, *Domination and the Arts of Resistance: Hidden Transcripts* (New Haven: Yale University Press, 1990), esp. chap. 7; Evelyn Brooks Higginbotham, "African-American Women's History and the Metalanguage of Race," *Signs* 17 (Winter 1992): 274.

14. John Dollard, *Caste and Class in a Southern Town* (New York: Doubleday, 1957), 310. See Raymond Gavins, "North Carolina Black Folklore and Song in the Age of Segregation: Toward Another Meaning of Survival," *North Carolina Historical Review* 66 (October 1989): 412–42; Trudier Harris, "Adventures in a Foreign Country: Humor and the South," *Southern Cultures* 1 (Summer 1995): esp. 459–60; and Lawrence W. Levine, *Black Culture and Black Consciousness: Afro-American Folk Thought from Slavery to Freedom* (New York: Oxford University Press, 1977), 342–43.

15. *Savannah Morning News*, April 14, 1894, quoted in Edward L. Ayers, *Vengeance and Justice: Crime and Punishment in the Nineteenth Century American South* (New York: Oxford University Press, 1984), 232.

16. *Washington Post*, April 25, 1897; *Alexandria Gazette*, April 26, 1897. For other examples of funerals becoming the stage for protest, see *Fairburn Campbell News*, March 17, 1899; *Savannah Tribune*, March 18, 1899; *Newnan Herald and Advertiser*, March 17, 1899; *Richmond Planet*, March 25, 1899. See also *Charleston News and Courier*, December 29, 31, 1889; George B. Tindall, *South Carolina Negroes, 1877–1900* (Columbia: University of South Carolina Press, 1952), 248–49. For a sophisticated discussion of the meanings of one funeral following a late lynching, see Ruth Feldstein, "'I Wanted the Whole World to See': Race, Gender, and Constructions of Motherhood in the Death of Emmett Till," in *Not June Cleaver: Women and Gender in Postwar America, 1945–1960*, ed. Joanne Meyerowitz (Philadelphia: Temple University Press, 1993), 263–303. See also Clenora Frances Hudson, "Emmett Till: The Impetus for the Modern Civil Rights Movement" (Ph.D. diss., University of Iowa, 1988). In contrast, Stephen J. Whitfield, *A Death in the Delta: The Story of Emmett Till* (New York: Free Press, 1988), has surprisingly little to say about Till's funeral.

17. William Faulkner, "Barn Burning," in *The Faulkner Reader: Selections from the Work of William Faulkner* (New York: Random House, 1954), 502. For one account of the misfortunes suffered by several white mob leaders, see "Not by Violence," *Independent* 53 (April 4, 1901): 496–97.

18. On arson as a means of black protest, see Albert C. Smith, "Down Freedom's Road: The Contours of Race, Class, and Property Crime in Black-Belt Georgia, 1866–1910" (Ph.D. diss., University of Georgia, 1982), esp. chap. 6; George C. Wright, *Racial Violence in Kentucky, 1865–1940: Lynchings, Mob Rule, and "Legal Lynchings"* (Baton Rouge: Louisiana State University Press, 1990), 163, 169.

19. See E. M. Beck and Stewart E. Tolnay, "When Race Didn't Matter: Black and White Mob Violence against Their Own Color," and Larry J. Griffin, Paula Clark, and Joanne C. Sandberg, "Narrative and Event: Lynching and Historical Sociology," in this volume.

20. Stewart E. Tolnay and E. M. Beck, "Black Flight: Lethal Violence and the Great

Migration, 1900 to 1930," *Social Science History* 14 (1990): 347–70; Tolnay and Beck, "Rethinking the Role of Racial Violence in the Great Migration," in *Black Exodus: The Great Migration from the American South*, ed. Alfredteen Harrison (Jackson: University Press of Mississippi, 1991), 20–35.

21. For examples, see *Savannah Morning News*, August 30, 1904; *Columbus Enquirer-Sun*, December 15, 1910; *Montgomery Advertiser*, August 27, 28, 1913; *Atlanta Constitution*, May 19–28, 1918; NAACP Memo, "Memorandum for Governor Dorsey from Walter F. White," July 10, 1918, and "Memo from Walter White, Nov. 12, 1918," Antilynching Files, Box C-353, NAACP Files, Library of Congress; Ray Stannard Baker, *Following the Color Line* (1908; rpt. New York: Harper & Row, 1964), 188–89; James R. Grossman, *Land of Hope: Chicago, Black Southerners, and the Great Migration* (Chicago: University of Chicago Press, 1989), 16–18. Strictly speaking, armed blacks were not anonymous, but they achieved a kind of anonymity by virtue of their numbers and the difficulty of determining who instigated the armed flight. On the dimensions of anonymous protest, see Scott, *Domination and the Arts of Resistance*, 140–52.

22. Ray Stannard Baker, *Following the Color Line* (New York: Doubleday, Page, 1908), 188–89.

23. *Norfolk Journal and Guide*, October 6, 1917. For a fictional rendering of a black economic boycott against white violence, see Bebe Moore Campbell, *Your Blues Ain't Like Mine* (New York: Putnam's, 1992).

24. M. M. Bakhtin, *The Dialogic Imagination: Four Essays*, ed. Michael Holquist (Austin: University of Texas Press, 1981), 293–94. The subsequent discussion draws upon Alan Hunt, "Rights and Social Movements: Counter-Hegemonic Strategies," *Journal of Law and Society* 17 (1990): 309–28; Marc W. Steinberg, "The Dialog of Struggle: The Contest over Ideological Boundaries in the Case of London Silk Weavers in the Early Nineteenth Century," *Social Science History* 18 (Winter 1994): 505–41; and Richard Terdiman, *Discourse/Counter-Discourse: The Theory and Practice of Symbolic Resistance in Nineteenth-Century France* (Ithaca, N.Y.: Cornell University Press, 1986).

25. Higginbotham, "African-American Women's History and the Metalanguage of Race," 267.

26. *Atlanta Constitution*, December 22–27, 1894; *Macon Telegraph*, December 24–26, 1894; *Savannah Morning News*, December 24–26, 1894; *New York Times*, December 24–26, 1894; *Valdosta Daily Times*, December 22, 29, 1894, January 5, 1895; *Richmond Planet*, December 29, 1894.

27. *Atlanta Constitution*, December 26, 1894.

28. Oliver Cox explained, "He [the black man] prostrates himself, as it were, before white men in recognition that Negroes enjoy a degree of well-being only by sufferance of their white neighbors" (*Caste, Class, and Race: A Study in Social Dynamics* [New York: Monthly Review Press, 1970], 564).

29. Couto, *Lifting the Veil*, 256. Howard Newby also makes the essential point that deferential behavior by a group cannot be assumed to represent the endorsement of the moral order that condones their subordination. See "The Deferential Dialectic," *Comparative Studies in Society and History* 17 (1975): 143–45.

30. Kelley, "'We Are Not What We Seem,'" 79–89. On the importance of social spaces for dissident culture, see Scott, *Domination and the Arts of Resistance*, chap. 5.

For case studies of black historical memory and the meaning attached to lynchings, see Couto, *Lifting the Veil*, 254–55; Charlotte Wolf, "Constructions of a Lynching," *Sociological Inquiry* 62 (February 1992): 83–97.

31. bell hooks has written evocatively about the importance of blacks' home sites in *Yearning: Race, Gender and Cultural Politics* (Toronto: Between the Lines, 1990).

32. For discussions of the NAACP and its campaign against violence in the rural South, see W. Fitzhugh Brundage, *Lynching in the New South: Georgia and Virginia, 1880–1930* (Urbana: University of Illinois Press, 1993), 221–38; Couto, *Lifting the Veil*, 127–45; Adam Fairclough, *Race and Democracy: The Civil Rights Struggle in Louisiana, 1915–1972* (Athens: University of Georgia Press, 1995), esp. chaps. 3–4; Shapiro, *White Violence and Black Response*, passim; Wright, *Racial Violence in Kentucky*, 192–205. On the explosiveness of unveiling previously masked dissent, see Scott, *Domination and the Arts of Resistance*, chap. 8.

33. *Chicago Defender*, January 24, 1920; *Messenger* 2 (March 1920): 7; *Half Century* 8 (March 1920): 17.

34. For examples, see *Norfolk Journal and Guide*, October 6, 1917; Robert F. Engs, *Freedom's First Generation: Black Hampton, Virginia, 1861–1890* (Philadelphia: University of Pennsylvania Press, 1979), 195; *Richmond Dispatch*, May 8, 1901; *Richmond Planet*, May 11, 1901. See also McMillen, *Dark Journey*, 226; Wright, *Racial Violence in Kentucky*, 162–63, 169–72, 189–90.

35. *Portsmouth Star*, October 24–27, 1904; *Norfolk Virginian-Pilot*, October 25–28, 1904; *Richmond Times-Dispatch*, October 25–28, 1904; *Washington Post*, October 24–28, 1904; *Baltimore Sun*, October 25–26, 1904; *Richmond News Leader*, October 24–31, 1904; *Richmond Planet*, October 29, 1904. For other instances of overt black protest in Virginia and South Carolina, see *Richmond Times-Dispatch*, August 5, 1904; *Norfolk Virginian-Pilot*, August 5, 1904; *Washington Post*, August 6, 1904; *Baltimore Sun*, August 6, 1904; *Charlottesville Daily Progress*, August 6–10, 1904; and *Columbia State*, January 21, May 22–25, 1907.

36. For various accounts of the events in Darien, see Adjutant General's Report, *Georgia Senate Journal, 1899*, 112–25; W. Fitzhugh Brundage, "The Darien 'Insurrection' of 1899: Black Protest during the Nadir of Race Relations," *Georgia Historical Quarterly* 74 (Summer 1990): 234–53; Brundage, *Lynching in the New South*, 133–36. Arthur Raper provides a factually inaccurate account of the Darien "Insurrection" and draws very different conclusions from mine in *The Tragedy of Lynching* (Chapel Hill: University of North Carolina Press, 1933), 232.

37. *Savannah Press*, August 26–27, September 1, 1899; *Savannah Morning News*, August 26–27, 1899; *Atlanta Constitution*, August 28, 1899; McIntosh County Superior Court Minutes, Book E, 1896–1905, 174–97, Georgia Department of Archives and History, Atlanta; *Darien Gazette*, February 24, 1900.

38. The term is borrowed from Scott, *Domination and the Arts of Resistance*.

39. Antonio Gramsci, *Selections from the Prison Notebooks*, ed. Quintin Hoare and Geoffrey Nowell Smith (New York: International Publishers, 1971), 196.

40. Brundage, "The Darien 'Insurrection' of 1889"; *Charleston News and Courier*, December 29, 1889; *Norfolk Virginian-Pilot*, October 25–28, 1904.

41. John Dollard provides an interesting discussion of the greater leeway given black women in *Caste and Class in a Southern Town*, 289–90. See also Kelley, "'We Are Not What We Seem,'" esp. 97–100; Kelley, *Race Rebels*, 27–28, 69–70.

42. McIntosh County Superior Court Minutes, Book E, 1896–1905, 174–97, 227–28; *Savannah Press*, September 1, 1899.

43. For a convenient overview of black newspapers, see Henry Lewis Suggs, ed., *The Black Press in the South, 1865–1979* (Westport, Conn.: Greenwood Press, 1983). Among the most valuable discussions of black editors are Ann F. Alexander, "Black Protest in the New South: John Mitchell, Jr., and the Richmond *Planet*" (Ph.D. diss., Duke University, 1973); Alexander, *John Mitchell, Jr.: Fighting Editor of the New South* (Urbana: University of Illinois Press, forthcoming), chap. 4; Henry Lewis Suggs, *P. B. Young, Newspaperman: Race, Politics, Journalism in the New South, 1902–62* (Charlottesville: University Press of Virginia, 1988); Julius E. Thompson, *The Black Press in Mississippi, 1865–1985* (Gainesville: University Press of Florida, 1993); Tindall, *South Carolina Negroes*, 149–52; John M. Matthews, "Black Newspapermen and the Black Community in Georgia, 1890–1930," *Georgia Historical Quarterly* 68 (Fall 1984): 356–81.

44. Gunnar Myrdal, *An American Dilemma: The Negro Problem and Modern Democracy*, 2 vols. (New York: Harper & Row, 1944), 2:910.

45. Ida B. Wells, "Southern Horrors: Lynch Law in All Its Phases," in *Selected Writings of Ida B. Wells-Barnett*, comp. and ed. Trudier Harris (New York: Oxford University Press, 1991), 42; Thomas C. Holt, "The Lonely Warrior: Ida B. Wells-Barnett and the Struggle for Black Leadership," in *Black Leaders of the Twentieth Century*, ed. John Hope Franklin and August Meier (Urbana: University of Illinois Press, 1982), 42.

46. Quoted in Alexander, *John Mitchell, Jr.*

47. Ida B. Wells-Barnett, *Crusade for Justice: The Autobiography of Ida B. Wells*, ed. Alfreda M. Duster (Chicago: University of Chicago Press, 1970), chap. 6; David M. Tucker, "Miss Ida B. Wells and Memphis Lynching," *Phylon* 32 (Summer 1971): 112–22. For two portraits of Wells and her leadership style, see Holt, "Lonely Warrior"; and Patricia A. Schechter, "Unsettled Business: Ida B. Wells against Lynching or, How Antilynching Got Its Gender," in this volume.

48. Nathan Huggins, "Afro-Americans," in *Ethnic Leadership in America*, ed. John Higham (Baltimore: Johns Hopkins University Press, 1978), 91–118. For two other interpretations of black leadership which reach similar conclusions, see August Meier, "Negro Class Structure and Ideology in the Age of Booker T. Washington," *Phylon* 23 (Fall 1962): 258–66; and Wilson J. Moses, *The Golden Age of Black Nationalism, 1850–1925* (New York: Oxford University Press, 1978), esp. 22–23.

49. For a cogent analysis of Wells and her campaign, see Gail Bederman, *Manliness and Civilization: A Cultural History of Gender and Race in the United States, 1880–1917* (Chicago: University of Chicago Press, 1995), chap. 2. For the larger context, see Deborah Gray White, "The Cost of Club Work, the Price of Black Feminism," in *Visible Women: New Essays on American Activism*, ed. Nancy A. Hewitt and Suzanne Lebsock (Urbana: University of Illinois Press, 1993), 247–69. On Mitchell, see Alexander, "Black Protest in the New South," passim; Alexander, *John Mitchell, Jr.*, chap. 4; W. Fitzhugh Brundage, " 'To Howl Loudly': John Mitchell, Jr., and His Campaign against Lynching in Virginia," *Canadian Review of American Studies* 22 (Winter 1991): 325–42; Brundage, *Lynching in the New South*, 164–65, 173–76.

50. Fairclough, *Race and Democracy*, esp. chaps. 3–5. See also Michael K. Honey, *Southern Labor and Black Civil Rights: Organizing Memphis Workers* (Urbana: Uni-

versity of Illinois Press, 1993); and Robin D. G. Kelley, *Hammer and Hoe: Alabama Communists during the Great Depression* (Chapel Hill: University of North Carolina Press, 1990).

51. These ideas draw upon Ranajit Guha, "The Prose of Counter-Insurgency," *Subaltern Studies* 2 (1983): 26–33; Rosalind O'Hanlon, "Recovering the Subject: *Subaltern Studies* and Histories of Resistance in Colonial South Asia," *Modern Asian Studies* 22 (February 1988): 222.

52. Scott, *Domination and the Arts of Resistance*, 56. George Lipsitz similarly observes that dominant groups "must make their triumphs appear legitimate and necessary in the eyes of the vanquished" ("The Struggle for Hegemony," *Journal of American History* 75 [June 1988]: 147).

53. *Savannah Tribune*, August 20, 1892. For other examples of "wild talk" leading to violence against blacks, see Executive Minutes, January 1, 1890–December 31, 1891, Reel 50-60, 203, Microfilm Library, Georgia Department of Archives and History, Atlanta; of an unnamed black man for protesting the lynching of two blacks: *Macon Telegraph*, June 28–29, 1908; *Atlanta Constitution*, June 28–29, 1908; *Way-cross Herald*, July 4, 11, 1908; of Henry Etheridge: *Atlanta Constitution*, April 27, 1912; *Macon Telegraph*, April 27, 1912; *Savannah Tribune*, May 4, 1912; *Forsyth Monroe Advertiser*, May 3, 1912; and of the threatened lynching of a black undertaker for questioning the cause of a black man's death: N. B. Young to Dr. W. E. B. Du Bois, November 14, 1916, Antilynching Files, Box C-336, NAACP Papers.

54. *Savannah Press*, August 29, 1899.

55. *Savannah Morning News*, August 29, 1899. For similar attitudes, see *Darien Gazette*, September 2, 1899.

56. Kelley, " 'We Are Not What We Seem,' " 112.

57. The task remains of carefully charting both the circumstances that gave rise to different forms of black resistance and the calculations made by blacks of their options when confronted by white violence.

58. Ralph Ellison, "A Very Stern Discipline," *Harper's* 263 (March 1967): 84.

Unsettled Business

Ida B. Wells against Lynching, or, How Antilynching Got Its Gender

Patricia A. Schechter

I n the late nineteenth- and early twentieth-century American South, lynching ended thousands of lives and politicized gender across and within racial lines. The archetypal "lynching story" reported in mainstream newspapers justified lynching as punishment for black men's alleged sexual assaults on white women. These accounts portrayed white males as patriarchal protectors of white females against African American men, the so-called black beasts or burly brutes who functioned as dark foils for true (white) manhood.[1] White women appeared as passive, dependent, usually silent victims. This conventional story, for all its drama, left out the white women, black women, and white men who were also historical victims of lynching and ignored the active role of white women in abetting or resisting mobs. Furthermore, black women were totally invisible in the dominant lynching story.[2] Yet middle-class black women, led by Ida B. Wells in the early 1890s, became lynching's most articulate and daring public critics.[3]

Ida B. Wells's initiative against lynching invites a reconsideration of educated black women's historic impact on organized antilynching protest.[4] Wells's pathbreaking critique of racial-sexual politics and her international publicity campaign represented a new departure in black women's public activity. It triggered a process of feminization within the ranks of American reform that channeled its radical impulses into a more domesticated form of "women's work." By the 1920s black women's activism against lynching, although still public, was marked more strongly by gender and gendered traditions of female-only organization, voluntarism, evangelicalism, and the rhetoric of womanhood and maternalism, all distinctly different from Wells's earlier crusade.

How do we account for the political and ideological changes that occurred between the work of Wells and that of the black women Anti-
Lynching Crusaders of 1922? And how, during these years, did black
women's agitation against lynching "prepare the way," in Jacquelyn Hall's
words, for the Association of Southern Women for the Prevention of
Lynching, founded by Jessie Daniel Ames, a white Texan, in 1930?[5] Almost certainly black women's public airing of the issue over thirty-five
years made it acceptable—if still not completely safe—for southern "ladies" to take on the mob. As Rosalyn Terborg-Penn suggests, previous
scholarly neglect of black women's activism against lynching is partly the
result of its being perceived and devalued as "women's work," which falls
through the cracks of narratives by Walter White and other prominent
male leaders of the antilynching fight.[6] But in exactly what ways was
antilynching *women's* work? How did antilynching become gendered?[7]

Though not recognized by scholars until recently, Wells's first published pamphlet, *Southern Horrors: Lynch Law in All Its Phases* (1892), is
a point of origin in American critical thought on lynching.[8] Wells's brief
but comprehensive account offered a stinging critique of southern society
as a "white man's country." After identifying lynching as a chief expression of "opposition . . . to the progress of the race," Wells made a creative
new analysis of sex-race politics that owed little ideological debt to maternalism or the rhetoric of womanhood typical of nineteenth-century wom-
en's writing.[9] Wells's reports of consensual and sometimes illicit sexual
contact between white women and black men and of white women's role
in abetting mobs undermined the assumption of white women's moral
purity used to justify lynching. Furthermore, Wells probed the politics of
"true manhood" in the lynching story and linked black men's oppression
through lynching to black women's oppression through rape. Finally, her
exploration and reworking of racial and sexual ideology claimed new
authority for black women with the goal "that justice be done though the
heavens fall."[10]

The pamphlet's distinctive style complemented its provocative theses.
Throughout *Southern Horrors*, Wells used unorthodox punctuation to
mark up the stories of lynching she copied from mainstream newspapers.
By disrupting these texts with quotation and question marks, Wells
mocked their authority and created space for her own findings and re-
readings of the material.[11] For example, Wells questioned how America
"legally (?) disfranchised the Afro-American" and whether black men
"always rape (?) white women."[12] She took issue with the " 'honor' " invoked by southerners to justify lynching and with what passed for "evi-

dence (?)" of black peoples' guilt of crime in the newspapers.[13] Wells warned her readers to "note the wording" of lynching reports, and in a chapter mockingly entitled "The Black and White of It," she reread some of them with a critical eye.[14] Playing on the supposed self-evident truth of texts/skin colors, Wells showed that the "facts," moral certainties, and racial divides portrayed in mainstream southern newspapers were not at all what they seemed.

Consistent with the emerging progressive, muckraking impulse in journalism, Wells's analysis of southern racism reworked the tenets of Christian civilization, bourgeois gender roles, and the rule of law in an appeal to protect all African Americans from violence and to create a blueprint for black self-help.[15] By disrupting and rereading mainstream press accounts of lynching, Wells attacked the dominant culture's values and ideology from within: "Out of their own mouths shall the murderers be condemned."[16] Nowhere was the power (and instability) of her rereading strategy more evident than on the issue of gender, which Wells placed at the center of her case for black protection and self-help against lynching.

IDA B. WELLS ON LYNCHING

In the late nineteenth century, gender was an important metaphor in Anglo-American moral and political discourse.[17] Gender politics were particularly resonant among the middle-class African Americans who were part of Wells's intended audience. Although lynching was a growing concern to African Americans all over the United States, black resistance to racism and gender consciousness both were especially visible in southern cities and towns, where white and black people lived in close proximity and where the streets, public accommodations, and press provided theaters in which dramas of power, status, and identity were played out.[18]

The post-Reconstruction generation of educated African Americans exercised an unprecedented, albeit circumscribed, autonomy. Many hoped that progress and prosperity in the South could be built on such notions of respectability as Christianity, thrift, sobriety, and adherence to middle-class gender roles shared across the color line. These values would help to secure a modicum of social access and to empower the entire black community.[19] It was in response to the very economic and political gains of black members of southern communities that negrophobes of the 1890s intensified their rhetoric about black inhumanity, innate mental deficiency, and corrupt morals.

During the 1880s, Memphis, Tennessee, where Ida B. Wells lived and worked as a teacher and journalist, was home to a thriving black community. Hoping to make Memphis the "Chicago of the South," city boosters fostered development with a degree of racial tolerance. But as black Memphians tried to turn progress into equality, white resistance appeared. In 1883, for example, Wells brought a suit against a railroad company that refused to honor her ticket for a seat in a first-class car after the trainman roughly, forcibly removed her from the car.[20] No major racial violence occurred in Memphis—the site of the post–Civil War South's bloodiest race riot in 1866—until 1892, when three black shopkeepers were lynched because they posed an unacceptable economic threat to a local white businessman. For Wells, the triple lynching of Calvin McDowell, Tom Moss, and Henry Stewart made plain the masking function of the rape charge in lynching. Wells (and later protesters) would focus relentlessly on the fact that less than 29 percent of all lynchings even involved the charge of rape.[21]

Wells understood lynching as sometimes arbitrary, sometimes tactical terrorism against an entire race of people and a particular assault on black males and black "manhood." In this context, the concept of a "race's manhood" evoked a historically specific set of male social functions (voting, economic independence, and protecting dependents) and symbolized the prestige of an entire community.[22] On a practical level, lynching usually targeted individual black men. On a symbolic level, the lynching story lied about the source of sexual and violent aggression in the South. "This cry [of rape] has had its effect," noted Wells bitterly in *Southern Horrors*. "It has closed the heart, stifled the conscience, warped the judgement and hushed the voice of press and pulpit on the subject of lynch law throughout this 'land of liberty.' "[23] Wells showed that mobs aimed especially at the "subjugation of the young manhood of the race."[24] She insisted that the so-called black beast rapist was in reality the innocent victim of both white male blood lust and, highlighting a previously suppressed element to the story, white female sexual lust.[25]

In an era partial to "black and white" views of social reality, Wells argued that lynching was both about sex and not about sex. She declared that "mob spirit has grown with the increasing intelligence of the Afro-American," and from the annual lynching statistics published in the white press, she showed that even according to whites, the rape charge against black men was neither dominant nor adequately proven in lynching cases. Wells also revised the connection between sexual order and social order proposed by the lynching-for-rape story. *Southern Horrors* "reduced to plain English" her belief that white mobs lynched the black man "not because he is always a despoiler of virtue, but because he succumbs to the smiles of white women." Thus the pamphlet provided "a defense for the Afro-American Sampsons who suffer themselves to be betrayed by white Delilahs."[26] It was simply not their fault.

Wells's evidence for consensual sexual liaisons between black men and white women provoked negrophobes' worst nightmare of miscegenation. Through the acknowledgment—even tacit endorsement—of the activities of "white Juliets [and] colored Romeos," she redeployed the white supremacist narrative of race mixing as a story of potential racial equality. Instead of marking the beginning of the end of Anglo-Saxon civilization, Wells reread interracial sex as a signifier of a shared culture and common humanity of all people. At the "bottom of this [lynching] business," argued Wells, was "the fact that coloured men, advancing as they are in intelligence and position, have become attractive to certain classes of white women."[27] *Southern Horrors* suggested that there were "many white women in the South who would marry colored men" if it were socially and legally permitted. She noted further that "some white women love the company of the Afro-American," as reported by the "daily papers of the South."[28] Wells had no reproach for "the white women of the South" on this point for, given her vindication of black men, "such need not be said."[29]

Most black commentators on lynching avoided explosive sexual issues, focusing instead on law and order. Yet many drew on Wells's reconstructed vision of black manhood to frame their protests. Two images of lynching from the *Richmond Planet* (Figures 1 and 2), for example, suggest the centrality of gender and manhood within antilynching discourse among African Americans in the age of Jim Crow. The image of crucifixion highlighted black men's status as victims ennobled by innocence. Black men also triumphed over mob violence by offering themselves as legitimate wielders of force in the nation's service. The black soldier of World War I protected both the black community and American society, exhibiting the restraint of Victorian manhood as well as more modern martial masculinity.[30] Echoing *Southern Horrors*, the *Planet* represented black manhood along a continuum of manly sacrifice ranging from innocent victimization to battlefield martyrdom. But unlike Wells, the *Planet* left black women as silent, faceless sufferers or out of the picture altogether.[31]

Southern Horrors, in contrast, made black women visible in the dynamics of southern lynching and sexualized racism. Wells documented not black women's sideline suffering but attacks—lynchings *and* rapes—

FIGURE 1. *"Not Kultur, but Americans Passed This Way,"*
by George H. Ben Johnson (Richmond Planet, *November 22, 1919)*

on black women and girls, including the heinous attack by a mob that
"legally (?) hung poor little thirteen year old Mildred Brown" in Columbia,
South Carolina, on suspicion of murder in 1890.[32] Instead of focusing on
black men as failed protectors, however, Wells drew attention to white
abuse of black women. She stressed the general public's ignorance of
black women's experiences and declared that even if the facts were
known, "when the victim is a colored woman it is different." Americans
knew "nothing of assault by white men on black women, for which no-
body is lynched and no notice is taken."[33]

Thus in addition to vindicating black manhood, *Southern Horrors* asserted black women's claim to outraged womanhood traditionally re-

FIGURE 2. *"Loyalty," by George H. Ben Johnson*
(Richmond Planet, *June 16, 1917*)

served only for white women and unthinkable under white supremacist
ideology. By refraining from criticism of black men, Wells avoided further
impugning "the race's manhood" and blunted potential complaints from
within the black community that she was "rather hard on the young men"
of her race.[34] Yet gender's hold on the terms of power in the late nineteenth century led Wells to frame the imperative for black protest and
resistance in gendered and potentially barbed terms, especially for men.

"Nothing, absolutely nothing," she insisted, "is to be gained by a further sacrifice of manhood and self-respect."[35] And in detailing black women's agony at the hands of white mobs, Wells revealed information that was painful or perhaps even shameful for some black men and women.

For all her maneuvering through gender and sexual politics, the graphic nature of Wells's exposé and the implications of her arguments unsettled her audiences. Indeed, the (gendered) questions of strategy, authority, and leadership within the black community and the boundaries of sexual discourse in U.S. society in general were precisely at issue at this historical moment.[36] Wells's subject matter—law and order, politics, and sexual practices across the color line—was understood by many to be either male terrain or best not broached loudly or publicly. An examination of what other African American intellectuals were saying about these subjects in 1892 brings the originality, daring, and radical potential of Wells's work into clearer relief.

ON RAPE AND LYNCHING

Anna Julia Cooper published *A Voice from the South* in 1892, the same year that Wells wrote *Southern Horrors*. The work was a compilation of speeches Cooper wrote for literary groups and women's clubs in Washington, D.C., where she worked as a schoolteacher. Cooper dedicated her book "with profound regard" and "sincere esteem" to Bishop Benjamin W. Arnett of the A.M.E. Church.[37] Cooper's dedication (and Wells's inclusion in *Southern Horrors* of a letter of endorsement by Frederick Douglass) suggests both the expectation of female social deference to powerful men in the community and black women's practical need for patronage to legitimize and distribute their work.[38] Yet within this deferential framework, Cooper produced a manifesto of possibility for black womanhood.

In her eloquent arguments for the development of an "elevated and trained womanhood," Cooper identified the sexual victimization of black women by white men as one of the many obstacles to black progress. As a remedy, she proposed the extension of fatherly and siblinglike protection over disadvantaged girls and women by those able to give help. "We need . . . men who can be a father, a brother, a friend to every weak, struggling, unshielded girl. We need women . . . to lend a hand to a fallen or falling sister." Cooper's moral vision was family-centered: "A race is but a total of families." Throughout *A Voice*, she identified black girls' need for protection from abuse, though, unlike Wells, she never used the word "rape." Her moral universe was a romantic fusion of chivalry and Christianity. At one point, Cooper suggested that a woman's sheer "pure-minded[ness]" could cause dangerous "rabble" and "vice" to "slink away" from her path in the street.[39]

A Voice promoted a modulated Christian patriarchal order in which strong, chivalrous fathers protected weaker females and, in the spirit of equality before God, welcomed more able ones to equal education with men.[40] Cooper likened the "*Colored Girls* of the South—that large, bright, promising fatally beautiful class" to "delicate plantlet[s]," "shivering" before the "fury of tempestuous elements . . . so sure of destruction." These girls were "without a father . . . often without a stronger brother" to "defend their honor with his life's blood." "Oh, save them, help them, shield . . . them!" implored Cooper. "Snatch them, in God's name, as brands from the burning!"[41] Like Wells, Cooper saw black women's physical vulnerability as a pressing problem. But unlike Wells, her overview downplayed unequal economic and political power between the races and made no mention of lynching.

Lynching, however, was a main concern of Frederick Douglass, the elder statesman among African Americans, who also wrote an analysis of the southern racial situation in 1892. In July, the prestigious *North American Review* carried "Lynch Law in the South," giving Douglass an audience, especially among white readers, that Wells and Cooper could not command at that time. In his essay, Douglass defined lynching as a case of race hate destroying law and order. Like Wells, he identified the rape charge against black men as a subterfuge, merely the newest "best excuse" available to conceal and legitimate white hostility to black achievement.[42]

Douglass appealed to commonsense notions of rational human behavior to undermine the rape charge. He began by pointing out that black men could not have become uncontrollable rapists "all at once" after having remained safely alone with white women and children on the plantations during the Civil War. Refuting white southerners' claims, Douglass argued that there could be no "rational doubt" about the certitude of punishment to the fullest extent of the law for any black person convicted of crime in southern courts. To end lynching, Douglass looked to education by the "press and the pulpit," a tactic Wells also endorsed but to which she added boycotts, migration, and political pressure through voting and lobbying.

Gender distinctly marked the social criticism of Cooper and Douglass. The dominant culture understood lynching as something men did to other men in public—it was publicized aggressively and its victims made a spectacle. Rape, by contrast, was coded "private"—it happened to women, often in private or domestic spaces. Consistent with this schema and Victorian reticence about sex, Cooper lamented the sexual victimization of black women in the context of an appeal to the black community, especially fathers, to protect women in the name of advancing the race. Her "feminine" critique delicately identified the problem of rape or sexual assault and kept the solution private and within the family.[43] Similarly, Douglass recognized lynching as a public crime, and his critique was characteristically "masculine." He was concerned with the breakdown of public authority and appealed to community institutions (press and pulpit) that could, in his mind, "easily" affect public sentiment to uphold law and order. But Wells bridged the ideological divide that separated Cooper's and Douglass's critiques.

Specifically, *Southern Horrors* connected the "private" crime of rape to the "public" crime of lynching.[44] Cooper used the naturalistic metaphor of the "tempestuous elements" for rape and pleaded for help from the fathers and brothers in the African American community. Wells instead understood the "legal (?)" attacks on black women not as fate but as politics, of a piece with the abuse of black men through lynching; the remedy for both was legal protection of black people. And by describing the sexual liaisons and personal betrayals that sometimes occurred between white women and black men and led to lynchings, Wells articulated the "private" origins of an issue which Douglass understood as a failure of public institutions. According to Wells, lynching and rape formed a web of racist sexual politics aimed at subjugating southern blacks. In breaking down the distinctions between public and private crimes against the bodies of black people, Wells moved beyond the gendered critique of southern racial practices produced by her peers and in so doing charted new ideological territory.

That territory contained more fluid boundaries between private and public social facts and allowed Wells to expand the existing discourse on sexuality.[45] In *Southern Horrors*, white women appeared as neither passive nor passionless but as agents of racism and illicit sexual desire—not unlike white men. Black women were presented as full historical subjects whose being was violated through assault—much like black men. Muting gender difference, these constructions privileged the racial divide to make the case about unequal power between blacks and whites. Yet at other moments Wells mocked the notion of settled racial distinctions—the supposed "black and white of it"—by pointing to ongoing sexual contact across the color line, to the growing class of mixed-race southerners (herself included), and to cases when white men committed crimes with "their faces blackened."[46] By contesting and refiguring the boundaries between public/private, male/female, black/white, *Southern Horrors* made visible information about sex and power hidden within the conventional lynching story.

WHO DOES SHE THINK SHE IS?

Wells's blurring of ideological lines permeated the structure of *Southern Horrors*. Though neatly divided into chapters, the pamphlet combined the features of a sociological tract, exposé journalism, sermonizing, and a rousing call to armed self-defense ("A Winchester rifle," she urged, "should have a place of honor in every black home"). Instead of providing neat narrative closure, the text is full of questions and commands. "The press is singularly silent," Wells cautioned her readers. "Has it a motive? We owe it to ourselves to find out." Rather than exhibiting ladylike tact, *Southern Horrors* has an unbounded quality, disrupted by creative punctuation and the use of asides and sarcasm. In the wake of Reconstruction's violence, Wells noted, "the race was left to the tender mercies of the solid South."[47] A single tone or voice is inadequate to carry Wells's message.

By contrast, Frederick Douglass, as a spokesman for all African Americans, positioned himself squarely within dominant notions of masculine authority, especially mastery over language, self, and environment.[48] Similarly, Anna Julia Cooper, who identified herself on the title page of *A Voice* as "A Black Woman of the South," invoked Victorian notions of womanhood and made her case from the philosophically essentialist position "woman" (with all its radical implications for black women).[49] Wells identified herself quite differently. The cover of *Southern Horrors* carried a specific name and face: a striking portrait of the author and her name in capital letters (Figure 3). This gesture qualified the effect of the authenticating introduction provided by Douglass's letter. Yet in the context of educated black women's cultural invisibility in late nineteenth-century America, the name and face of Ida B. Wells raised as many questions about power and identity as did Cooper's proud label "A Black Woman of the South."[50]

In the body of her text, Wells identified herself as an exile, claiming the authority of the margins, of one who is dislocated or out of place. In the preface to *Southern Horrors*, she cited her pen name "Exiled," over which

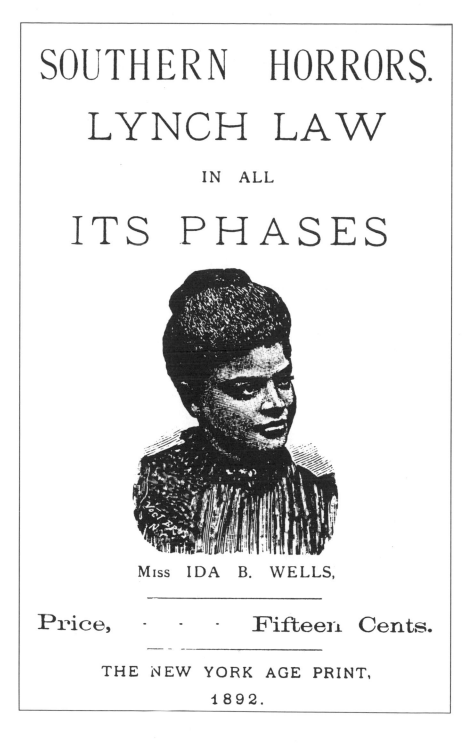

SOUTHERN HORRORS.

LYNCH LAW

IN ALL

ITS PHASES

Miss IDA B. WELLS,

Price, · · · Fifteen Cents.

THE NEW YORK AGE PRINT,

1892.

FIGURE 3. *Cover of* Southern Horrors

an earlier newspaper version of her material had appeared. A few pages later, she again identified herself as "an exile from home" because her press office had been destroyed by a white mob in Memphis in May 1892 in response to the publication of a scathing editorial against lynching.[51] The exile functions as a dialectic with access to the knowledge of the insider/outsider, southerner/northerner, victim/survivor. The ambiguous gender symbolics of the exile forfeited some of the ideological ground under the category "woman." Wells as exile instead embraced liminality and gained a richer if less stable ideological terrain from which to work.

The exile as victim/survivor was a powerful construction of black female subjectivity for Wells. It resonated historically with black women's experience of sexual (and other) victimization during and after slavery. Western literary tradition tends to erase the female victim of rape through madness or death. In conventional lynching accounts, for example, the "raped" white woman (dis)appears as a silent, comatose, or dead victim. But black women's narratives of victimization tend to stress survival and provide an alternative moral economy through which to represent and resist sexual exploitation.[52]

The ideological underpinning of the black woman as victim/survivor contrasted sharply with that of the black man as victim of/victor over lynching. As dramatized by the antilynching cartoons published in the *Richmond Planet*, the black soldier's status derived from his formal relationship to the state, a legitimately constituted social authority (as did Christ's from God). Wells's exile status by definition placed her outside such patriarchal institutions as the state, church, or male-headed family. Wells often represented herself as "homeless" and an "orphan" in these years, identities that legitimized both her physical mobility/autonomy and her claim to assistance from powerful members of her community.[53]

Wells's critique thus reclaimed and updated a powerful construction of black female subjectivity as it broke new analytic ground on lynching and southern sexual politics. She redrew the boundaries between private and public on the issues of race and sex and, in so doing, remapped the authority of the black woman intellectual. By insisting that lynching and rape constituted connected domains of racial oppression, Wells rewrote the dominant southern narrative about race relations and female subjectivity in powerfully unsettling terms.[54] Those uncomfortable with a black woman out of (her) place quickly moved to reprimand or silence her. Indeed, the racist Memphians who wrecked her press office also threatened Wells with a lynching replete with castration—"a surgical operation with a pair of tailor's shears"—since they assumed that the speaker of such strong words was male.[55]

Like white Memphians, many white Americans ignored Wells's message of black suffering in the South and instead attacked the messenger. White criticism of Wells vividly expressed the racist sexism black women faced in the 1890s. Transgressive white females were viewed as "unsexed"; black females were assumed to be sexually loose. These two images formed ideological counterpoints in rhetorical moves designed to discredit and control unacceptable female speech.[56] White supremacists defined any person who failed to condemn sex across the color line as a dangerous race-mixer. For relating information about illicit interracial sex to white audiences in 1893–94, southern racists labeled Wells a "black harlot" in search of a "white husband," a "strumpet," a "saddle-colored Sapphira [sic]," an "adventuress of a decidedly shady character," and "a prostitute bent on miscegenation."[57] The *New York Times* disparaged her as a "slanderous and nasty-minded mulatress."[58] Even northern white women who protested lynching at this time were ridiculed in the South as "the short-haired, strident-voiced sisterhood of Boston."[59]

In this context of heightened racism and volatile gender politics, few people, white or black, were comfortable with Wells's treatment of sex and race. In her autobiography, Wells recalled that a "delegation" of black men in New York City asked her in 1894 to "put the soft pedal on charges against white women and their relations with black men."[60] Apparently they felt she unduly complicated and sensationalized the already difficult job of ending lynching. Some black women understood Wells's findings about these liaisons as evidence not for liberalized sexual contact across the color line but for better policing of it. "The Afro-American shall be taught, that whatever folly a white woman may commit the suspicion of participation in that folly means torture and death for him," decreed the Ladies' Home Circle of the A.M.E. Church in St. Paul, Minnesota, in 1894.[61]

In general, the black community welcomed Wells's statistical refutation of the rape charge. Yet at a time when hundreds of blacks were being murdered each year in the South, much of the commentary on Wells's work took shape not around the issue of stopping racial violence, which reform-minded readers agreed about, but around gender politics, which were exacerbated by conflict on both sides of the color line. Wells did not hide her femininity (the cover of *Southern Horrors* and letter from Frederick Douglass calling her a "Brave woman!" announced it), but neither did she base her authority on essentialist claims about womanhood or female moral superiority over men. The pamphlet's grateful dedication to the "Afro-American women of Brooklyn and New York" who supported her work contained no paean to Woman. Yet some were uncomfortable with Wells's claim to individual self-possession, even in exile, and recoiled at the negative publicity surrounding her work.

Many gauged Wells by a standard of true womanhood. Julia Coston of Cleveland, Ohio, editor of *Ringwood's Afro-American Journal of Fashion*, did so when she declared that "essentially feminine" women were "not troubled with affairs of State, nor [were] agents of reform." In 1894, when Coston criticized those black women who would "throw off the veil of modesty, and . . . in the name of reform, pose as martyrs, sacrificing themselves to a great work," she easily could have been referring to Wells.[62] Others were patronizing. Clubwoman Fannie Barrier Williams of Chicago remarked in 1895 that "the public has been so accustomed to think of Miss Wells' remarkable zeal for the cause of law and order that, I suppose, no one ever reads of a case of lynching without associating with it the indignant protest of our plucky little friend." Evoking both the canons of true womanhood and black women's concern in the 1890s with public appearances and safety, Williams complained that Wells's "unique career" opened her private life to unbecoming public scrutiny. Williams's tart observation in 1895 that Wells planned to "marry a man while still married to a cause" conveyed disapproval through a metaphor of polygamy, even promiscuity. By speculating that Wells's wedding to Ferdinand Lee Barnett would be a "topic of national interest and comment," Williams hinted that such publicity might bring on more name-calling, contempt, and perhaps even danger for black women.[63]

At a moment when middle-class black women were striving to define black womanhood in positive terms, some members of the club movement disapproved of unorthodox female behavior. At the founding conventions of the National Association of Colored Women (NACW) in 1895–96, some women criticized the "fierce denunciation[s] made by 'mercurial persons' of the race" which they felt fell outside the proper tone of club work.[64] Sharing sentiments with black male leaders and white women reformers as well, some black women were uncomfortable with political speeches and confrontation, dubbing them tactics of mere "complaint," as opposed to the desire to be "actually noble." Public agitation and strong language unsettled genteel standards of decorous ladyhood to which many clubwomen aspired. True womanhood was a class-based gender ideal that formed part of the ideological basis for clubwomen's resistance to negative stereotypes about black females. But Wells's work and the resistance to it suggest little consensus on these ideals in 1895.

A strong core of black supporters in the 1890s, however, found Wells's womanliness everywhere in evidence. Her success on the lecture platform offered many African Americans, especially women, a renewed sense of pride.[65] Katherine Davis Tillman wrote a poem praising Wells as a model for black children.[66] Playing a reverse gender card, Wells's supporters recast her unique boldness and alleged appetite for praise as proof of her femininity. "To our mind, therein lies one of the chief charms of Miss Wells' crusade," the *Indianapolis Freeman* explained, "in that she has not permitted the cares and labors of the same to unsex her. The full blown rose of a blameless womanhood abideth within her."[67] Publicist Monroe Majors agreed. In spite of her "forcible pen [and] caustic oddness," Wells taught the nation "that sublime lesson of *modesty unchanged* even at the severest test."[68] Wells was also likened to Old Testament heroines Esther, Deborah, and Jael, mythic women who came forth in times of emergency to lead at moments of "lost courage" among men.[69] These images of purity, chastity, and selfless, temporary, service defused anxiety that Wells violated precepts of traditional femininity.

But even Wells's supporters determined that she trespassed on the male territory of politics and agitation. Some put the matter in friendly (and gendered) terms. "The hour had come, where was the man?" asked the *Freeman*. "Unfortunately, the man was not forthcoming—but Miss Wells was!"[70] In discussing lynching, Wells "handle[d] her subjects more as a man than as a woman," admitted New York editor T. Thomas Fortune.[71] "We regret we have not a hundred more Ida B. Wells [*sic*] to proclaim and defend the truth," lamented the A.M.E. Church's *Christian Recorder*. "But where, oh where are our leading men?"[72] These comments suggest that publicly representing the prestige of the community or speaking for "the race" was properly men's work, and for a woman to do it was at least a little troubling. Defenders of the courtly tradition in gender relations were outright offended by Wells's defense of black men at the "expense" of white women's moral reputation. For example, two black men complained in the pages of the *New York Times* that it was "dishonorable in the extreme to attempt any defense based upon an attack on the virtue of any class of women."[73] No proper, knightly (soldierly?) male could accept a vindication that undermined the moral economy of chivalry as did Wells's. Thus there seems to have been as little consensus on gender ideals for men as for women at this time.

When Wells emerged at the crest of a wave of black women's intellectual achievement and political initiative in the 1890s, her work both shaped and was shaped by a moment of flux and debate over women's roles as intellectuals and leaders. As Deborah Gray White has argued, black women's confidence was not enough to secure them an equal place in the work of racial reform.[74] Anna Julia Cooper was not optimistic about men's receptivity to female initiative. She noted that "the average man of our race is less frequently ready to admit the actual need among the sturdier forces of the world for woman's help or influence." The prestige of the "whole *Negro race*" might become visible in the "quiet, undisputed dignity of [her] womanhood," in Cooper's moving phrase, but Ida B. Wells was far from quiet and talked more about politics and economics than womanhood.[75] She was regarded by some as an odd female usurper of male privilege.

Because male power and community prestige (black *and* white) were at stake in the lynching scenario, African American women's initiative against racial violence promoted gender anxiety. As an intellectual and social project, Wells's antilynching work blurred the boundaries between public and private on issues and responsibilities that were ideally, if not always neatly, coded and divided by gender. Wells's work created anxiety because it destabilized gender dualisms and racial hierarchies and thereby threatened the very terms by which power, order, and legitimacy were understood by many middle-class Americans, black or white, clubwomen or clergy. Wells's exposé of white women's illicit sexual initiatives across the color line caused America's most influential woman, Frances E. Willard (president of the Woman's Christian Temperance Union), to publicly admonish Wells for attacking the ideological pillar of white women's reform: female moral purity.[76] White supremacists lashed out at the specter of an unloosed black female—among the most disempowered of Americans—as a dangerous menace to racial purity and the sexual-social order. And as Jim Crow hardened in the early twentieth century, a pattern of gender tension and black female creativity seemed to emerge around the lynching question in African American communities.

For example, in 1915, the *Chicago Defender* lamented the rarity of black men's forcible resistance to mobs, which, according to one writer, required fighting unto death. "Since there are no men, women come to the front; protect the weaklings that still wear the pants from the lynch mobs."[77] When a mob searched out a boy in a black neighborhood for a lynching in Louisiana, the next year, the paper reported that "several girls and women of the Race saw the mob coming and they hid the children till things cooled down. They jeered the mob and refused to run. The men were at the mills working."[78] When human life was at stake, black men and women resisted by whatever means were at hand. But in the aftermath of lynchings and particularly where issues of community prestige and leadership were at stake, gender shaped and defined ideal responses.[79]

Over time, gender anxiety, so easily sparked in the tinderbox context of extreme racism, undermined Ida B. Wells's authority and access to resources within the ranks of American reform. For example, in 1894, the ministers of the powerful A.M.E. Church in Philadelphia denied Wells institutional backing, claiming that the church already "had representative women . . . whom they could endorse unhesitatingly."[80] Wells was also squeezed out of leadership positions in national race organizations, including the all-female NACW, the mostly male Afro-American Council, and later the biracial NAACP. Wells's election to financial secretary of the council in 1899 elicited criticism from those who thought her better placed in "an assignment more in keeping with the popular idea of women's work."[81] This was achieved by making Wells head of the newly created Anti-Lynching Bureau.[82]

The "feminization" of antilynching, which began with the council's gesture toward Wells, continued in subsequent decades. This process was neither linear nor complete by the 1920s. Black women's protests against lynching (especially Wells's) never divided rigidly between "feminine" moral suasion or "masculine" politics but were inclusive.[83] And, of course, black and white men critical of white supremacy also protested lynching during the same period.[84] But the potential for equal leadership among black men and women, so evident in the 1890s, had eroded by the 1920s.

The feminization of antilynching culminated in the 1920s with the founding of the black women's Anti-Lynching Crusaders, led by NACW president Mary Talbert. The Crusaders worked under the aegis of the NAACP and organized around the feminine vocations of prayer, networking with white women through letter writing, and fund-raising. The *Crisis* trumpeted their work in deeply religious terms as "The Ninth Crusade."[85] Calling their objective "A Million Women United to Stop Lynching," the Crusaders focused on financial support of the NAACP's lobbying for the Dyer Anti-Lynching Bill.[86] Marking the distance from Wells's call to arms of the 1890s, the Crusaders engaged in a "moral battle" aimed at fostering a "new sense of personal responsibility" among Americans on the lynching question.[87] Meanwhile, Wells continued her front-line investigations, fund-raising, and independent agitation against lynching outside of the NAACP. But W. E. B. Du Bois, Walter White, and other male antilynching activists conspicuously overlooked her work even as they celebrated the efforts of the Anti-Lynching Crusaders.[88]

Two decades earlier, Ida B. Wells's antilynching lectures had been an nounced as "the simple story of an eloquent woman."[89] But as I have tried to show, her story about lynching was far from simple and, despite her eloquence, parts of that story would not be listened to. In *Southern Horrors* a black woman announced herself in a pamphlet with a picture of her face over the name "Miss IDA B. WELLS." The pamphlet contained stories about lynching and posed questions and challenges to the reader. But how readers understood the face, the stories, and the challenge was a volatile matter indeed.

Ida B. Wells defied categorization. She was described variously as unsexed, supersexed, unladylike, too feminine, the "man for the job," a "black" woman, and a "mulatress." Hortense Spillers's insight into African American women's historic potential to gain the "*insurgent* ground as female social subject" is suggestive here. Spillers writes: "Actually *claiming* the monstrosity (of a female with the potential to 'name') which her culture imposes in blindness, 'Sapphire' might rewrite after all a radically different text for a female empowerment."[90] Ida B. Wells was such a writer and *Southern Horrors* such a text.

NOTES

1. Jacquelyn Dowd Hall, *Revolt against Chivalry: Jessie Daniel Ames and the Women's Campaign against Lynching* (New York: Columbia University Press, 1979); Hazel V. Carby, "'On the Threshold of Woman's Era': Lynching, Empire, and Sexuality in Black Feminist Thought," *Critical Inquiry* 12 (August 1985): 262–77; Gail Bederman, "'Civilization,' the Decline of Middle-Class Manliness, and Ida B. Wells' Anti-Lynching Campaign," *Radical History Review* 52 (Winter 1992): 5–30; Nancy MacLean, "The Leo Frank Case Reconsidered: Gender and Sexual Politics in the Making of Reactionary Populism," *Journal of American History* 78 (1991): 917–48.

2. For excellent treatments of this issue, see Elsa Barkley Brown, "Imaging Lynching: African American Women, Communities of Struggle, and Collective Memory," in *African-American Women Speak Out on Anita Hill–Clarence Thomas*, ed. Geneva Smitherman (Detroit: Wayne State University Press, 1995), 100–124; and Nell Irvin Painter, "Who Was Lynched?" *Nation*, November 11, 1991, 577.

3. On Wells see Thomas Holt, "The Lonely Warrior: Ida B. Wells-Barnett and the Struggle for Black Leadership," in *Black Leaders of the Twentieth Century*, ed. John Hope Franklin and August Meier (Chicago: University of Illinois Press, 1982), 39–61; Herbert Shapiro, *White Violence and Black Response: From Reconstruction to Montgomery* (Amherst: University of Massachusetts Press, 1988), 58; David M. Tucker, "Miss Ida B. Wells and Memphis Lynching," *Phylon* 32 (Summer 1971): 112–22; Vron Ware, *Beyond the Pale: White Women, Race, and History* (New York: Verso, 1992), 169–224; Paula Giddings, *When and Where I Enter: The Impact of Black Women on Race and Sex in America* (New York: Bantam, 1984), 17–31.

4. On black women and lynching, see Bettina Apthcker, "Lynching and Rape: An Exchange of Views," *Occasional Paper #25* (San Jose, Calif.: American Institute for Marxist Studies, 1977), 1–33; and Aptheker, *Woman's Legacy: Essays on Race, Sex, and Class in American History* (Amherst: University of Massachusetts Press, 1982), 53–76; Nellie Y. MacKay, "Alice Walker's 'Advancing Luna—and Ida B. Wells': A Struggle toward Sisterhood," in *Rape and Representation*, ed. Lynn A. Higgins and Brenda R. Silver (New York: Columbia University Press, 1991), 248–60; Valerie Smith, "Split Affinities: The Case of Interracial Rape," in *Conflicts in Feminism*, ed. Marianne Hirsch and Evelyn Fox Keller (New York: Routledge, 1990), 271–87; Rosalyn Terborg-Penn, "African American Women's Networks in the Anti-Lynching Crusade," in *Gender, Class, Race, and Reform in the Progressive Era*, ed. Noralee Frankel and Nancy S. Dye (Lexington: University Press of Kentucky, 1991), 295–312; Jacquelyn Dowd Hall, " 'The Mind That Burns in Each Body': Women, Rape, and Racial Violence," in *Powers of Desire: The Politics of Sexuality*, ed. Sharon Thompson, Anne Snitow, and Christine Stansell (New York: Monthly Review Press, 1983), 328–49; Alice Walker, "Advancing Luna—and Ida B. Wells," in *You Can't Keep a Good Woman Down* (New York: Harcourt Brace Jovanovich, 1971); Wilson Jeremiah Moses, *The Golden Age of Black Nationalism, 1850–1925* (New York: Oxford University Press, 1978), 103–31.

5. Hall, *Revolt*, 167.

6. Terborg-Penn, "African American Women's Networks," 159.

7. My exploration is shaped by current feminist reevaluations of women's politics in the modern era, especially the ways in which distinctions between public and private, domestic and political, and male and female, have been shaped, challenged, or subverted in women's history. See Mary P. Ryan, *Women in Public: Between Banners and Ballots, 1825–1880* (Baltimore: Johns Hopkins University Press, 1990); Carole Pateman, "Feminist Critiques of the Public/Private Dichotomy," in *Public and Private in Social Life*, ed. S. I. Benn and G. F. Gaus (New York: St. Martin's Press, 1983), 281–306; Paula Baker, "The Domestication of Politics: Women and American Political Society, 1780–1920," in *Unequal Sisters: A Multicultural Reader in U.S. Women's History*, ed. Ellen Carol DuBois and Vicki L. Ruiz (New York: Routledge, 1990), 66–91; Sara M. Evans, "Women's History and Political Theory: Toward a Feminist Approach to Public Life," in *Visible Women: New Essays on American Activism*, ed. Nancy Hewitt and Suzanne Lebsock (Urbana: University of Illinois Press, 1993), 119–39; Elsa Barkley Brown, "Negotiating and Transforming the Public Sphere: African American Political Life in the Transition from Slavery to Freedom," *Public Culture* (Fall 1994): 1–40; Barbara Bair, "True Women, Real Men: Gender, Ideology, and Social Roles in the Garvey Movement," in *Gendered Domains: Rethinking Public and Private in Women's History*, ed. Dorothy O. Helly and Susan M. Reverby (Ithaca, N.Y.: Cornell University Press, 1992), 154–66.

8. Traditionally, the most often cited American authorities are Walter F. White, *Rope and Faggot: A Biography of Judge Lynch* (New York: Knopf, 1929); Arthur F. Raper, *The Tragedy of Lynching* (Chapel Hill: University of North Carolina Press, 1933); James Elbert Cutler, *Lynch-Law: An Investigation into the History of Lynching in the United States* (New York: New Universities Press, 1905); National Association for the Advancement of Colored People, *Thirty Years of Lynching in the United States, 1889–1918* (1919; rpt. New York: Arno Press and the New York Times, 1969).

9. See especially Hazel V. Carby, *Reconstructing Womanhood: The Emergence of the Afro-American Woman Novelist* (New York: Oxford University Press, 1984); and Claudia Tate, *Domestic Allegories of Political Desire: The Black Heroine's Text at the Turn of the Century* (New York: Oxford University Press, 1992). See also Mary Helen Washington, "Plain, Black and Decently Wild: The Heroic Possibilities of Maud Martha," in *The Voyage In: Fictions of Female Development*, ed. Elizabeth Abel, Marianne Hirsch, and Elizabeth Langland (Hanover: Dartmouth College, 1983), 270–86.

10. Ida B. Wells, "Southern Horrors: Lynch Law in All Its Phases," in *Selected Writings of Ida B. Wells-Barnett*, comp. and ed. Trudier Harris (New York: Oxford University Press, 1991), 19.

11. For this framework, I owe a deep intellectual debt to Mae Gwendolyn Henderson, "Speaking in Tongues: Dialogics, Dialectics, and the Black Woman Writer's Literary Tradition," in *Feminists Theorize the Political*, ed. Judith Butler and Joan W. Scott (New York: Routledge, 1992), 144–66.

12. Wells, "Southern Horrors," 29, 19.

13. Ibid., 27, 44; Ida B. Wells, *United States Atrocities: Lynch Law* (London: Lux Newspaper and Publishing Co., [1893]), 19. *Atrocities* is a slightly edited version of "Southern Horrors" published during Wells's British speaking tour in 1893.

14. Wells, "Southern Horrors," 20.

15. In Gail Bederman's reading of Wells's antilynching rhetoric, it was her play on traditional notions of Victorian manhood that piqued white Americans' anxiety over masculinity and moral fiber. Lynch mobs were not chivalrous, manly avengers of white womanhood, but true barbarians. But Wells did more than switch the roles of "barbarian" and "civilized man" in her rendition of southern race relations. Wells observed that "Red Indians and cannibals" were guilty only of living by their precepts; at least they were not hypocrites. The white South professed Christianity and the "majesty of law," defied both, and then lied about its actions. She thus revealed the corruption of language and meaning which accompanied the rape charge and exposed the white mob to be even more degraded than the so-called barbarians and uncivilized races. See Bederman, " 'Civilization,' " 11. For a concise statement of Wells's argument, see her 1893 article, "Lynch Law in America," reprinted in Mildred I. Thompson, ed., *Ida B. Wells-Barnett: An Exploratory Study of an American Black Woman, 1893–1930* (Brooklyn: Carlson, 1990), 241–43.

16. Wells, "Red Record," in *Selected Writings*, comp. and ed. Harris, 150.

17. See Joan W. Scott, *Gender and the Politics of History* (New York: Columbia University Press, 1988); and Mary Poovey, *Unequal Developments: The Ideological Work of Gender in Mid-Victorian England* (Chicago: University of Chicago Press, 1988).

18. W. Fitzhugh Brundage, "The Roar on the Other Side of Silence: Black Resistance and White Violence in the American South, 1880–1940," in this volume. See also Shapiro, *White Violence and Black Response*, passim.

19. Kevin Gaines, "Uplifting the Race: Black Middle-Class Ideology in the Era of the 'New Negro' " (Ph.D. diss., Brown University, 1991); Glenda Elizabeth Gilmore, "Gender and Jim Crow: Sara Dudley Pettey's Vision of the New South," *North Carolina Historical Review* 68 (July 1991): 261–85.

20. Ida B. Wells, *Crusade for Justice: The Autobiography of Ida B. Wells*, ed. Alfreda M. Duster (Chicago: University of Chicago Press, 1970), 18–20.

21. The most comprehensive recent survey of lynching data in ten southern states also concludes that alleged sexual crimes accounted for approximately 30 percent of all lynchings. See Stewart E. Tolnay and E. M. Beck, *A Festival of Violence: An Analysis of Southern Lynchings, 1882–1930* (Urbana: University of Illinois Press, 1995), chap. 4.

22. Ryan, *Women in Public*, 3–18.

23. Wells, "Southern Horrors," 30.

24. Ibid., 37. Anna Julia Cooper also referred to "the race [being] . . . just at the age of ruddy manhood" in *A Voice from the South*, ed. Mary Helen Washington (1892; rpt. New York: Oxford University Press, 1988), 26.

25. Martha Hodes, "Wartime Dialogues on Illicit Sex: White Women and Black Men," in *Divided Houses: Gender and the Civil War*, ed. Catherine Clinton and Nina Silber (New York: Oxford University Press, 1992), 230–45.

26. Wells, "Southern Horrors," 31, 19.

27. Ibid., 19.

28. Ibid., 21.

29. Wells, "Red Record," 147.

30. On military service and black manhood, see Jim Cullen, " 'I's a Man Now': Gender and African American Men," in *Divided Houses*, ed. Clinton and Silber, 76–96.

31. Wells reworked these notions of duty, self-sacrifice, and Christian morality into the amalgam of the Christian soldier in her pamphlet about the death of Robert Charles in the New Orleans race riot of 1900. See Ida B. Wells-Barnett, *Mob Rule in New Orleans* (Chicago: Ida B. Wells-Barnett, 1900). Another important thread of antilynching protest involved the theme of outraged motherhood, especially the heinous lynching of the pregnant Mary Turner in Georgia in 1918, memorialized notably through the writing of Angelina Weld Grimké, among others. See Tate, *Domestic Allegories*, 217–18.

32. Wells, "Southern Horrors," 44–45; see also Wells, "Red Record," 212–15.

33. Wells, "Southern Horrors," 26, 44.

34. Wells suggested that this criticism was in the air in a magazine short story she wrote in 1895, "Two Christmas Days: A Holiday Story," in *Ida B. Wells Barnett*, ed. Thompson, 227.

35. Wells, "Southern Horrors," 42.

36. The literature on both of these historical problems is voluminous. My goal is to show the ideological linkages and political contingencies within and between each. Briefly, see August Meier, *Negro Thought in America 1880–1915: Racial Ideologies in the Age of Booker T. Washington* (Ann Arbor: University of Michigan Press, 1966), and John D'Emilio and Estelle B. Freedman, *Intimate Matters: A History of Sexuality in America* (New York: Harper & Row, 1988), 171–235.

37. Cooper, *Voice*, flyleaf.

38. In her text, Cooper noted Alexander Crummell's pioneering essay "The Black Woman in the South" (1881) as follows: "For is it not written, 'Cursed is he that cometh after the king?' and has not the King already preceded me in 'The Black Woman from the South?' " Cooper then "beg[s] . . . with the Doctor's permission, to add [her] plea for the Colored Girls of the South" (ibid., 24). She went on, however, to make stinging criticism of discrimination against black women in education and the "16th century logic" exhibited by men in marriage dealings in the black community.

39. Ibid., 32–33, 29, 55–56.

40. "Will not the aid of the Church be given to prepare our girls in head, heart, and hand for the duties and responsibilities that await the intelligent wife, the Christian mother, the earnest, virtuous, helpful woman, at once both the lever and fulcrum for uplifting the race?" Cooper asked (ibid., 45).

41. Ibid., 24–25.

42. Frederick Douglass, "Lynch Law in the South," *North American Review* (July 1892): 17–24.

43. At moments in *Voice*, Cooper chafed at maintaining feminine tact. In her struggle to contain her rage at the abuse of black women on public transportation, she penned the following near contradiction: "I purposely forbear to mention instances of personal violence to colored women travelling in less civilized sections of our country, where women have been forcibly ejected from cars, thrown out of seats, their garments rudely torn, their persons wantonly and cruelly injured" (*Voice*, 91).

44. Aptheker, *Woman's Legacy*, 53–76; and Lynn A. Higgins and Brenda R. Silver, "Introduction," *Rape and Representation*.

45. Wells articulated, in Joan W. Scott's words, "politics as the expanding production of discourses on sex." See Scott, "Women's History," in *Gender and the Politics of History*, 26.

46. Wells, "Southern Horrors," 22–23, 44. Indeed, Wells's mixed racial ancestry would later become an ironic litmus test of her authenticity as a "black" spokesperson. Her father was the son of his slave mother and his white master, and her mother's father was "half Indian." See Wells, *Crusade for Justice*, 8.

47. Wells, "Southern Horrors," 42, 44, 29.

48. Richard Yarborough, "Race, Violence, and Manhood: The Masculine Ideal in Frederick Douglass' 'The Heroic Slave,'" in *Frederick Douglass: New Literary and Historical Essays*, ed. Eric J. Sundquist (Cambridge, Eng.: Cambridge University Press, 1990).

49. Mary Helen Washington, "Introduction," in Cooper, *Voice*, xxvii–liv. See also Elizabeth Alexander, "'We Must Be about Our Father's Business': Anna Julia Cooper and the In-Corporation of the Nineteenth-Century African-American Woman Intellectual," *Signs* 20 (Winter 1995): 341, who notes the "extremely essentialist" positions adopted by Cooper in *Voice*.

50. On the politics of gender and racial difference in black women's identity see Nell Irvin Painter, "Difference, Slavery, and Memory: Sojourner Truth in Feminist Abolitionism," in *The Abolitionist Sisterhood: Women's Political Culture in Antebellum America*, ed. Jean Fagan Yellin and John C. Van Horne (Ithaca, N.Y.: Cornell University Press, 1994), 139–58. On portraiture and representation in the life of a black woman, see Nell Irvin Painter, "Representing Truth: Sojourner Truth's Knowing and Becoming Known," *Journal of American History* 81 (September 1994): 482–87.

51. Wells, "Southern Horrors," 14, 19.

52. Missy Dehn Kubitschek, "Subjugated Knowledge: Toward a Feminist Exploration of Rape in Afro-American Fiction," in *Studies in Black American Literary: Black Feminist Criticism and Critical Theory*, ed. Joe Weixlman and Houston A. Baker Jr. (Greenwood, Fla.: Penkeville, 1988). Kubitschek writes: "The Afro-American literary tradition both addresses rape more frequently than the Euro-American tradition and offers a more realistic, complex vision of the meaning of the experience for the victim

and her community" (45), and "The Afro-American tradition . . . grant[s] the woman an identity beyond that of rape victim" (46). See also Valerie Smith, "'Loopholes of Retreat': Architecture and Ideology in Harriet Jacob's *Incidents in the Life of a Slave Girl*," in *Reading Black, Reading Feminist: A Critical Anthology*, ed. Henry Louis Gates Jr. (New York: Meridian, 1990), 212–26.

53. Wells, *Crusade for Justice*, 15–20, 80, 238. Wells exhibited her sarcasm and "dialogic" expressiveness in an 1894 letter to Helen Pitts Douglass. She wrote from London: "I shall spend this month of May here, doing what I can, and then in the early part of June will be coming home again. Home did I say? I forgot that I have no home, but back to the 'land of the free and home of the brave'" (Ida B. Wells to Helen Pitts Douglass, April 26, 1894, Frederick Douglass Papers, Library of Congress).

54. Dorothy O. Helly and Susan M. Reverby, "Introduction: Converging on History," in *Gendered Domains*, 1–24.

55. *Memphis Commercial* quoted in Wells, "Southern Horrors," 18.

56. See Ryan, *Women in Public*, 3–4, for a Civil War precedent linking women's political speech and gestures to prostitute status.

57. *Memphis Commercial*, December 15, 1892, May 26, 1894; *Memphis Appeal-Avalanche*, May 23, 1893, quoted in *Chicago Inter-Ocean*, August 21, 1899, Tuskegee Institute Clippings File, Schomburg Center for Research in Black Culture, New York.

58. *New York Times*, August 2, 1894.

59. Quoted in *Chicago Inter-Ocean*, August 21, 1899, Tuskegee Institute Clippings File.

60. Wells, *Crusade for Justice*, 220.

61. *Ida B. Wells in England* (St. Paul: The Appeal, 1984), 3.

62. Quoted in Monroe A. Majors, *Noted Negro Women: Their Triumphs and Activities* (1893; rpt. Chicago: Donohue and Henneberry, 1986), 253, 254.

63. *Woman's Era* (Boston), 2 (July 1895): 5.

64. Women of Bethel Church, New York, in *Historical Proceedings of the Conventions of 1895–96 of the Colored Women of America* (N.p., N.d.), 19.

65. See Gertrude Mossell's detailed account of Wells's crusade in *The Work of the Afro-American Woman* (Philadelphia: George S. Ferguson, 1894), 32–45; and *Topeka Weekly Call*, July 13, 1894.

66. *Christian Recorder*, July 5, 1894.

67. *Indianapolis Freeman*, August 25, 1894.

68. Majors, *Noted Negro Women*, 188.

69. Evelyn Brooks Higginbotham, *Righteous Discontent: The Women's Movement in the Black Baptist Church, 1880–1920* (Cambridge, Mass.: Harvard University Press, 1993), 143; Rev. Reverdy C. Ransom, *Deborah and Jael: A Sermon to the I.B.W. Woman's Club* (Chicago, 1897), passim.

70. *Indianapolis Freeman*, September 29, 1894.

71. T. Thomas Fortune, "Ida B. Wells, M.A.," in *Women of Distinction: Remarkable in Works and Invincible in Character*, ed. Lawson Scruggs (Raleigh: L. A. Scruggs, 1893), 39.

72. *Christian Recorder*, August 9, 1894.

73. J. W. Mans and John S. Durham, letter to the editor, *New York Times*, May 30, 1894.

74. Deborah Gray White, "The Cost of Club Work, the Price of Black Feminism," in *Visible Women*, ed. Hewitt and Lebsock, 260, 257.

75. Cooper, *Voice*, 135, 31.

76. Willard stated at the WCTU convention in 1894: "It is my firm belief that in the statements made by Miss Wells concerning white women having taken the initiative in nameless acts between the races she has put an imputation upon half the white race. . . . All such allusions [are] a source of weakness to the cause she has at heart" (Wells, "Red Record," 226–39).

77. *Chicago Defender*, September 4, 1915.

78. "Mob Dispersed by Women," *Chicago Defender*, December 2, 1916.

79. Toasts provided one such public space where such ideals were expressed. Wells and fellow newspaper editor T. Thomas Fortune of New York exchanged toasts at an Afro-American Press Association banquet in 1892. He toasted "The Ladies" and she "The Gentlemen" in a gesture that suggested a gender division of labor but also complementarity, even potential equality. A shift in sensibility was evident in 1907, when Wells offered a toast to "The Ideal Negro Manhood" after a speech on the Constitution and black rights in Chicago and no one offered one to womanhood (*Indianapolis Freeman*, October 8, 1892, and *Chicago Broad Ax*, December 14, 1907). The latter occasion was Rev. Reverdy Ransom's address "The Constitutional Rights of the Afro-American." Other toasts saluted "The Niagara Movement" and "Negro Enterprises."

80. Wells, *Crusade for Justice*, 222.

81. Quoted in Giddings, *When and Where I Enter*, 111.

82. Ida B. Wells-Barnett, "The National Afro-American Council," *Howard's American Magazine* 6 (May 1901): 416. John Mitchell Jr., editor of the *Richmond Planet* and a strong opponent of lynching, lamented Wells's resignation from the council in 1903 as "the worse blow of all" in the unraveling of that organization, noting that she "stands first and foremost among the agitators against lynching in this country." See John Mitchell Jr., "Shall the Wheels of Race Agitation Be Stopped?" *Colored American Magazine* 5 (1903): 386.

83. Elsa Barkley Brown's work has been most illuminating in this respect. See her "Maggie Lena Walker and the Independent Order of St. Luke" in *Unequal Sisters*, ed. DuBois and Ruiz, and her "Imaging Lynching."

84. W. Fitzhugh Brundage, " 'To Howl Loudly': John Mitchell, Jr., and His Campaign against Lynching in Virginia," *Canadian Review of American Studies* 22 (Winter 1991): 325–41. See Shapiro, *White Violence and Black Response*.

85. "The Ninth Crusade," *Crisis* 25 (March 1923): 213–17.

86. For the prayer circulated by the crusaders, see "The Anti-Lynching Crusaders," *Crisis* 25 (November 1922): 8. For a copy of their flyer, *The Shame of America*, see *Crisis* 25 (February 1923): 167–69. See also Claudine L. Ferrell, *Nightmare and Dream: Antilynching in Congress, 1917–1922* (New York: Garland, 1986).

87. "The Anti-Lynching Crusaders," 213, 214.

88. "The Arkansas Cases," *Crisis* 24 (September 1922): 216; and Walter White, "The Defeat of Arkansas Mob Law," ibid., 259–61. Several years earlier, Wells investigated the 1919 riot at Helena, Arkansas, and published *The Arkansas Race Riot* (Chicago: Mrs. Ida B. Wells-Barnett, [1920?]). See also Wells, *Crusade for Justice*, 397–404. On the *Crisis* ignoring Wells's work on another, earlier Arkansas case, see

Charles Flint Kellogg, *NAACP: A History of the National Association for the Advancement of Colored People* (Baltimore: Johns Hopkins University Press, 1967), 63 nn. 73–76; and Wells, *Crusade for Justice*, 336–37. Wells's participation in a delegation of fourteen black women from the NACW who petitioned President Warren G. Harding on the lynching question in August 1922 was picked up by the *Crisis*. See Jessie Fauset, "The 13th Biennial of the N.A.C.W.," *Crisis* 24 (October 1922): 260. In the 1930s and 1940s, white women of the Association of Southern Women for the Prevention of Lynching opposed federal antilynching legislation in favor of education and local initiatives, occupying an even more traditionally "feminine" position on the political spectrum, though they were criticized for even this in the South. See Hall, *Revolt against Chivalry*, chap. 6.

89. *Washington Bee*, October 22, 1892.

90. Hortense Spillers, "Mama's Baby, Papa's Baby: An American Grammar Book," *Diacritics* 17 (Summer 1987): 80.

Afterword

William S. McFeely

t would be fitting, as a postscript to these fine essays, to shut the door. Lynching, as every scholar writing in this book would agree, is one of the ugliest aspects of the American past. No matter how dispassionate the scholarly demeanor, each essayist senses the horror of the actions studied. They, along with other decent citizens, would be pleased to consign their subject firmly to the past tense.

Perhaps they can. With some confidence, we can anticipate that killings in the manner described and analyzed here are behind us. Horsemen no longer circle a remote country house brandishing torches. Obscene shouts outside the cabin, ominous knocks at its door have been silenced. The terror of the family inside is over, along with the wrenching away of a man dragged to a tree at the edge of a clearing, the mocked plea for mercy, the mutilations, the shrieks of pain, the hanging, the death—the cheers. Behind us, we hope, are similar scenes after a jail is broken into or entered through a door left unlocked. The force of law, if not societal discipline, reaches now to prevent such killings.

It has been a century since excursion trains carried spectators to the torturing to death in a town south of Atlanta of a fellow Georgian. I still find it chilling to drive through the town near where I live in which our state's last recorded lynching state took place in 1947, but it is true that it took place almost fifty years ago. Can't we say that the door is not only closed but firmly locked?

Not quite. Historians know that the past can never be erased and that the ugliest human actions cast the longest shadows. It will take no feat of imagination by readers to sense the horror of the death of John—simply John—the slave burned to death in Missouri in 1859 or of the people we meet in the other essays who might yet be alive if it were not for their lynchings. But what might be missed is the memory of those occasions. Have we adequately taken stock of lynching's legacy in the community from which a vastly disproportionate number of such victims were drawn, the world of black southerners?

In 1987 Bill Winn, a journalist for the *Columbus* (Ga.) *Ledger*, wrote a long, sensitive account of a 1912 lynching in that city.[1] Teasy McElhaney, a barefoot fourteen-year-old black boy, was sentenced in the Muscogee County courthouse, not to be hanged but to three years at hard labor for the death of Cleo Land, a white playmate. As he was being taken from the courtroom to jail, McElhaney was seized from the bailiffs by relatives of the dead boy, dragged to a trolley car—they paid his fare—taken to the edge of town, and shot. As word of the death spread, a crowd of curious white people went out to have a look. Finally, Alex Toles, the black undertaker, came and took the body away.

Winn had to find a way to end his story. Effectively, he imagined the hymns that might have been sung in the black churches as people gathered to mourn in that 1912 November. But that did not put the matter to rest. Those mourners remembered, and though details blur over time, their children and their children's children carry forward memories of such acts of inhumanity.

In 1956, Dr. Thomas H. Brewer Sr., an early and courageous worker for civil rights in Columbus, was murdered in a downtown store.[2] The grand jury, refusing to indict his killer, ruled the death a justifiable homicide. In scholarly accounts, Brewer's death is recorded, correctly, as a telling, early event in the civil rights movement, but Winn reports that African Americans in Columbus saw Brewer's death as belonging to a chain running back to the McElhaney lynching and to others still more terrible in detail.

Reactionary critics of liberal scholarship would deny not only the element of racism in the history of lynching but also the extent of its horror.[3] This latter point can be argued only on the grounds of statistics. In a century in which we speak, almost routinely, of genocidal death of millions, should we be troubled by the death, by lynching, of hundreds of Americans? The answer, of course, is yes. Just as history requires us to measure the hatreds of our wars, we must not refrain from taking stock, with precision, of more local deaths. As the historian Rhys Isaac, reminding us of the obvious, has pointed out, each of us dies singly and feels the pain alone, no matter how many of our fellows fall next to us.

Critics who refute the centrality of race in lynchings in our past also deny that racism is a force today in the making of a new illiberal order for the society. The citing of white men and women lynched or even of black men carrying out a lynching simply denies the evidence that the suppression of black Americans by white Americans was the motivation in an overwhelming number of cases. It is also true that most lynchings took place not, as myth would have it, to protect white women from rape, but as punishment for criminal behavior. The crime, however, was not the alleged murders and other crimes but the threat posed to a repressive social order by ambitious African Americans.

That ancient animosities linger does not mean that they must. Racism, indeed, the very concept of race is not immutable. Much has been achieved in the establishment of civil rights for African Americans since the years covered in this book's essays, but much remains to be done in the field of criminal justice. Evidence abounds that, with good reason, black Americans distrust our courts. Despite the Supreme Court's claim that equity exists in its implementation, the death penalty, in the eyes of many, remains a potent tool of racism and contributes fundamentally to the distrust of the law's workings. There are valiant people at work seeking the death penalty's end. As with lynching, the long, hard work of change, of abolition, will not end soon, but there are, and will be more, like Ida B. Wells to take up the struggle.

In this note, I speak of Georgia; the authors of these studies speak of the South—here defined as the former slaveholding states—but we must remember that lynchings also took place in the North and in the West. This method of death is part of a national past. Properly, the essays in this book concentrate on the subject at hand, lynching. But they are, as well, part of a larger meditation on death, or, rather, on the act of putting to death—on the deliberate killing of human beings. Our society almost sanctifies guns and their possession. They do not go unused; our murder rate is alarming. The urge to be violent, to kill a fellow being runs deep and wide. Think, for example, of the recent rush of applicants to be part of the firing squad when Utah prepared to carry out an execution.

Many keen observers of our society, including some in the legal profession, see a direct link between lynchings and the death penalty. Fitzhugh Brundage, the editor of this volume, has, in an earlier work, written: "With the decline of lynching, many southern whites renounced the inhumanity of the mob, preferring instead to rely on the harsh justice of the state."[4] Many question whether the inhumanity has been greatly lessened.

The title of this book is *Under Sentence of Death*. Death as a result of accident or natural causes is not its subject. Death as a willful human act is. The question that lingers from the work of this volume is, What are we, as a people, when we countenance the deliberate killing of our fellows, whether outside the law by lynching or within it by execution? Or, indeed, in the home or schoolyard. The door of our minds should be open to such contemplation.

NOTES

1. Bill Winn, "Incident at Wynn's Hill," *Columbus* (Ga.) *Ledger*, January 25–31, 1987.

2. Bill Winn, "Brewer's Life, Death Helped Shape Our History," *Columbus* (Ga.) *Ledger-Enquirer*, April 24, May 1, 8, 1988.

3. For a recent egregious example, in which Dwight D. Murphey argues that "lynching, even in the South, was only in small part an act of racism," see "Issues in American History: Lynching in Perspective," *Conservative Review* 6 (July–August 1995): 8–15.

4. W. Fitzhugh Brundage, *Lynching in the New South: Georgia and Virginia, 1880–1930* (Urbana: University of Illinois Press, 1993), 259.

Notes on the Contributors

Bruce E. Baker holds an M.A. in folklore from the University of North Carolina at Chapel Hill. His thesis is entitled "Lynching Ballads in North Carolina." He is also a contributor to the forthcoming *Handbook of North Carolina History*.

E. M. Beck is professor and department head of sociology at the University of Georgia. With Stewart E. Tolnay, he has published numerous articles in *Social Forces*, the *American Sociological Review*, and other journals. Their book, *A Festival of Violence: An Analysis of Southern Lynchings, 1882–1930* (1995), received the President's Book Award from the Social Science History Association.

W. Fitzhugh Brundage is associate professor of history at Queen's University in Ontario, Canada. He has been a Fellow at the National Humanities Center and is the author of *Lynching in the New South* (1993) and *A Socialist Utopia in the New South: The Ruskin Colonies in Tennessee and Georgia, 1894–1901* (1996).

Joan E. Cashin is associate professor of history at Ohio State University. She is the author of *A Family Venture: Men and Women on the Southern Frontier* (1991), editor of *Our Common Affairs: Texts from Women of the Old South* (1996), and is currently completing a biography of Varina Howell Davis.

Paula Clark is a graduate student in history at Vanderbilt University. She is writing her dissertation on race and race relations in the Appalachian South.

Thomas G. Dyer is professor of history at the University of Georgia. He is former editor of the *Georgia Historical Quarterly* and author of *Theodore Roosevelt and the Idea of Race* (1980) and *The University of Georgia: A Bicentennial History*. A version of his essay in this collection received the 1995 award for best article published in the *Missouri Historical Review*.

Terence Finnegan is assistant professor of history at William Paterson College. He completed his Ph.D. at the University of Illinois in 1993 and is revising his dissertation, " 'At the Hands of Parties Unknown': Lynching in Mississippi and South Carolina, 1881–1940," for publication.

Larry J. Griffin is professor of history at Vanderbilt University. A past Fellow at the Center for Advanced Study at Stanford University, he has published articles on lynching, organized labor, and sociological-historical methodology in the *American Journal of Sociology*, *Social Science History*, *Historical Methods*, and *Sociological Methods and Research*. He also is coeditor of *The South as an American Problem* (1995).

William S. McFeely is Abraham Baldwin Professor of Humanities at the University of Georgia. He is the author of *Yankee Stepfather: General O. O. Howard and the Freedmen* (1968), the Pulitzer Prize–winning *Grant: A Biography* (1981), *Frederick Douglass* (1991), and *Sapelo's People: A Long Walk into Freedom* (1994).

Nancy MacLean is associate professor of history at Northwestern University. She has published in the *Journal of American History* and *Gender and History* and is author of the multiple award-winning book, *Behind the Mask of Chivalry: The Making of the*

Second Ku Klux Klan (1994). She is currently working on a history of affirmative action in employment.

Joanne C. Sandberg is a graduate student in sociology at Vanderbilt University. In addition to issues of race, her research interests include gender and the interrelations of family and work.

Patricia A. Schechter is assistant professor of history at Portland State University. She received her Ph.D. from Princeton University and taught at Hunter College before moving to Portland State. She is currently revising her dissertation on Ida B. Wells-Barnett for publication.

Roberta Senechal de la Roche is associate professor of history at Washington and Lee University. She is the author of *The Sociogenesis of a Race Riot: Springfield, Illinois, in 1908* (1991) and "Collective Violence as Social Control," *Sociological Forum* 11 (March 1996).

Stewart E. Tolnay is director of the Center for Social and Demographic Analysis and professor of sociology at the State University of New York at Albany. He and E. M. Beck are longtime collaborators, with numerous publications to their credit.

George C. Wright, provost of the University of Texas–Arlington, is a former William R. Kenan Professor of American History, vice-provost, and director of the African and Afro-American Studies Program at Duke University. He is the author of *Life Behind a Veil* (1985), *Racial Violence in Kentucky, 1865–1940* (1990), and *A History of Blacks in Kentucky: In Pursuit of Equality, 1890–1980* (1992).

Index

Abrahams, Roger D., 228

Adams, Mitchell, 197

Adams County, Miss.: legal process in, 101

Addams, Jane, 4

Afro-American Council, 309

Alexandria, Va., 274

American Civil Liberties Union, 258

Ames, Jessie Daniel, 11

Amite County, Miss., 207

Anson County, N.C., 28, 232–33

Arrow Rock, Mo., 87, 100

Arthur, Benjamin, 125, 126

Association of Southern Women for the Prevention of Lynching, 5, 293

Atlanta: postwar expansion, 161–62

Attempted lynchings: significance of, 25–28; Neshoba County, Miss., 26; Obion County, Tenn., 26; number of, 26–27, 34–35; Anson County, N.C., 28; Deadon, Tenn., 28; Colleton, S.C., 196; McIntosh County, Ga., 278–79

Ayers, Edward L., 12–13

Bakhtin, M. M., 275

Baldwin, Susan, 118, 120, 126

Ballard County, Ky., 250

Barnwell County, S.C., 196–201, 279

Batson v. Kentucky, 266

Beard, W. P., 210

Bederman, Gail, 284

Benjamin, Robert C. O., 189

Black, Donald, 23; theories of social control, 49–50, 52, 63

Blackmun, Justice Harry A., 268

Black newspaper editors: and anti-lynching campaign, 280–82

Black participation in lynchings: explanations for, 36–38

Black resistance: armed self-defense as form of, 27, 278–79; in S.C., 196, 197, 200; varieties of, 271–85; flight as

form of, 275; role of women in, 279–80

Black retaliation: against black informers, 274

Blacks: and southern justice, 36–37. *See also* Criminal justice

Black women: resistance to white violence, 279–80; feminization of anti-lynching campaign, 308–9; Anti-Lynching Crusaders, 309

Bolivar County, Miss., 32–40

Bossier Parish, La., 138–39

Boyd, Samuel, 86

Bradley, William O., 259; and legal lynching, 262–63, 264

Brennan, Justice William J., 268

Brewer, Thomas H., Sr., 319

Brice, Mitchell, 276

Bricker, L. O., 168

Brooks County, Ga., 275–76

Brown, John, 83, 84

Brown, Joseph Mackey, 176

Bulloch County, Ga., 275

Burns, William J., 164

Caddo Parish, La., 138–39

Capital punishment. *See* Legal executions

Carson, Fiddlin' John, 175

Cash, Wilbur J., 7, 98

Chase, Benjamin, 101, 102; prosecutes Saline County mob leader, 96–97

Child, Francis J., 219

Chivers, Walter, 31

Choctaw County, Ark., 146

Class tensions: in postbellum Ga., 162–63

Coahoma County, Miss., 34, 36

Cobb, James, 35

Cohen, Anne, 224

Colleton, S.C., 196

Colored Farmers' Alliance: violence against, 194–95

Hix, Martha, 116, 117, 119
Hobsbawm, Eric, 10
Hofstadter, Richard, 10
Houston, Charles H., 255
Hovland, Carl, 8
Hurricane Creek, Ark., 147
Hurston, Zora Neale, 271
Hutchinson, Joseph L., 89

Intraracial lynchings, 132–51; pattern of over time, 133–36; distribution of black-on-black violence, 137–39; alleged offenses of victims, 140–41, 147–48; brutality of black mobs, 143–44; distribution of white-on-white violence, 144; brutality of white mobs, 148; explanations for, 148–51
Isaac, Rhys, 319

Jackson, Andrew, 94
Jefferson County, Ark., 142
Johnson, Ripley, 197
Joiner, Saxe: lynching of, 109–26; sketch of, 116; controversial letters by, 117–18; arrest of, 120; trial of, 124
Jones County, Miss., 141–42

Keenan, James, 111, 121, 122
Keenan, William, 121
Kelley, Robin D. G., 285
Kemper County, Miss., 26
Kentucky: legal executions in, 250–68; politics, regarding opposition to mob violence, 259–60. *See also* Black resistance
Kentucky Court of Appeals: and legal lynching, 261–62, 263–64
Kiser, Giles, 84
Ku Klux Klan, 51, 119, 125, 176, 179

Lake City, S.C., 204, 208–10
Lamon, Lester C., 273
Laws, G. Malcolm, 219, 235
Leflore County, Miss., 194–95

Legal executions: in Kentucky, 250–68; of blacks for rape, 256–57; of blacks for self-defense, 257–58; by race since 1930, 268
Lester, Julius, 248
Lexington, S.C., 201
Lincoln, Abraham, 2
Lincoln, Bruce, 237, 238
Lipsitz, George, 272
Little Rock, Ark., 27
Logan County, Ky., 250
Lomax, Alan, 220
Lowry, Robert, 195
Lynching: antebellum history of, 2–3; and honor, 3; in the West, 3; postbellum history, 3–4; southern defenses of, 5; official complicity in, 26, 34–36, 39; definition of, 50–51; in international context, 51–52; and black migration, 60–61, 275; relationship to rioting, 61–63; estimates of in antebellum Missouri, 98–99; intraracial, 132–51; and political competition, 189–215; alleged causes of in South Carolina, 202; alleged causes of in Mississippi, 202–3; and disfranchisement, 204–5; in Kentucky, 250–51; legal, in Kentucky, 250–68. *See also* Attempted lynchings; Lynching victims
Lynching ballads, 219–42; as part of folk culture of lynching, 220–21; Emmett Till, 221; In a Little Country Schoolyard, 221; The Strayhorn Mob, 221; The Ashland Tragedy, 221, 230; Emma Hartsell, 221–26; treatment of race in, 224; sentimentality in, 225; Alec Whitley, 226–32; J. V. Johnson, 232–35; The Fate of Gladys Kincaid, 241
Lynchings: Kemper County, Miss., 26; Little Rock, Ark., 27; Bolivar County, Miss., 32–40; Saline County, Mo., 81–103; Arrow Rock, Mo., 87, 100; Union County, S.C., 109–26; Leo Frank, 132, 155–56; Caddo Parish,

ment of Colored People (NAACP), 5, 40, 255, 271, 309; antilynching activities of, 277–78; cross-class alliance during 1930s, 282
National Association of Colored Women (NACW), 306, 309
Neshoba County, Miss., 26
New Orleans, La., 144–45
Norfolk, Va., 280
North Carolina, 219–42
Northumberland County, Va., 275

Obion County, Tenn., 26–27
Odum, Howard W., 7
Oglethorpe County, Ga., 272

Park, Robert, 6
Perry County, Ark., 146
Phagan, Mary, 158, 159; as icon, 163, 165, 174, 175; and sexual anxieties, 166–68, 170, 172
Phillips County, Ark., 144
Phoenix, S.C., election riot, 210–13
Pike County, Ark., 148
Pine Hills, Miss.: lynchings in, 205–6
Porter, Dale, 30
Powell, Lewis, 267
Power-threat hypothesis: as explanation of lynching, 190–91
Psychological interpretations of lynching, 7–8

Raper, Arthur F., 7, 9, 10, 31
Reactionary populism: and lynching of Leo Frank, 160–61
Red Hills, Miss.: lynchings in, 205–6
Relational distance: and lynching, 52–55
Resnikoff, Philip, 7
Richardson, John P., 197
Robertson, William J., 171
Rosser, Luther Z., 179
Rude, George, 10

St. Francis, Ark., 148
Saline County, Mo.: description of,

81–82; lynching in, 81–103; slavery in, 82–84
Schwarz, Philip, 98
Scott, James C.: theory of resistance, 273, 283
Sears, Robert, 8
Shackleford, James M., 90, 96, 97, 101; defends lynching, 92–94
Sharp, Cecil, 219
Sherman, William T., 115, 161
Slaton, John Marshall, 159, 167, 177, 179
Slavery: and planter paternalism, 117
Smelser, Neil, 21
Smith, Ola D., 171
Smith v. Commonwealth of Kentucky, 255
Social polarization: and lynching, 60–61
Social status: and lynching, 56–58
Sociological interpretations of lynching, 5–6, 24–25, 29–31
Somerville, Henderson, 190
South Carolina: lynchings in, 189–215; disfranchisement and lynching in, 195–96
Southern Tenant Farmers Union, 236
Stampp, Kenneth, 98
Stanly County, N.C., 226–27
Steadman, James, 122, 123, 125
Straker, David Augustus, 189
Strauder v. West Virginia, 254
Strother, John P., 89

Talbert, Mary, 309
Talladega County, Ala., 140
Terborg-Penn, Rosalyn, 293
Thomas, J. Park, 121, 122, 125, 126
Thomas, William, 125
Thompson, E. P., 30
Till, Emmett, 54, 59
Tillman, Benjamin, 199, 200
Tillman, Katherine Davis, 307
Tilly, Charles, 10, 21
Tolbert, Robert, 210, 211, 212, 213
Tolbert, Tom, 211, 212, 213

Trexler, Harrison A., 98
Twain, Mark, 1, 4, 77

Union County, S.C.: early history of, 110–11; planter elite in, 111–12; town elite in, 112–14; during Civil War, 114–15
United Confederate Veterans, 174
United Daughters of the Confederacy, 174
U.S. Supreme Court: and legal racism, 267–68

Van Buren County, Ark., 147
Vance, Rupert B., 7
Vesey, Denmark, 110
Virginia v. Rives, 255

Watson, Tom, 166, 173, 176, 179
Wayne, Michael, 101
Wayne County, Ga., 284
Weems, Frank, 236
Wells-Barnett, Ida B., 5, 214, 249, 284; antilynching activities of, 280–81, 292–310; on race and sexuality, 295–96; views on black sexual victimization, 301–2; as exile, 303–4; responses to antilynching campaign of, 305–6; marginalized by black organizations, 309

West, Cornel, 272
West, Rebecca, 155
Wharton, Vernon L., 10
White, Deborah Gray, 308
White, Walter, 309
Whitecapping: in Miss., 206–7; in Greenwood County, S.C., 213
White women: in Atlanta mills, 161–62; exploitation of, 168–70
Willard, Frances E., 4; criticizes Ida B. Wells-Barnett, 308
Williams, Fannie Barrier, 306
Williamson, Joel, 12, 266
Willson, Augustus E.: opposes lynching, 263–64; and legal lynchings, 264–66
Wilmer, C. B., 164
Women. *See* Black women; White women
Woodward, C. Vann, 10
Woodward, James G., 178
Woofter, Thomas J., Jr., 7
Wright, Richard, 2, 15
Wyatt-Brown, Bertram, 12, 98

Yancey, J. F.: defends lynching, 94–95
Yazoo Delta, Miss.: lynchings in, 194–95
Yell County, Ark., 146–47
York County, S.C., 200